THEORIES OF
URBAN POLITICS

THEORIES OF URBAN POLITICS

edited by

David Judge, Gerry Stoker
and Harold Wolman

SAGE Publications
London • Thousand Oaks • New Delhi

First published 1995

SAGE Publications Ltd
6 Bonhill Street
London EC2A 4PU

SAGE Publications Inc
2455 Teller Road
Thousand Oaks, California 91320

SAGE Publications India Pvt Ltd
32, M-Block Market
Greater Kailash – I
New Delhi 110 048

British Library Cataloguing in Publication data

A catalogue record for this book is available
from the British Library

ISBN 0 8039 8864 8
ISBN 0 8039 8865 6 (pbk)

Typeset by Mayhew Typesetting, Rhayader, Powys
Printed in Great Britain by The Cromwell Press Ltd,
Broughton Gifford, Melksham, Wiltshire

Contents

Preface

The idea for this book emerged in 1992 and gained more concrete form in 1993. We were amazed and delighted when so many scholars quickly agreed to write chapters to match our outline vision and not at all surprised when some failed to meet the deadlines we set. Especially as we at times fell behind the deadline ourselves. All authors responded to our criticism and comments on the first draft of their chapters and we thank them all for their considerable efforts. The task of editing was slightly complicated by David Judge departing in 1993/4 from Strathclyde to Houston University as a Visiting Professor. Hal Wolman in turn left Wayne State University for a six month sabbatical in England in June 1994. Gerry Stoker, unusually for him, stayed in one place but did manage the occasional transatlantic trip and enjoyed discussing the book at various stages in Detroit, Cleveland, New Orleans and Houston. This book then through its authors and the activities of its editors is a true multi-site production. It was made in the United States and Britain, a further product of the special relationship between two countries who almost share the same language.

The final stages of editing were greatly assisted by the secretarial support provided by Fiona Thorpe. Thanks also go to Lorraine, Deborah and Dianne and not forgetting Andy, Ben, Hannah, Bethany, Robert and Benjamin.

David Judge, Hal Wolman and Gerry Stoker

About the Contributors

Laura Brunell is a doctoral candidate in the Department of Political Science at the University of Colorado at Boulder.

Susan E. Clarke is an Associate Professor of Political Science and Director of the Centre for Public Policy Research at the University of Colorado at Boulder.

Susan S. Fainstein is Professor of Urban Planning and Policy Development at Rutgers University.

Michael Goldsmith is a Professor at the Department of Politics and Contemporary History, Salford.

Alan Harding is a Professor at the European Institute for Urban Affairs, Liverpool John Moores University.

Clifford Hirst is a PhD candidate in the Programme in Urban Planning and Policy Development at Rutgers University.

Bryan D. Jones is a Professor at the Department of Political Science, Texas A&M University.

David Judge is a Professor at Strathclyde University, Glasgow, in the Department of Government.

Michael Keating is a Professor at the Department of Political Science, University of Western Ontario, London, Ontario.

Vivien Lowndes is a Lecturer at the Institute of Local Government Studies, University of Birmingham.

Joe Painter is a Lecturer at the Department of Geography, University of Durham.

Christopher Pickvance is a Professor of Urban Studies at the University of Kent.

Lynn A. Staeheli is an Assistant Professor of Geography and a Research Associate at the Institute of Behavioural Science at the University of Colorado at Boulder.

Gerry Stoker is a Professor at Strathclyde University, Glasgow, in the Department of Government.

Clarence N. Stone is a Professor in the Department of Government and Politics, University of Maryland.

Harold Wolman is a Professor in the Department of Political Science and the College of Urban, Labor and Metropolitan Affairs at Wayne State University.

1

Urban Politics and Theory:
An Introduction

David Judge, Gerry Stoker and Harold Wolman

A book with the title *Theories of Urban Politics* should obviously be concerned with 'theories' and 'urban politics'. And that is what this book is: all of the chapters deal, in their various ways, with theories of urban politics. Indeed, it is the sheer eclecticism of theories and the variety of approaches to theoretical issues which makes the study of urban politics so vibrant in the 1990s – but which also generates a need for a book of this type. There are now *so many* theories that it is increasingly difficult for scholar and student alike to keep pace with them, let alone comprehend or evaluate their respective merits.

The purpose of this edited volume, therefore, is to bring together leading scholars from both sides of the Atlantic to explain and assess the major theories underpinning the study of urban politics. The authors, pre-eminent scholars in their own right, not only review the theories but stake out their own positions and contribute to the debate. Authors were asked to follow a common, but flexible, format (although it was understood that the coherent development of argument might vary from chapter to chapter and thus preclude too rigid an adherence). Authors were asked to deal with the exposition and explanation of the theory, illustrations and applications of it, critiques and criticism, and to provide their own overall evaluation and original insights.

Nonetheless, the chapters and the subjects they cover are quite diverse and inevitably raise the question of what we mean by 'theory'. We are very encompassing in our conception of theory, and, as a consequence, we have cast our net widely. Theories, as we conceive them, can be normative or empirical; they can also be models, conceptual frameworks or perspectives. We also include, under our broad tent of theories, 'theorizing' – systematic thinking about or speculation concerning important issues in urban politics. Most of our chapters include more than one, and in some cases several, of these approaches to theory.

Normative theories concern how the world ought to be; the theorist posits a desired state or set of conditions and argues why it is to be preferred. As Judge (Chapter 2) and Harding (Chapter 3) make clear, both pluralism and elite theory can be conceived as normative theories to the extent, they argue, that urban politics *ought* to be pluralist (power should be dispersed) or elitist (power should be concentrated). Lowndes, in her chapter 'Citizenship and Urban Politics' (Chapter 9) deals with normative theory as does Wolman, who examines and contrasts the basic values that are pursued by American and British systems of local government in Chapter 8, 'Local Government Institutions and Democratic Governance'.

Prescriptive theories are instrumental; they are concerned with the best means of achieving a desired condition. Wolman's discussion of the extent to which different local government institutions contribute to normative values of local government involves an exercise in prescriptive theory. Jones, in Chapter 5, is concerned with how local bureaucracies can best be subjected to democratic control.

Empirical theory, on the other hand, is concerned with explaining and interpreting reality (although all theory is obviously related to 'reality' to some extent). In its broadest sense explaining means an understanding of reality. In a narrower sense empirical theory is concerned with establishing causal relationships – what factors (independent variables) account for the phenomenon to be explained (dependent variable). Elitist theory, as discussed by Harding in Chapter 3, can be seen as empirical theory in the sense that it explains the nature of policy decisions produced by urban governments as a function of the decision-making structure (it can also be a normative theory if theorists advocate decision making by an elite as the preferred mode of political decision making). Goldsmith, in his discussion on local autonomy in Chapter 12, considers, among other things, the causes or preconditions of local autonomy in an effort to explain why local autonomy is relatively stronger in some systems of local government than in others.

Empirical theory can be inductive, based on empirical observation and an accumulation of evidence from hypotheses testing. The vast amount of research on the decision-making structure of urban governments discussed in Chapters 2–4 constitutes an example of inductive empirical theory. Empirical theory can also be deductive, starting from a premise or set of premises and deducing conclusions about causal relationships and behaviour from these premises. The premises may or may not be empirically valid, but utilizing them produces plausible results about and an understanding of (that is, explains) reality. Public choice theory, discussed by Keating in Chapter 7, starts from the economists' premise of individual utility maximization and derives from that explanations of individual, community and jurisdictional behaviour within metropolitan areas. While the assumptions underlying the theory may not be empirically verifiable, they lead to, it is argued, accurate predictions (explanations) about behaviour; individuals behave *as though* they were utility maximizers. Similarly Marxist and neo-Marxist theory discussed by Pickvance in Chapter 13 is, to a substantial extent, deductive theory. It starts from the premise that capitalism cannot guarantee its own reproduction because it has prerequisites which the market cannot secure and produces conflicts which need to be regulated.

It is frequently argued that empirical theory is not, despite claims sometimes made, value free and devoid of normative bias. The selection of research questions, the defining of concepts, the research design, and, in particular, interpretation of results all are likely to reflect unconscious (and sometimes conscious) normative values of the researcher. This has been a particular theme in debate on the pluralist-elitist research and is discussed by Judge in Chapter 2 and by Harding in Chapter 3.

Strict interpretations of empirical theory require explanation to be concerned with causal relationships or, at least, associations; in order to have the status of a theory some phenomenon (variable) must be linked to or related to others consistently. But more relaxed interpretations of theory can also contribute to explanation or understanding. Models, conceptual frameworks, and perspectives all fall under this rubric.

Models are representations or stylized and simplified pictures of reality. They include the most important components or categories, but they do not posit relationships among the variables. Systems theory, for example, is a model through which analysis of urban political phenomena can be examined. (However, in econometric and associated studies, a specified model includes the hypothesized relationships among the variables.)

Conceptual frameworks or *perspectives* are ways of looking at or conceiving of an object of study. They provide a language and frame of reference through which reality can be examined and lead theorists to ask questions that might not otherwise occur. The result, if successful, is new and fresh insights that other frameworks or perspectives might not have yielded. Conceptual frameworks can constitute an attempt to establish a paradigm shift. Regime theory, discussed by Stoker in Chapter 4, is an example of the productive use of a new conceptual framework for examining urban politics. Regime theory sees the world through the lens of building governing coalitions to accomplish public purposes. It leads us to focus our attention not on how decisions are made, but on how important goals are set forth and achieved, on social production rather than social accounting. Regulation theory, discussed by Painter in Chapter 14, also provides a new language and frame of reference for the study of urban politics. Its focus is on the social and politico-economic institutions that underlie the prevailing set of relationships between production, consumption and investment and the implications of these changing relationships for urban government and governance. Marxist and neo-Marxist theory looks at the urban world through the lens of class relationships and interests. As Pickvance indicates (Chapter 13) it is particularly concerned with the role of the state in the reproduction of capitalism. Clarke, Staeheli and Brunell utilize the perspective of gender in Chapter 11 (or the feminist lens as they call it) to approach urban political phenomena. Such conceptual frameworks may be heuristic in the sense that they stimulate the generation of hypotheses that may be tested and lead to the development of more formal empirical theory.

We also speak of theories in the sense of *theorizing* or thinking about some aspect of urban phenomena. These theories specify an object of interest – social movements which Fainstein and Hirst focus on in Chapter 10, political leadership which Stone covers in Chapter 6 – and set forth a claim that these are important urban political phenomena that 'drive' or lie behind much that is of interest in urban politics. Stone, in his chapter, attempts to derive the characteristics of urban leadership through a consideration of the careers of several well-known American mayors. Fainstein and Hirst consider a series of issues related to urban social movements. Such *theorizing* can cover a range of other theoretical concerns: under what conditions will urban social movements occur (empirical theory), have such movements displaced class as the most useful category for neo-Marxist analysis (conceptual framework), do urban social movements bring about progressive (that is, desirable) change (normative and prescriptive theory)?

Finally we wish to distinguish between theories and theorists. The latter have careers and their ideas and theories may develop and change over time. Theories, on the other hand, are the product of the activity of the community of scholars, even though they may be strongly associated with or have been originated by a specific individual. Although it may sometimes be of interest to trace how theorists change, the focus of this book is on theories rather than theorists.

It is important to note that, although we have presented these differing conceptions of theory serially, they are frequently intermingled and linked to one another. Theories contest against and respond to one another. In addition, theories change and develop over time, frequently as a result of refinement and modification occasioned by criticisms from other theoretical perspectives.

The way in which theories are contested and change over time is well illustrated in Part I of this volume (Chapters 2–4). In considering the key issue of power in urban communities, pluralist, elite and regime theorists have been prompted into refinements and reconsideration of their initial hypotheses by criticisms and counter-arguments made by their 'competitors'. Each theory makes very different assumptions about the nature and meaning of power, and each claims to be 'correct' in its conceptualization and measurement of power. In the process of questioning and criticism, inconsistencies or omissions have been discovered, commonalities identified, and refinements and modifications generated within and between the diverse theories. In other words, theories develop in response to other theories, they are not static. Moreover, different emphases and considerations emerge *within* theoretical positions over time, so that internal variation characterizes the major general theories. Hence, there is no single, homogeneous theory of 'pluralism', or 'elites', or 'regimes', or for that matter 'Marxism' or 'feminism': there are only theor*ies*. In which case it is of considerable importance to specify *which* variant is being considered at any particular time.

A classic example of theoretical contestation and development is provided in the 'community power debate' between pluralism and elite theory. As Judge notes in Chapter 2 the original urban pluralists – Dahl, Wolfinger and Polsby – sought to reject the elitist findings of Hunter's study of Atlanta. What is common to all pluralist theories, therefore, is the rejection of the view that political power is highly stratified. Instead, they are agreed that power, and resultant inequalities within society, should be seen to be dispersed. This is often taken as a statement both that such dispersion is a fact – and one that can be empirically validated – and also as a prescription, as a desirable feature of a modern liberal democracy. However, beyond a basic set of claims about the decentralization of power, 'pluralism' rapidly fragments into a series of models or types of theory, where different 'pluralisms' are apparent in different cities at different times. In part, this fragmentation is a response to comparative empirical investigations – across cities, countries and time – but, in large part it also results from counter-responses to these findings by other theories. It is important therefore to be clear about which 'type' of pluralism is being considered at what time. Thus as Chapter 2 makes clear we should speak of 'hyper-', 'bounded', or 'neo-' pluralism and be sensitive to the spatial, temporal and socioeconomic contexts of each.

Harding's chapter on elite theory – the contention that urban governments are (or, in its normative version, should be) ruled by a relatively small number of people with like-minded, usually business, interests – similarly indicates the breadth and heterogeneity of elite theory. It also chronicles how elite theory has developed over time in response to empirical 'testing', and to criticism and 'competition' from other theories. From the starting point of Hunter's reputational analysis of Atlanta – the first rigorous attempt at systematic quantitative and qualitative assessment of elite theory in an urban setting – elite theory had to respond to the pluralist criticism that Hunter's commitment to the scientific method and empirical verification had been compromised because of the original 'bias' of his conceptualization of power. In other words, he was accused of taking for granted exactly what needed to be proved. In developing their own 'decisional methodology' pluralists maintained that theirs was truly an 'empirical descriptive' theory. Their focus was upon the *exercise* of power: it was a capacity, a form of control and its results were observable. Yet, this assumption led to a counter attack by neo-elitists, most notably by Bachrach and Baratz, and their identification of a 'second face' of power, of 'non-decisions'. As Harding points out, it rapidly became apparent in this debate that the competing sides were using different methodologies to answer different questions about how power was conceived and measured.

While the contest between pluralists and elite theorists became even more abstruse, intense and parallel (in the sense that both sides talked past each other, rather than engaging in a 'debate' about their commonalities and divergences), their arguments became more focused, in fact re-focused, by the theoretical challenge posed by neo-Marxism in the 1970s. As Pickvance notes in Chapter 13 Marxist studies of urban politics in that decade highlighted the importance of class interests and the 'systemic' nature of the power of capital over local decision making. We will return to Marxist theory shortly, but its importance at this stage of the discussion is that it led both pluralists (in neo-pluralism) and elite theorists (in the literature on growth machines) to consider the wider socioeconomic and state contexts and constraints within which local decision makers had to operate.

As pluralists and elite theorists responded respectively to neo-Marxist studies, so too a new 'theoretical force' – regime theory – emerged in the mid-1980s. Regime theory changes the focus of the pluralist-elitist debate from 'social control' or 'power over' to 'social production' or 'power to'. It directs our attention away from the question of 'who rules' to the question of how public purposes are accomplished and, in particular, to how long-term effective governing coalitions to achieve such purposes are constructed and sustained. In addition to directing our attention to this phenomenon, regime theory provides a framework for examining it. Stoker's exposition of this new theory in Chapter 4 reveals clearly how it took on board the central tenets of neo-Marxist inspired studies of urban politics – that power should be conceptualized 'systemically', and that business exercises a privileged position in governmental decision making, but that, within those constraints, political institutions and actors could still exert influence through complex and interrelated networks. Complexity is thus seen to be at the heart of urban governance. In these circumstances Stoker argues that regime theory 'focuses on efforts to build more stable and intense relationships in order that governmental and non-governmental actors accomplish difficult and non-routine goals'. Ultimately though this is a diffuse focus, with regime theorists themselves acknowledging commonalities with some variants of pluralist theories. Equally there are some similarities with neo-elite theory, and certainly neo-Marxism informs a significant part of 'regime theory'. Nonetheless, Stoker argues that regime theory is conceptually distinct from its 'competitors'. As a relatively new theory it is still evolving, and in its infancy it has suffered, in Stoker's words, from 'the tendency of most of its main propositions to emerge inductively from observation of the urban scene'. Yet Stoker is confident that regime theory has established a new agenda for researchers. Exactly how that agenda will unfold remains uncertain, but a large part of it will be concerned with delimiting the 'distinctiveness' of regime theory from other theoretical perspectives on urban power.

'Democracy' is a general theme underpinning the chapters in Part II, and provides an analytical thread linking them together. In Chapter 5 Jones considers the problem of how non-elected bureaucrats can be subjected to effective control in urban political systems, a fundamental

problem of modern democratic theory. He starts from an assessment of
the deficiencies of existing models of 'overhead democracy' – that is,
voters elect public officials who reflect the public will by enacting policies
and hiring bureaucrats to implement them. Democratic control of the
bureaucracy is thus effected through control of bureaucrats by local
elected officials. But Jones argues that empirical studies of implementation
and principal-agent relations do not support the idea of popular control
through elected representatives. This then raises the question of 'who
controls' the bureaucracy, and leads Jones to seek the answer in terms of
'who benefits' and a recognition that who benefits is time dependent. From
this perspective he proceeds to sketch out an alternative approach based
upon the different incentives that may be generated from different
institutional designs for the delivery of services. In this approach the
contingency of control, particularly the contingency of time, is recognized:
'Because of the complex interactions between goals, means, and institutions, particular controls over public agencies are highly time-
contingent'. Thus, in highlighting the inadequacies of the existing model
of 'overhead democracy', Jones outlines an analytical model designed to
discover how incentive structures can be modified 'to encourage bureaucrats to adapt to proper objectives'. At this juncture Jones's chapter
reveals both its prescriptive nature and its contribution to *theorizing* (as a
process of conceptualization).

In Chapter 5 Stone examines the nature of democratic political
leadership in an urban context. He makes it clear that there is no well
developed theory of political leadership. His purpose therefore is to define
the concept of 'leadership' and to identify the challenge of leadership in
the urban arena. In examining the careers of four prominent mayors in the
United States, Stone uses these observations to construct hypotheses about
how to measure leadership performance. Then, in an attempt to discover
what American experience can teach us about urban leadership more
generally, he contrasts leadership styles in the US with those in the United
Kingdom. In this process, Stone specifies the relationships between
political variables and provides the necessary insights to understand those
connections.

In contrast, Keating's attention in Chapter 7 is upon *competing* theories
that underlie debate about the most appropriate size for municipalities and
the most appropriate organization for metropolitan areas. Public choice
theory views municipalities as producers of local goods and services and
individuals as consumers paying for these local products through the tax
system. The metropolitan area is thus viewed as a market analogue with
municipalities competing with each other by offering varying mixes of
services at different (tax) prices and individuals choosing the tax/service
package they prefer by moving to the locality that offers it (voting with
their feet). As in product markets, efficiency is enhanced by large numbers
of producers competing with one another; thus a fragmented system of
local government in metropolitan areas, consisting of large numbers of

small municipalities, is said to promote efficiency. Consolidationists, on the other hand, argue a more diffuse case. Their emphasis is on economies of scale as a promoter of efficiency. In addition, they contend that large, consolidated units are more efficient since they can bring about better coordination of activities. They are also better able to engage in redistribution. Consequently, consolidationists advocate large units of government, preferably at the metropolitan scale. In analysing the issues of principle that have divided 'consolidationists' from public choice theorists Keating illuminates the normative dimensions of this debate. Indeed, like so many other debates in urban politics it is one often driven by ideology, 'interest' and value judgements. Keating is particularly critical of public choice theory for attempting to conceal its normative principles behind deductive principles. Overall his conclusion is that theories about the size and efficiency of local government cannot be separated from broader political and value judgements.

Wolman's examination of local government institutions and democratic governance in Chapter 8 reveals both the normative and empirical dimensions of the debate. Wolman's concern with institutional structure includes not only the internal arrangements of local government, but also informal norms, roles, relationships and operating practices that are so stable, structured and accepted that they can be said to be 'institutionalized'. He notes that institutional structure is important because it is the vehicle through which the basic purposes and values a society wishes to pursue through local government are carried out. Accordingly, Wolman begins by setting forth and contrasting the fundamental values that underlie local government in the United States (a sometimes contrasting mix of participation, representation and economy and efficiency) and Britain (efficiency in local service delivery) and the way in which local government structure in each country reflects these values. He then asks whether local government structure in each country does, in fact, promote the intended values – that is, does structure matter in that it produces intended results? Wolman reviews both the political and academic debate related to structure and its impact in both the US and Britain, including empirical research that sheds light on this debate in both countries. He concludes that the traditional debate has reached a dead end in both countries and that the recent change in focus from more formal institutional structure to institutional norms underpinning local government activity is likely to be more productive.

Part III is concerned with the role of citizens in urban politics. In Chapter 9, Lowndes provides an overview of the treatment of citizenship in urban debate. She notes citizenship has a long association with the city. The urban setting has been seen as an appropriate locus for the exercise of the rights and duties of citizenship. The debate is brought up to date and is seen by Lowndes to underlie a number of the current reforms and debates about the future of urban government.

In Chapter 10 Fainstein and Hirst address urban social movements, which they define as a new category of social movement (collective social actors defined by both their organization and aims) differing from traditional social movements in their non-class basis, operation outside the realm of production, and participatory ethos. As previously discussed, a concern with urban social movements is a contribution to urban theory in that it identifies specific features of reality that are worthy of attention – of being in the foreground of analysis; and raises questions about why, and with what effect, these aspects have been differentiated from the background of other experiences. Thus Fainstein and Hirst point out that before the urban protests and civil disturbances of the 1960s and early 1970s, urban scholars had a largely non-conflictual view of city life. However, changes in the political terrain of American and European cities from the 1960s onwards, and the emergence of urban social movements, led to a questioning of these dominant theories of urban politics. Chapter 10 is important therefore in noting that the existence of urban social movements 'challenged the earlier preoccupation with decision making at the top, forced recognition of social divisions resulting from other bases of solidarity besides class, and broadened the definition of urban politics to include interactions within the realm of civil society that were not necessarily tied to the state'. Moreover, in reviewing recent developments in the theorization of urban social movements, Fainstein and Hirst make clear the necessity of understanding the relationship between these movements and the sociopolitical framework within which they operate.

A particularly striking example of how theories selectively 'foreground' some concepts rather than others is provided in Chapter 11. There Clarke, Staeheli and Brunell argue for a more gendered perspective on urban politics. They contend that a feminist perspective contributes to urban analysis in three significant ways: first, by providing an epistemological critique of existing gendered, analytical frameworks; second, by contributing to the theoretical debate on gendered local restructuring processes; and third, by providing a normative perspective on urban governance and citizenship. Clarke and her colleagues argue that, in the absence of a feminist perspective, urban scholars construct a view of localities that is partial and misleading. By looking at localities through a 'feminist lens' their intention is to 'bring into focus a number of features neglected by other perspectives'. In calling for gender to be taken seriously in urban research they also highlight the need to develop more historically and empirically grounded feminist theories of 'interest', and for a recognition of the importance of contextual variables (especially changes in political opportunity structures) in feminist analyses. More particularly, they call for an enlarged research agenda; one that will 'require rethinking of existing theories in terms of their sensitivity to gender relations and then attempting to disaggregate analytical categories by gender'.

Part IV is concerned with the economic and political framework in which urban politics takes place. In Chapter 12 Goldsmith examines the political and economic limits to local autonomy. He establishes a typology in which countries can be placed and then reviews the available evidence to see how far the typology is supported. He concludes that 'there is pressure on local autonomy in many political systems today'.

In Chapter 13 Pickvance provides a good example both of how theories choose to foreground some concepts rather than others, so identifying new issues for analysis, and of the conceptual diversity to be found within some theories. Marxist and neo-Marxist theories are essentially deductive theories in that they start from the premise that the mode of production basically determines the nature of social and political relations within a capitalist state and that the state, in capitalist systems, supports the interests of capital. Pickvance states that Marxist theories of urban politics view urban political institutions as part of the state apparatus and hence are inescapably marked by the role which the state plays in capitalist society. Linked to this premise is a rejection of the basic tenets of most other theories on urban politics. Hence, Marxists argue that non-Marxist theories are 'biased' in favour of western capitalism in their choice of which questions are deemed to be of importance in the first instance and how then to test for that importance. Indeed one characteristic feature of Marxist theories is a general dismissal of rival theories in favour of the 'scientific' methodology of historical materialism.

However, if there is agreement about what Marxist theory *is not* there is considerable disputation, even among Marxists, as to what *it is*. Pickvance reveals these differences by distinguishing between 'instrumentalist' theorists, those who see the state as a class instrument, and 'structuralists', those who are willing to concede some relative autonomy to the state. In outlining and reviewing Marxist writings on urban politics Pickvance examines the respective influence of instrumentalist and structuralist analyses in this field. He also maps out the scope and levels of external criticisms – revolving around the concepts of 'class', 'class reductionism', and 'class conflict' – and concludes that 'the argument that the local state is capitalist remains no more than a theoretical assertion'. Nonetheless, Pickvance credits Marxist theories with drawing attention to the significant roles played by economic and class interests in the formation of urban policies. In doing so they have impacted upon other theories – most notably pluralism, elite theory and regime theory – causing them to address central issues about systemic power and the relationship between economic forces and political action. Certainly, Pickvance is correct in his conclusion that Marxist theories have 'widened the questions asked and suggested new explanations'. Equally, they have generated a series of conceptual and methodological controversies along the way.

In Chapter 14 Painter addresses regulation theory. One of the new questions posed by Marxist theorists in the 1970s was how and why had capitalism survived over time and across space? The answers were sketched out by Marxist economists in what was to become 'regulation theory'. The prime concern of this variant of Marxist theory was with the explanation of economic change and development. Political institutions, structures and practices were undoubtedly part of the explanation but not the central focus of the theory itself. Indeed, the primary concern of most regulationist writers remains the regulation of the economy rather than a conceptualization of the role of the state. Where the regulationist approach has been applied to urban politics it tends to draw an analogy between the organization of the process of production ('Fordist' or 'post-Fordist') and the organization of local government institutions and the manner in which local services are provided (centralized/bureaucratic or decentralized/non-hierarchical). The labour process within local government is thus seen to be of central significance, with some 'regulationists' arguing that information technology has affected both state production processes and the nature of collective provision of local welfare services. However, as Painter observes there is no single and unified regulation theory. Further it is only within the past decade that the concepts of regulation theory and post-Fordism have been applied to the field of urban politics. Attempts to operationalize these theories have at best been sporadic and far from systematic. In these circumstances Painter calls for greater refinement of the concepts associated with regulation theory, for more empirical testing, and for more comparative studies to be undertaken at the urban level.

Theories in comparative perspective

In this book we are concerned primarily with urban theories that have currency in the United States and/or Britain (although many of the theories have relevance in – indeed, in some cases, may have originated in – other countries). Within this context it is as well to ask the question of how generalizable are these theories across countries – that is, how well do these theories travel? Clearly theories that are pitched at a high level of generality – macro level theories – such as those concerned with the relations of capital and the state, local autonomy or who rules, are likely to be of relevance in most countries, at least in terms of the questions they pose. However, theories that focus attention on behavioural phenomena that may not exist to the same degree in all countries – urban growth machines, regime theory, urban social movements – or exist in institutional contexts that differ substantially – urban leadership, bureaucratic control – may be more or less relevant across countries. Empirically based theories explaining relationships or phenomena must, of course, be tested in each country (even though theories may posit an invariant relationship across all countries); pluralism, for example, may characterize urban political systems in one country, while elitism does so in another. Throughout this book readers should be alert to the potential applicability of the various theories not only in their own country but also in a comparative context.

It may also be helpful if readers note certain fundamental differences between the urban government systems of Britain and the United States. These differences are explored in various chapters throughout the book and in some instances – notably the chapters by Goldsmith, Keating and Pickvance – the comparative analysis moves farther afield. By way of an introductory orientation certain fundamental contextual differences between Britain and the United States can be identified:

- Differences in governmental structure that result in a greater emphasis on spatial politics in the United States and party politics in Britain. The federal structure of the United States means that urban governments are in effect creatures of state governments. Party conflict and partisanship are central to the unitary British system. The weaker party politics of the United States creates greater scope for a local politics.
- The more direct role of central government in Britain (and greater local autonomy in the United States) provides less scope for British local governments to engage in activity of their own choosing but a greater central government interest in local services and policies.
- A much more fragmented local government structure in the United States that encourages economic competition among localities. The US system is incredibly more complex. There are some 80,000 local government agencies in the United States, approximately 200 times more agencies than there are elected local authorities in Britain.
- The lack of a focused local executive in Britain compared with the United States where the elected mayor, or in some instances the city manager, has a prominent role in urban politics.
- A local fiscal structure in Britain that substantially reduces incentives for local governments to compete against each other's tax base. The British system retains a strong emphasis on resource equalization with funding being brought into line between richer and poorer localities. The contrast with the US system is clear where the heavy reliance on local property-based taxes creates a considerable incentive to attract businesses to sustain the tax base of local government.

Cross-national research requires conceptual and theoretical rigour if comparison is to advance beyond description into the realm of expla-nation. This book, by reviewing various theories and examining their application on both sides of the Atlantic, aims to make a modest contribution to the development of cross-national urban research. In effect it is a ground-clearing exercise to enable a serious assessment of the conceptual foundations that might be available for the comparative study of urban politics.

Part I

UNDERSTANDING URBAN POWER

2

Pluralism

David Judge

Pluralism is perhaps the most important theory to be examined in this book. Naturally this bold statement needs some qualification. It does not mean that pluralism is either more 'correct' or 'convincing' than any of the other theories and perspectives examined in the chapters hereafter, nor does it mean that 'pluralism' constitutes a singular, coherent and immutable concept. What it does mean, however, is that pluralism is the theory from which many perspectives on urban politics have developed, or against which many others have set themselves. Thus, for example, 'regime theory' has commonalities with pluralism, and much of the literature on social movements accepts a 'plurality' of organizations as the dynamic of urban politics. In addition, pluralism has been seen to exert 'ideational hegemony' over the political science professions on both sides of the Atlantic. In urban studies especially it has served as the 'dominant paradigm used to explain the distribution of power in American society' (Waste, 1986: 117). But, simultaneously, pluralist theory has also served as 'a warning sign to all good radicals . . . [to] gather themselves up to do battle against its complacent defence of the status quo' (Phillips, 1993: 139). In fact, pluralism, or rather 'the critique of pluralism', has been credited with rejuvenating academic interest in urban issues and of being the 'starting point of much of the recent work on urban politics' (Hampton, 1991: 239). So in either direction – for or against – pluralism has been remarkably influential in the study of urban politics. If anything, given the developments within pluralism itself and among its critics, there is the danger that in the 1990s 'we are all pluralists now'. If we are, then pluralism is everything and nothing. What this chapter seeks to establish therefore is what pluralism 'is'; what successive chapters seek to demonstrate is what pluralism 'is not'.

What is pluralist theory?

There is no simple answer to this question. First, there is little agreement as to the defining characteristics of 'pluralism' and, second, there is disagreement as to whether 'pluralism' constitutes a 'theory'. Indeed, it is now commonplace to start consideration of pluralism with the disclaimer that in the past 'critics have attacked a crude model of pluralism' (Smith, 1990: 302); or that a 'naive version of pluralism' has developed and one that is 'untenable as a description of power in Western liberal democracies' (Cox et al., 1985: 107); or that the debate has revolved around a 'critique of a rather simplistic pluralist model' (Stoker, 1991: 118). If anything critics of pluralism are credited with 'redefining' pluralism 'in a more positive and exaggerated form' than pluralist writers intended (Jordan, 1990: 290). Hence, the first point of importance is to ensure that in analysing 'pluralism' the theory under consideration is what 'pluralists' say it is, rather than what their critics have reinterpreted them as saying it is. As far as possible in this chapter, therefore, the actual words of pluralists (and primarily the words of those pluralists operationalizing the concept at the *urban level*) will be used. In this respect the chapter deals with only one particular stream of pluralist thought − urban pluralism (to borrow Stone's (1993) phrase) − and its conceptual tributaries.

With these caveats in mind, it is possible, nonetheless, to offer an indicative outline of the 'core' or 'principal tenets' of urban pluralism. These tenets reflect the elements of a 'general pluralist model' that can be derived more broadly from pluralist writings beyond the urban level (see Jordan, 1990: 293). In pulling together these elements Jordan identifies the main characteristics of a general pluralist model as: first, that power is seen to be fragmented and decentralized; second, there is dispersed inequalities in so far as all groups have some resources to articulate their case, even if their demands are not necessarily, or successfully, acted upon; third, that this dispersion of power is a 'desirable feature in any system approaching the status of democracy' (Jordan, 1990: 293); fourth, that political outcomes in different policy sectors will reflect different processes, different actors and different distributions of power within those sectors; fifth, that the exercise of political power extends beyond the formal institutional structures of elections and representative institutions in liberal democracy; sixth, 'the interaction of interests would supply a practical alternative to the "general will" as the source of legitimate authority' (Jordan, 1990: 293); finally, that the disaggregated nature of decision making, and the very uncertainty of outcomes of the bargaining process, helps bind participants to the process itself.

When reduced to this 'core' the basic ideas are few in number and, moreover, do not amount to a single model. Indeed, as the rest of this chapter demonstrates, subsequent elaborations and qualifications to these ideas have generated a *series* of models. In fact, perhaps the central defining feature of pluralism is what it sets itself against. In this sense, as

Jordan points out, it is 'no more than an anti-theory. What it is rejecting is more important than what it is establishing' (1990: 295). What the original urban pluralists, Dahl, Wolfinger and Polsby (the latter in particular), were rejecting was the elitist view discovered by Hunter's reputational study of Atlanta (see Hunter, 1953; Harding, Chapter 3, this volume). Pluralists rejected the highly stratified view of the power structure identified in Atlanta, where a small group of economically and socially pre-eminent men, by determining policy informally behind the scenes, were seen to have subordinated the roles of civic and political leaders. While not disputing that community decision making was restricted to small numbers of people, Dahl and his associates maintained that electoral politics had not been residualized in the manner described by Hunter; for them, urban elected decision makers were still of significance in shaping issues, still operated in the context of a 'democratic creed', and were still subject to popular control. The political system was thus seen to be relatively permeable in that 'it remain[ed] open to groups who are active, organized and want to be heard' (Dahl, 1986: 182–3). For pluralists society was 'fractured into congeries of hundreds of small special interest groups, with incompletely overlapping memberships, widely diffused power bases, and a multitude of techniques for exercising influence on decisions salient to them' (Polsby, 1980: 118). This was an important 'characteristic of New Haven and most cities in the United States' (Dahl, 1986: 183). In essence, pluralist democracy combined social pluralism – the existence of relatively autonomous groups and organizations – with electoral mechanisms of choice and a 'set of beliefs on democracy, relatively widely held, if unequally held and diffused' (Dahl, 1986: 186). Underpinning the political system, therefore, was a widespread popular consensus and support for the basic features of that system.

Beyond this basic set of claims urban pluralism rapidly fragments into diverse variants where prefixes – 'stratified', 'hyper-', 'neo-' – become necessary indicators of the type of pluralism and reminders that there is no single, simple model of 'pluralism' as such. These variants will be examined shortly but, in preface, the other area of disagreement – whether pluralism constitutes a 'theory' – needs some preliminary discussion. Certainly Dahl (1984: 240), as a leading 'pluralist', maintains that *Who Governs?* (Dahl, 1961) 'was not written to advance a general "pluralist theory of politics"'. For him, pluralism is an 'empirical descriptive' analysis of decision making. It seeks to explain 'how things really are' and 'how decisions are really made'. If it is 'theory' then it is 'empirical democratic theory' in the tradition of Plato and Machiavelli; whom Dahl believes to be 'the two political theorists who did most to develop a descriptive political science' (1961: vi).

While Dahl might not regard himself as a 'theorist' of pluralism his mode of analysis has been seen to operationalize an underpinning 'normative theory' and he has consistently been accused of being an apologist for western liberal democracy. In part both views are accurate.

On the one side, the purpose of *Who Governs?* was to describe the reality of urban decision making, and to this end Dahl used the term 'pluralism'; but, on the other side, throughout most of his other work he was concerned to theorize the concept of 'polyarchy' which had prescriptive and normative dimensions. 'Polyarchy' was often used as a normative benchmark, as an idealized institutional arrangement, against which the actual performance of existing political systems could be assessed. In this sense polyarchy is more than pluralism. As Dahl has consistently argued the existence of a significant number of relatively autonomous social groups and organizations 'is what has come to be called *pluralism*' (Dahl 1989: 219, original emphasis), but that pluralism is only one constituent element of 'polyarchy'. In keeping open the question of how closely polyarchy actually approximates representative democracy as an idea', Dahl has also 'kept open' the exact meaning and normative dimensions of 'polyarchy' (Dahl, 1990: 60). Fortunately there is no need to enter into the confused and confusing debate about what 'polyarchy' is and what the concept has been used for. Instead, a distinction may be drawn between 'polyarchy' as a normative theory – as a prescription – and 'pluralism' or even more precisely 'urban pluralism' as an empirical descriptive theory. But even here it has to be acknowledged from the outset that urban pluralism in its initial 'empirical descriptive' formulation had a strong normative element: it preferred western democratic systems to authoritarian regimes; it did not dissent from the 'common view' that 'our system is not only democratic but is perhaps the most perfect expression of democracy that exists anywhere' (Dahl, 1961: 316); and generally it believed that no minority group is permanently excluded from the political arena or suffers cumulative inequalities. Critics have subsequently argued that the normative expectations built into pluralism were in fact the current conditions under which the US political system operated (see Connolly, 1966; Walker, 1966). But this is to afford priority to what the critics of pluralism say rather than what pluralists themselves say. What needs to be established first of all, however, is what pluralists say themselves. The logical starting point is thus to review the original works of Dahl, Polsby and Wolfinger and their attempts to answer the question: 'Who Governs?' in an urban community.

For Dahl the question was an empirical one: 'How does a "democratic" system work amid inequality of resources' (1961: 3). In examining one urban American community, New Haven, Connecticut, Dahl (1961: 7–8) sought to answer the specific questions:

- Are inequalities in resources of influence 'cumulative' or 'non-cumulative'?
- How are important political decisions actually made?
- What kinds of people have the greatest influence on decisions?
- What is the relative importance of the most widely distributed political resource – the right to vote?

- Are the patterns of influence durable or changing?
- How important is the nearly universal adherence to the 'American creed' of democracy and equality?

The answers were to be provided through describing 'who' was involved and 'how' they were involved in the making of 'important decisions'. Nelson Polsby in *Community Power and Political Theory* (1980) later specified three questions designed to elicit the 'indices of the power of actors' in New Haven: who participates in decision making, who gains and who loses, and who prevails. One of the themes of Polsby's book was that 'what social scientists presume to be the case will in great measure influence the design and even the outcome of their research' (1980: 4). Critics agreed, but turned this statement against Polsby and pluralists generally. Thus, in one of the earliest and most influential critiques of the New Haven studies, Bachrach and Baratz contended that: 'the pluralists' ... approach to and assumptions about power predetermine their findings and conclusions' (1962: 952).

Methodological excursion: beginning and end of the story?

Before outlining Dahl's findings, and certainly before these findings can be assessed, it is necessary to examine the methodology employed in the New Haven study: a methodology variously characterized as 'decisional', 'positional', or 'the issue outcome method' (Bell and Newby, 1971: 234). Accompanying such characterization is normally a critique of Dahl as a 'faulty methodologist'. In other words, in choosing to describe and explain the process of decision making, Dahl is accused variously of selecting too few decisions, of 'stacking' the issues, or of choosing the 'wrong' issues (for an overview see Waste, 1987: 77–88).

In seeking 'to examine decisions to see what processes of influence are at work' (Dahl, 1961: 103) – and so 'to identify participants in policy-making and describe what they did' – the New Haven study focused upon three 'issue areas' – urban redevelopment, public education, and political nominations. In *Who Governs?* the choice of issues is simply justified in the statement that they constitute 'important decisions requiring the formal assent of local governmental officials' (1961: 102). It was left to Polsby (1980: 70–84) to explain why these decisions were deemed to be of such importance. Urban redevelopment 'was an obvious choice' in that it 'was by most criteria the biggest thing in New Haven'; public education was 'by far the largest item in the municipal budget'; and the nomination of public officials had to be treated as of major significance 'if public office is a base of influence in determining the outcomes of public policy'.

One immediate criticism was that Dahl and his colleagues had selected too few issues. Even Dahl's defenders are willing to concede that 'in all probability, the New Haven study is weakened by the inclusion of only three main issues' (Waste, 1987: 79). However, on the more substantial charges the defence of pluralist methodology is far more robust. When accused of choosing the 'wrong issues', of examining issues which were not particularly salient to economic and social notables in New Haven (Anton, 1963; Ricci, 1971), pluralists such as Waste (1987: 80) respond by admitting that there might be 'some merit' in examining other issue areas, but then quibble over which areas would provide useful alternatives to the original three. More importantly, they argue that Dahl cannot be accused simultaneously of choosing issues of low political salience but at the same time of 'stacking the issues'.

Yet this is precisely what other critics accused Dahl and his colleagues of doing – of choosing those issues which were politically salient and so contested by multiple actors. The charge to be answered now was that the 'decisional' methodology was guaranteed to find a pluralistic process. As Bachrach and Baratz (1970: 10) argue Dahl's findings were 'foreordained', because he 'accepts as issues what are reputed to be issues'. This leads Bachrach and Baratz to raise the possibility that many issues in a community do not become the site of public contestation. Instead, 'bias' within the political system is mobilized, ensuring that vitally important issues do not reach the public agenda, and so do not become 'decisions'. Such issues remain 'undecided' and so constitute 'non-decisions'. In this manner, power is exercised – but not overtly. Hence, pluralists in their search for 'decisions' would miss 'covert influence' and the 'suffocation' of demands for change 'from entering the political process' (Bachrach and Baratz, 1970: 44–6). This has become known as the second (undisclosed) face of power. Other Marxist and radical critics went still further and conceptualized a 'third face' of power arising out of 'socially structured and culturally patterned behaviour of groups, and practices of institutions' (Lukes, 1974: 22; see also Connolly, 1972). In other words there are structural constraints imposed by the capitalist economy and state which by their very nature exclude certain issues from the policy agenda.

The response to these 'second face' criticisms by pluralists has been combative. On non-decisions some pluralists maintain that whereas decisions can be observed 'precisely because of their visibility . . . They can be studied, agreed upon, and analyzed', in contrast, 'invisible issues almost by definition present the opposite problem' (Waste, 1987: 83). Other pluralists, most notably Polsby, however, argue that a non-decision is itself a certain sort of decision, in that it is an observable act not to act. If this is the case then 'the second face of power in practice merges with the first face and becomes identical' (Polsby, 1980: 212–13). On these grounds the work of Bachrach and Baratz is summarily dismissed as 'utterly fail[ing] to contribute to the solution of the dilemma they posed so dramatically for the scholarly community' (Polsby, 1980: 213). While it is conceded that findings about the second face of power may 'qualify, supplement, or amend' findings about the first face 'they do not erase these findings'

(Polsby, 1980: 218). Ultimately, the disagreement resolves itself into a problem of research strategy and methodology: with pluralists contending first, that it would be an extremely difficult task to design and execute a strategy capable of discerning the mobilization of bias in a local setting; and, second, that those studies which have attempted to do just that, are in practice methodologically deficient (Crenson, 1971; Gaventa, 1980; for criticism see Polsby, 1980: 217; Waste, 1987: 82–4).

Indeed, what particularly aggrieves Dahl and Polsby is criticism by caricature. As Dahl states:

> One of my disappointments was that my professional colleagues often have not fully grasped the diversity of techniques that we used. We were probing at the beast [of community power] with lots of different instruments . . . [but] for some reason, a number of readers seem to have come to the conclusion that all we did was study three decisions. (1986: 198–9)

Indeed, in *Who Governs?* an 11 page appendix reveals the methodological eclecticism of the New Haven study: historical surveys; interviews, and reinterviews, with 46 'active participants' in the three key decisions; questionnaires to 1063 members of organized groups and parties, 286 follow-up interviews; qualitative surveys of registered voters; quantitative analysis of voting and census data; and 'in addition, Dr Wolfinger spent a year in two highly strategic locations in City Hall and provided invaluable background information' (Dahl, 1961: vi).

Findings: New Haven and stratified pluralism

What this research strategy produced was the finding that over 'the course of the past two centuries, New Haven has gradually changed from oligarchy to pluralism' (Dahl, 1961: 11). Nonetheless, the pluralist city was 'stratified' in that there was, 'as in other political systems, a small stratum of individuals [who are] much more highly involved in political thought, discussion, and action than the rest of the population' (Dahl, 1961: 90). The politically active were *homo politicus*, the politically inactive *homo civicus*. However, the political system remained 'pluralist' to the extent that 'if leaders lead, they are also led' (1961: 102). The outcomes of decisions are uncertain given 'a stubborn and pervasive ambiguity that permeates the entire political system' (1961: 102). Thus, in the analysis of the three key issue areas in New Haven (urban redevelopment, public education and political nominations), only a small number of persons were found to have much *direct* influence (1961: 163), but 'most citizens . . . possess a moderate degree of indirect influence' in so far as elected leaders keep in mind 'the real or imagined preferences of constituents . . . in deciding what policies to adopt or reject' (1961: 164).

Decision making was 'stratified', therefore, in that its essential feature was a 'pluralism for and among active citizens' (Waste, 1987: 126). But the active citizenry did not constitute a single power elite. In each of the three issue areas different decision-making processes and participants were observed. In each area 'different actors appeared, their roles were different, and the kinds of alternatives which they had to choose among were different' (Polsby, 1980: 90). In other words different elites made different decisions in different issue areas. (This has led some commentators to argue that the dispute between elite theorists and pluralists is a 'non-controversy' (Perry and Gillespie, 1976), as what is at issue is the *number* of elites, not their existence – see Chapter 3.) What was seen as 'the most striking characteristic of influence' was the extent to which influence was *specialized*, that is, influential individuals and groups in one issue area were not necessarily, or normally, influential in other areas.

Moreover, Dahl argued that, whereas in the past there was cumulative inequality, with economic inequality translating into social and political inequality, 'in the political system of today inequalities in political resources remain, but they tend to be *noncumulative*. The political system of New Haven, then, is one of *dispersed inequalities*' (1961: 85, original emphasis). Dahl (1961: 228) proceeds to list six characteristics which mark a system of dispersed inequalities. First, different citizens have many different kinds of resources for influencing officials; second, these resources are invariably unequally distributed; third, individuals endowed with one resource are often 'badly off' with respect to many other resources; fourth, no one type of resource ('whatever may be used as an inducement is a resource' (1961: 226)) dominates all others; fifth, a resource may lead to influence in some but not in all issue areas; finally, virtually no individual or group is entirely lacking some influence resources.

What pluralists claim to provide is a 'realistic evaluation of the actual disposable resources of actors' (Polsby, 1980: 120). What is important is not mere possession of resources, therefore, but the 'processes of bargaining, negotiation, salesmanship and brokerage, and of leadership in mobilizing' those resources (Polsby, 1980: 120). The starting premise is that 'a political resource is only a *potential* resource' (Dahl, 1961: 271, original emphasis). The frequency and the range of issues upon which resources are expended needs to be considered, alongside the fact that most decisions 'move along in an atmosphere of apathy, indifference, and general agreement' (Dahl, 1961: 198).

Dahl is quite clear that as an empirical proposition it is axiomatic that 'inequality of influence is a characteristic of virtually all political systems, in all times and all places . . . those of us who came to be called pluralists, and certainly I, have never believed that all groups in politics are equal' (1986: 184). *Who Governs?* makes this point repeatedly:

> Within a century a political system dominated by one cohesive set of leaders had given way to a system dominated by many different sets of leaders, each having access to a different combination of political resources. It was in short a pluralist system. If the pluralist system was very far from being an oligarchy, it was also a long way from achieving the goal of political equality advocated by the philosophers of democracy. (Dahl, 1961: 86)

Like every other political system, of course, the political system of New Haven falls far short of the usual conceptions of an ideal democracy; by almost any standard, it is obviously full of defects. (Dahl, 1961: 311)

In summary, the political system was not oligarchical because policy success depended upon 'a capacity for anticipating what the organized interests, the political stratum, and the voters in general would tolerate or support'. The system might be stratified but it was also differentiated: different groups/elites wielded different degrees of influence in different policy areas at different times. In other words, there was a plurality of political institutions, elites, organized interests, individuals, and voters involved in decision making. Twenty-five years after the publication of *Who Governs?* Dahl still saw a pluralist process: 'New Haven was and is a community in which a diversity of groups exist and bear on the making of public policy'. But what Dahl also conceded upon reflection was that the New Haven study was 'a case study of one city at one time' (1986: 189).

Different 'pluralisms'? Different cities, different times, different countries

Considerable energy has been expended since 1961 both upon the extension of empirical case studies to other cities, and on advancing the case of the comparative conceptual utility of 'pluralism'. Dahl (1961: v) himself was careful to make no claims that his findings represented 'cities in general' though he did suggest that 'New Haven is in many respects typical of other cities in the United States' (1961: v). This latter phrase was interpreted by some critics to mean that pluralist findings would be apparent in 'any community' (see Crenson, 1971: 107). But pluralists themselves are careful to point out that 'to say that such statements [about the distribution of power] are true in New Haven is not to say that they are true elsewhere. That remains an empirical question' (Polsby, 1980: 164).

Cross-national comparison: Britain and pluralism

'Pluralist theory underlies most of the case studies of local politics in Britain': so states Hampton (1991: 238). More accurately, it is a *critique* of pluralist theory that has underpinned most British case studies (see, for example, Dearlove, 1973; Saunders, 1983). One major case study, conducted by Newton in Birmingham between 1966 and 1972, starts with a sceptical view of pluralist theory (1976: 73–88), and ends with an equally jaundiced view. Of more significance for present purposes, however, is Newton's discovery – no matter how grudgingly presented – of patterns of decision making compatible with pluralist theory (as stated by Dahl rather than by his critics). Indeed, just as Dahl believed that New Haven was in many respects typical of other American cities, so Newton took Birmingham 'as a fairly typical example of British cities in general'

(1976: 1). Newton employed a mixture of quantitative and qualitative techniques (interviews with 66 council members and 70 officers of politically active organizations, questionnaire responses from 466 'politically active' and 84 'politically inactive' organizations). In addition, he examined three issue areas – housing, education and race relations – which were chosen 'because all . . . are important, involving large numbers of people, large sums of money, or both' (Newton, 1976: 194). Newton's methodology was designed to discover the extent to which groups had been active when decisions taken by the council or public officials 'affected the interests of their organization' (1976: 37). What Newton found was different levels of group activity in each of the three areas. Housing was characterized by an 'extraordinarily high level of public involvement' and 'a high level of pressure group activity' (1976: 221). Education was more of a party political battle but nonetheless 'local pressure groups played a full part in th[e] sequence of events' (1976: 222). Race relations on the other hand provided an example of 'the politics of the powerless' with the issue of race 'gently shunted onto a political siding where it has been left for powerless and harmless bureaucrats to handle' (1976: 222). Newton therefore was confronted by his own findings: on education he concedes that 'in some important ways the pluralists are right about the issue' (1976: 225); on housing he notes that both producers and consumers were organized with access to decision makers. But he still takes pluralism to task because, even in these areas, group organization was 'lop-sided'. Yet, Dahl had already recognized that there were 'extensive inequalities in resources' (1961: 1) and that although there are many different kinds of resources 'with few exceptions, these resources are unequally distributed' (1961: 228). Newton then proceeds to argue that on the issue of race the 'pressure group system is not merely lop-sided, it is largely one-sided' (1976: 227). The position in Britain was soon to change (see below); even so – even in 1976 – Newton was forced to conclude:

> Birmingham's political system appears to be a pluralist democracy, but only in part. Political elites do respond with varying degrees of alacrity or reluctance to some publics . . . . To return once more to Robert Dahl's famous phrase, the city is a pluralist system, warts and all, but the warts are not simply unaesthetic; they disfigure the body politic and, in some instances, appear to be associated with a malign disease which gives grave cause for concern. (1976: 224)

This statement has been taken by many to be anti-pluralist (see Stoker, 1991: 119–20). Undoubtedly, it is meant to be. *But*, it is so largely in the sense of creating a 'straw man' version of pluralism that certainly Dahl and Polsby have difficulty in recognizing or accepting (see Polsby, 1980: 194–5). Thus, for example, Newton maintains that 'pluralist theory tends to work on the assumption that each and every interest is equally capable of organizing and defending itself' (1976: 228). This is an exaggeration. Dahl's 'theory' of urban pluralism did not combine the words 'each', 'every' and 'equally' in the manner ascribed to him by Newton (see Dahl, 1982: 207). Similarly, as noted above, pluralists were keenly aware of the inequality of resources available to groups and individuals. Thus, Newton chooses to ignore Dahl's statement that 'man for man an individual of low income is likely to have fewer total resources than a person of higher income' (Dahl, 1961: 243). Instead, Newton asserts simply that pluralists fail to acknowledge research indicating that 'people of lower socio-economic status have fewer political resources than people of higher status' (1976: 231). For this reason it is important to understand what pluralists say rather than to accept what their critics say that they say. This is not to deny the force of Newton's finding that in Birmingham a 'pattern of cumulative inequalities' is to be found among voluntary organizations. Indeed, in later reformulations, pluralist theory more explicitly acknowledged that 'organizational pluralism is perfectly consistent with extensive inequalities' (Dahl, 1982: 40); that there were indeed different 'types' of inequalities (Dahl, 1986: 185) and that 'pluralism . . . may also have undesirable consequences' (Dahl, 1984: 235). That pluralism was refined in this manner is indicative of the need both to respond to the weight of criticism heaped upon the original New Haven study and to take account of other political contexts in other cities at other times.

Comparison across time and space

While cross-national 'comparison' is important in understanding how the concept of pluralism has been operationalized, and in identifying different constellations of groups and their contribution to decision making, it is also important to make 'cross-time' comparisons. Simply stated, chronology is of importance because cities and the issues confronting them change over time. Moreover, developments and refinements in the conceptualization of research questions and methodology occur over time.

Pluralists sought not simply to encourage empirical comparative studies, but also to derive 'more general, comparative statements' from their own work from which expressed relations between variables can be discovered and 'general explanatory statements derived' (Polsby, 1980: 165). In so doing, they drew attention, no matter how unwittingly, to the wider national political and economic frame in which cities operated. If comparison was to be made then there was at least a prima facie case for the common constraints of the broader political system and capitalist economy upon individual cities to be brought into the research equation – at least as independent variables.

Hyperpluralism

Just such a direct link between temporal and economic change is made by Trounstine and Christenson: 'As cities grow, they diversify; elites can't command all the community's organizations; competition and pluralism increase' (1982: 40). Similarly, Ross et al. argue that 'the rise of taxpayer associations, neighborhood and minority groups, and environmentalist organization have all helped to make power in . . . cities more pluralistic' (1991: 58). Leaving aside, for the moment, the crucial question of whether social pluralism (the number of groups) is necessarily correlated with political pluralism (the diffusion of power), the impact that the very increase in the number of organized groups had upon the conceptualization of pluralism itself needs to be considered.

It was noted above that an underpinning assumption of the study of New Haven in the 1950s was that apathy and indifference characterized public attitudes towards the political process. In Dahl's words: 'Most citizens are indifferent about public matters unless public actions encroach upon their own primary activities (which is not often or for long)' (1961: 191). However, Thomas and Savitch claim that this was not unique to New Haven and that at the time 'most big cities [had] relatively few active or influential political groups' (1991: 9). This position was to change rapidly in the 1960s as the combined effects of the growth in the size of urban ethnic/minority communities, urban riots, and federal programmes (community action, model cities, etc.) 'signalled an expansion in the number, power, and stridency of political groups in America's big cities' (Thomas and Savitch, 1991: 10). This increase in political activism led some analysts to reformulate the original pluralist question of 'Who Governs?' into 'Does Anybody Govern?' The starting assumption was thus: given, on the one side, the number, diversity and scope of organized interests, and, on the other, the diminution in the capacity of elected politicians to control city bureaucrats, there would be policy instability and a fragmented and ineffective process of decision making.

Yates is in no doubt that:

> The environment of policy making and the character of urban problems determine the shape of urban policy. Policy outcomes are a product of highly fragmented and unstable problem and policy contexts. And it is precisely because urban policy makers must deal with so many different, fragmented problem and policy contexts that urban policy making as a whole is so fragmented, unstable and reactive. (1977: 85)

In other words, instead of the benign process of group competition and responsive political leadership identified in earlier pluralist studies, Yates's experiences of New York and New Haven (again!) lead him to argue that policy making was 'fragmented to the point of chaos'. What existed was 'an extreme pluralism of political, administrative, and community interests which produces . . . "street fighting pluralism"' (1977: 34). This new pluralist variant reflected an intricate process characterized by 'diversity, variability, complexity, instability, and interdependence of interests and decision games and by the fact that policy making involves direct and well-crystallized conflicts about urban goods and services' (Yates, 1977: 37). On this basis such cities were deemed to be 'ungovernable'. Indeed, Lineberry (1980: 50) later underscored Yates's argument by pointing to the 'exaggerated', 'extreme' and 'perverted form' of hyperpluralism – a system in which 'too many groups, each refuse to take "no" for an answer'.

Significantly, Yates chose to criticize Dahl's New Haven study (and Banfield's (1961) *Political Influence*) on methodological grounds. His contention was that the issues chosen by Dahl reveal as much about the character of urban policy making in particular issue areas as they do about the general power structure (Yates, 1977: 89). Hence the conclusions reached about power relations in earlier pluralist studies are seen to be a reflection of the decisions chosen for study. Yates claims, instead, that his analysis of 'decision games' in New York City supports the proposition that governing the city becomes more difficult the greater the number of participants; the more the major participants are independent of city hall; the more zero-sum conflicts are involved; and the more issues become 'symbolic' – in that they become defined in terms of 'racism', 'power to the people' or 'oppression of the ordinary citizen' (Yates, 1977: 138). In these circumstances 'urban decision games turn into unstructured, unstable free-for-alls (street-fighting pluralism)' (Yates, 1977: 144).

It is instructive to note that Yates did not employ sophisticated qualitative or quantitative research techniques to arrive at his conclusions. Indeed, his findings are based primarily upon his 'personal observation of events and on notes kept in a diary', his 'own experience', 'personal conversations' and 'on coverage in the *New York Times*' (Yates, 1977: 204–6). In other words, Yates could not substantiate his claim empirically. (In fact, to argue that a city is 'ungovernable' requires the qualification of evidence to the contrary – that large areas of policy are entirely 'governable', not to mention routine.) Yet, his 'perception' was that contemporary city politics is incoherent and ineffective, where nobody really makes decisions, or if decisions are made it is remarkably difficult to trace exactly who exerted what amounts of influence at which stage in the process of decision.

A strong resemblance to Yates's 'street-fighting pluralism' has recently been discerned in a study of 13 American cities (Savitch and Thomas, 1991). This study offers a 'profile' of each major city 'with an eye toward what kinds of groups, coalitions, or actors have emerged since the 1960s and what portends for big city politics in the 1990s' (Thomas and Savitch, 1991: 12). Common to all these cities was a 'splintering' of their political composition and an 'intensification of the old pluralism' (Savitch and Thomas, 1991: 246). This led to the conclusion that 'few if any of the elite power structures of the Floyd Hunter era survive today' (1991: 246). But if pluralism had 'triumphed' – in the limited and negative respect of the demise of elite findings – it was a pyrrhic theoretical victory because the assumed *inherent benignity* of pluralism itself could not be defended. The pluralism of the 1980s and 1990s according to Savitch and Thomas is 'hyperpluralism'. To be more precise still it is 'contemporary hyper-pluralism'. In this 'contemporary' form it differs from Yates's 'street-fighting pluralism' in that it has moved from the streets of the city to the corridors of city hall, transitioning from the pitched battles of 'street fighting pluralism' to the periodic negotiations for a share of the pie in the 'corridors of power'. With that transition has come a muting of the stridency that characterized the earlier hyperpluralism but no lessening of the demands on the resources of the city. (Savitch and Thomas, 1991: 246)

However, once back in city hall the influence of public leaders is brought back into the research equation, and the concerns of Dahl re-emerge: that is, how does an executive-centred coalition emerge in the context of group diffusion and competition? Thus, Savitch and Thomas are led to concede: 'Much as we may interpret and debate the meaning of our 13 city profiles, the direction of change is toward some kind of pluralist or hyperpluralist system' (1991: 248). Indeed, Houston alone of the 13 cities was seen to be run in much the same elitist manner as 30 years ago (Parker and Feagin, 1991: 187). Even here, however, this conclusion has recently been challenged. Richard Murray, of the University of Houston, argues that

the reality is that Houston has become more pluralistic over time. One reason is simply that the city has grown . . . power must now be shared with more and more participants. This means that political power in Houston is now *coalitional* in nature because no single ethnic, ideological, or economic group dominates the city. Successful leaders have to pull together diverse coalitions to get elected and move their policies forward. (1992: 186)

If anything 'political power is likely to become more fragmented, more pluralistic' (Murray, 1992: 187).

Antiregimes, regimes and neo-pluralism

Perhaps nowhere is fragmentation of social and political structures better illustrated than in San Francisco. In 1974 Frederick Wirt described the city's combination of decentralized governmental system and highly fragmented interest group politics as 'hyperpluralistic'. Manuel Castells (1983: 326) in *City and the Grassroots* identifies a 'wild city' where urban social movements emerge in a negative and reactive way to resist change, growth and progress as defined by business elites. DeLeon in *Left Coast City* notes that San Francisco's hyperpluralism is even greater than it was at the time of Wirt's (1974) study (DeLeon, 1992: 31). From this observation DeLeon then proceeds to argue:

the 'wild city' is another name for the kind of chaos that San Franciscans have made for themselves and are trying to escape today. . . . Leaders of the progressive coalition somehow have to solve the problems of endemic hyperpluralism, crises of governance, internal conflicts, and mounting conservative opposition. What the city has at best is an *antiregime*. (1992: 7–8, original emphasis)

An antiregime is 'a defensive system of governance designed to block and filter big business power and to protect [the city] . . . from unregulated market forces and grandiose progrowth schemes' (DeLeon, 1992: 11). The antiregime is seen as the first line of defence in the protection of social diversity, and its primary instrument is local government control over land use and development. It constitutes a 'kind of latter day urban feudalism that preserves local diversity by complicating the exercise of centralized power' (1992: 139).

DeLeon's findings and analysis are located within the conceptual language of regimes, discussed in Chapter 4. Much of the discussion of urban regimes revolves around the informal arrangements that exist between a city's political and business elites to facilitate economic development. But, according to DeLeon (1992: 136), two of the key assumptions of regime theory do not apply in San Francisco: first, that an urban regime increases governability through the promotion of economic and physical development; and, second, that political order is secured through the imposition of elite will over that of the masses. (In fact, most regime theorists would not accept these assumptions.) What does apply, however, is social and ethnic diversity where there is 'no natural majority' and where 'majorities are made, not found' (DeLeon, 1992: 13). San Francisco is now 'the Balkans by the Bay. Everything is *pluribus*, nothing is *unum*. Hyperpluralism reigns' (1992: 13). In which case, 'antiregime' turns out to be a particular form of obstructive hyperpluralism. While DeLeon identifies the urban regime concept as being 'central to the theoretical, empirical, and polemical arguments of this study' (1992: 4) most of his attention thereafter is focused upon its conceptual and practical limitations.

Indeed, it is worth taking a slight detour here (without impinging too much upon the territory of Chapter 4) to examine the conceptual distinctiveness of 'regime theory'. This examination is necessary because Stone, who is most closely associated with the concept of urban regime, acknowledges that 'to a casual observer, regime analysis might appear to be a return to classical urban pluralism . . . . After all, the executive-centred coalition described in *Who Governs?* [Dahl, 1961] bears all the earmarks of a regime' (1993: 1). But Stone is adamant that 'fundamental differences separate the two approaches to urban politics' (1993: 1). He chooses to make the distinction by rejecting *what he identifies* to be three basic assumptions of pluralist analysis: first 'voting strength [as] the key factor in political power'; second, the treatment of 'the public and private sectors as politically distinct and the downplaying [of] the complex interrelationships between government and the economy'; and, third, 'the assumption of an autonomous state' (Stone 1993: 4).

In elaborating the 'pluralist position' Stone identifies the centrality of elections and voting to the exercise of political power. In fact, he maintains that pluralists treat the 'problem of inequality as being election-centred', and cites in evidence Dahl's statement that 'running counter to th[e] legal equality of citizens . . . is an unequal distribution of the resources that can be used for influencing the choices of voters, and between elections, of officials' (Dahl, 1961: 4). Stone chooses to emphasize voters and elections in this sentence, but equally 'between elections' and 'officials' could have been emphasized – but to different effect. Similarly, Stone chooses to argue that Dahl treats the public and private sectors as politically distinct and so downplays the complex interrelationships between government and the economy (1993: 4). This might have been true in 1961, but even in *Who Governs?* there are sufficient passages to sustain a case that Dahl was aware of the linkage of the private and public sectors. Dahl was willing to acknowledge the existence of governing coalitions 'of public officials and private individuals who reflect the interests and concerns of different segments of the community' (1961: 186). In the case of redevelopment, Dahl identifies the key actors as being 'with few exceptions officially, professionally, or financially involved in its fate' (1961: 183). 'In origins, conception, and execution, it is not too much to say that urban redevelopment has been the direct product of a small handful of leaders' (1961: 115). However, Stone's argument is even more difficult to sustain in the 1990s given the acceptance by Dahl of the manifest linkages between public and private spheres, and between the economy and the polity.

Upon reflection Dahl was willing to accept that the structural constraints of the capitalist economy should have been more explicitly acknowledged in *Who Governs?*:

> I took for granted that New Haven, like any other city in the United States, operates as a part of a capitalist system – an economic system in which many crucial decisions are made with some degree of autonomy, though not necessarily local autonomy by corporate leaders. That being the case, not only are some decisions important in the life of the community that lies outside the conventionally defined political realm of municipal politics, but also within the realm of the conventionally defined political life of municipality, decision makers will be influenced – directly and indirectly – by the need to take into account the decisions and influences of the market system. A lot of that I took for granted. (1986: 192)

Indeed, Dahl in his earlier work with Charles Lindblom – *Politics, Economics and Welfare* (1953) – had begun to examine the relationship between business and government. In his later work Dahl came to acknowledge the severe political violations of political equality produced by corporate capitalism (Dahl, 1985: 102) and to conclude generally that 'capitalism is persistently at odds with values of equity, fairness, political equality among all citizens, and democracy' (Dahl, 1990: 83). But Dahl essentially left it to Lindblom (1977: 170–221) to explain in detail the 'privileged position of business'. Lindblom is insistent that the political role of business is not merely an interest group role. At most business interest group activity is 'only a supplement to its privileged position' (1977: 193). More profoundly, there is a tacit understanding shared by government and business 'with respect to the conditions under which enterprises can or cannot profitably operate' (1977: 179). In other words, Lindblom identifies systemic constraints imposed upon public policy by the requirements of private accumulation. He acknowledges, therefore, the 'early, persuasive, unconscious conditioning . . . to believe in the fundamental politico-economic institutions' of capitalist society. And by the time Dahl wrote *Democracy and its Critics* there is an explicit recognition of the special importance of 'business firms' and 'economic enterprises' in the state (1989: 327). These bear a close resemblance to the constraints examined by Stone (1980). Indeed, Stone (1993: 14) eventually redirects his attention from Dahl to Polsby, to make the case that pluralists see 'the economy and political affairs as separate arenas'. Yet, in quoting the latter to support his case – 'If a man's major life work is banking, the pluralist presumes he will spend his time at the bank and not in manipulating community decisions' (Polsby, 1980: 117) – Stone leaves out Polsby's next sentence: 'This presumption holds until the banker's activities and participations indicate otherwise'. In other words, Polsby's comments were made in the context of a discussion about the measurement of influence and of assessing 'overt' as opposed to 'covert' action (rather than of the separation of economic from political activity).

The fact that both Dahl and Lindblom (who by the 1970s could be designated as 'neo-pluralists' (see Dunleavy and O'Leary, 1987: 283)) and regime theorists were responding to Marxist critiques of urban decision making undoubtedly led them to address common issues and so to reconsider and refract their arguments through the analytical challenge posed by neo-Marxist theory (see Chapter 13). Yet, in seeking to differentiate themselves from Marxist analyses these theories seem to have backed into each other – no matter how unwittingly and partially.

So does the difference between regime theory and pluralism ultimately distil into a dispute over the degree of 'imbalance in abilities to contribute to the capacity to govern' (Stone, 1989: 223)? In Stone's analysis the business elite is 'uniquely able to enhance the capacity of a local regime to govern'. This stems from its 'systemic power' (see Stone, 1980). The concept of systemic power attempts to deal with the problems raised variously in the radical, Marxist and neo-Marxist debates about non-decisions, the third face of power and ruling class hegemony. As such it focuses upon how a highly stratified socioeconomic system constrains the autonomy of urban public officials in decision making. In so doing Stone (1989: 988) argues the concept 'throws off the pluralist prediction that electoral competition and administrative fragmentation will yield shifting coalitions and unpatterned biases'. Ultimately, Stone is left to differentiate regime theory from pluralism in terms of the conception of power as 'power to' rather than 'power over', of a 'systemic' versus a 'social control' model of power. But even here the distinction is not entirely clear cut. As much is acknowledged by Stone: 'there is an admitted kinship between pluralism and the social production model of power. In regime theory, the capacity to govern is always partial and it is subject to the centrifugal forces to which pluralists are sensitive' (1993: 8). Yet still Stone wants to sustain 'a basic difference' from pluralism and to do so on the grounds that 'nongovernment resources are highly skewed and reflect a stratified society' (1993: 8). But Dahl, in his 'neo-pluralist' guise, would presumably have few qualms in accepting that!

Britain and neo-pluralism

In Britain recognition of the impact of temporal considerations upon both the theory and practice of pluralism has led Stoker to challenge elitist interpretations of local decision making in so far as they 'do not match the complexity of current relationships between local authorities and local interest groups. The principal claim is that times have changed' (1991: 123). What had changed in particular was the tendency of many local authorities from the mid-1970s onwards (the very time of the publication of Newton's study of Birmingham) to seek the active involvement of organized interests in decision making. Combined with this was a 'strengthening and a widening of the base of local interest group activity' (Stoker, 1991: 128). Indeed, these two developments were often inter-connected. Whereas Newton found ethnic minorities to be ignored in, let alone excluded from, the processes of urban decision making, a decade later Ben-Tovim et al. (1986) and Jacobs (1986) pointed to the activism and 'inclusion' of ethnic organizations in local politics. Moreover, the rise of a state-sponsored community work 'profession', with explicit political goals of stimulating community action and participation on the part of voluntary organizations and local welfare groups (see Lees and Mayo, 1984; Stoker, 1991: 130–2), served to enhance the pluralist characteristics of British local politics. The picture was now one of social pluralism paralleling an institutional pluralism. In Stoker's words: 'the reality . . . is often of different interests attracting support from different sections of the local authority' (1991: 135).

   But Stoker then went on to argue that this was 'very much a "surface" picture of local interest group politics' (1991: 136). More specifically he advanced an argument, very similar to Lindblom's, about the privileged position of business: 'certain interests – especially business interests – have such a crucial role in society that no government, local or central, can afford to ignore their interest' (Stoker, 1991: 136). The same position is thus reached on the British side of the Atlantic as on the American side – there are pluralist processes at work (both social and political) – but that these processes are 'constrained' or 'bounded' by systemic socioeconomic variables which have to be included in the research equation.

We are all pluralists now?

So the question raised in the introduction now needs to be answered. Perhaps the safest answer is yes and no: we are pluralists in the sense of recognizing the diversity and the inevitable 'social plurality' of large cities, we are pluralists in recognizing the 'process' of group competition; but we are not necessarily 'normative pluralists' (if the latter is seen to be a defence of liberal capitalist society). But that is too easy an answer. If nothing else this chapter has demonstrated that pluralist theory is not the monochromatic picture often painted by its critics. It has to be seen through the eyes of pluralist writers themselves, or more accurately read from their own words. As an empirical descriptive theory it is as complex and as changing as the reality it seeks to describe. The argument here has been that when the qualifications and conceptual hesitations of pluralists are acknowledged, then it becomes essential to add prefixes to the term pluralism. We should speak of 'stratified', 'hyper-', 'bounded', or 'neo-' pluralism and be sensitive to the spatial, temporal and socioeconomic contexts of each variant. When these qualifications are put in place then the elite versus pluralist debate is at best a 'non-controversy' as what is at issue is 'competitive elitism'. Similarly, the later debate between pluralist theory and regime theory (or more accurately the dismissal of the former by the latter) resolves itself into the nature of 'governing coalitions'. By the time neo-pluralism has been elaborated then fine distinctions have to be drawn in order to separate Lindblom's 'neo-pluralism' from Stone's notion of 'systemic' power. Ironically, Stone (1980: 985), in advancing his thesis of 'systemic power', actually quotes Lindblom – but identifies the latter as a 'radical critic' (Stone, 1993: 5) rather than as a pluralist! Even the newer concept of 'anti-regime' turns out in practice to be a variant of 'hyper-pluralism'.

In part this conclusion is consciously reductionist and is designed to provoke thought about successive chapters. If it is 'overly' reductionist then it is so because it is easy to be so. Most of the recent theorizing about urban politics has often forgotten about pluralism (other than as some straw man argument) and so rediscovers, by default and unawares, elements of pluralism. Moreover most recent theorizing has been precisely that: theorizing. As Bryan Jones points out:

> Empirical work has lagged far behind this cutting theoretical edge. As theory has gotten better, empiricism has, if anything, gotten worse. I do not mean that empirical work is less competent technically – it is vastly superior to that produced a decade or two ago. But it is less relevant to theory. (1989: 39)

This is a major point, for methodology is both the beginning and end of the 'testing' of theory. For a variety of reasons (not the least of which is financial cost) methodologies have become less extensive since *Who Governs?* (see Yates, 1977; Dahl, 1986: 190; Stone, 1989: 258–60). One consequence has been that assertion has often replaced detailed evidence. Another factor has been that much of the debate has been ideologically driven. Dahl, as noted above, has been accused of being an apologist of liberal democracy. And, indeed, if the explicitly normative dimensions of 'polyarchy' are admitted, then 'polyarchy' (note not 'pluralism') could be seen to have an ideological purpose. Precisely this point has traditionally been made by radicals and Marxist critics.

Yet, a reassessment of the importance of Dahl's work is underway – at least among leftist writers in Britain. Thus, for example, Paul Hirst regards it to be 'a pity that Marxists have spent so long decrying and systematically misunderstanding promising and rigorous theories like those of R.A. Dahl' (1990: 56). Similarly, Anne Phillips acknowledges that the deep gulf between 'pluralism and the left is being bridged' (1993: 141). She then notes a particular element in the 'recuperation of pluralism' to be the growing emphasis on the political significance 'of sub-groups that are defined through gender, ethnicity, religion, sexuality, language and so on'. In other words, there is a 'new pluralism' of social movements (see Chapters 10 and 11 on social movements and feminism, respectively). Even within the more routine concerns of local government studies, Desmond King has called for 'the traditional community power approach pioneered by Robert Dahl in his pluralist analysis' to be 'resurrected and broadened to capture the dynamics of the new post-Thatcher local government system' (1993: 215). Ultimately, what these developments reveal is that if we are not yet 'all pluralists now', at least it is now academically respectable to take pluralism seriously. Dahl is in danger of becoming one of the 'good guys'!

Note

My thanks to Grant Jordan, Mike Keating, Bob Lineberry, Gerry Stoker and Hal Wolman for their comments on an earlier version of this chapter.

References

Anton, T. (1963) 'Power, pluralism and local politics', *Administrative Science Quarterly*, 7 (2): 425–57.

Bachrach, P. and Baratz, M.S. (1962) 'Two faces of power', *American Political Science Review*, 56 (4): 947–52.

Bachrach, P. and Baratz, M.S. (1970) *Power and Poverty*. New York: Oxford University Press.

Banfield, E.C. (1961) *Political Influence*. New York: Free Press.

Bell, C. and Newby, H. (1971) *Community Studies*. London: Allen and Unwin.

Ben-Tovim, G., Gabriel, J., Law, I. and Stredder, K. (1986) *The Local Politics of Race*. London: Macmillan.

Castells, M. (1983) *The City and the Grassroots*. Berkeley: University of California Press.

Connolly, W.E. (1966) *The Bias of Pluralism*. Chicago: Aldine Atherton.

Connolly, W.E. (1972) 'On "interests" in politics', *Politics and Society*, 2 (4): 459–78.

Cox, A., Furlong, P. and Page, E. (1985) *Power in Capitalist Society: Theory, Explanations and Cases*. Brighton: Wheatsheaf.

Crenson, M. (1971) *The Un-Politics of Air-Pollution*. Baltimore: Johns-Hopkins University Press.

Dahl, R.A. (1961) *Who Governs? Democracy and Power in an American City*. New Haven: Yale University Press.

Dahl, R.A. (1982) *Dilemmas of Pluralist Democracy*. New Haven: Yale University Press.

Dahl, R.A. (1984) 'Polyarchy, pluralism and scale', *Scandinavian Political Studies*, 7 (4): 225–40.

Dahl, R.A. (1985) *A Preface to Economic Democracy.* Berkeley: University of California Press.

Dahl, R.A. (1986) 'Rethinking *Who Governs?* New Haven revisited', in R.J. Waste (ed.), *Community Power Directions for Future Research.* Newbury Park, CA: Sage.

Dahl, R.A. (1989) *Democracy and its Critics.* New Haven: Yale University Press.

Dahl, R.A. (1990) *After the Revolution?* (2nd edn). New Haven: Yale University Press.

Dahl, R.A. and Lindblom, C. (1953) *Politics, Economics and Welfare.* New York: Harper and Row.

Dearlove, J. (1973) *The Politics of Policy in Local Government.* Cambridge: Cambridge University Press.

DeLeon, R.E. (1992) *Left Coast City: Progressive Politics in San Francisco, 1975–1991.* Kansas: University of Kansas.

Dunleavy, P. and O'Leary, B. (1987) *Theories of the State.* London: Macmillan.

Gaventa, J. (1980) *Power and Powerlessness: Quiescence and Rebellion in an Appalachian Valley.* Urbana: University of Illinois Press.

Hampton, W. (1991) *Local Government and Urban Politics* (2nd edn). London: Longman.

Hirst, P. (1990) *Representative Democracy and its Limits.* London: Polity.

Hunter, F. (1953) *Community Power Structure.* Chapel Hill: University of North Carolina Press.

Jacobs, B.D. (1986) *Black Politics and Urban Crisis in Britain.* Cambridge: Cambridge University Press.

Jones, B. (1989) 'Why weakness is a strength: some thoughts on the current state of urban analysis', *Urban Affairs Quarterly*, 25 (1): 30–40.

Jordan, G. (1990) 'The pluralism of pluralism: an anti-theory?', *Political Studies*, 38 (2): 286–301.

King, D. (1993) 'Government beyond Whitehall', in P. Dunleavy, A. Gamble, I. Halliday and G. Peele (eds), *Developments in British Politics 4.* London: Macmillan.

Lees, R. and Mayo, M. (1984) *Community Action for Change.* London: Routledge and Kegan Paul.

Lindblom, C.E. (1977) *Politics and Markets.* New York: Basic Books.

Lineberry, R. (1980) *Government in America: People, Politics, and Policy.* Boston: Little Brown.

Lukes, S. (1974) *Power: A Radical View.* London: Macmillan.

Murray, R. (1992), 'Power in the city: patterns of political influence in Houston, Texas', in K.L. Tedin, D.S. Lutz and E.P. Fuchs (eds), *Perspectives on American and Texas Politics* (3rd edn). Iowa: Kendall Hunt.

Newton, K. (1976) *Second City Politics: Democratic Processes and Decision Making in Birmingham.* Oxford: Oxford University Press.

Parker, R.E. and Feagin, J.R. (1991) 'Houston: administration by economic elites', in H.V. Savitch and J.C. Thomas (eds), *Big City Politics in Transition.* Newbury Park, CA: Sage.

Perry, R.W. and Gillespie, D.F. (1976) 'Community power: a controversial "non-controversy"', *Scottish Journal of Sociology*, 1 (1): 45–56.

Phillips, A. (1993) *Democracy and Difference.* Cambridge: Polity.

Polsby, N.W. (1980) *Community Power and Political Theory* (2nd edn). New Haven: Yale University Press.

Ricci, D. (1971) *Community Power and Democratic Theory.* New York: Random House.

Ross, B.H., Levine, M.A. and Stedman, M.S. (1991) *Urban Politics: Power in Metropolitan America.* Illinois: Peacock Publishers.

Saunders, P. (1983) *Urban Politics; A Sociological Interpretation.* London: Hutchinson.

Savitch, H.V. and Thomas, J.C. (1991) 'Conclusion: End of the millennium big city politics', in H.V. Savitch and J.C. Thomas (eds), *Big City Politics in Transition.* Newbury Park, CA: Sage.

Smith, M.J. (1990) 'Pluralism, reformed pluralism and neopluralism: the role of pressure groups in policy making', *Political Studies*, 38 (2): 302–22.

Stoker, G. (1991) *The Politics of Local Government* (2nd edn). London: Macmillan.

Stone, C.N. (1980) 'Systemic power in community decision making: a restatement of stratification theory', *American Political Science Review*, 74 (4): 978–90.

Stone, C.N. (1989) *Regime Politics: Governing Atlanta, 1946–1988*. Kansas: University of Kansas Press.

Stone, C.N. (1993) 'Urban regimes and the capacity to govern: a political economy approach', *Journal of Urban Affairs*, 15 (1): 1–28.

Thomas, J.C. and Savitch, H.V. (1991) 'Introduction: big city politics, then and now', in H.V. Savitch and J.C. Thomas (eds), *Big City Politics in Transition*. Newbury Park, CA: Sage.

Trounstine, P.J. and Christenson, T. (1982) *Movers and Shakers: The Study of Community Power*. New York: St Martin's Press.

Walker, J. (1966) 'A critique of elitist democracy', *American Political Science Review*, 60 (2): 285–95.

Waste, R.J. (1986) 'Community power and pluralist theory', in R.J. Waste (ed.), *Community Power Directions for Future Research*. Newbury Park, CA: Sage.

Waste, R.J. (1987) *Power and Pluralism in American Cities*. New York: Greenwood Press.

Wirt, F.M. (1974) *Power in the City: Decision Making in San Francisco*. Berkeley: University of California Press.

Yates, D. (1977) *The Ungovernable City: The Politics of Urban Problems and Policy Making*. Cambridge MA: MIT Press.

3

Elite Theory and Growth Machines

Alan Harding

The nature and development of elite theory

Anyone who ever thinks about the world in terms of what *they* are doing to or for *us* carries an implicit elite theory in his or her head. *They* are the elite, the group(s) of individuals whose decisions play a crucial part in shaping the lives, choices and futures of the mass of people. To speak of an elite is to have a mental picture of the way power is distributed. Whether we live in democratic or authoritarian societies, with market or command economies, 'common sense' generally tells us that control over crucial resources like property, money, the legitimate use of violence, political influence, scientific knowledge and so on is concentrated in the hands of a few. Social structures resemble pyramids, with a relatively small number of very powerful people at the top gradually giving way to a large mass of unpowerful individuals at the bottom. Elite theory is based on this hierarchical conception of society and concerns itself with relations between the rulers and the ruled, the powerful and the powerless.

Modern elite theory[1] has developed over the last century but rigorous conceptions of elites and elitism date back at least as far as Ancient Greece (Plato, 1974). Indeed, such terms have probably been in currency for as long as distinctions have been made between individuals or groups on the basis of possessions, status and leadership capacity. The *Oxford English Dictionary* defines elitism as 'advocacy of or reliance on leadership or domination of a select group'. The distinction between leadership and domination implies important differences in the level of consent accorded to elites by the rest of society. Leadership suggests a willingness to follow whereas domination implies a simple inability to resist. The distinction between advocacy and reliance is even more critical. To argue that society *is* controlled by an elite is very different from arguing that this is how things *should be*. It may be possible to demonstrate reliance on elite leadership and domination without believing it to be natural, just, efficient or satisfactory when measured against a range of criteria which might define a good society. At the other extreme, one might positively favour rule by the few and attempt to show that major problems only arise when elites are challenged or are not allowed to rule. Alternatively, one could view evidence of elite rule with trepidation but conclude, reluctantly, that it is a necessary evil for the functioning of society.

In fact, these three positions summarize the main approaches within elite theory. Only one could be described as elitist. That is the *normative* approach associated mainly with early (modern) elite theorists from the Italian school.[2] The subtly different arguments of Mosca (1939), Pareto (1935) and their acolyte Michels (1959) deserve separate discussion[3] but their nineteenth and early twentieth century works were clearly 'part of a political doctrine which was opposed to, or critical of, modern democracy, and still more opposed to modern socialism' (Bottomore, 1966: 15). They saw human history as dictated not by class struggle but by the domination of a disorganized majority by an organized minority. Irrespective of the form government takes, the victors in the intense competition for political and economic power guard their privileges jealously. Normative elite theorists mainly used this basic argument to dismiss the strong egalitarian and democratic claims of the then burgeoning working class movement. Other questions, like whether the competition for power was an equal one, whether the organized elite deserved its position, whether it could be displaced if it did not, and whether elites ruled in their own interests or those of society as a whole, were seen as less important.

Normative elite theorists viewed the leading features of liberal democracy – the universal franchise and free competition between political parties – as at best making no difference to the 'fact' of elite rule. At worst, they could lead to responsible elites being replaced with others that were intellectually, morally and economically inferior or raise unrealistic expectations of political and economic equality among the masses. Either way, destabilization, national decline or more authoritarian government would ensue. Michels's contribution was to argue that even ostensibly democratic organizations pursuing egalitarian goals – socialist political parties and trade unions – are rendered undemocratic and conservative by the 'iron law of oligarchy' that governs all bureaucracies. The hierarchy, discipline and competitiveness essential to organizational survival means that party and union leaders inevitably become remote from ordinary members and follow courses of action that are good for their organizations rather than the constituencies they were designed to serve. For Michels, such organizations either become indistinguishable from non-socialist ones or, at worst, centralize power and rule more autocratically than their rivals.

A *technocratic* approach suggests that elites, for good or ill, are necessary for the management of increasingly complex modern societies. The analysis is similar to the Italian school's but the conclusions are less pessimistic. Weber, the classical sociologist and major influence on Michels, argued (1968) that the extended division of labour associated with industrialization generated forms of human organization that were more efficient than those of earlier ages. In place of the traditional authority of the feudal era, based on the divinity of Church and Crown, came rational authority, based on bureaucratic efficiency and meritocracy. Bureaucracy relies on specialized tasks being performed according to formal rules and procedures within a well-defined hierarchy. Power is therefore concentrated in the hands of the few who occupy commanding positions within society's leading bureaucracies. Weber realized that growing bureaucratization could result in self-serving rule by senior government and business figures, working in tandem. He was optimistic, however, that liberal democratic systems of representative government could harness bureaucratic power for broader purposes. Elected politicians, utilizing charismatic authority, were the key to maintaining social control over powerful bureaucratic forces.

Critical elite theory is the flip side of the normative approach but takes on board many aspects of the technocratic approach. It is also the perspective that informs most of the applications of elite theory to urban studies. Critical elite theorists like the sociologist C. Wright Mills (1956) see the 'power elite' as neither natural nor desirable but as the worrying product of historical trends. Mills suggests power in the US was once widely dispersed and decentralized. Countless small-scale leaders in business, politics and military affairs shared power and influence with social institutions like the family, the church and schools. However, with growing bureaucratization, power became concentrated within large business corporations, the central executive machinery of government and the military establishment. The US became a military-industrial complex[4] in which a few senior decision makers in the three key power centres were afforded the capacity to monopolize crucial national decisions by virtue of their organizations' control over vast physical, financial, political and intellectual resources. The elements of the power elite might sometimes disagree among themselves or fail to use their ruling capacity. But it is they alone who have that capacity. For Mills, representative democratic institutions as organized and configured at the time had effectively surrendered sovereignty to a mainly unelected power elite.

This brief review indicates the breadth and heterogeneity of elite theory. It accommodates a range of positions from virulent anti-Marxism to neo-Marxism[5] and can be applied to all forms of society, not just capitalist ones. Relatively few elite theorists talk of a ruling *class*[6] and even classical Marxists (Trotsky, 1972) adapted the language and concepts of elite theory when analysing the stubborn persistence of centralized, minority rule within the one-party systems of socialist states. Among the few general tendencies to be discerned within elite theory is that political scientists concentrate somewhat narrowly on elite-formation in and around the machinery of government whereas sociologists see political leaders as one element of a wider elite, usually encompassing military and business leaders. Beyond this, there is little internal agreement on basic themes such as the precise composition of elites, whether they rule by consent, right, force or duplicity, whether they evolve over time to reflect wider social change or hang on to power by manipulation, and so on.

Elite theory and urban politics

Classical elite theorists used 'societies' – effectively countries – as their
basic units of analysis. Before long, though, researchers were asking
whether elite analysis was valid at different spatial levels. After all,
societies are not the only entities associated with specific geographical
boundaries, particular cultures, certain divisions of labour and a given set
of institutions. If it was worth asking whether societies were dominated by
elites, could the same question not be posed about cities? Furthermore, if
cities are effectively microcosms of societies, and since cities are smaller
and more manageable for the purposes of empirical research, couldn't
urban elite studies generate insights that might be applied more generally?

In answering these questions affirmatively, scholars who applied elite
theory to studies of urban politics triggered a major development in
empirical work on cities. They also opened up a methodological can of
worms. With the partial exception of Michels, the work of classical elite
theorists contained little in the way of contemporary empirical study.
Their arguments were developed from theoretical principles and the
marshalling of 'facts' provided by ancient and modern historians. Mosca
identified a dilemma for researchers when he suggested that members of an
elite never admit to – or perhaps even recognize – their own power. Elites
always try to legitimize the status quo with reference to an abstract
principle like divine right or representative democracy – what Mosca
called a 'political formula' – which makes their rule seem more palatable
or natural to the majority they rule over. If this was true, how were
(urban) elites to be identified through empirical study?

The first rigorous attempt to apply elite theory to urban studies was
made by Hunter (1953). In his study of Regional City (actually Atlanta,
Georgia), Hunter attempted to solve the methodological dilemma by
applying what became known as reputational analysis. In reputational
analysis, the basic data employed to 'prove' the power of individuals is
their reputation for having that power. Hunter's 'objective' method began
with the identification of community influentials; individuals 'in prominent
positions within four groups that *may be assumed to have power connections* . . . business, government, civic associations, and "society" activities'
(Hunter, 1953: 11, emphasis added). A long list of individuals within these
four groups was assembled, drawing on the personal knowledge of Hunter
and his key contacts and formal lists held by local organizations. A panel
of judges was then asked to rank people within each group according to
their reputation for power. The 40 top-ranked people were then inter-
viewed in depth in order to ascertain who among them was perceived to be
most powerful, how they interacted, how they grouped themselves in
relation to key 'community projects' and how their influence over these
projects was channelled.

Hunter found that his community influentials formed themselves into
'crowds' depending on their main interests but that the leaders of each

crowd together comprised a powerful and coherent cadre of perceived 'policy makers'. Virtually all of them were senior executives within key Atlanta businesses. Few were visible to the lay community. They generally left it to others, less important or senior than themselves, to be most active within business and civic associations. Neither did they make policy in a political or administrative sense. Atlanta's mayor was the only government figure seen as belonging to the policy-making group. But the textbook process of policy making, whereby the electorate's desires are translated into policies by elected representatives and implemented by officials, allegedly bore no relation to the reality. Rather, 'institutions and the formal associations play . . . a vital role in the execution of determined policy . . . but the formulation of policy often takes place outside these formalized groupings. Within the policy-forming groups the economic interests are dominant' (Hunter, 1953: 82). In other words, nothing in the governance of Atlanta moved if it did not originate within, or gain the approval of, a business-dominated elite.

Hunter's seminal study offered 'scientific' evidence that local representative democracy in the US was just a smokescreen for dominant economic interests. It triggered the 'community power debate' between elite and pluralist theorists that dominated studies of urban politics – at least in the United States – for the next 20 years (Polsby, 1963, 1980). The pluralist counter-attack (Judge, Chapter 2, this volume) concentrated on methodological issues. Hunter was accused of using empirical methods that were inadequate and predetermined his findings. First, the way the list of community influentials was generated and refined was said to reflect the mere hunches of Hunter and his panellists about where power would lie. Having started from this position, though, the research methodology effectively ruled out alternative conclusions and interpretations. Second, the reputational method was said not to place powerful individuals within a local economic, political and social context; that is, it was not known *why* they were powerful. Hunter had ignored 'positional characteristics' – the power that different jobs and social roles give to people – and made it seem that power was simply the property of individuals. Third, critics argued that the reputation for power had not been backed up with evidence of individuals using that power in particular situations.

The first two criticisms were hardly insurmountable and did not invalidate the reputational method Hunter had pioneered. The first rightly criticized Hunter's rigid pursuit of evidence of a single dominant elite but it is difficult to see how any researchers, whatever their methodology, could begin exploring power without using some sort of working hypothesis about who is powerful and why. All that can be asked is that the hypothesis was set out and tested clearly and that potentially counterfactual evidence was not automatically ruled out by the methodology. The second is a little unfair in that Hunter clearly *did* use positional analysis, albeit in an intuitive and implicit way, in specifying the sectors of Atlanta society where he expected to find the most powerful people. The third criticism was entirely justified, however, and formed the basis of the very different approach adopted by pluralists.

As Judge's chapter explains, the decisional methodology used by pluralists focused on 'controversial' local government decisions on which there were obvious clashes of interest or on others deemed to be important by the researcher in question. The pluralists claimed that the decisional approach, which involved looking at what they said was the actual exercising of power in real decision-making situations, was superior to one that relied on reputational analysis. They also claimed their results refuted the notion that urban politics was dominated by a single, coherent elite. In pinpointing the individuals who had greatest direct influence over decisions in a number of policy areas, and finding them to be different in each case, they found a plurality of elites. None of these mini-elites operated behind the scenes, as Hunter's business elite had, and no one group of decision makers dominated all the others.

Decisional analysis was attacked, in turn, by neo-elite theorists. The crux of their case was that the findings of pluralists were also predetermined by the methods of empirical verification they used. Bachrach and Baratz (1962, 1970) argued that the decision points studied by pluralists were purely arbitrary and that decisional analysis was blind to the way policy agendas are set. Pluralists could not prove that the decision points they studied represented the most important points at which power was exercised, nor that the issues those decisions dealt with were critical to the city's most powerful people. Bachrach and Baratz argued that the power used to make concrete decisions represented only one face of power. A second face, involving 'non-decision making', sees the powerful act to ensure that only those issues that are comparatively innocuous to them ever reach the point of decision. Thus the weak mini-elites identified by pluralists may have been decisive in disputes over issues that were on the agenda before them but that agenda could already have been neutralized so as to be unthreatening to the 'real' elite. In other words, the truly powerful might already have mobilized bias[7] to keep those issues they did not want debated off the public agenda.

The competing sides of the community power debate used different methodologies to answer slightly different questions. The original elite school asked 'who rules?', the pluralists 'does anybody rule?' and the neo-elitists 'who sets the agenda and why aren't they challenged?' The conceptual and methodological debate about power certainly did not end with neo-elitism but it did become ever more abstract to the point that any concern with the sort of urban empirical data that had helped fuel it disappeared (Lukes, 1974; Foucault, 1980). In fact the phrase 'community power debate' is really a misnomer, since the debate was overwhelmingly about definitions of power and the way it might be measured. There was virtually no debate about community. This is unfortunate, since some of the limitations of the debate can be put down as much to very vague notions of community.

Urban elite theorists and pluralists operated within worlds defined by the geographical boundaries of cities.[8] Their 'communities' were the people residing within those boundaries; communities lying beyond were of scant interest.[9] Within the defined geographical area, researchers asked which community members – by definition, local residents – were most influential in determining decisions made within local government politics. The choice of study area and subject matter caused problems for analyses of power. Both pluralists and elite theorists conflated geographical places with 'communities', and power over local government decisions with power per se. In so doing, they implicitly imputed an unrealistically high degree of local autonomy. On one hand, the powerful, whoever they were and however they were identified, were assumed to reside within the relevant boundaries. On the other, the most significant expressions of power were to be seen in an ability to shape local government policies and agenda.

Non-local influences on the extent and nature of power exercised by local people, whether inside or outside local government, were assumed away as either constant and therefore unproblematic, non-existent, or too difficult to cope with empirically. Important factors were therefore ignored, such as non-local ownership of productive assets and the capacity of higher levels of government to influence the structures, processes and outcomes of local government decision making. Change in these fields clearly affects the level of local political and economic autonomy in that it helps determine who controls resources and hence holds power, what decisions local governments are empowered to make, how they make them, what magnitude they have and therefore what importance they assume for other local interest groups. Such changes were very difficult to account for within the confines of the community power debate.

Growth machines: elite theory revisited?

During the 1970s the community power debate was substantially overtaken by neo-Marxist and neo-Weberian approaches to urban theory. The work of these two schools was much less concerned with the actions of individuals or groups in guiding urban change or with the particular role of urban politics in the wider state system (Saunders, 1979: 66–136; Dunleavy, 1980: 39–50; Pickvance, Chapter 13, this volume). However recent work in the US on growth machines (Molotch, 1976, 1990; Logan and Molotch, 1987) marks a partial reversion to the concerns of the community power debate: that is to account for aspects of urban change by examining the actions of, and interrelationships between, the main human agents that help produce them. Along with regime theory (Elkin, 1987; Stone and Sanders, 1987; Stone, 1989; Stoker, Chapter 4, this volume) the growth machine thesis represents the most systematic recent attempt to develop a political economy of 'place'.

The growth machine thesis in some ways further refines elite theory but it focuses on the broad field of urban development and not just on what affects local government decisions in this field. It is deliberately voluntaristic. Logan and Molotch emphasize the role of individuals and interest groups because they want to challenge the structuralist accounts that had dominated the field and made it seem that human actions were immaterial to social change. Like earlier urban elite theorists, they emphasize the power of the business community and argue that 'the activism of entrepreneurs is, and always has been, a critical force in shaping the urban system' (Logan and Molotch, 1987: 52). Logan and Molotch borrow from classical Marxism in distinguishing between use-values and exchange-values with regard to property. Most people value their land or buildings for the day-to-day uses they get from them but a small group of owners are mainly interested in making financial gain from their assets. These 'rentiers' lie at the core of the urban development process. They constantly strive to maximize the value of their holdings, by intensifying the uses they are put to or developing higher-value uses, in order to increase the rents they can charge for using them.

Rentiers cannot achieve their aims alone. For example, landowners do not have the expertise, resources or inclination to develop successful factories but they will try to persuade corporations or developers to do the job for them and take a cut of the profits in the form of rent. In Logan and Molotch's terms, rentiers are 'parochial capital'. They own assets that cannot be shifted from place to place. They need to attract investment that is more mobile – 'metropolitan capital' – by bargaining directly with non-local investors or by helping create the sort of business climate that will attract investment. The allies rentiers need to pursue their objectives are found in the other members of the growth machine. Some of them are also 'place-bound' while others are geographically unconstrained. What unites them is a commitment to economic growth, based on the tangible benefits it will bring them. A growth machine tries to legitimize the gains of its members and disarm critics by espousing an ideology of 'value-free development' which claims economic growth is good for all.

Rentiers have three sets of allies within the growth machine. One, which may or may not be place-bound, comprises businesses that profit directly from the development process, for example developers, financiers, construction interests and professional practices in areas like architecture, planning and real estate. A second set comprises those who benefit indirectly because development projects boost demand for their products and services. Typically, this includes local media and utility companies who are place-bound and achieve higher sales as a result of most forms of growth. A third set of auxiliary members includes agencies and interests that have local ties and can benefit from some, but not all types of growth. Thus universities, cultural institutions, professional sports clubs, labour unions, the self-employed and small retailers may be part of growth machines when their interests coincide with core members'.

This list of key players roughly describes a business elite that collectively wields power over the pattern of urban development by virtue of its control over substantial material and intellectual resources and its ability to smooth access to external investment. In Logan and Molotch's view, growth machines need not always embrace all these interests, far less those of the wider community. Challenges by groups defending the use-values of property over their exchange-values – principally neighbourhood organizations – are not impossible. Anti-growth movements, or others prepared to tolerate only selective growth, can be particularly powerful in affluent areas where residents think the benefits of growth might be outweighed by the costs, for example in environmental degradation or the loss of a neighbourhood's exclusive feel (Clavel, 1986; Molotch, 1990; Molotch and Logan, 1990; Schneider and Teske, 1991). When growth machines lose momentum though, corporate capital, normally aloof from local affairs, can often remobilize them. In Cleveland, for example, lobbying and campaigning by big corporations helped bring down a populist mayor the business community disliked (Swanstrom, 1985).

Logan and Molotch are unclear whether local governments are actually members of growth machines but they are certainly strong supporters because they are 'primarily concerned with increasing growth' (Logan and Molotch, 1987: 53). Quite why local governments should be so predisposed to support growth strategies is not developed at length. Partly this is because Logan and Molotch expect their readership to be knowledgeable about American institutional arrangements. But they are also inconsistent, effectively saying that local governments back growth machines apart from when they do not. In explaining why they usually do, Logan and Molotch briefly contrast the US with other liberal democracies and argue that the US local government system is marked by fragmentation into a large number of units, a high level of control over land-use decisions by urban authorities, a depoliticized local bureaucracy, and heavy reliance on taxes raised locally from businesses and residents. Local politicians and officials are thus particularly receptive to the needs of businesses and there is far more vigorous competition for investment and development between American cities than, say, in the United Kingdom (Logan and Molotch, 1987: 149).

Logan and Molotch remain true to critical elite theory tradition in arguing that the decision-making system works to the advantage of the most powerful and the detriment of the least powerful. The systematic favouring of exchange-values over use-values in urban areas means that: 'In many cases, probably in most, additional local growth under current arrangements is a transfer of wealth and life chances from the general public to the rentier groups and their associates' (Logan and Molotch, 1987: 53). Growth is not good for all. Its costs fall disproportionately on low income communities and marginal local businesses which are often physically displaced by redevelopment strategies and, in the former case, can rarely compete with new residents and commuters for new employment opportunities. Neither does local economic growth necessarily generate, rather than relocate, economic activity. The intense inter-urban competition for development encouraged by growth machines therefore provides questionable net benefits at a regional or national scale. For the losers in the competition it can be very costly. Local authorities which commit growing resources to competitive growth strategies often face budget problems when their attempts are unsuccessful.

The growth machine thesis is not just an extension of urban elite theory. The focus on 'urban development' issues is more specific than in the more diffuse community power studies but the scope is in some ways expanded in that the central concern is with the broad politics of development, not just the local government politics of development. This makes it considerably easier to analyse the influence of the business community without making business leaders seem omnipotent in local politics. The question of power is also made more manageable. Logan and Molotch are less concerned with the intractable 'who, if anyone, rules?' and more with who has the greatest influence over the physical restructuring of places, why, and with what effect. The focus, for convenience, is still on geographical areas but there is no assumption that those who wield power and influence over local development patterns necessarily reside within them. Within the business community at least, Logan and Molotch clearly recognize the importance of connections between local and non-local decision making, as in the arranged marriages between parochial and metropolitan capital.

Like classical elite theorists, Logan and Molotch develop their case through conceptual argument. American critics (see Feagin, 1987; Clark, 1988; Cox and Mair, 1988, 1989; Clarke, 1990) concentrate on their core conceptual assumptions and argue that, while the growth machine thesis has considerable strengths, they are too simplistic and sweeping for the argument to be swallowed whole. The main charges against Logan and Molotch concern their 'limited conceptualisation of the local state' (Clarke, 1990: 191) and their narrow view of the economic development process. On the former, the growth machine thesis, like earlier elite approaches, is excessively 'localist'. It takes the institutional features of US local governance as read and unchanging. Higher levels of government are seen as having local influence only through federal programmes that support urban property development. Logan and Molotch's arguments here are less sophisticated than those of regime theorists who demonstrate the more profound effects that the actions of higher levels of government can have on the nature and direction of local policies and the coalitions of interests that support them.[10]

On economic development, it is said that Logan and Molotch focus disproportionately on just one aspect of local economies and business concerns: property development. They further assume that easy distinctions can be made between rentiers and non-rentier business interests and between parochial and metropolitan capital. This allows them to boil the economic development process down to one where rentier-led coalitions compete to offer the lowest-cost sites to footloose corporate investors. But, say the critics, the world is not so simple. The rentiers of the growth machine thesis are a dying breed. On one hand, growing property speculation, often on an international scale, means fewer and fewer assets are locally-owned. On the other, such property that remains locally-owned often lies in the hands of complex large firms who supplement their mainstream business with property ownership in order to spread business risk. These types of owner are unlikely to assume the driving role of Logan and Molotch's local, single-purpose rentier.[11]

Neither is capital necessarily as footloose as Logan and Molotch suggest. The needs of corporate investors – indeed of any business in the information age – are not only for low-cost sites. Locational choices are affected by many other factors such as the availability of local skills, relations between employers and unions/workforces, appropriate local networks of suppliers and business services, access to modern communications technologies, the proximity of supportive higher education institutions and so on. Each of these factors make businesses dependent on, or desirous of, particular places to varying degrees at different times. There is massive variety in these 'local social relations of production' (Eisenschitz and Gough, 1993: Chaps 5 and 6) but they have a number of important implications for the growth machine thesis.

First, they mean that companies can rarely play local administrations off against each other for subsidies and incentives in the decisive way suggested by Logan and Molotch. Second, they mean that local economic strategies to lure external capital or retain and build local businesses need to extend well beyond property development packages. Local governments would not otherwise become involved in initiatives promoting research and development, capital formation, training, technology transfer, product development and so on. Third, as a result, the interests involved in growth machines must extend beyond, and even sometimes ignore, the property interests mentioned by Logan and Molotch if their efforts are to be effective. Fourth, while businesses are locally-dependent to varying degrees, it is not necessarily at the urban scale. Coalitions of business and government actors are therefore not found only in cities and there is nothing conceptually distinct or important about analyses pitched at the urban level.

None of the above points suggest that the notion of cities effectively being governed by business-government coalitions is not very valuable but they do pose questions about the appropriate objects of empirical research. What is therefore surprising, particularly given the legacy of the community power literature, is the lack of debate over the methodology used in growth machine analysis. One searches in vain through the growth machine literature for details of the way empirical material was assembled. This makes it difficult to make useful comparisons between the various US studies and doubly difficult to assess whether and how the growth machine concept might be applied in cross-national comparative research.

Elite theory, growth machines and comparative urban research

Are urban elite theory and the growth machine thesis robust enough to be relevant in other national contexts? The question is particularly pertinent just now when interest in meaningful cross-national comparison is keener than ever and there are signs of a new community power debate taking shape at two inter-related levels of analysis (Harding and Garside, 1993). At the broader level, theorists from a number of disciplines are asking whether 'places' are becoming more important within an increasingly globalized economic, political and cultural 'system'. One emerging strand of argument is that global economic change has reinforced the importance of urban-regional economies and reduced the capacity of national governments to respond to economic change through traditional policy instruments. Almost by default, decisions made at subnational level are becoming more important and urban redevelopment efforts are taking on added significance for local and national decision makers in the public and private sectors (Harding and Le Galès, 1994).

More specifically, researchers are exploring cross-national similarities in the way the structures of local governance in advanced liberal democracies are changing, particularly the tendencies towards decentralization, fragmentation, a shift in the balance of local policy priorities towards 'productive' and away from welfare goals and an enhanced role for the private sector in defining and delivering public goods (Stoker, 1990; Mayer, 1993). These trends do not mean that systems of local governance in liberal democracies are everywhere being 'Americanized' but they do raise interesting questions about the extent of convergence between countries and about possible cross-national explanations for that process. Given this context, theories that are concerned with bargaining between public and private interests in defining urban development agenda and programmes are of growing interest. But does this mean that the literatures on urban elites and growth machines are now the basis for comparative, cross-national research?

Looking to the recent impact of the US literatures in the UK, there is a paradox. On the positive side, some researchers are reflecting once more on the lessons of the community power debate in an attempt to develop research methodologies more befitting of contemporary circumstances (Dowding et al., 1993). Others have made rudimentary attempts to apply the growth coalition concept to empirical study in the UK (Cooke, 1988; Lloyd and Newlands, 1988; Bassett and Harloe, 1990). On the other hand there is a powerful tradition of scepticism among UK political scientists about imported US theories and methods (Harding, 1994). US approaches are generally dismissed as ethnocentric and insensitive to fundamental differences between the two countries. Below the surface, though, are more profound doubts about the usefulness of a political economy approach to urban studies.

On the former, it is clear that the range of economic, institutional and cultural characteristics which separate US and UK experiences of urban development and governance should make researchers wary of simplistic, direct comparisons between the two. Urban business interests in the UK lack the strength, organization and political linkages of their US counterparts. Urban political activity by business leaders in the UK is very low and there is no significant private sponsorship of local electoral candidates. The urban system in the UK is also more centralized than in the US. With the exception of London, UK cities are less important to big business fortunes and contain fewer local resources to facilitate economic growth – the absence of regional banking structures is one obvious example. This means they also provide less fertile environments for the business social networks which offer US business interests a solid platform from which to contribute to discussions on urban redevelopment strategies. There is also less entrepreneurialism with property assets in the UK, with land often being owned by aristocratic families, the Crown, the Church, universities, charitable trusts or local authorities, none of which are as aggressive in promoting economic development as Logan and Molotch's rentiers.

The local government context is also different. Despite recent central government reforms, which have fragmented local service delivery and constrained local authority actions (Stewart and Stoker, 1989, 1994), UK local authorities remain the more significant service providers, particularly in social welfare, and are much more firmly integrated into national systems of policy making. They do not depend so heavily on finance from local taxes and market borrowing as their US counterparts. There is therefore a weaker trade-off between local economic health/income levels and the provision of services. Logan and Molotch recognized that the UK provided less fertile ground for growth machines when they argued that 'central government, working closely with élites in the production sphere, has relatively greater direct impact on the distribution of development than in the US, where parochial rentiers have a more central role' (Logan and Molotch, 1987: 149). Molotch subsequently conceded that the growth machine model was ethnocentric but countered that something fairly similar nonetheless developed in cultural, political and institutional environments as different as those of Japan and Italy (Molotch and Vicari, 1988).

Molotch's cross-national research confirms what others (Harding, 1991; Shaw, 1993) have argued with respect to the UK: that a simple replication of US-style growth machines should not be expected. But neither can it be argued that there are no signs of convergence between the two countries on important features of local governance or that local authorities and business interests in the UK are, or ever have been, unconcerned with the relative economic vitality of 'their' localities. In other words there is, and always has been, pressure for some form of public-private cooperation in urban development in the UK even if the larger economic and political environment did not induce it to the same extent as in the US.

Urban political scientists in the UK have largely ignored the implications of this observation. This has usually led them to reject not only specific models like the growth machine but the wider political economy approach into which they, along with urban elite theory, fit. Recent UK usage of the notion of growth machines is no exception to this general rule. It has been applied, post hoc, to redescribe urban phenomena rather than used, conceptually, as a basis for empirical study.[12] Bassett and Harloe (1990), for example, appropriate the terminology in arguing that the 'growth coalition' which drove Swindon's postwar expansion comprised entrepreneurial local authority officers and politicians and central government departments. But they assert, rather than demonstrate, that the various elements of the private sector played virtually no role in the strategy for expansion.

Bassett and Harloe's work is part of a UK urban political science which has long been characterized by a narrow, institutional approach wherein 'the assumption has usually been made that the contours of political power at the local level correspond to the formal institutions of local government; that power resides in the town hall . . . and nowhere else' (Saunders, 1979: 328). The community power debate was virtually ignored and critics found it 'astonishing . . . that with the exception of some unpublished doctoral theses, there exist no studies of community power in Britain' (Crewe, 1974: 35). The apparent lack of interest in looking at the influence of forces outside the formal local political system, particularly the business community, is all the more surprising given that the one UK attempt to do so – Saunders's case study of Croydon – unearthed evidence of close public-private sector cooperation based on 'a relatively dense and cohesive network of business and political activists, interacting regularly and relatively informally in a variety of institutional contexts' (Saunders, 1979: 313).

For Saunders, and other critics like Dunleavy (1980), urban political scientists in the UK assumed, rather than proved, that the public and private spheres in cities operate independently. The actions of the business community were assumed not to have implications for those of the local public sector, and business leaders were assumed not to have the capacity to shape the public agenda or to influence the nature and direction of specific programmes developed by local governments. Such assumptions, while they might be valid at some level, reflect a failure to distinguish between local government politics, the politics of urban government and local governance. Dunleavy (1980) demonstrated that urban government differs from local government in that the sources of formal authority affecting urban life extend well beyond local authorites to a large number of other public agencies. Furthermore, the way each of these agencies exercise their authority is conditioned by a range of non-local and non-governmental forces. Local government therefore lacks autonomy in the narrow sense that the levers it can pull are limited and the ways it can pull them are subject to external influence.

Local government also has restricted autonomy in the deeper sense that it has relatively little purchase over many factors which contribute to, or detract from, citizen well-being (Wolman and Goldsmith, 1992: 22–47). If local governance can be defined as the making of decisions intended to protect and enhance local citizen well-being, then local government is clearly just one of many important 'bit players'. On the many issues where it has interests but little power to control events, local government needs to elicit the support of non-governmental forces and other parts of the fragmented public sector in trying to achieve some of its aims. Local governance is therefore about different interests clarifying what they want for or out of particular places, assessing how feasible their desires are, courting those interests who might support their objectives, bargaining with others on what place their desires might have within a wider urban development agenda and setting up formal or informal coalitions with others to achieve at least some of their aims. It is local governance that UK political scientists have largely chosen not to study and that the American literature covered in this chapter grapples with, albeit sometimes in an ethnocentric way.

The attitudes of political scientists in the UK are beginning to change as a result of recent reforms of the structures of local governance. The local government literature now abounds with words like 'partnership' and 'enabling' which suggest a role for local authorities in building elite consensus and forming coalitions to achieve various governing aims. Critics might argue that, in the urban redevelopment field at least, this new terminology simply recognizes processes which were once informal and hidden but are now more formal and visible. In other words, the sort of research agenda addressed by American approaches like those examined in this chapter have always been relevant to the UK. What is needed to take urban research forward, however, is a common methodological approach which can be applied to case study areas cross-nationally but is sensitive to national differences in the way functions are shared within and between different levels of government. While acknowledging that local governments cannot simply stay out of development debates, we need to know how far they are structurally predisposed towards a growth agenda and how and why such predispositions change.

A comparative methodology would need to be much less 'localist' than the US approaches examined here, but at least three of the strengths of urban elite theory and the growth machine thesis demand consideration. First, Logan and Molotch's notion of place-boundedness, as expanded by Cox and Mair (1988), is central to analysing why certain sections of the business community are committed to the prosperity of particular places and prepared to become actors in redevelopment. Second, while reputational analysis does not offer compelling evidence about power and influence in and of itself, it still has considerable potential as a starting point for research. Business leaders who are active within the growing array of quasi-public and public-private development agencies are becoming increasingly visible to the researcher. The technology also exists to undertake vast and rapid media searches of more general business activity within cities. Researchers studying the role of business influentials no longer have to guess, Hunter-style, at 'behind the scenes' manoeuvring but can increasingly base reputational analysis, and further decisional study, on hard evidence of business activism. Finally, researchers could do worse than adopt the spirit of enquiry that pervades elite theory in all of its guises; that it is the mission of social science to debunk 'political formulae' and find out how things really operate.

Notes

Work for this chapter forms part of a research project entitled 'Coalition-formation and urban redevelopment: a cross-national study', financed through the UK Economic and Social Research Council's *Local Governance Initiative* (Project Reference: L311253002). The author wishes to thank the ESRC for its support.

1 Early modern elite theory (late nineteenth, early twentieth century) is often called 'classical' elite theory. For general introductions to modern elite theory, see Bottomore (1966), Welsh (1979: 1–17), Dunleavy and O'Leary (1987: 136–203), and Moyser and Wagstaffe (1987: 1–15).

2 The normative approach dates back to Plato. Like the Italian elite school, Plato despaired of all political systems operating during his lifetime, including the democratic and oligarchic alternatives tried in his native Athens. Adjudging politics to be too important to be left to politicians, he advocated government by a small group of dispassionate, highly educated, self-selecting 'philosopher rulers' (see Plato, 1974, particularly Parts IV, VI and IX).

3 See, for example, Meisel (1962) and Albertoni (1987).

4 For Mills, the last World War deepened both the interconnections between the military, business and political establishments and the control they jointly exercised over civil society. That power was not relinquished but continued into the Cold War period.

5 Miliband (1969), for example, uses elite concepts to support a neo-Marxist argument that Britain has a ruling class. He shows that key decision makers in all sections of society tend to have privileged origins and educations from which they derive certain values and access to exclusive social networks.

6 Mosca's *The Ruling Class* only had that title in the English translation.

7 Schattschneider (1960: 71) argued that organization is, by definition, the mobilization of bias. By this he meant that within all organizations some forms of conflict are tolerated while others are routinely suppressed.

8 Political scientists, with their preference for examining territories clearly covered by particular decision-making units, tended to use local government boundaries. Sociologists sometimes preferred slightly larger territories such as travel-to-work areas or SMSAs.

9 Hunter (1953: 151) accepted that '[n]o community is an isolated entity'. But the chapter of *Community Power Structure* that puts Atlanta into its larger context deals mainly with the influence of the city's community influentials within higher levels of government, not vice versa.

10 Elkin (1987), for example, proposes a distinction between federal (local) political economies, which are heavily influenced by federal government interventions, and pluralist

and entrepreneurial forms. Each is associated with a particular regime, that is a governing coalition, but only in the latter case does it resemble a growth machine.

11 It is rarely acknowledged, but Logan and Molotch do recognize that more complex and less local patterns of control over property assets can reduce the energy of growth machines. However it is still valid to question the importance the growth machine thesis attaches to particular sorts of rentiers rather than property owners per se.

12 Parallel developments in Australian urban studies (Caulfield, 1991; Wanna, 1991) have seen the growth machine thesis applied more rigorously and have produced somewhat different conclusions.

References

Albertoni, E.A. (1987) *Mosca and the Theory of Elitism*. Oxford: Basil Blackwell.

Bachrach, P. and Baratz, M.S. (1962) 'Two faces of power', *American Political Science Review*, 56: 947–52.

Bachrach, P. and Baratz, M.S. (1970) *Power and Poverty: Theory and Practice*. New York: Oxford University Press.

Bassett, K. and Harloe, M. (1990) 'Swindon: the rise and decline of a growth coalition' in M. Harloe, C. Pickvance and J. Urry (eds), *Place, Politics and Policy: Do Localities Matter?* London: Unwin Hyman.

Bennett, R.J. (ed.) (1990) *Decentralisation, Local Government and Markets: Towards a Post-welfare Agenda?* Oxford: Oxford University Press.

Bottomore, T.B. (1966) *Elites and Society*. Harmondsworth: Penguin.

Caulfield, A. (1991) 'Community power, public policy initiatives and the management of growth in Brisbane', *Urban Policy and Research*, 9 (4): 209–19.

Clark, G.L. (1988) 'Review of urban fortunes: the political economy of place', *Political Geography Quarterly*, 7 (4): 374–5.

Clarke, S.E. (1990) '"Precious" place: the local growth machine in an era of global restructuring', *Urban Geography*, 11 (2): 185–93.

Clavel, P. (1986) *The Progressive City: Planning and Participation, 1969–1984*. New Brunswick, NJ: Rutgers University Press.

Cooke, P. (1988) 'Municipal enterprise, growth coalitions and social justice', *Local Economy*, 3 (3): 191–9.

Cox, K.R. and Mair, A. (1988) 'Locality and community in the politics of local economic development', *Annals of the Association of American Geographers*, 78 (2): 307–25.

Cox, K.R. and Mair, A. (1989) 'Book review essay: Urban growth machines and the politics of local economic development', *International Journal for Urban and Regional Research*, 13 (1): 137–46.

Crewe, I. (1974) *British Political Sociology Yearbook, Vol. I: Elites in Western Democracy*. London: Croom Helm.

Dowding, K., Dunleavy, P., King, D. and Margetts, H. (1993) 'Rational choice and community power structures: a new research agenda', Paper to the American Political Science Association conference, Panel 12, Washington, D.C.

Dunleavy, P. (1980) *Urban Political Analysis*. London: Macmillan.

Dunleavy, P. and O'Leary, B. (1987) *Theories of the State: The Politics of Liberal Democracy*. London: Macmillan.

Eisenschitz, A. and Gough, J. (1993) *The Politics of Local Economic Policy: The Problems and Possibilities of Local Initiative*. London: Macmillan.

Elkin, S.L. (1987) *City and Regime in the American Republic*. Chicago, IL: University of Chicago Press.

Feagin, J.R. (1987) 'Urban political economy: the new paradigm matures', *Contemporary Sociology*, 16 (4): 517–19.

Foucault, M. (1980) *Power/Knowledge*. New York: Pantheon.

Harding, A. (1991) 'The rise of urban growth coalitions, U.K.-style?', *Government and Policy*, 9 (3): 295–317.

Harding, A. (1994) 'Urban regimes and growth machines: towards a cross-national research agenda', *Urban Affairs Quarterly*, 29 (3): 356–82.

Harding, A. and Garside, P. (1993) 'Globalization, urban political economy and community power', Paper to the American Political Science Association conference, Panel 12, Washington, D.C.

Harding, A. and Le Galès, P. (1994) 'Globalization, urban change and urban policy', in A. Scott (ed.), *The Limits of Globalization*. London: Routledge.

Hunter, F. (1953) *Community Power Structure: A Study of Decision Makers*. Chapel Hill: University of North Carolina Press.

Lloyd, M.G. and Newlands, D.A. (1988) 'The "growth coalition" and urban economic development', *Local Economy*, 3 (1): 31–9.

Logan, J. and Molotch, H. (1987) *Urban Fortunes: The Political Economy of Place*. Berkeley: University of California Press.

Lukes, S. (1974) *Power: A Radical View*. London: Macmillan.

Mayer, M. (1993) 'Urban governance in the post-Fordist city', Paper to the 'Challenges to Urban Management' seminar, Newcastle University.

Meisel, J.H. (1962) *The Myth of the Ruling Class*. Westport, CN: Greenwood Press.

Michels, R. (1959) *Political Parties: A Sociological Study of the Oligarchical Tendencies of Modern Democracy*. New York: Dover.

Miliband, R. (1969) *The State in Capitalist Society*. London: Weidenfeld and Nicolson.

Mills, C. Wright (1956) *The Power Elite*. Oxford: Oxford University Press.

Molotch, H. (1976) 'The city as growth machine', *American Journal of Sociology*, 82 (2): 309–55.

Molotch, H. (1990) 'Urban deals in comparative perspective', in J. Logan and T. Swanstrom (eds), *Beyond the City Limits: Urban Policy and Economic Restructuring in Comparative Perspective*. Philadelphia, PA: Temple University Press.

Molotch, H. and Logan, J. (1990) 'The space for urban action: urban fortunes; a rejoinder', *Political Geography Quarterly*, 9 (1): 85–92.

Molotch, H. and Vicari, S. (1988) 'Three ways to build: the development process in the US, Japan and Italy', *Urban Affairs Quarterly*, 24 (2): 188–214.

Mosca, G. (1939) *The Ruling Class*. New York: McGraw-Hill.

Moyser, G. and Wagstaffe, M. (eds) (1987) *Research Methods for Elite Studies*. London: Allen and Unwin.

Pareto, V. (1935) *The Mind and Society*. London: Cope.

Plato (1974) *The Republic* (2nd edn). Harmondsworth: Penguin.

Polsby, N.W. (1963) *Community Power and Political Theory*. New Haven, CN: Yale University Press.

Polsby, N.W. (1980) *Community Power and Political Theory* (2nd edn). New Haven CN: Yale University Press.

Saunders, P. (1979) *Urban Politics: A Sociological Interpretation*. London: Hutchinson.

Schattschneider, E.E. (1960) *The Semi-Sovereign People*. New York: Holt, Rinehart and Winston.

Schneider, M. and Teske, P. (1991) 'The antigrowth entrepreneur: challenging the "equilibrium" of the growth machine', Paper to the American Political Science Association Conference, Washington D.C., August.

Shaw, K. (1993) 'The development of a new urban corporatism: the politics of urban regeneration in the North East of England', *Regional Studies*, 27 (3): 251–9.

Stewart, J. and Stoker, G. (eds) (1989) *The Future of Local Government*. London: Macmillan.

Stewart, J. and Stoker, G. (eds) (1994) *Local Government in the 1990s*. London: Macmillan.

Stoker, G. (1990) 'Regulation theory, local government and the transition from Fordism', in D.S. King and J. Pierre (eds), *Challenges to Local Government*. London: Sage.

Stone, C.L. (1989) *Regime Politics: Governing Atlanta 1946–1988*. Lawrence: University Press of Kansas.

Stone, C.L. and Sanders, H.T. (eds) (1987) *The Politics of Urban Development.* Lawrence: University Press of Kansas.

Swanstrom, T. (1985) *The Crisis of Growth Politics: Cleveland, Kucinich, and the Challenge of Urban Populism.* Philadelphia, PA: Temple University Press.

Trotsky, L. (1972) *The Revolution Betrayed.* New York: Pathfinder Press.

Wanna, J. (1991) 'Community power debates: themes, issues and remaining dilemmas', *Urban Policy and Research*, 9 (4): 193–218.

Weber, M. (1968) *Economy and Society: Parts I and II.* Berkeley: University of California Press.

Welsh, W.A. (1979) *Leaders and Elites.* New York: Holt, Rinehart and Winston.

Wolman, H. and Goldsmith, M. (1992) *Urban Politics and Policy: A Comparative Approach.* Oxford: Blackwell.

4

Regime Theory and Urban Politics

Gerry Stoker

Regime theory came to the fore in the study of urban politics from the mid-1980s onwards. In contrast, then, to pluralist and elitist accounts it is a relatively new theoretical force and indeed cannot claim to be as well developed as either of those two currents. It also lacks the extent and range of empirical work surrounding pluralist and elitist studies. Yet this chapter argues that regime theory offers a distinctive approach to the study of urban politics and in particular the issue of power. It provides a framework for analysis which captures key aspects of urban governance at the end of the century. It provides a new conceptual framework and more particular theoretical statements about causal relationships and behaviour in urban politics.

Regime theory holds substantial promise for understanding the *variety* of responses to urban change. Its emphasis on the interdependence of governmental and non-governmental forces in meeting economic and social challenges focuses attention upon the problem of cooperation and co-ordination between governmental and non-governmental actors. While significant differences persist from country to country, it is clear that the need for some form of public/private cooperation exists in all advanced capitalist societies. Growing competition between cities for investment, and the role of business interests in local decision making have increasingly shaped the urban terrain. Decentralization and shifting responsibilities within the state, increased financial constraints, and the development of privatized services utilizing both for-profit and non-profit organizations, have also created additional complexities for local governments. Urban governments are increasingly working through and alongside other interests. This concern with 'governance' emerges in a range of policy areas: economic development, human capital and training programmes, crime prevention, environmental protection and anti-drug campaigns. In the UK the word 'enabling' has emerged to describe the shifting role of government (Cochrane, 1993). In the US the talk is of government being 'reinvented' and having a catalytic rather than a direct provision role (Osborne and Gaebler, 1992). Because of its emphasis on the way governmental and non-governmental actors work across boundaries, regime theory is especially relevant, given the shifting role of urban government.

Regime theory provides a new perspective on the issue of power. It directs attention away from a narrow focus on power as an issue of social control towards an understanding of power expressed through social production. In a complex, fragmented urban world the paradigmatic form of power is that which enables certain interests to blend their capacities to achieve common purposes. Regime analysis directs attention to the conditions under which such effective long-term coalitions emerge in order to accomplish public purposes.

In the first two sections of the chapter the core elements of regime theory are presented. These core propositions are unfortunately for regime theory often buried within detailed case studies. An effort is made to provide a more general statement drawing in particular on the work of Clarence Stone. The differences between regime theory, elitist and pluralist interpretations are explored. In doing so the assessment made of regime theory in Chapter 2 is challenged and a more positive judgement about its potential presented.

The next section of the chapter explores the application of regime analysis in the urban context. One of the problems of the regime concept is that it provides a descriptive label that can be used in single city case studies that in the United States especially have a prominent position in publishing schedules and listings. Regime terminology is used but a regime analysis is not really provided. To address this problem the most suitable case study to take is that provided by Stone of Atlanta. A brief account of Stone's regime analysis of the politics of that city is provided.

The final main section of the chapter raises a series of questions about regime theory identifying areas of criticism or where further development is required. The pioneering efforts of Stone, Elkin and others in relation to regime theory leave a number of issues unexplored. First, it is necessary to examine the understanding of power offered in regime analysis and how that understanding can be explored through empirical study. Second, regime theory needs to escape the 'localist' trap and place its analysis in the context of the broader political environment. Third, regime theory lacks a coherent approach to the issue of regime continuity and change. A brief concluding section provides an overall assessment of the theory.

Regime theory, pluralism and neo-pluralism

Stone comments that 'regime theory has many antecedents' (1989a: 145). The work of Fainstein and Fainstein (1986), Jones and Bachelor (1986) and Elkin (1987) would seem particularly relevant in the context of urban politics. According to Elkin:

> The way in which popular control operates in contemporary cities is largely a consequence of the division of labour between state and market as that is manifest in cities. This division, which stems from the corresponding arrangement of the national political economy, means that ownership of productive assets in the city is largely placed in private hands. Public officials share responsibility for the level of citizen well-being with these private

controllers, but these officials cannot command economic performance, only induce it. The concern of public officials with citizen well-being stems largely from their being subject to election or appointment by those who themselves have been elected. (1987: 18)

Regime theory takes as given a set of government institutions subject to some degree of popular control and an economy guided mainly but not exclusively by privately controlled investment decisions. A regime is a set of 'arrangements by which this division of labour is bridged' (Stone, 1993: 3).

David Judge is right to argue in Chapter 2 that regime theorists have taken on board the central thrust of much Marxist inspired work of the 1970s (reviewed in Chapter 13). Namely that business control over investment decisions and resources central to societal welfare give it a privileged position in relation to government decision making. In the words of Stone 'we must take into account these contextual forces – the facet of community decision-making I label "systemic power"'. He continues: 'public officials form their alliances, make their decisions and plan their futures in a context in which strategically important resources are hierarchically arranged . . . Systemic power therefore has to do with *the impact of the larger socioeconomic system on the predispositions of public officials*' (1980: 979, original emphasis).

Regime theorists argue that 'politics matters'. In this sense their work challenges economic determinists such as Peterson (1981) and some neo-Marxist work. The founding premise of regime theory is that urban decision makers have a relative autonomy. Systemic power is constraining but scope for the influence of political forces and activity remain. Regime theorists argue that the organization of politics leads to very inadequate forms of popular control and makes government less responsive to socioeconomically disadvantaged groups. As Elkin argues 'the roots of the city's failures are not in the necessity of earning its keep but in how that impulse gets translated into action' (1987: 98). The organization of politics does not facilitate large-scale popular participation and involvement in an effective way.

Elkin (1987: 95–7) argues that urban politics suffers not only from a systematic basis in the benefits provided to certain interests but also is undermined by failures in social intelligence. In the policy debate within cities one solution and one view about how to proceed tends to dominate. Problem solving in these circumstances is not likely to be to the benefit of citizens because desirable alternatives go unexplored.

All this suggests that regime theory stands on different ground to the 'classical urban pluralism, the reigning wisdom of 30 years ago and earlier' (Stone, 1993: 1). Yet David Judge is right to suggest that regime theorists do share common ground with the revised statements of pluralists such as Dahl and Lindblom. In many respects regime theory takes as its starting point many of the concerns of 'neo-pluralists' (as defined by Dunleavy and O'Leary, 1987: Ch. 6). It accepts the privileged position of business. It is concerned about the limits to effective democratic politics. It also shares the 'neo-pluralist' concern with the fragmentation and complexity of governmental decision making. Stone comments: 'we have a special need to think about what it means politically to live under conditions of social complexity ... about the special character of power relationships in complex social systems' (1986: 77).

Thus far then regime theory shares common ground with the 'neo-pluralists'. Who deserves most credit for carving out this common ground is a matter of debate. In the urban field regime writers can reasonably claim a stronger track record. Dahl and Lindblom's revised statements are of a more general nature. Pluralists in the urban world have rather developed hyperpluralist visions (see Chapter 2 for a fuller discussion) which sit rather uncomfortably alongside the thrust of 'neo-pluralist' and regime arguments. For hyperpluralists (Yates, 1977; Thomas and Savitch, 1991) the number of organized interests, the weakness of government and the scale of social and economic problems lead to a process of policy instability and a fragmented and ineffective decision-making process. Regime theory stands in contrast to hyperpluralism. It is about how in the midst of diversity and complexity a capacity to govern can emerge within a political system.

Regime theory can thus be distinguished from classical pluralism and from the dominant thrust of urban pluralism – hyperpluralist models. It has, however, as David Judge argues 'backed into' the same ground as the 'neo-pluralists'. If on the surface it can appear that we are all pluralists now then this phenomenon tells us more about the changing nature and diversity of pluralism than it does about how regime theorists and others are supposedly rediscovering the past wisdoms of pluralist writers.

The contribution of regime theory

What is attractive about regime theory is that it begins to address the questions which flow from the common ground it shares with 'neo-pluralists'.

- What are the implications of social complexity for politics?
- What does the systemic advantage of certain interests imply for the nature of urban politics?
- What forms of power dominate modern systems of urban governance?
- What role is there for democratic politics and the role of disadvantaged groups?

Regime theory moves beyond 'neo-pluralism' by offering a series of distinctive answers to these questions and provides a broad framework for analysis to examine the variety of politics within cities.

In this section of the chapter the discussion concentrates on the work of Clarence Stone. His work represents the most advanced application of regime analysis. However, some of his core insights are submerged in the details of his intensive case study of Atlanta (Stone, 1989b). Moreover it is necessary to free the regime perspective offered by Stone from its exclusive focus on the United States (cf. Stoker and Mossberger, 1994b). What is offered, then, is a general statement of the regime conceptual framework drawn largely from the original insights of Stone.

Complexity is central to the regime perspective (Stone, 1986). Institutions and actors are involved in an extremely complex web of relationships. Diverse and extensive patterns of interdependence characterize the modern urban system. Lines of causation cannot be easily traced and the policy world is full of unpredicted spillover effects and unintended consequences. Fragmentation and lack of consensus also characterize the system. 'Many activities are autonomous and middle-range accommodations are worked out. In some ways the . . . world is chaotic; certainly it is loosely coupled, and most processes continue without active intervention by a leadership group' (Stone, 1989b: 227).

This kind of society 'does not lend itself to the establishment of direct and intense control over a large domain in a wide scope of activity' (Stone, 1986: 89). Such command or social control power is limited to particular aspects or segments of society. The study of regime politics focuses on how these limited segments or domains of command power combine forces and resources for 'a publicly significant result' – a policy initiative or development.

Complexity and fragmentation limits the capacity of state as an agency of authority or control. Nor can the state simply be seen as an arbiter or judge of competing societal claims. Rather 'as complexity asserts itself government becomes . . . more visible as a mobilizer and co-ordinator of resources' (Stone, 1986: 87). It is this third type of governmental activity which is particularly the target of regime analysis. As was argued in the introduction to the chapter, it is this form of urban politics which is becoming more important.

The state can on occasion still impose its will. It can also mediate between parties. Yet authoritative action and pluralist bargaining capture 'only a small part of political life in socially complex systems' (Stone, 1986: 88). Politics in complex urban systems is about establishing overarching priorities and 'the issue is how to bring about enough cooperation among disparate community elements to get things done' (Stone 1989b: 227). Politics is about government working with and alongside other institutions and interests and about how in that process certain ideas and interests prevail.

The point is that 'to be effective, governments must *blend* their capacities with those of various non-governmental actors' (Stone, 1993: 6, original emphasis). In responding to social change and conflict governmental and non-governmental actors are encouraged to form regimes to facilitate action and empower themselves. Thus following Stone (1989b: 4) a regime can be defined as 'an informal yet relatively stable group *with access to institutional resources* that enable it to have a sustained role in making governing decisions' (original emphasis). Participants are likely to have an institutional base – that is, they are likely to have a domain of command power. The regime, however, is formed as an informal basis for coordination and without an all encompassing structure of command.

Regimes operate not on the basis of formal hierarchy. There is no single focus of direction and control. But neither is regime politics governed by the open-ended competitive bargaining characteristic of some pluralist visions of politics. Regimes analysts point to a third mode of coordinating social life: the network. The network approach, like regime analysis, sees effective action as flowing from the cooperative efforts of different interests and organizations. Cooperation is obtained, and subsequently sustained, through the establishment of relations promised on solidarity, loyalty, trust and mutual support rather than through hierarchy or bargaining. Under the network model organizations learn to cooperate by recognizing their mutual dependency.

Relationships within the regime then have a character that is different to the mayor-centred coalitions identified in some pluralist work, especially that of Dahl's study of New Haven (Dahl, 1961). Regime partners are trying to assemble long-running relationships rather than secure for themselves access to immediate spoils: 'Governance is not the issue-by-issue process that pluralism suggests . . . Politics is about the production rather than distribution of benefits . . . Once formed, a relationship of cooperation becomes something of value to be protected by all of the participants' (Stone, 1993: 8–9). Politics is not then the fluid coalition building characteristic of many versions of pluralism. Regime theory focuses on efforts to build more stable and intense relationships in order that governmental and non-governmental actors can accomplish difficult and non-routine goals.

Politics is about achieving governing capacity which has to be created and maintained. Stone (1989b) refers to power being a matter of social production rather than social control. In contrast to the old debate between pluralists and elitists which focused on the issue of 'Who Governs?' the social production perspective is concerned with a capacity to act: 'What is at issue is not so much domination and subordination as a capacity to act and accomplish goals. The power struggle concerns, not control and resistance, but gaining and fusing a capacity to act – power to, not power over' (Stone, 1989b: 229).

Unlike elite theorists, regime theory recognizes that any group is unlikely to be able to exercise comprehensive control in a complex world. Regime analysts, however, do not regard governments as likely to respond to groups on the basis of their electoral power or the intensity of their preferences as some pluralists do. Rather, governments are driven to cooperate with those who hold resources essential to achieving a range of policy goals. As Stone argues: 'Instead of the power to govern being something that can be captured by an electoral victory, it is something created by bringing cooperating actors together, not as equal claimants, but often as unequal contributors to a shared set of purposes' (1993: 8). Regime theorists emphasize how the structure of society privileges the participation of certain interests in coalitions. As Stone (1986: 91) comments, for actors to be effective regime partners two characteristics seem especially appropriate: first, possession of strategic knowledge of social transactions and a capacity to act on the basis of that knowledge; and second, control of resources that make one an attractive coalition partner.

The US-based regime literature (see, for example, Stone and Sanders, 1987) sees two groups as the key participants in most localities: elected officials and business. Beyond this, however, there is recognition that a variety of other community interests may be drawn in based on minorities, neighbourhoods or even organized labour. Writing with a comparative perspective means that it is useful to add a fourth broad category: technical/professional officials. Such officials may well be influential participants in some US coalitions but in other western democracies, especially in Europe, their leading role is difficult to deny. These officials (for examples see Harloe et al., 1990) may be employed by elected local government, work for various non-elected local agencies or be local agents of various central or regional government departments. Knowledge joins economic position as a key resource that gives groups privileged access to decision making.

Regime theory is concerned more with the process of government-interest group mediation than with the wider relationship between government and its citizens. Regime theory views power as structured to gain certain kinds of outcomes within particular fields of governmental endeavour. The key driving force is 'the internal politics of coalition building' (Stone, 1989b: 178). If capacity to govern is achieved, if things get done, then power has been successfully exercised and to a degree it is irrelevant whether the mass of the public agreed with, or even knew about, the policy initiative.

Yet regime theory gives some recognition to the role of popular politics, elections and public participation in liberal democratic politics. Opposition to policy agendas that are being pursued can be mobilized and disrupt established policy regimes (see DeLeon 1992). Established regimes, however, can be expected to seek to incorporate certain marginal groups, to make them part of their project. People are brought in, it is suggested, less by being sold 'big ideas' or 'world views' and more by small-scale material incentives (Stone, 1989b: 186–91). Regimes may also practise a politics of exclusion, seeking to ensure that certain interests are not provided with access to decision making. Generally all regimes have to develop strategies for coping with the wider political environment.

A further distinction between pluralism and regime theory is highlighted by Stone (1993). Politics from a regime perspective is not the aggregation of preferences since this neglects the prior question of how preferences are formed. In a complex differentiated world preferences are likely to emerge through action, social relationships and experience. Regime theory sees preference formation as critical whereas much pluralist work regards the matter as unproblematic. Policy preferences do not simply exist; rather in the messy, uncertain world of politics they have to be formed. From a regime perspective preferences are developed within the dynamic of the political process and as such are subject to the influence of the logic of the situation and judgements about what is possible.

The task of regime formation is about gaining a shared sense of purpose and direction. This in turn is influenced by an understanding of what is feasible and what is not. Feasibility favours linking with resource-rich actors. It also favours some goals over others whose achievement may be more intractable and problematic. The 'iron law', as it were, governing regime formation is that 'in order for governing coalition to be viable, it must be able to mobilize resources commensurate with its main policy agenda' (Stone, 1993: 21).

This 'iron law' is then operationalized by Stone (1993) to identify four types of regime to be found in American cities. The logic of the typology is driven by the concern to demonstrate how different regimes have to match resources to the requirements of their proposed agenda. The difficulties and challenges of collective action become more intense as regimes propose more radical and socially inclusive change. Maintenance regimes seek no major change but rather to preserve what is. Their core governing task of routine service delivery requires relatively straightforward relationships between government officials and non-governmental actors. A development regime in contrast needs more resources and is attempting a more complex governing task. Such regimes are concerned to take positive action to promote growth or counter decline. Middle-class progressive regimes in contrast seek environmental protection and control over growth and/or social gains from growth. Such regimes engage in a complex form of regulation as their core governing task. Finally Stone identifies lower class opportunity expansion regimes which in order to achieve their ends require substantial mass mobilization. Such regimes face resource and coordination prerequisites that are often absent in American cities.

Regime theory, then, is ultimately a model of policy choice in the urban setting. Regime theory according to Stone: 'holds that public policies are shaped by three factors: (1) the composition of a community's governing coalition, (2) the nature of the relationships among members of the governing coalition, and (3) the resources that members bring to the governing coalition' (1993: 2). Regime members make their policies in the context of a socioeconomic environment which presents problems as well as opportunities. Achieving cooperation among regime partners is assumed to be problematic in a fragmented and uncertain world. The essence of the regime approach to politics is not to identify an elite partnership of governmental and non-governmental actors, but rather to explore the conditions for such a partnership to be created and maintained. The underlying issue is the extent to which a regime achieves a sustained capacity to act and influence developments in key policy areas.

The application of regime theory

Urban regime has in the United States become a familiar and popular phrase. The pages of *Urban Affairs Quarterly* and the *Journal of Urban Affairs* have throughout the 1990s seen a constant flow of references to 'regimes'. The phrase has entered the urban political vocabulary with a considerable force. However, there is a great danger that this very popularity has created a new descriptive catchword – a regime – in place of an explanation of the phenomenon under question (cf. Garvin, 1994). Not every study of a city that refers to its political regime constitutes a regime analysis or a contribution to regime theory.

The difficulties caused by a loose use of the regime concept are illustrated by Savitch and Thomas's book on *Big City Politics in Transition*. The book contains some valuable and interesting case studies of many of the major cities of the United States. In the final chapter Savitch and Thomas (1991: 224–50) use regime terminology to draw some general conclusions. Different cities are seen to have their politics dominated by various types of governing coalition or political regime. Pluralist regimes are dominated by strong political leaders who bring together a mixed, diffuse and competitive set of private actors. Elitist regimes are run primarily by a strong cohesive business elite with weak political leaders taken along with them. Corporatist regimes combine both strong political leaders, who set their own agenda, and a unified business elite, who knows what it wants (p. 248). The final category is the hyperpluralist regime in which 'neither political leaders or private actors are powerful enough to pull together the strings of the urban political economy' (p. 248). The direction of change within city politics is seen as 'towards some kind of pluralist or hyperpluralist system' (p. 248).

Plainly Savitch and Thomas (1991) mean their analysis to capture broad trends. As a description of developments in various cities it has a certain value. But is it a regime analysis? First, no explanation is offered as to why certain political leaders or business elites are strong or cohesive. Indeed the argument is somewhat circular along the lines that if political leaders are strong then that city's politics is dominated by strong political leaders. Second, no regime analysis is provided of the nature of the partnership forged between governmental or non-governmental leaders. For example in the corporatist regime how is it that political and business elites agree a joint agenda from their own clearly defined and strongly-held positions? Third, no effective distinction is made between power exercised as social control and power as social production. Fourth, the term regime is used as a convenient descriptive label for any political system whereas in Stone's analysis a regime is a particular type of long-term stable relationship between governmental and non-governmental partners. Indeed it is difficult to be certain whether any of the regimes identified by Savitch and Thomas could be counted as a regime in terms of Stone's definition. Finally, the identification of pluralist and in particular hyperpluralist tendencies in city politics by Savitch and Thomas overlooks the claim of regime analysis that beyond the surface of fragmented and disjointed interest group conflicts certain partnerships between government and non-governmental actors may be formed that gives its members a 'pre-emptive occupancy of a strategic role' (Stone, 1988: 82).

Regime is a label that scholars have used for different purposes. The regime framework and theory which is the focus of attention in this chapter has at its core certain key propositions and a way of understanding urban politics. A regime analysis as defined here needs to make use of that particular framework and conceptualization. To illustrate a regime analysis in practice the obvious example to take is Stone's study of Atlanta.

Stone (1989b) provides an account of Atlanta's politics between 1946 and 1988. What is observed is a single regime which despite some elements of change retains a stable means of cooperation and a resolute commitment to an activist agenda of economic growth. The dominant policy push towards full tilt development represents the triumph of a particular perspective and the pursuit of measures that involve extensive government spending and considerable risk. The regime has worked to maintain its overarching policy aim against significant opposition and the context of alternative policy options.

Two groups dominate the regime. The first is the downtown business elite which has operated and structured itself to have a single voice: 'The banks, the utilities, the major department stores, the daily newspapers, and Coca Cola, in particular, have a long history of acting in concert, and they draw other businesses that may be new to the Atlanta scene into the same pattern of unified public action' (Stone, 1989b: 169). The other main coalition partner is the political force represented by black mayors in the context of the emerging postwar black electoral majority in the city. Black political leaders have proved adept at mobilizing their supporters and with the help of the black clergy of Atlanta have been able to present a relatively unified front and stable political position. Ultimately it is the black middle class that manipulates this political resource for its benefit.

These two change-oriented elements came to share a commitment based on the increased opportunities presented to them by a full-tilt development strategy. Business saw the attraction of economic success and expansion. For the black middle-class it was the selective incentives of high quality housing, employment and small-business opportunities that encouraged a desire to go along. These material incentives were matched by the development of trust and cooperation between the regime partners through a series of shared civic institutions and informal exchanges. Both elements of the regime developed an attachment to their alliance.

Both partners were able to position themselves in a way that made them indispensable to the strategic decision making of the city. Business interests offered a groupwide view, selective incentives to encourage cooperation and established a network of civic organizations to make and maintain partnership in practice. Yet business could not pursue its objectives on its own and relied on government support and therefore an alliance with black leaders and more broadly the black middle class. The active mobilization of the resources of both sides through a network of civic cooperation created a regime that was capable of pursuing a development agenda that was beneficial to both partners. The Atlanta regime was thereby imbued 'with a means to achieve [a] publicly significant result that an otherwise divided and fragmented system of authority could not provide' (Stone, 1989b: 198).

Criticisms and developments

This section of the chapter reviews various criticisms of regime theory and the way in which regime analysis can be taken forward and developed.

The need for care in defining and applying the regime understanding of power

The regime framework is still evolving and perhaps suffers from the tendency of most of its main propositions to emerge inductively from observation of the urban scene. The 'groundedness' of regime theory is a value that should not be overlooked but it may be helpful to state in more abstract terms its approach to community power.

The regime approach is premised on the view that power in urban politics can be observed in a variety of forms. There are at least four forms of power in operation. The first is systemic power which is available to certain interests because of their position in the socioeconomic structure. Business, for example, because of its control over investment decisions and resources crucial to societal welfare is seen as having a privileged position in policy making. So much so that it may not need to act in order for its interests and concerns to be taken into account in community decision making. This form of power 'is a matter of context, of the nature of or "logic" of the situation' (Stone, 1980: 979). A participant need not make a conscious effort to obtain a structurally advantaged position for that position to be power relevant. Further the participant need not be aware of the particular consequences of their power position. Systemic power reflects the advantages and disadvantages conferred on certain groups in society based on their position within the socioeconomic structure.

The second form of power is less positional and more active. In regime terms the second form of power is that of command or social control. Power in this sense involves the active mobilization of resources (information, finance, reputation, knowledge) to achieve domination over other interests: 'The emphasis is, therefore, on one actor's capacity to achieve compliance and the other's capacity to resist' (Stone, 1988: 88). Regime theory argues, however, that command power typically only extends over a limited domain and a restricted set of activities in most urban politics. The resources, the skill and the time to achieve command power are only likely to be available to certain interests in limited arenas. Because of the limited capacity for domination and control in urban politics a third type of power can also be observed: coalition power.

Coalition power involves actors not seeking to dominate but rather to bargain on the basis of their respective autonomous basis of strength. The bargaining depends on seeking others that share compatible goals and complementary resources and for this reason coalitional arrangements tend to be relatively unstable.

Systemic, command and coalitional power are all seen as having a role in urban politics. However, the distinctive contribution of regime theory is its emphasis on a fourth form of power. Pre-emptive power or the power of social production forms a crucial axis within regime theory. Power here rests on the need for leadership in a complex society and the capacity of certain interests in coalition to provide that leadership. This leadership control is not achieved through ideological indoctrination (as in Lukes's (1974) third face of power), rather it is a result of a group of interests being able to solve substantial collective action problems to put together a structure capable of performing the needed function. The act of power is to build a regime and achieve the capacity to govern. This form of power is intentional and active.

Regime theory contends that certain interests are at an advantage when it comes to building regimes – those with systemic power and those with resources associated with command power. Yet to turn that advantage to pre-emptive power they have to manipulate their strategic position and control over resources into an effective long-term coalition which is able 'to guide the community's policy responses to social change and alter the terms on which social cooperation takes place' (Stone, 1988: 102). What is needed is a capacity for collective action to achieve significant results. The coalition needs to be able to attract participants. It needs to succeed or at least convince people that it can or is succeeding in obtaining an attractive goal. It needs to offer a range of incentives to keep partners committed to a common sense of purpose. It needs to manage its relationship with the wider political environment. Its aim is to achieve 'the strength and mastery of resources to make control of the leadership responsibility difficult for anyone else. That is the act of pre-emption' (Stone, 1988: 102). A regime once established is a powerful force in urban politics. Opponents 'have to go along to get along' or face the daunting task of building an effective counter-regime.

The above makes it clear that care is needed in defining the approach to power taken within regime theory. The regime analyst may be operating with four understandings of power. Regime studies require a considerable degree of care and subtlety from researchers in developing and presenting their findings. The sharpness of distinctions made in the abstract may become blurred in the detail of empirical application. Studies need to move from theory through empirical application and back to theory. For this reason the regime approach does not need a stack of case studies which discover regimes to bolster its position against pluralists and elitists. It rather needs to be able to substantiate the claim that its framework for analysing urban politics is robust and flexible enough to both describe and explain a variety of power distributions in different localities.

To make the same point in a more particular way: there is no need for a regime analysis to discover an effective and operational regime in a city. Indeed Orr and Stoker's (1994) regime study of Detroit in the 1990s finds a city with a limited and weak regime building capacity. It explores factors such as the nature of the potential regime partners and the weakness of civic organizations to explain how the collective action obstacles to effective city leadership were not overcome.

At the height of the community power debate in the 1950s and 1960s elitists got the result they want when they discovered an elite; pluralists claimed victory when they showed there was no elite. The regime approach cannot be subject to such simple testing. Regime theory holds that causal relationships underlying policy development are very complex and so it offers a broad conceptual framework to guide analysis. Case studies test that framework by being able to demonstrate its application in practice. The test is of a capacity to explain a process rather than to predict an outcome.

The need to put regimes in context

Urban regime analysis holds that public policies are shaped by the composition, relationships and resources of the community's governing coalition. It also acknowledges the way that the socioeconomic environment frames the options open to the governing coalition and how federal grants or state-level policies are necessary to make certain options feasible. However, the focus in Stone's case study of Atlanta (Stone, 1989b) is on the internal dynamics of the governing coalition to the detriment of contextual forces. A dilemma facing all studies of community power is how to place the analysis within the context of wider processes of change. There is a problem with the regime model if it exclusively 'locates causes for policy actions in agents that are too proximate to the action' (Jones, 1993: 1). The crucial challenge is to connect local and non-local sources of policy change.

Regimes exist within the broader external regional or national environment, as well as a local environment (cf. Horan, 1991). The capacity of local regimes can be substantially enhanced by their access to non-local powers and resources. Equally non-local forces can constrain or influence the direction of regimes. Regimes need to be placed in the architecture of governmental complexity. Keating comments:

> The wider political context is critical in determining the terms of the relationship. The central state can be oppressive, or it can be a resource allowing localities to escape other forms of dependence. . . . This, in turn, depends on the weight of local elites in the national political system and their ability to forge coalitions to extract resources on their own terms. (1991: 66)

A crucial dimension to regime formation is the way local elites are able to manage their relationship with higher levels of government and the wider political environment.

The argument for putting regimes in context is taken a step further by Jones and Bachelor (1993) and Jones (1993). They argue that in particular eras certain policy ideas become so dominant that urban regimes become locked into that way of seeing the world. There are echoes here of Elkin's concern with the limited social intelligence that guides decision making in urban politics. These dominant policy ideas may have a dynamic that reflects national or even cross-national forces at play (Stoker and Mossberger, 1994a). Trends in economic development ideas from physical renewal to more human capital based schemes would, for example, seem to follow that pattern. Urban regimes are affected by these trends in policy ideas about what is appropriate and what is feasible. They 'codify solutions and problem definitions into a solution-set that tends to dominate policy-making for a period of time' (Jones and Bachelor, 1993: 18). Regimes come to be defined as much by the solution-sets they adopt as the nature of the participants involved in the regime. Indeed the position of some groups in terms of their ability to form a regime may be enhanced by the dominance of policy ideas and a definition of 'the problem' that suggest that their participation and the kind of solutions they can offer are particularly appropriate or apt.

As Harding concludes in Chapter 3 a comparative framework for the analysis of urban politics needs to be much less 'localist' than many of the approaches dominant in the United States. Regime theory must escape from the 'localist' trap. Indeed it needs to do so to operate successfully in the United States let alone as a framework for broader cross-national comparison.

The need to explain regime continuity and change

Regime studies need to explore the dynamics of regime change as well as regime continuity. Community power needs to be viewed within a dynamic perspective. Stone (1989b) in his study of Atlanta focuses on the forces of continuity and on how the collective action problems for those challenging the established order are considerable. Yet changes do occur in regimes. DeLeon (1992), for example, analyses a shift in San Francisco from a pro-growth to a progressive or at least a slow growth regime. Shifts in the patterns of funding from Federal government and the arrival of a business leadership that held their position as managers and had fewer direct ties to San Francisco are seen as having weakened the grip of the pro-growth regime. These processes of continuity and change need to be located within a developing framework of regime theory. What is needed is a recognition of the impact of shifts in exogenous conditions as well as developments in the internal dynamics of coalition building.

The role of policy ideas in explaining both regime continuity and change is emphasized in the work of Jones and his colleagues referred to earlier. The stability of a regime is explained by the solution-set it adopts. Once in place, solution-sets tend to dominate policy search and sustain the regime's policy perspective allowing some scope for incremental change. This condition of policy stasis, however, can break down and be punctured by rapid policy development and change (for a wider discussion see Baumgartner and Jones, 1993). In these circumstances 'fresh policy proposals and symbolic representations of them have the capacity to attract new participants to politics, altering the existing governing arrangements' (Jones and Bachelor, 1993: 250). When the regime's favoured policy solution falls into disrepute the promotion of an attractive alternative policy more 'in tune with the times' can rapidly gain supporters and generate considerable positive feedback: 'that is changes cascade in a kind of urban bandwagon that sweeps through the system' (Jones, 1993: 3).

Orr and Stoker (1994) propose a model of regime transition which gives recognition to the influence of non-local forces – reflecting broader shifts in the political and economic environment – as well as the internal dynamics of coalition building. They argue it is useful to think of regime transition in terms of a three-stage scheme.

The first stage revolves around the questioning of the established regime. Doubts may be raised about its capacity and about the goals it is pursuing. Such questions are most likely to be raised where developments in the wider environment appear to contradict or challenge the established regime. Questions and doubts have to find some vehicle of expression among corporate, political or other potential leaders.

The second stage involves a conflict about redefining the scope and purpose of the regime. Here competing groups of elite actors may organize to seek new ways forward and a new policy direction. This is a period of much uncertainty and debate. Hostility between opposing camps may find public expression. There will be a battle for 'hearts and minds' of established actors and a search for new actors to support a new way forward. Experiments and pilot initiatives may also form the useful function of visible flags around which the challenging forces can assemble, gathering strength and gaining in mutual understanding.

A third stage involves the institutionalization of the new regime. The institutionalization of a new regime involves the establishment of a new set of material incentives and ideological outlook. In short a new solution-set would need to be established alongside appropriate institutional arrangements and selective incentives.

Regime transition is not likely to be a simple and straightforward process. To challenge a regime is a difficult task. To assemble an alternative regime, as has been argued throughout this chapter, reflects a considerable expression of power.

Conclusion

Regime theory has made a useful contribution to the study of urban politics. It provides a framework for analysis which encourages attention to be directed to important aspects of urban politics. In particular the attempt to push urban political science beyond a narrow focus on power as an issue of social control is to be welcomed. To understand the politics of a complex urban system it is necessary to move beyond a notion of power as the ability to get another actor to do something they would not otherwise do. Politics is not restricted to acts of domination by the elite and consent or resistance from the ruled. Social control or command power because of the cost of obtaining compliance is likely to be restricted to limited domains of action. In a complex society the crucial act of power is the capacity to provide leadership and a mode of operation that enables significant tasks to be done. This is the power of social production. Regime theory suggests that this form of power involves actors and institutions gaining and fusing a capacity to act by blending their resources, skills and purposes into a long-term coalition: a regime. If they succeed they pre-empt the leadership role in their community and establish for themselves a near decision-making monopoly over the cutting-edge choices facing their locality.

The framework for analysis offered by regime theory and its layered conception of power provides the basis for a more subtle understanding of urban politics than that provided by the hyperpluralist-models reviewed in Chapter 2 and the growth coalition literature examined in Chapter 3. It is a theory in need of further development. It needs to avoid the trap of a narrow localism and enhance its capacity to explain regime change. Above all it needs to avoid its terminology and language being usurped to serve the needs of a multitude of atheoretical case studies of city politics.

Finally regime theory has the capacity to travel. If some of its ethnocentric assumptions are removed it may be able to offer an effective framework for analysis in other countries. As Alan Harding notes in Chapter 3, UK political scientists have in the past been reluctant to undertake such empirical tests. Yet in its concern with the blending of capacities between governmental and non-governmental actors regime theory would seem to highlight processes which are now more to the fore in the British system. It may also be possible to go further and use regime theory as a framework for cross-national comparison. Some of the groundwork for such a move has been provided already (Stoker and Mossberger, 1994b). Regime theory will need to grow and develop if it is to survive. It has succeeded in establishing a new agenda for researchers. If in ten years' time regime analysts have a track record of empirical research and theoretical development on both sides of the Atlantic then regime theory will really have come of age.

References

Baumgartner, F. and Jones, B. (1993) *Agendas and Instability in American Politics*. Chicago, IL: University of Chicago Press.

Cochrane, A. (1993) *Whatever Happened to Local Government?* Milton Keynes: Open University Press.

Dahl, R. (1961) *Who Governs?* New Haven, CT: Yale University Press.

DeLeon, R. (1992) *Left Coast City: Progressive Politics in San Francisco 1975–1991*. Lawrence: University Press of Kansas.

Dunleavy, P. and O'Leary, B. (1987) *Theories of the State*. London: Macmillan.

Elkin, S. (1987) *City and Regime in the American Republic*. Chicago, IL: University of Chicago Press.

Fainstein, N. and Fainstein, S. (1986) 'Regime strategies, communal resistance and economic forces', in S. Fainstein, R.C. Hill, D. Judd and M. Smith (eds), *Restructuring the City: The Political Economy of Urban Redevelopment*. New York: Longman.

Garvin, J. (1994) Personal communication.

Harloe, M., Pickvance, C. and Urry, J. (eds) (1990) *Place, Policy and Politics*. London: Unwin Hyman.

Horan, C. (1991) 'Beyond governing coalitions: analyzing urban regimes in the 1990s', *Journal of Urban Affairs*, 13 (2): 119–35.

Jones, B. (1993) 'Social power and urban regimes', *Urban News*, Newsletter of the Urban Politics Section of the American Political Science Association, 7 (3): 1–3.

Jones, B. and Bachelor, L. with Wilson, C. (1986) *The Sustaining Hand: Community Leadership and Corporate Power*. Lawrence: University of Kansas Press.

Jones, B. and Bachelor, L. (1993) *The Sustaining Hand: Community Leadership and Corporate Power* (2nd edn, revised). Lawrence: University of Kansas Press.

Keating, M. (1991) *Comparative Urban Politics: Power and the City in the United States, Canada, Britain and France*. Aldershot: Edward Elgar.

Lukes, S. (1974) *Power: A Radical View*. London: Macmillan.

Orr, M. and Stoker, G. (1994) 'Urban regimes and leadership in Detroit', *Urban Affairs Quarterly*, 30 (1): 48–73.

Osborne, D. and Gaebler, T. (1992) *Reinventing Government: How the Entrepreneurial Spirit is Transforming the Public Sector*. Reading: Addison-Wesley.

Peterson, P. (1981) *City Limits*. Chicago: University of Chicago Press.

Savitch, H. and Thomas, J. (1991) 'Conclusion: End of the millennium big city politics', in H. Savitch and J. Thomas (eds), *Big City Politics in Transition*. Newbury Park, CA: Sage.

Stoker, G. and Mossberger, K. (1994a) 'The dynamics of cross-national policy borrowing: frameworks for analysis in the urban setting', Paper presented at the Urban Affairs Association Annual Conference, New Orleans, 2–5 March.

Stoker, G. and Mossberger, K. (1994b) 'Urban regime theory in comparative perspective', *Government and Policy*, 12: 195–212.

Stone, C. (1980) 'Systemic power in community decision making: a restatement of stratification theory', *American Political Science Review*, 74 (4): 978–90.

Stone, C. (1986) 'Power and social complexity', in R. Waste (ed.), *Community Power: Directions for Future Research*. Newbury Park, CA: Sage.

Stone, C. (1988) 'Pre-emptive power: Floyd Hunter's "Community Power Structure" reconsidered', *American Journal of Political Science*, 32: 82–104.

Stone, C. (1989a) 'Paradigms, power and urban leadership', in B. Jones (ed.), *Leadership and Politics*. Lawrence: University Press of Kansas.

Stone, C. (1989b) *Regime Politics: Governing Atlanta, 1946–1988*. Lawrence: University Press of Kansas.

Stone, C. (1993) 'Urban regimes and the capacity to govern: a political economy approach', *Journal of Urban Affairs*, 15 (1): 1–28.

Stone, C. and Sanders, H. (eds) (1987) *The Politics of Urban Development*. Lawrence: University Press of Kansas.

Thomas, J. and Savitch, H. (1991) 'Introduction: Big city politics, then and now', in H. Savitch and J. Thomas (eds), *Big City Politics in Transition*, Newbury Park, CA: Sage.

Yates, D. (1977) *The Ungovernable City: The Politics of Urban Problems and Policy Making*. Cambridge, MA: MIT Press.

Part II

URBAN GOVERNMENT AND DEMOCRACY

5

Bureaucrats and Urban Politics: Who Controls? Who Benefits?

Bryan D. Jones

Any analysis of bureaucracies inevitably centres on the fundamental issue of *control*. It looks so simple: most citizens think of democratic government as consisting of elected officials who reflect the 'will of the people' by enacting policies and hiring bureaucrats to implement them. Thus, fundamental to democracy is control of the bureaucrats by the elected officials.

It is the purpose of this chapter to show that such a simple model of democratic government is seriously misleading. It is not supported by the day-to-day facts of government, and it is a poor model for the conduct of popular business. The reason is that the very nature of control is fundamentally inappropriate in trying to understand government, urban and otherwise. After reviewing the issues in control, I develop a new approach to the issue, which involves viewing governments and their bureaucracies as *adaptive systems*, responding to forces in their environments as they influence these forces.

By misunderstanding control, we may become overly cynical about the conduct and promise of democratic government. *From the right*, it is argued that 'budget-maximizing bureaucrats' use their superior information about the requirements of implementation and their natural political constituencies to implore elected officials to expand government beyond what is efficient. *From the left*, it is claimed that bureaucracies are responsive to the needs of business, driven by the necessity of increasing the tax base as capital flees the confines of the statutory city. *Both views* are pessimistic about the potential for democratic government, because of a failure of popular control of bureaucrats. But both views are incomplete, and hence of limited utility in understanding how communities are governed.

This chapter has four parts. The first examines the issue of who controls urban bureaucracies, treating bureaucracies as units. The issue addressed in this section is the extent to which the elected, or 'political', branches of government can and do control the behaviour of the officials appointed to implement legislation and directives from the political branches. The problem is that elected officials cannot spend all of their energies in supervising bureaucrats, and it might not be good policy to do so in any case. In the United States, the doctrine of pluralism developed to counteract the notion that overhead supervision by legislators was desirable. In this doctrine, agencies were to receive considerable delegated power, and they were to respond to the needs and demands of interests affected by the policies that they were responsible for implementing. In the case of local governments in federal systems, it is not clear just who is supposed to be doing the supervising. In the United States, local bureaucrats are legally responsible to the council, but because local governments, including city councils, school boards, county governments, and special authorities, are all legal creatures of the state, they are also responsible for the implementation of state law. They are also accountable for implementing many federal mandates.

The second part of this chapter looks at the issue of internal control of bureaucracies. Bureaucracies are not wholes; they are complex organizations themselves. Even if agency heads want to control bureaucracies, they may not be able to do so. Here we enter the world of the 'street-level bureaucrat'; the official who is legally part of an agency hierarchy (so there is no question of the existence of 'multiple principles' wherein the lines of authority are blurred), yet local forces cause the street-level official to act somewhat independently of the dictates of the rules and customs established in the agency.

The third section studies the question of institutional design; that is, can bureaucracies be controlled by changing the incentives that bureaucrats face by, for example, inducing competition through privatization or through contracting, where private contractors can be terminated for not obeying the strictures of the contract? If bureaux and the bureaucrats they employ are so difficult to control, can central authorities actually make use of the tendencies inherent in governmental organization to enhance the probability that the policies they desire actually get implemented?

Finally, I offer a model of bureaucratic control based on the adaptive nature of complex systems that is considerably more optimistic about the potential for successful local democracy within the administrative state than is currently in vogue. The model downplays the issue of control by viewing the political branches not as controllers but as occasional meddlers in the affairs of localities. When attention is drawn to policy areas that are the basic responsibilities of local officials, central authorities may act to correct the course of local officials. This is best done by creating proper institutional incentives of the type that will be discussed in the third section of the paper. But it means giving up hope of completely dictating the behaviour of local officials, who generally respond to local forces in any case.

It is important that any discussion of control of bureaucracies simultaneously deal with the issue of local control. Public service agencies exist at all levels of government. So do political entities, from city councils and local school boards to national legislatures. In a federal system such as exists in the United States, functions are so intertwined that it is not possible to assign a set of priorities that are exclusively national, and a set that are exclusively local. In many cases, the federal government uses the intergovernmental grant system to require the states and localities to implement national priorities. This is the case for almost all domestic programmes except social security. If Congress and the President cannot control the behaviours of local politicians and bureaucrats, then they cannot control the implementation of national policies. Even in a more centralized state such as the United Kingdom the issue emerges, as is indicated by the efforts of Conservative governments to rein in the spending of Labour-dominated local councils. So the issue of bureaucratic control, viewed from a comprehensive national-level perspective, is so intertwined with the issue of local discretion that they ought to be treated holistically.

Popular control of bureaucracies

The notion that citizens elect representatives who then enact policies that are straightforwardly implemented by public agencies is known as the *overhead democracy* model (Redford, 1969). There are two linkages in the model: citizens control elected officials (which is termed *electoral accountability*), and elected officials control bureaucrats *(bureaucratic accountability)*. Both run into empirical difficulties.

Electoral accountability is difficult because the relationship between elected officials and citizens is complex. Numerous studies in the United States and in the United Kingdom, as well as elsewhere, have shown that most citizens do not cast their votes on the basis of policies. Rather, such facets as party identification and candidate appeal are also critical. If citizens do not vote for policies, then elected officials do not carry with them policy mandates when they take office. Various lines of argument may save the linkage; for example, citizens may switch parties if their party consistently offers policies that are inimical to their interests. And citizens may judge parties retroactively; that is, they may reject policies enacted by a party rather than prospectively endorse party platforms. But in the United States, policy responsibility is so diffuse that it is difficult for citizens to judge. Public powers are divided at the national level and in most state governments; often different parties hold different branches of government. And in local governments, many elections are non-partisan, making it difficult to hold any set of office holders accountable electorally. So electoral accountability, at least as a global concept, is difficult at best, and more so in the United States than in the United Kingdom.

The issue of bureaucratic accountability

Bureaucratic accountability is even more problematic, because it is not even so clear that it is a good idea in the first place. And here lies one of the great debates of American politics: overhead democracy versus pluralism. With the expansion of the national state in the US in the 1930s, the type of national government that was to emerge became critical. The administration of President Roosevelt was busy establishing the 'alphabet soup' of public agencies designed to curb the excesses of capitalism, to stimulate the economy, and to protect those devastated by the depression. But open government meant that 'special interests' could directly influence the operation of these agencies. Hence the national government devolved into *policy whirlpools* or *policy subsystems* (Griffith, 1939), within which regulated interests, interested members of Congress, and the regulators worked out policy solutions. But such a pluralistic system of policy subsystems necessarily implied weak control by the elected branches of government.

Hence the debate between the proponents of overhead democracy and those of pluralistic government debated the very nature of democracy. To the pluralists, the system of policy subsystems was open and fluid, allowing the easy entry of those interested. As the affected countermobilized, a pluralist balance would result. To the proponents of overhead democracy, a pluralist system always fell prey to those with the most resources, thereby denying the national majorities forged by the less fortunate through their access to the ballot.

In the US, prior to the 1930s the states and localities were responsible for the vast bulk of policy activity in the nation. And the states and localities were struggling with the consequences of the industrial revolution and vast waves of immigration that occurred after the Civil War. If pluralistic government was an issue at the national level, it dominated academic concern in the states and localities. The early 1960s yielded the great trilogy of pluralist thinking about cities: Banfield's *Political Influence* (1961), analysing Chicago; Sayre and Kaufman's *Governing New York City* (1960); and Dahl's *Who Governs?* (1961), a study of New Haven, Connecticut. These works differed among themselves. Sayre and Kaufman defended the drastically decentralized government of New York City, which they characterized as consisting of 'islands of functional power' dominated by policy experts and the interested. Dahl viewed executive power as capable of spanning the pluralist politics of issue-areas by means of 'executive-centred coalitions' that changed as policies changed. But taken together, these works both codified a theory of city government and established the primary method for studying cities, the case study of actual decision making.

The counter-attack was not long in coming. For the purposes of this chapter, the most important critic of the pluralist city was Theodore Lowi. Examining New York as part of the Sayre-Kaufman project, Lowi's *At the Pleasure of the Mayor* (1964) analysed the problems of the elected mayor in establishing city-wide priorities in the face of limited control over budgeting; a federal system of boroughs (which were independent municipalities prior to their merger to form the City of New York at the turn of the century); and the vast archipelago of functional power vested in city administrative agencies. In such a system, city-wide popular majorities were regularly denied; bureaucratic agencies were uncontrollable. Lowi extended his critique of pluralism to the national government in his *The End of Liberalism* (1979). There he called for 'juridical democracy', which relied on tightly-controlled bureaucratic agencies through the wording of statutes that would constrain the discretion of bureaucrats.

In the US, the overhead democracy model carried the day, both in academic and popular opinion, but not in fact. Special interests have come to be viewed almost exclusively not as the dynamos of open government but as the opponents of popular majorities, and bureaucratic discretion less a tool for problem solving and more a barrier to the 'will of the people'. Two academic versions of this theme may be found in *implementation studies* and in *principal-agent analysis*. Both are models of legislative control of bureaucracies. Both lead to pessimistic conclusions about democratic governance. Implementation studies start with the premise that there exist stages of policy making, two of which are policy enactment and policy implementation. Legislative majorities enact policies, and then leave it up to bureaucracies to implement them. In the US, most domestic policies are implemented both by national agencies and state and/or local agencies, usually through a combination of *grants in aid* and *mandates* or directives. But virtually all empirical studies of implementation have found the intrusion of local forces into the idealized hierarchical implementation process.

Principal-agent analyses assume that the legislature is a principal while a bureaucratic agency serves as an agent of the principal, somewhat like when a manufacturing firm (the principal) retains an accounting firm (the agent). The agent has more information about the policy area than does the principal on whose behalf the agent is acting; this is known as the *information asymmetry problem*. Hence a grant of discretionary power, either formally or informally, occurs. But because agents may act on their own behalf, special control measures are necessary on the part of the principal. Most principal-agent analyses assume that the legislative branch is the principal. This is more descriptive in unitary, parliamentary systems such as Great Britain. In law the central bureaucracy is a servant of the crown, and hence bureaucrats owe their allegiances to the political executive. Local officials are employees of the local authority, but have the legal responsibility to implement central government policies. Local bureaucrats also owe formal allegiance to the local council. Even in unitary states, dual authority may be an issue.

The analogy becomes considerably more strained, however, when applied to federal, presidential systems. Just who is the principal? Either one must maintain that Congress is the principal, and decry bureaucratic autonomy, or postulate *multiple principals*, including the president and the courts in addition to Congress. Chubb (1985), for example, chooses the former strategy, depicting a dual implementation structure that involves first the national tier of bureaucrats, controlled by Congress, and then the State and local bureaucrats, controlled by the national bureaucrats. Quantitative studies show little support for the second linkage (Scholtz et al., 1991; Wood, 1991). More realistic is a model of bureaucratic adaptation in which 'bureaucracies . . . are continually adjusting to concurrent, multiple, and diverse stimuli' (Wood and Waterman, 1993: 523). But that leads to a conclusion that *nobody* controls the bureaucracy. So we ought to ask (but we haven't): if there are multiple principals, who benefits? And under what conditions do they benefit?

At the local level, the problem becomes even more severe. Is a local council supposed to be an agent of the national or state government? In law, they are creatures of the state, not the nation (but *home rule charters* have granted substantial independence to municipalities). On the other hand, cities exist in a complex federal system, one in which functional agencies of the city are linked to their functional equivalents at the state and nation in what Deil Wright (1978) terms *picket fence federalism*. In the localities in strong federal systems such as the US, the principal-agent metaphor breaks down and is not useful. It leads back to the 'multiple influences (multiple principals) from diverse sources' analysis, and thus fails to specify the conditions of control.

Who controls bureaucracies if legislatures do not?

In the end, studies of implementation and principal-agent relations, at least in the federal US, lead to frustrations over models of overhead democracy and accountable bureaucracies. But saying that democratic control fails does not speak to the issue of who does control. There are two potential answers: the interests and the bureaucrats themselves.

The bureaucrats   It has, of course, been long recognized that bureaucrats have an interest themselves. Sporadic outbursts of charges of 'feathering their own nests' have been levelled at government officials, elected and appointed. These inchoate observations have been brought to full flower in *public choice theories* of bureaucracies. These theories postulate that government officials maximize their self-interests, and then go on to analyse the conditions within government that provide incentives and opportunities for such maximization. And, according to the public choice theorists, the opportunities are legion. In the most recognized version of the public choice thesis, that by Niskanen, agency officials are assumed to maximize the size of their agency's budgets (Niskanen, 1971). The model was modified by Migue and Belanger (1974), who assumed that agency chiefs maximize their agencies' *discretionary* budget, defined as the difference between the total agency budget and the cost of producing a level of output that will be accepted by political authorities to which the agency heads report. Niskanen (1991: 18) has accepted that modification, suggesting that such a model actually looks more like a profit-maximizing firm, which was the analogy for his study of bureau behaviour.

In the United Kingdom, the notion that urban bureaucrats govern in their own interests is known as *managerialism*. Under the 'pure managerialist' model, 'control of access to local resources is held by the professional officers of the authority concerned'. These public managers hold a common ideology and 'manipulate their elected representatives so that the political composition of the council makes little difference to the policies pursued' (Pahl, 1975: 270). Pahl attempted to explain the distribution of urban resources through the action of urban managers, who served as gatekeepers in the allocation of scarce urban resources. In this approach, public bureaucrats are not so much rational maximizers as they are captive of their own powerful attitudes and values, which may include self-interest, but also embody a full theory of state intervention. Indeed, rather than defer to economists, he suggests that sociologists should study the constellations of values that public managers hold. Pahl has modified his pure managerialist model to allow for the 'structural' deference of the state to capitalist interests and the dictates of the central state (Pahl, 1975), but this seems to undermine the point of the argument (Saunders, 1981).

Both of these models of the actions of public bureaucrats are essentially static. In the case of the public choice models, Niskanen and others assume an incentive structure for bureaucrats, but it may not hold at all times and places. Similarly, Pahl's equivocation on the role of capital could have been a response to changing deference to capital during a period of economic difficulty. This is a point to which I will return presently.

The interests The second answer to the question of bureaucratic control in the absence of supervision by the policy-making branches (and hence national majorities) is that control falls to those interested and active in the political process. It is a grand truism of political science that those who have an interest or stake in a policy outcome are most active in attempting to influence that outcome. It is also often argued that government ought to respond to the interested and active, and that this is the essence of democracy. The problem is that a different constellation of interests prevails during the implementation stage of the policy process than in the enactment stage. At least with respect to major policy initiatives, there is generally widespread interest by the media, and substantial involvement by political parties, the president, and the activist strata of citizens at the enactment stage. National mobilization in the public debate may be an overstatement, but widespread interest and involvement clearly occurs. But when the policy moves to the implementation stage, the gradient of attentiveness falls rapidly. This leaves the field to the most affected groups. Bernstein's (1955) classic bureau 'life cycle' points to the loss of mission over time after a regulatory agency is established. The conditions for this loss of mission (and consequent decline into 'capture' by the affected interests) comes about as legislative overseers lose interest and the regulated industry becomes adept at working with the regulators, pointing out the problems caused by the regulations.

At the local level, Stone (1976) has shown how business groups may have to make major compromises in the enactment stage of the policy process, but during the implementation stage can reassert themselves. It can be a mistake, however, to assume that business can always win in the implementation stage. In a study of nuclear power, Campbell (1988) shows how the nuclear power industry was more effective in the legislative stage, but citizen groups were able to influence the implementation process dramatically. The broader point is that bureaucratic agencies are subject to influence by fairly small groups during the implementation stage because of the lack of large-scale mobilization that is typical of major policy enactments.

Business power   The role of interests in politics always raises the issue of the power of business in politics. Two different strands of thought have been developed on the issue of business power. The first is the *instrumentalist* position. Instrumentalists argue that business is powerful because business interests possess the political resources (or instruments) to get governmental officials to do their bidding. This approach, which is the dominant one among political scientists in the United States, leads scholars to examine such things as the role of lobbyists, campaign contributions to politicians, and the connections between high-level appointed officials and business concerns.

The second position, the *structuralist* position, views democratic politics as the handmaiden of capitalist accumulation. Capitalism is premised on the accumulation of wealth in the hands of capitalists, who invest it in productive enterprises. Governments capture part of the productive increment to operate. Hence governments are responsive to business interests because they are dependent on capitalism. This special relationship gives what Charles Lindblom (1977) terms a 'privileged position' in the councils of government: because business in a capitalist system is responsible for growth creation, governments must pay business interests special heed.

One does not have to adopt the full-blown structuralist position to see that the instrumentalist position is too limited to understand the role of business interests in government. On the other hand, trying to understand the relationship between business and government in structural terms alone has not been successful. Vogel (1989; see also Jones, 1986) points out that business interests organize and try to influence politics when things are not going well for them. Under a structuralist model, it is difficult to explain why business would ever lose political battles.

It seems futile to try to develop a model of interest influences in government that holds for all times at all places. If one constellation of interests were able to control government activity, as is implied in the business power models, then we would expect that business would be powerful at all times and in all places. But it has been shown that the different levels of government may be responsive to different constellations of interests. In the UK, Peter Saunders argued that by the late 1970s a *dual state* had emerged, with the national government developing a tendency towards promoting investment (that is, towards policies that aid in the accumulation of capital and economic growth), and local councils emphasizing collective consumption policies, such as housing and public works (Saunders, 1979). In his sophisticated analysis of urban service provision in the UK, Dunleavy defines urban politics 'in terms of the study of decision making on collective consumption processes' (1980: 50). Ironically, Peterson (1981) has argued that in the United States, local governments are highly dependent on their export industries, and hence shift towards investment policies in an attempt to nurture these industries. In comparison, the national government is preoccupied with consumption policies (or what are termed redistributive policies, because they shift resources from the better off to the worse off citizens). Hence we have a situation in which different types of interests 'control' different levels of government, but in which the levels of government controlled vary across countries. This would seem to cause considerable problems for the unbridled business domination thesis, whether in its structuralist or instrumentalist guise.

The reconciliation of the dual state problem has much to do with the differences in the manner in which central governments relate to their subnational governments. In the United States, local governments are and have always been heavily reliant on the local tax base for raising revenue, particularly in the form of the property tax. Grants come to localities from both the state governments (in many states, a major source of revenue) and the national government (not a major source, except during the 1970s). In the United Kingdom, the central government has provided much revenue to the localities through grants, making the local councils less dependent on local revenue. Conservative governments in the 1980s curtailed grants, but, not trusting the design of institutions to have their effect, also capped the property tax rate and then moved to a local 'head tax' and now to a 'council tax' to finance locally provided services and legislated the details of public policies. In general, a direct connection between spending and taxing will shift expenditure policies towards investment-style policies. One investment-style approach is to keep tax rates low, but this can interfere with the provision of physical and human infrastructure that is critical to business growth. So the broader point is that policies will shift from consumption to investment where governments are small and not affected by intergovernmental grants. Where grants from one level of government to another are plentiful, the priorities of local dependency on the tax base can be modified. So one answer to the problem of 'who controls' the bureaucracy is that it very much depends on how governmental institutions are arranged. We shall return to a more extended analysis of this point later in this chapter.

Arrangement of functions among levels of government does not, however, tell the whole story. Investment or developmental policies have become a major theme among governments in the United States, Canada, the United Kingdom and France (Keating, 1993). This hints at a different perspective on the issue of investment versus consumption policies: the mix for any level of government can change a great deal over time. State and local governments in the US for example, maintained an average ratio of investment to consumption expenditures of around 2.0 for the period 1945 to 1990, while the national government's investment consumption ratio was estimated to be around 0.3 (Baumgartner and Jones, 1993: 223–4). The state ratio, however, varied greatly through the period, with the peak investment period coming between 1955 and 1965. Investment policies dominated state governments when the economy was good, but declined as the economy deteriorated during the 1970s. The role of federal grants-in-aid and mandates, rather than a more vigorous consumption-based state and local level politics, seems to be the reason (Baumgartner and Jones, 1993: 224–5).

Above I suggested that if one wants to answer the question of 'who controls' the bureaucracy, one must look at who benefits from the operation of bureaucracies. Now we can discern two partial answers. First, in regard to local governments, who benefits depends mostly on local forces, filtered through the manner in which public sector resources are raised (local taxes versus intergovernmental grants). Second, who benefits seems time dependent; the mix of investment versus consumption policies varies over time. So any understanding of bureaucratic control must incorporate change.

The picture is even more complex when we move to an exclusive focus on localities. Within levels of government, different bureaucracies may respond to different interests. Friedland reports 'two worlds of municipal expenditures: one oriented to providing services and public employment for the city's residents, the other to constructing the infrastructure necessary to profitable private investment' (1982: 202). So local government can be pushed in the direction of both consumption and investment policies. The overall mix of policies may be less of a reasoned balance (or a result of capture of the entire structure of government by business interests) and more the result of historical pressures to deal with existing problems, leaving a bureaucratic legacy of the contradictory demands on government. That is, government bureaucracies are the present traces of past struggles over public policies, and cannot really be understood outside of that historical context.

Controlling bureaucrats in agencies: street level bureaucrats and service delivery rules

Bureaucracies, urban or otherwise, are complex organizations. They are not easily controlled, both because the sub-units of government agencies themselves have interests and are affected by the interests, and because agencies are composed of individuals, who themselves are self-interested. But internal bureaucratic politics is not a game that is played without consequences. Urban officials, such as police, teachers, building inspectors, and zoning officials make daily decisions that impact so heavily on the lives of citizens. Some citizens and their neighbourhoods can be greatly aided by the actions of urban officials, while others can be irreparably harmed.

Before we move further into an examination of control processes within urban service delivery agencies, we ought to be more explicit about the sources of control. In the classic work on the subject, Dahl and Lindblom (1953) distinguish among four social processes that may act to control human behaviour: the price system, hierarchy, polyarchy and bargaining. Of the four, only hierarchy serves to impose direct, intended control. The others are modes of interaction in which there is no central control. This means that in any system of human interaction, there will be multiple sources of control in addition to that imposed by hierarchy. Just how an individual chooses among the competing incentive systems that compete for a role in directing his or her behaviour is a major source of enquiry in organization theory.

One of the classic criteria of bureaucratic organizations is that they operate according to formal rules. These rules, in theory, are imposed by the political branches of government in order to carry out the mandates of law enacted by these bodies. That is, they are the handmaidens of hierarchy, allowing managers to pre-specify the appropriate actions of agency personnel, and then to monitor compliance with the rules. Hammond (1986) has shown how different hierarchical arrangements dictate an agency's decision-making agenda; that is, the structure of an organization implies an organizational strategy (Hammond, 1986). But examining the formal rules is not enough, because the behaviour of agency personnel responds to other incentives than hierarchy. In almost all cases the proper implementation of statutes involves a *grant of discretion*; that is, it is left to the public employee to decide just what situations are in need of intervention. This grant of discretion has a firm basis in reality: it is extremely difficult, if not impossible, to pre-specify all conditions that require action, and then to pre-specify the appropriate action. Even if this were possible, it would not be desirable. When management–employee relations deteriorate in urban service delivery agencies, sometimes employees 'work to rule', meaning they follow the letter of the rules they are supposed to obey. The result is inevitably great case backlogs and irate citizens who are 'written up' for every possible violation. On the other hand, this grant of discretion can lead to substantial discrimination among citizens by the 'street-level bureaucrats' that deliver services to citizens (Lipsky, 1980).

As a consequence, formal rules interact with the very nature of the task to generate a set of *behavioural* rules; that is, rules that agency personnel actually use to govern their actions (Cyert and March, 1963). Within an organization, rules may be imposed through the hierarchy, as explicit mechanisms of control, but they may also emerge from the diverse sources of demands on agency personnel. Grappling with the task can generate rules that are quite contrary to the formal rules of the organization. These behavioural rules have a very important impact on the distribution of services to citizens (Jones, 1980). That is, it is not enough to point to the grant of discretion to street-level bureaucrats in the study of the distribution of services to citizens. One must also examine the set of behavioural rules that actually govern the behaviour of street-level bureaucrats, attending to the sources of these behavioural rules. While formal rules may impact the behavioural rules, they are not the only source for them.

But there is a more severe problem with the set of formal rules that are supposed to govern the behaviour of bureaucrats and impartially implement the statutes and directives emanating from the political branches of government. The rules themselves are made in response to political pressures, only some of which are related to the implementation of statutes. In a study of building regulation in Chicago, I found a *dual* policy-making system. On the one hand, there was a policy subsystem concerned with making and enforcing building regulations. The relevant actors were the commissioner of buildings, the chair of the city council committee on buildings, the head of the fire prevention bureau, and the private interests: architects, developers, builders and representatives of the craft trades (electricians, plumbers, etc.). Relationships were regularized, and characterized by bargaining between the representatives of the government bureaux and the private interests (Jones, 1985: Ch 2).

On the other hand, a second policy-making system existed in parallel with the substantive one, and it was concerned with issues of management control. I characterized this management control policy subsystem as *regularized, adversarial, unstable, and non-incremental* (Jones, 1985: 45). It was regularized because the same actors, primarily reform groups and the media, tended to raise problems with management control – usually as corruption or misfeasance. As a consequence, the charges brought against the bureau were highly symbolic. The response of the attacked agency was reactive and non-incremental, in order to meet the major challenge to its way of doing business. And the response inevitably involved the imposition of more central control in the bureau; that is, a withdrawal of the grant of discretion to agency personnel.

In such an environment, government inevitably ends up with a panoply of formal rules that are so detailed (at least in respect to the issues raised in the scandal) that choices among the formal rules are necessary just to conduct agency business. Overspecifying in order to impose hierarchical control can have the opposite affect of granting discretion through the necessity of choosing among the voluminous formal prescriptions that are adopted to try to ensure management control. And in the case of regulatory policies, such overspecification can impose massive inefficiencies on the marketplace. Here is the way that the commissioner of buildings in Chicago described the problem:

> You try to stop the 'bad guys' by putting in checks [in the building permit process]. They figure a way around the check, and you put in another check. And so on. Meanwhile the normal person has to go through the same checks, and gets frustrated . . . So you review the system of checks, and drop some . . . Then, all of a sudden, someone says that there is a building that is not going up right, and it's not. So you put in the checks again. (Jones, 1985: 59).

There are three primary sources of the distribution of public output to citizens: hierarchy and formal rules; behavioural rules; and street-level discretion. There are actually two types of behavioural rules: decision rules and attention rules (Jones, 1985). *Decision rules* are those rules that emerge from task performance. They specify the triggering of intervention and the nature of the response to the problem or situation. They are those parts of the formal rules that are employed in practice. Most services in cities in the United States, at least, are delivered according to such decision rules (Mladenka, 1978; Jones, 1980). *Attention rules* are behavioural rules that force attention to situations that are not, strictly speaking, related to the performance of the service task (Crecine, 1969). Attention rules are pre-specified rules for the allocation of special attention depending, say, on the race of the service recipient or the voting patterns of a neighbourhood. Unlike the task-relevant decision rules, they are not in conformity with the *norm of neutral competence* (Kaufman, 1956), the ideal that services ought to be delivered without regard to the characteristics of citizens receiving the service contact, that is a cornerstone of professional bureaucracy.

Clearly street-level discretion can result in discrimination against citizens (Lipsky, 1980). But task performance rules can also operate, unintendedly, in what might be characterized as a discriminatory manner (Levy et al., 1974; Jones, 1980). For example, if it is the policy of a city department to operate on a service-on-demand rule, then citizens that complain most will receive the most services. If, for example, neighbourhoods in which large numbers of recent immigrants are reticent about contacting authorities, those neighbourhoods will receive fewer services than they might receive if they were objectively rated regarding the severity of the problems that they face. Should attention rules operate against recent immigrants, then these neighbourhoods would receive service levels that were attenuated from both sources.

Decision rules, attention rules and direct discrimination from service agencies can interact in complex ways, so their relative effects are difficult to disentangle. One approach has been to model the distributional effects of decision rules, and then examine deviations from those rules in service allocations to neighbourhoods (Jones, 1981). In using this approach in a study of building code enforcement in Chicago, I found that 'machine' wards (those most supportive of the local Democratic party) were favoured, and that 'reform' wards were denied adequate enforcement services. Black wards that were supportive of the machine received a level of service close to the machine's 'best' white ethnic wards, but black wards that did not support the machine received far less service than would be expected on the basis of decision rules alone (Jones, 1984). Attention rules (support those who support the party) counter-acted decision rules, and allowed discriminatory practices within the service organization to prevail in the service delivery process. Where, however, minorities have been disadvantaged by the operation of supposedly-neutral bureaucratic decision rules, politics can force attention rules on the bureaucracy that compensate for the unintended discrimination of decision rules. Meier et al. (1991), in a study of 140 urban school districts, show how political forces cause changes in educational policy that benefits minorities. They write: 'Black school board members influence the selection of black administrators who in turn influence the hiring of black teachers. Black teachers then mitigate the impact of bureaucratic decision rules and provide black students with better access to educational opportunities' (Meier et al., 1991: 174). Politics can shift the operation of bureaucratic decision rules by instituting attention rule overrides, but the direction of the override cannot be predicted. Attention rule overrides can compensate or they can aggravate discriminatory patterns.

Manipulating the incentive structure through institutional design

It should be clear at this point that a simple model of democratic policy making based on electoral accountability and bureaucratic control is not viable empirically. Efforts at control by central political authorities tend to be sporadic and can be counter-productive in terms of the efficient delivery of public services. But a second approach to bureaucratic control is available: changing the incentive structure that public bureaucrats face through institutional design. I noted above that small governments whose operating resources must come from the local tax base are more likely to pursue investment policies than are large, encompassing governments or small governments whose operating revenues come from intergovern-mental grants. The underlying dynamic is *competition*; the more severe the

competitive pressures that governments feel, the more they are likely to try
to enact policies to bolster the tax base. This tendency towards *tax base
maximization* (Schneider, 1989) can skew the mix of public policies away
from those preferred by democratic majorities, either within the city
boundaries or within the broader unit of government within which the
municipality is situated. Hence collective goods – those that benefit all
citizens – will be undersupplied. Moreover, redistribution, which can be in
the collective interest by maintaining the social peace, cannot be
accomplished in small governments bent on tax base maximization. On the
other hand, governments insulated from the pressures of competition can
become quite inefficient in the delivery of services, in both senses of the
word *efficiency*. First, large governments do not do a very good job of
matching public preferences to policies in diverse societies, because there
will always be large minorities who are dissatisfied (Dahl, 1967). This is
efficiency in the *economic* sense. Second, large governments are more prone
to waste, partly because of the increased difficulty in monitoring the
behaviour of bureaucrats in large organizations, discussed above as the
principal-agent problem. This is efficiency in the *public administration*
sense. Neither large governments nor small ones can maximize both
efficiency and the provision of collective goods at once.

We need to note that the dynamic of tax base maximization is
dependent on the nature of the institutional design of governments, and on
the tax and revenue systems used to fund those governments. If revenue is
dissociated from the benefits of economic growth, then local governments
will not have the incentives to put in place policies that will attract
industry. In Great Britain, businesses pay what is basically a national tax,
thereby severing the link between the stimulation of economic growth
through the attraction of business and the benefits that the authority might
receive from business.

Directing attention to the different incentives that are generated from
different institutional designs for delivering services moves us from a
frustrating attempt to impose central control on large organizations to a
greater appreciation for the complex patchwork of governments connected
through intergovernmental grants and mandates, on the one hand, and the
open lobbying of governments at the higher tier by governments at the
lower tier, on the other. That is, in intergovernmental systems in their
entirety, the issue is never simply the size of governments. How they are
interlinked is also critical. Intergovernmental grants can relieve pressures
for tax base maximization; mandates from higher to lower tiers can make
sure national needs, such as anti-discrimination provisions, are set. On the
other hand, intergovernmental grants for mandated public services can fail
to relieve local fiscal pressures, and actually add to them by requiring
matching funds. Allowing open lobbying by lower levels of government
can mitigate the tendency of higher levels to enact policies and push the
costs off on lower levels through mandates (but raises the spectre of
interests-within-government again). This complexity is the prevailing

pattern in the US, and may be viewed as a complex system of governments dealing with complex problems of governance (Ostrom et al., 1988).

Western democracies seem to be in the middle of a trend towards greater local control and more sporadic state intervention. It is true in the United States, with a decline in the intergovernmental aid structure. It is true in Europe as well, with the exception of the UK, where a more centralized state is evolving (Parkinson, 1987; King and Pierre, 1990; Batley and Stoker, 1991). 'In Britain, there seems to be a lack of faith in local political control and democracy' (G. Stoker, 1991: 9). The central government has questioned the electoral legitimacy of local councils, regionalized many functions, legislated the detail of service provision, and required the contracting out of services. It is strange behaviour. Conservatives in the UK had a powerful tool to limit the collective consumption policies of its local governments – make the localities reliant on the local tax base, and then let the natural necessity of bolstering the tax base change the nature of local politics. Indeed, this was the theory behind the rate grant cuts in the early 1980s (Parkinson, 1987: 5). Instead, they enhanced the central state, almost certainly inefficient in its ability to direct local policy. It is a prime example of ignoring the 'natural inclinations' of the local public economy in a frenetic effort to direct the behaviour of local authorities.

We may conceive this slightly differently, in terms of costs of control in the process of implementation (R.P. Stoker, 1991). Central policy makers gain when the policies they want are implemented; they lose when local politicians and bureaucrats are able to undermine the implementation and act in accordance with the dictates of local forces. There are two kinds of control costs: compliance costs (getting the local bureaucrat to comply) and opportunity costs (associated with missed opportunities to implement the policy because the bureaucrat is constrained with the rules that bind compliance, and the rules can never pre-specify all alternatives). Now the correct way for a central authority to evaluate the situation is to compare the costs with the benefits from implementation, and find a way to minimize costs. Institutional designs that alter the incentives of local bureaucrats towards the policy aims of the central authorities can minimize both compliance costs and opportunity costs in the implementation process. Dowding (1991) distinguishes between what he terms *political power*, in which an actor influences outcomes, and *social power*, in which an actor changes the incentive structure facing others in order to achieve a desired result. By focusing only on political power, Conservatives in the UK would seem to have missed an opportunity to shift more forcefully the incentive structure facing local public managers.

A second manner in which the incentive structure facing public bureaucracies may be changed is through *privatization*. There are two dimensions to privatization. The first is the actual movement of services from the public to the private sector, best represented by the waves of denationalization of industries in the United Kingdom in the early 1980s and France in the late 1980s. In France, the theory that a strong national state was needed to forge modernization after the Second World War resulted in large-scale nationalization of industries in the 1944–6 period, and included electric power, major manufacturing industries, and insurance and banking. The result of *étatisme* was a modern economy and high economic growth, one of the unheralded economic success stories of modern times. By the late 1980s, however, the large, central state had come into disrepute, and the Chirac government in 1986 moved to denationalize. When the Socialists returned to power, they did not reverse this trend. *Étatisme*, once the salvation of a poor country, had become dysfunctional in a rich one.

The second dimension of privatization is *contracting out*. Here the public authorities will contract with private firms to perform services that public employees performed previously. While this is thought of by many students of public administration as a new approach, it definitely is not. America's urban infrastructure was modernized during the early part of the twentieth century by contracting: street and sewer construction, electrification, traction, and housing development was all accomplished through one form of privatization or another. The result was modern infrastructure and great profit to private firms and the politicians who let the contracts (through bribes, kickbacks, and 'honest graft' such as investment opportunities). Most contracts were let through a grant of monopoly power to the private entrepreneur. In many cases, this system was developed only after a failure of competitive enterprise to provide proper services; in the early years train tracks did not meet because different gauges were used, for example. But while government-granted monopolies allowed the imposition of uniform standards, many of the efficiency benefits of private competition were lost.

Whatever the history of government contracting, the idea has now become a driving force in western democracies, leading to what Milward et al. (1994) term 'the hollow state'. Contracting with the private sector, with other units of government, and with 'non-profits' has become so pervasive that, in many communities, even though 'services are funded by public agencies, the distribution of those funds is controlled and monitored by nongovernmental third parties who themselves determine which agencies to subcontract with for the actual provision of services' (Milward et al., 1994: 2). Contracting in the hollow state has vast implications for the control of bureaucracies. If governments place the normal set of bureaucratic limitations on the service providers, they will lose all the benefits of contracting in the first place – the presumed flexibility of private firms. Second, the 'interests in government' problem intensifies, since private corporations are not just regulated by government, they are sustained by it. In effect, the costs of control increase dramatically in systems of contracting out, further undermining the 'overhead democracy' model that is so popular in academic lore in the US, and in practice in the UK.

Adaptive systems and administrative complexity

Approaches to control of public bureaucracies, urban and otherwise, have been afflicted by 'one-dimensional thinking'. There has always been an underlying assumption that someone controls the bureaucracy, and the search is on for who it is that is doing the controlling. These answers have been diverse: the legislatures control the bureaucrats; the special interests control the bureaucrats; the capitalists control the bureaucrats; the bureaucrats control the bureaucrats. Something is clearly wrong here, and I will argue that what is wrong is our very conception of 'control'.

The search for control is misplaced because control is contingent, and is particularly contingent in time. During some eras, ideas that act to underpin an urban regime are so powerful that they hand control to different groups *without those groups even being aware that ideas hand them power*. Margolis (1993) has argued that, in the case of scientific discovery, the difficulty of the new idea is far less important than ingrained 'habits of mind' that serve as barriers to new ways of thinking. Urban regimes operate similarly; they become locked into a way of seeing the world and applying solutions to the problems they isolate. Lynn Bachelor and I term this connectivity between solutions and problems *solution-sets* (Jones and Bachelor, 1993). These solution-sets, we argue, are as important as the participants in an urban regime in defining that regime. Because governments create bureaucracies to enable the solutions they envision, bureaucracies are intimately linked to the solution-sets of a regime. But solution-sets change; and, by changing, shift the 'control' of bureaucrats. Indeed, they shift the very function of the state.

In a remarkable book, historian Joel Schwartz documents housing and urban renewal policies in New York City from the 1920s through the 1960s (Schwartz, 1992). He focuses a re-evaluation of the career of housing 'tsar' Robert Moses, who has become a 'villain' for his engineering of wide-scale destruction of old New York tenements and factories, ruthless relocation of tenants, and the replacement by what turned out to be dysfunctional high-rise public housing. Schwartz shows conclusively that Moses operated 'within the groove of municipal policy' (1992: 297); that is, while he was entrepreneurial and aggressive, he did not make policy on his own. Second, Schwartz devastates the notion that business people have their way when it comes to redevelopment. Moses tried valiantly to induce business people to invest in the city, and turned to public housing only when land 'write downs' and other inducements failed to interest the capitalists. Third, Schwartz notes that local elected officials, far from genuflecting to business interests, were very concerned about tenant relocation, even to the extent of thwarting several Rockefeller-inspired projects. Moreover, the city, as a matter of policy, simply destroyed its export (manufacturing) industries in an effort to replace the factories with upper-middle class housing.

Schwartz really does not relate his work to debates in political science and other circles about the nature of the city and control of public agencies such as the housing agencies that Moses headed. But the work turns topsy-turvy almost every conventional wisdom we have about city government. None of the standard models hold. What happened, according to Schwartz, is that the career of Moses rose and fell on the 'liberal vision' of the city; grandiose in scale, governmentally planned and directed, and envisioning a city inhabited by appreciative middle-class professionals making their peace with an idealized working class. Moses was 'the instrument of this legacy' (Schwartz, 1992: 297). This is too strong; ideas were important, but they were elaborated and modified by Moses and other public officials. Indeed, Schwartz argues that New York's urban redevelopment policies were piecemeal and opportunistic, unified only by 'horse trading' by politicians and 'conjured visions', 'dreamy metaphors', and 'self-fulfilling prophecies' (1992: 300).

As a city bureaucrat, Robert Moses had enormous power and great discretion. He was an able manipulator of politics, dealing with business, elected politicians, and state and federal officials with a complex mixture of 'sweetness and light'. But the real source of his power was his ability to exemplify the liberal dream of the city. When the dream failed, he failed. During the era, New York politics were primarily about renewal, transportation and housing. These problems were connected to 'solutions' that seemed to flow so directly out of the network of isolated problems – using public power to clear land for redevelopment by either private or public authorities. But these solutions yielded their own problems, and that was their downfall. In their heyday, however, they made it easier for the housing commissioner than, say, the education commissioner to obtain resources and exercise expertise and discretion.

There is an ebb and flow in the politics of ideas that is critically important to the issue of bureaucratic control. We cannot even discuss control without an appreciation of how these changes affect the incentives and opportunities that bureaucrats face and exploit daily. Control cannot be viewed as something static; it must be viewed in dynamic perspective. To explore this further, we look briefly at the state functions that bureaucrats are supposed to implement.

One pastime of urbanists has been to try to figure out the 'functions' of the state. Indeed, few have been willing to postulate singular state functions (although Peterson (1981) does so for cities, but not for broader units of government). Two ambitious attempts to define governmental (state) functions have come to similar conclusions. Shefter (1985) writes of the 'imperatives' of city governments in democracies – the needs to maintain order, win votes and maintain city finances (hence becoming dependent both on the local tax base and the municipal bond market). Gurr and King (1987), in a sophisticated analysis of the role of cities within the broader state, note the primary state interests of public order, legitimation, and economic growth. Not everyone agrees on the existence of fixed state functions; Stone and Sanders, for example, argue that the 'collective interest' is too amorphous to define so precisely, allowing different governing coalitions to form at different times and places (Stone and Sanders, 1987). On the other hand, there must be some limits to this contingency; a city with no tax base cannot govern.

At any rate, if, as a starting-point, we adopt the state functions of legitimacy, order and growth, we still have no guidelines concerning just what mix of these goals at what particular time the state will pursue. Stone and Sanders adopt a *spatial contingency* approach, detailing the differences in governing coalitions that can emerge in different cities. But the approach I suggest here is *temporally contingent*: the same state will face different problems at different times in its development. But these problems, although they have a firm basis in the 'facts', are also defined in the public debate about the proper role of government. Because these problems cannot be measured on the same 'metric', they cannot easily be compared. Hence cities, like other governments, have much to do, and must select for attention only some things at any one time. In so doing, they can be guided by changes in underlying conditions (deterioration in revenues stemming from the local tax base; voter dissatisfaction with corruption in public agencies; a crime 'wave'), but the conditions themselves are never enough to determine the actions of government (Baumgartner and Jones, 1993). As a consequence, a government's solution-set is a function both of objective conditions and the process of issue definition in public (or elite) debate.

Governments, however, have both present and past solution-sets. Bureaucracies, in effect, are the residues of the problems that governments have worked on in the past; they are the past solution-sets. To the extent that their 'missions' reflect aspects of the current solution-set, they have added claims for resources and, frequently, discretion in dealing with the problems they have been assigned. Perhaps police departments do well in budgetary negotiations and politics more generally in the US because of their special legitimacy. But it may also be the case that police do well because crime is such an integral part of American urban life. That is, they benefit from aspects of the current solution-set. As Schwartz's study of urban renewal in New York makes clear, only with such an agenda-based understanding of urban regimes can we place such figures as Robert Moses and his accomplishments in perspective.

Recall from the discussion above about 'principal-agent' problems that some observers have suggested that bureaucratic agencies respond to 'multiple principals'. Unfortunately, this approach fails to specify the nature of the contingencies – that is, to explain when and where some principals rather than others control. Bureaucratic control is both *cross-sectionally* and *temporally* contingent. It is cross-sectionally contingent because it is contingent on the structure of public institutions that affect a public agency. These include, in particular, the extent of competition facing an agency and the intergovernmental grant and mandate arrangement. As cross-sectional institutional variables, they may be changed explicitly, as would be the case in privatization, or in a major restructuring of the grant-in-aid programme. Temporal contingency exists because changes in control happen even within a specified set of institutional rules. Bureaucratic control is temporally contingent because the policies that governments pursue are embedded in a set of ideas about desirable courses of action, courses that are related to the core functions of governments. But just what core functions are emphasized at any one point in time is difficult to predict; today it may be economic growth, tomorrow legitimation. Indeed, it is a false dichotomy to view legitimation as opposed to growth; mayors have mobilized voters around the concept of 'jobs' (Jones and Bachelor, 1993). Because of the complex interactions between goals, means and institutions, particular controls over public agencies are highly time-contingent. Temporal contingency is more slippery than cross-sectional contingency, because so many more variables can act to change the parameters of control. A major source of temporal contingency, however, centres on agenda processes – how policy ideas affect the problem of control. In turn, agenda processes hinge on the *attentiveness* of the policy-making branches of government – what problems they are focusing on.

If the very concept of control is so contingent on a combination of the incentives generated by institutional arrangements and the agendas of governments, then how should we approach the nature of bureaucratic control? First, we must, I believe, jettison *both* the concept of overhead democracy (electoral control of politicians + hierarchical control of bureaucrats) *and* the notion that business controls city governments. Both democratic accountability and capitalism are forces in a complex administrative and political reality. Then we must realize that changes in institutional structure always affect the issue of control, but that the cause and effect in complex systems may be far removed and surprising (the story of New York redevelopment is a case in point). Forrester (1969) of MIT made this point a quarter of a century ago; it still is not sufficiently appreciated. Finally, we must open a place for the politics of ideas in the politics and administration of cities.

Doing this will force us to examine bureaucracies as *adaptive systems* in a manner analogous to the approach developed by biologists and computer scientists (see Jones (1994) for a discussion). In complex systems, effects can be separated in time and space from causes, and all causes have unintended effects. More hierarchical control can lead to poorer perform-ance in bureaucracies (Jones, 1985). Temporal contingency means that control techniques that once worked may not do so now. It also means that control will vary with the policy agendas that governments pursue. The overhead democracy model of democratic accountability leads to increasing specification of a task that may be obsolete tomorrow, denying bureaucratic agents the discretion to deal with change. The model of the helpless city embedded in a capitalist economy leads to inaction and cynicism about local democracy. But a complex systems perspective implies that things change, and change in part because of the currency of policy ideas. Affecting ideas through the public debate affects the course of government. This perspective also implies that, at some times, all the work in the world will not yield much in the way of results, while at other times a modest intervention may 'snowball' into important changes (Baumgartner and Jones, 1993).

'Who controls' in a hierarchical, overhead democracy model is, in the end, a misplaced question. The proper question is: how do bureaucracies, as active agents adjusting to a changing political and economic environment, adapt, and how can the incentive structure be modified to encourage bureaucrats to adapt to the proper objectives? Clearly this would involve an analytical model much closer to the pluralist than to the overhead democracy model. But it still resembles certain schools of thought in public management that stress performance monitoring and policy evaluation. The problem with this approach is that what is monitored is not always what is important in the broader sweep of changing political and economic conditions. There is nothing wrong with these monitoring approaches, if it is realized that they are quite incomplete. Both political demands and economic performance are in themselves important feedback processes, giving great information to policy makers about what will work and what will not; where there are windows of opportunity and where there exist few prospects for change.

References

Banfield, E. (1961) *Political Influence*. Glencoe, IL: Free Press.

Batley, R. and Stoker, G. (eds) (1991) *Local Government in Europe*. New York: St Martins.

Baumgartner, F.R. and Jones, B.D. (1993) *Agendas and Instability in American Politics*. Chicago, IL: University of Chicago Press.

Bernstein, M. (1955) *Regulating Business by Independent Commission*. Princeton, NJ: Princeton University Press.

Campbell, J. (1988) *The Collapse of an Industry: Nuclear Power and the Contradictions of US Policy*. Ithaca, NY: Cornell University Press.

Chubb, J.E. (1985) 'The political economy of federalism', *American Political Science Review*, 79: 994–1015.

Crecine, J.P. (1969) *Government Problem-Solving*. Chicago, IL: Rand McNally.

Cyert, R.A. and March, J.G. (1963) *A Behavioural Theory of the Firm*. Englewood Cliffs, NJ: Prentice-Hall.

Dahl, R. (1961) *Who Governs?* New Haven, CT: Yale University Press.

Dahl, R.A. (1967) 'The city in the future of democracy', *American Political Science Review*, 61: 953–70.

Dahl, R.A. and Lindblom, C.E. (1953) *Politics, Economics, and Welfare*. New York: Harper and Row.

Dowding, K.M. (1991) *Rational Choice and Political Power*. Aldershot: Edward Elgar.

Dunleavy, P. (1980) *Urban Political Analysis*. London: MacMillan.

Forrester, J. (1969) *Urban Dynamics*. Cambridge, MA: MIT Press.

Friedland, R. (1982) *Power and Crisis in the City*. London: Macmillan.

Griffith, E. (1939) *Congress: Its Contemporary Role*. New York: New York University Press.

94   *Theories of Urban Politics*

Gurr, T.R. and King, D.S. (1987) *The State and the City*. Chicago, IL: University of Chicago Press.

Hammond, T.H. (1986) 'Agenda control, organizational structure, and bureaucratic politics', *American Journal of Political Science*, 31: 379–420.

Jones, B.D. (1980) *Service Delivery in the City*. New York: Longman.

Jones, B.D. (1981) 'Party and bureaucracy: the role of intermediary groups in urban public service delivery', *American Political Science Review*, 75: 688–700.

Jones, B.D. (1984) 'Political decision-making and the distribution of public benefits: a political science perspective', in A. Kirby, P. Knox and S. Pinch (eds), *Public Service Provision and Urban Development*. London: Croom-Helm.

Jones, B.D. (1985) *Governing Buildings and Building Government*. Tuscaloosa, AL: University of Alabama Press.

Jones, B.D. (1986) 'Government and business: the automobile industry and the public sector in Michigan', *Political Geography Quarterly*, 5: 369–84.

Jones, B.D. (1994) *Receiving Decision-Making in Democratic Politics*. Chicago, IL: University of Chicago Press.

Jones, B.D. and Bachelor, L. (1993) *The Sustaining Hand* (2nd edn). Lawrence: University Press of Kansas.

Kaufman, H. (1956) 'Emerging conflicts in the doctrines of public administration', *American Political Science Review*, 50: 1057–73.

Keating, M. (1993) 'The politics of economic development', *Urban Affairs Quarterly*, 28: 373–96.

King, D. and Pierre, J. (1990) *Challenges to Local Government*. London: Sage.

Levy, F., Meltsner, A. and Wildavsky, A. (1974) *Urban Outcomes*. Berkeley: University of California Press.

Lindblom, C.E. (1977) *Politics and Markets*. New York: Basic Books.

Lipsky, M. (1980) *Street-Level Bureaucracy*. New York: Russell Sage.

Lowi, T. (1964) *At the Pleasure of the Mayor*. New York: Free Press.

Lowi, T. (1979) *The End of Liberalism* (2nd edn). New York: Norton.

Margolis, H. (1993) *Paradigms and Barriers*. Chicago: University of Chicago Press.

Meier, K., Stewart, J. and England, R. (1991) 'The politics of bureaucratic discretion: educational access as an urban service', *American Journal of Political Science*, 35: 155–77.

Mladenka, K. (1978) 'Rules, service equity, and distributional decisions', *Social Science Quarterly*, 59: 192–202.

Migue, J.-L. and Belanger, G. (1974) 'Towards a general theory of managerial discretion', *Public Choice*, 17: 24–43.

Milward, H.B., Provan, K.G. and Else, B. (1994) 'What does the hollow state look like?', in B. Bozeman (ed.), *Public Management Theory*. San Francisco, CA: Jossey Bass.

Niskanen, W.A. (1971) *Bureaucracy and Representative Government*. Chicago, IL: Aldine Atherton.

Niskanen, W.A. (1991) 'A reflection on "Bureaucracy and Representative Government"', in A. Blais and S. Dion (eds), *The Budget-Maximizing Bureaucrat*. Pittsburgh, PA: University of Pittsburgh Press.

Ostrom, V., Bish, R. and Ostrom, E. (1988) *Local Government in the United States*. San Francisco, CA: ICS Press.

Pahl, R. (1975) *Whose City?* Harmondsworth: Penguin.

Parkinson, M. (1987) *Reshaping Local Government*. Rutgers, NJ: Transaction Books.

Peterson, P. (1981) *City Limits*. Chicago, IL: University of Chicago Press.

Redford, E. (1969) *Democracy in the Administrative State*. New York: Oxford University Press.

Saunders, P. (1979) *Urban Politics*. London: Hutchinson.

Saunders, P. (1981) *Social Theory and the Urban Question*. New York: Holmes and Meier.

Sayre, W. and Kaufman, H. (1960) *Governing New York City*. New York: Russell Sage.

Schneider, M. (1989) *The Competitive City*. Pittsburgh, PA: University of Pittsburgh Press.

Scholtz, J., Twombley, J. and Headrick, B. (1991) 'Street-level political controls over federal bureaucracy', *American Political Science Review*, 85: 829–50.

Schwartz, J. (1992) *The New York Approach: Robert Moses, Urban Liberals, and the Redevelopment of the Inner City*. Columbus: Ohio State University Press.

Shefter, M. (1985) *Political Crisis/Fiscal Crisis*. New York: Basic Books.

Stoker, G. (1991) Introduction, in R. Batley and G. Stoker (eds), *Local Government in Europe*. New York: St Martins.

Stoker, R.P. (1991) *Reluctant Partners*. Pittsburgh, PA: University of Pittsburgh Press.

Stone, C. (1976) *Economic Growth and Neighborhood Discontent*. Chapel Hill: University of North Carolina Press.

Stone, C. and Sanders, H. (eds) (1987) *The Politics of Urban Development*. Lawrence: University Press of Kansas.

Vogel, D. (1989) *Fluctuating Fortunes: The Political Power of Business in America*. New York: Basic Books.

Wood, B.D. (1991) 'Federalism and policy responsiveness: the clean air case', *Journal of Politics*, 53: 851–9.

Wood, B.D. and Waterman, R.W. (1993) 'The dynamics of political-bureaucratic adaptation', *American Journal of Political Science*, 37: 497–28.

Wright, D. (1978) *Understanding Intergovernmental Relations*. North Scituate, MA: Duxbury Press.

6

Political Leadership in Urban Politics

Clarence N. Stone

There is no well developed theory of political leadership, perhaps not even a universally accepted definition.[1] Consequently the treatment of leadership in the urban literature is largely ad hoc, and much of the discussion is embedded in various biographies. Most of the relevant writing concerns the occupants of the office of mayor, but they by no means monopolize the field of urban leadership even in the United States.

Why examine urban leadership as a topic? Why not focus on office holding and study the formal powers attached to elected positions? The answer is that governance is broader than office holding. The actions of office holders *qua* office holders are at most only an anaemic version of leadership; these actions give an inadequate account of interactions with followers.

Office holding bestows authority, but the authority conferred is highly limited (Barnard, 1968). Particularly at the local level, governmental authority commands only modest resources. Energetic governance requires more than office holding alone can provide. The weakness of formal authority thus gives added importance to the personal leadership of prominent urban actors, especially in the loosely structured context of local politics in America. Elusive as the personal may be as a research target, its importance nevertheless makes leadership a fitting topic of study, more so than the formal structure of government.

This chapter begins with the task of defining leadership and identifying the leadership challenge in the urban arena. Then it moves on to a consideration of existing studies of urban political leadership. Next the chapter turns to the issue of how to assess leadership performance. The chapter concludes with an appraisal of the part that personal factors play in the behaviour of mayors and other urban leaders.

Defining leadership

Aimless interaction requires no leadership. Leadership revolves around purpose, and purpose is at the heart of the leader-follower relationship. Indeed, in some cases a compelling statement of mission not only gives direction to a group, but is its formative experience, shaping the identity of group members by highlighting a shared aim.

Purposefulness does not mean that leaders and followers hold identical goals. While leader-follower interaction centres on purpose, that interaction is quite complex. James MacGregor Burns thus defines leadership as 'the reciprocal process of mobilizing . . . various economic, political, and other resources . . . in order to realize goals independently and mutually held by both leaders and followers' (1978: 425; see also 18–19). In this definition, the leader's goals need not be the same as those of followers, and followers themselves may have diverse ends. The effort to realize aims is, however, one that involves an interaction between leader and followers.

For Burns, the leader-follower relationship is central, and it is not one-way. Leaders as well as followers engage in an ongoing process of defining and reshaping goals, in part, on the basis of their interaction with one another. What, then, distinguishes leaders from their followers? According to Burns:

> Leaders and followers may be inseparable in function, but they are not the same. The leader takes the initiative in making the leader-led connection; it is the leader who creates the links that allow communication and exchange to take place. . . . The leader is more skillful in evaluating followers' motives, anticipating their responses to an initiative, and estimating their power bases, than the reverse. . . . Finally, . . . leaders address themselves to followers' wants, needs, and other motivations, as well as to their own, and thus serve as an *independent force in changing the makeup of their followers' motive base through gratifying their motives.* (1978: 20, original emphasis)

Burns talks about gratifying the motives of followers because he distinguishes between leadership and 'naked power-wielding' (1978: 19). Leaders may engage in persuasion, offer inducements, rely on emotional appeals, and even mix coercion with other incentives; but, Burns argues, leaders, in their role as leaders, never lose sight of the fact that their *followers are persons who are to be motivated*, persons whose wants and needs are to be taken into account.

Although Burns distinguishes between leadership and 'naked power wielding', he sees leadership as a form of power. It is a way of making something happen that would otherwise not take place. Hence Burns offers 'contribution to change' as a test of leadership (1978: 427).[2] Thus, from Burns, we have a conception of leadership with three essential elements: leadership is purposeful activity, it operates interactively with a body of followers, and it is a form of power or causation. Put succinctly, leadership is 'collectively purposeful causation' (Burns, 1978: 434).

The leadership challenge

When difficulties arise, a call for leadership is inevitably sounded. The called-for leader is seen as someone with vision, someone with a plan of action, and perhaps someone with the ability to summon people to extraordinary effort. Leadership goes to the heart of politics, that is, to the capacity of a people to act together on their shared concerns. They act in order to change what would otherwise be the course of events.

Arendt has explored the matter in depth. Politics, she argues, is about what people can do together. It is a creative process, one in which we 'call something into being which did not exist before' (Arendt, 1961: 151). As Arendt sees it, life is enmeshed in various ongoing processes, and politics – acting together out of shared concerns – makes it possible to break out of these processes. Such actions constitute what she terms political freedom; they are 'interruptions of some natural series of events, of some automatic process' (1961: 168). The 'automatic process' could be a matter of convention or established routine or even a large historical trend already in motion.

Sometimes processes take on a crisis-generating character. When people face increasing difficulties and call for leadership, they are seeking a means to 'interrupt' the movement towards greater crisis. They want a way out of what otherwise promises to be a certain path to disaster.[3] Political leadership is, of course, not restricted to crisis conditions, but a crisis highlights what in other respects might not be so plain, that leadership is a means for acting outside routine processes (Selznick, 1957). Moreover, leadership alters events, not as an individual act of heroism, but through interaction with followers. In that context, Burns, as we saw, offers 'contribution to change' as a measure of leadership, but change is not a concept without ambiguity. I would suggest that we follow Arendt and think of change in relation to an established course of events. Because a course of events can be threatening, someone who takes the initiative in order to halt a trend or head off an impending threat is no less a leader than someone whose ultimate goal is innovation. A person does not cease to lead because the goal is one of conserving.

If the test of leadership is one of having an impact on the flow of events, then leadership is not a mere matter of holding office or even exercising authority. Similarly, speaking for a group does not in itself constitute leadership. The word 'posture' is often used to describe the actions of individuals who speak, sometimes flamboyantly, but bring about no change. It is helpful, then, to think about leadership in reference to a base point, perhaps a path of least resistance. The leadership challenge is to produce departures from this base point, to produce in Arendt's words 'interruptions of some natural series of events, of some automatic process.'

Urban political leadership in action

Let us turn now to urban political leadership in action, looking first at the American experience. Because the American system of government is much more decentralized than the British system, problem-solving

COURSE READER MATERIAL ©
Copyright Permission ■ Free Pick-up & Delivery

THINGS TO DO

✓	ITEM	PRIORITY
	"Tipico ~'73 TL 11252	
	Love Enny ~ Alegpes of Ramatn TL 2666	
	Org. Aragon "The Heart of Heaven" v.e." TL 11628	
	Org. Ritmo Oriental "Trenced Habana" TL 11209	
	438 Bunche Hace	
	Ismael	

WESTWOOD VILLAGE

Tel. 310.443.3303
Fax 310.443.3305

1743 Westwood Blvd
Los Angeles CA 90024

responsibilities are more localized than is the case in the United Kingdom. Within the United States and its candidate-centred politics, the office of mayor makes a particularly visible leadership platform (Svara, 1990; Schneider and Teske, 1995).

Let us begin by considering two mayors prominent in the first half of the twentieth century, James Curley of Boston and Fiorello La Guardia of New York. Both put themselves forward as champions of have-nots and had followerships composed substantially of ethnic minorities. La Guardia, however, is regarded as a highly effective mayor (Kessner, 1989; Bayor, 1993), while Curley is dismissed as a demagogue (Beatty, 1992: Connolly, 1993).

Boston's James M. Curley

By all accounts Curley was an exceptionally skilled politician, an accomplished speaker, and a figure with extraordinary personal charm. He was quick to offer assistance and make gestures of concern, especially to Boston's immigrant poor. In office he raised the wages of ordinary city workers while cutting salaries of higher-level employees. He expanded hospital facilities, built new schools, increased services and spent freely on public improvements. He relished being called 'Mayor of the Poor' (Beatty, 1992: 297).

Throughout his career, whether as mayor or as a member of Congress, Curley championed the cause of immigrants and those disparaged for minority status. During the Second World War, a period in which he was a member of the US House of Representatives, there was an upsurge of anti-Jewish sentiment among the Boston Irish. While reform Mayor Tobin and Massachusetts Governor Saltonstall remained silent, Curley took the occasion to make an eloquent defence of American Jews and their contributions to the country, including service in the military (Beatty, 1992: 455).

On what grounds, then, is Curley dismissed as a demagogue? There are two. In rallying the Irish and other have-nots to his many candidacies, Curley never put into effect a systematic policy of expanded opportunity for the poor. Mostly he offered help on an individual basis and favoured the kind of public works projects that would perpetuate a system of patronage. However, lower-level public service jobs were not an especially effective channel of upward mobility, though they did provide Curley and other patronage politicians with a secure vote base (Erie, 1988).

Even public works were handled in a self-serving manner. Thus, when the New Deal was in place, Curley was primarily concerned about how to get 'his "cut" from the federal largesse, and his constant feuding with New Deal officials . . . slowed the relief effort in Boston' (Beatty, 1992: 335, see also 381–2). Under Curley and others, Boston spent lavishly, but not well. Corruption was widespread, inefficiencies common place, and tax favouritism rampant. Curley achieved the worst combination – a poor climate for business investment and ineffectiveness in redistributing opportunities to the poor. He took a spoils system as given and exploited it ruthlessly for personal gain.

How was Curley able to hold his base of support with so little change in material condition for his followers? Was it patronage alone that sustained him? Curley's biographer answers no. In the first place, Curley's exploitation of the spoils system, especially for personal gain, weakened him as a political figure on a number of important occasions. But more to the point about leader-follower relations, Curley was an adroit practitioner of the 'politics of ethnic and religious resentment' (Beatty, 1992: 395). He was able to do this because, dating back to the Know-Nothing period of the nineteenth century, Massachusetts was the scene of intense bigotry on the part of Yankee Protestants towards the Irish and other recent immigrants. Skilful in the exploitation of immigrant indignation, Curley's hold on voters, his biographer argues, had 'more to do with the communal resentments he articulated' than with the favours he dispensed (Beatty, 1992: 501). When Curley attacked and was attacked by the forces of 'good government', led by bankers and other business figures and by such Yankee respectables as Lodge and Saltonstall, he could play the martyr and distract attention from his personal shortcomings as a political leader. The resentments he expressed had a strong basis in reality:

> Economic frustration and class hatred, wounded pride and ethnic resentment, thwarted hope and strangled aspiration – these were the mute causes that found their tribune in James Michael Curley. Boston was in decline, the Boston Irish were caught in a spiral of downward mobility, throughout the first half of the twentieth century. (Beatty, 1992: 67)

Beatty adds: 'Curley rose as Boston fell' (1992: 67).

How was this possible? Curley's biographer draws a parallel with Peron in Argentina and quotes a Peronist as saying: '"Before Peron I was poor and I was nobody; now I am only poor"' (Beatty, 1992: 501). It is gratifying to a followership when they have someone in a position of authority give voice to their resentments and taunt those they see as their oppressors. It delivers the followers from being nobody. Curley expressed such resentments, but did not restrict himself to negative appeals. One of his tactics was ethnic pride, 'to insist that there was an Irishman at the bottom of everything' (Beatty, 1992: 168).

While an appeal to ethnic pride and solidarity is not in itself a matter for reproof, Curley comes under criticism for the manner in which he played the 'politics of division', pandering to a 'conspiratorial worldview' and reinforcing in his followers 'the habit of suspicion' (Beatty, 1992: 454). 'In using "wedge issues" to split people apart', Curley, it is charged, encouraged the habit of scapegoating (Beatty, 1992: 343). That Curley himself encouraged neither the anti-Semitism of the 1940s nor the anti-Black sentiments of more recent years is not the point. He fortified a pattern of inter-group resentment and can claim no exemption when the Boston Irish chose targets different from his.

Despite Curley's considerable ability as a political leader, he made little of his talents. He furthered his own career, but left his followers in much the same situation they were in when he entered politics. While he himself travelled widely and became a national figure, Curley reinforced rather than changed the provincialism of his core constituency – the poor and working class Irish of Boston. Over the many years that he interacted with his followers, there is little evidence that a larger social purpose was advanced in the process. Instead, the energies of his followers were dissipated in inter-group resentments. By playing on these resentments, Curley was able to distract the attention of his followers from the extent to which he was furthering his personal aims instead of meeting the leadership challenge. His innovation was in using the mass media to mould a personal following, not in altering the conditions of his followers (Connolly, 1993).

New York's Fiorello La Guardia

La Guardia's career followed a different path. Whereas Curley left a patronage system intact and used it for personal gain, La Guardia not only maintained a record of unassailable personal honesty, he overturned New York's spoils system.

Like Curley, La Guardia related to that followership in a different way and included in his camp of supporters a significant body of good government reformers. La Guardia expanded New York's merit system, thereby weakening Tammany's base of power and at the same time opening city positions to those who were younger, better educated and non-Irish. Thus La Guardia benefited new immigrants eager to use education as a means of upward mobility.

The merit system combined with La Guardia's practice of hiring excellence for top posts and pursuing progressive aims enabled him to bring together followers who were not exactly natural allies, such as the new immigrants and labour along with good government reformers. La Guardia certainly practised the politics of giving recognition to various groups, but did so in a way that not only 'articulated their concerns and shielded them from a sense of isolation', but did so by invoking larger purposes and positioning himself 'as a defender of humanity' (Kessner, 1989: 400, 403). As a response to frictions between Italian and Jewish workers, La Guardia emphasized 'their shared interest in better conditions, breaking down ethnic antagonisms' (Kessner, 1989: 29).

In pursuing an activist government, La Guardia lessened the city's financial squeeze by turning to the federal government, working with officials in other cities to encourage new forms of assistance. Whereas Curley's opportunism made federal administrators unwilling to deal with him except in the most guarded terms, La Guardia instilled confidence and enabled New York to receive a generous flow of federal monies (Kessner, 1989: 294–5). New schools, parks, infrastructure, low-income housing, relief money, a modern airport, the preservation of free tuition at the city university, and even public art and sculpture became part of an exciting agenda for action. More was involved than just bringing in federal grants. As a biographer observed: 'for the first time in a very long while, individuals of goodwill felt that by their efforts, the commonwealth, their city, could be changed for the better, that the good fight had a powerful, decisive leader' (Kessner, 1989: 290).

La Guardia's leadership was thus more than assembling a coalition of followers. His leadership energized followers by linking them to purpose and possibility: 'His assault on corruption and favouritism raised civic morale and won back for New Yorkers not only the respect of the nation but their own self-respect. By recapturing the charmed capacity of politics to instruct, care, and transform, he attracted to it some of the best-intentioned individuals of his time' (Kessner, 1989: 290). In the words of one member of his administration, 'his was the most exciting show in town' (quoted in Kessner, 1989: 290).

As La Guardia put together his team of talented and highly motivated staff members, he raised expectations and expanded possibilities. He pioneered in appointing women to major city posts, and in putting African Americans into significant and visible posts. In a variety of ways he opened up participation in the governance of the city and did it in a way 'that made good government exciting and immediate' (Kessner, 1989: 342).

La Guardia's achievements need to be kept in perspective. There is much that he did not accomplish. Genuine reform of the police and law-enforcement eluded him. His efforts in expanding affordable housing were tempered significantly by what he saw as 'politically possible' (Kessner, 1989: 335). Perhaps the clearest example of his acceptance of constraints is his response to the Harlem riot of 1935, during his third year as mayor. Although he was someone on good terms with the major black organizations and an outspoken champion of racial equality and tolerance, La Guardia was nevertheless surprised by the outbreak of disorder and the alienation that it signalled. He responded in constructive ways, appointing a Commission on Conditions in Harlem and initiating new projects in the community, but he was unwilling to give a full public airing to the many deep-seated grievances that the commission gave voice to. 'His commitment to correcting the plight of blacks was circumscribed', his biographer argues, because the problems were so large and so intractable – 'other problems seemed more promising of solution' (Kessner, 1989: 371, 374).

Even though there were substantial gaps in La Guardia's action agenda, his ability to combine good government reform with a progressive programme was a considerable accomplishment. He changed what he inherited to fashion a new system of governance. When La Guardia came into office, New York had not yet become a modern city. It was a set of 'antiquated boroughs, dingily administered and divided into political and bureaucratic fiefdoms' (Kessner, 1989: xii). The city was riddled with corruption and saddled with fiscal crisis. La Guardia led the move to a new way of governing, fashioning a new structure by reorganizing the formal structure and insisting on scrupulous adherence to reform principles and then imbuing the process with a new spirit as well.

Tammany had been little concerned with tangible achievements and was content to rely on the system that Curley relied on in Boston – 'an essentially unskilled, labor-intensive system of municipal service made up of political hacks who did loyal party work in return for their patronage appointments' (Kessner, 1989: 210). The consequence was to destroy 'the delicate fabric of civic virtue that underlies all good government' (Kessner, 1989: 237). Restoring civic virtue was, then, a major feat, all the more impressive because, in order to do it, La Guardia had to replace an entrenched system of patronage. So while not successful on every count, La Guardia met the challenge of leadership by instituting reformed and progressive governance and initiating a wide range of new programmes. In doing so, he energized followers and made them integral parts of the process of change.

Richard Daley and Harold Washington in Chicago

Richard J. Daley was Chicago's chief executive from 1955 until his death during his sixth term in 1976.[4] During that time, he was a force at the state and national levels as well as in city affairs. Daley's style of leadership was mainly to work behind the scenes, presenting himself more as broker than entrepreneur (Banfield, 1961). At the same time, he attended to the details of managing the city and promoted the slogan that, under his leadership, Chicago was 'the city that works'.

In creating a system of personal control, Daley neither overturned the city's patronage system nor created powerful new agencies outside its operation. Instead, by assuming the dual positions of Mayor of Chicago and Chair of the Cook County Democratic party, Daley consolidated control of the patronage system under his personal direction. Through an expansive programme of infrastructure improvements and downtown redevelopment, Daley successfully courted business support. Since an active programme of construction served well the patronage requirements of the Democratic machine, Daley had no need to restructure the city's dominant political organization. His leadership consisted largely of knitting together and working with established centres of power.

In recent years, Daley's leadership record has come under criticism for its unresponsiveness to the changing demography of the city. Even though African Americans provided essential support in his initial capture of the mayoralty, Daley, in office, pursued policies that pandered to his white constituents and restricted opportunities for an expanding black population. Because the city was engaged in an immense programme of redevelopment concentrated in the inner city, African Americans were displaced in large numbers at the same time that they were a growing part of the population, even as they were constricted residentially by white neighbourhood resistance. Under these circumstances racial hostilities were sure to increase and Daley had no policy for combating this trend. Though Daley was responsive to the anxieties of his white followership, he did nothing to promote inter-racial understanding or to expand opportunities for a growing minority population.

Daley's mode of operation was highly paternalistic (Greenstone and Peterson, 1973). Indeed when redevelopment was at work, the Daley machine was as autocratic in dealing with white as with black neigh-bourhoods (Royko, 1971: 126–9). As part of its strategy of holding popular discontent in check, the Daley organization cultivated an image of invincibility. Hence, crushing a white neighbourhood was as consistent with Daley's strategy as was the manipulation of representation within the black community (Grimshaw, 1992).

Given the tight control that Daley exercised during his 21 years as mayor, one would expect his organization to display considerable staying power. But this was not the case; after his death the machine incurred a succession of defeats. Harold Washington's election as mayor was a particularly dramatic demonstration of the machine's weak hold in Chicago's African American community. Daley had handled his follower-ship in such a way as to intensify racial polarization and alienate the city's growing black population.

Whereas Daley had tight control of the party and city hall over more than two decades, Harold Washington had firm control of neither and was mayor for less than five years.[5] Much of this short time was spent battling the white majority on the city council. Yet, Washington still had a lasting impact on the city's politics. He put together the original 'rainbow coalition'. Hispanics, liberal whites, middle-class and poor African Americans, the city's small Asian American population, and the city's gay and lesbian community were among those who formed part of what Washington's biographer calls 'an improbably broad coalition', the coalition that put him into the mayoralty (Rivlin, 1992: 290). Washington even achieved a limited rapprochement with some of the city's white ethnics (Rivlin, 1992: 376–7).

The core of Washington's support was in the black community, and it was only through their extraordinary turnout that he was elected mayor. Without being inattentive to this core constituency, Washington put together a diverse administration, including a record number of women in management positions. He also adhered to reform practice by signing the Shakman decree and forgoing patronage as a means for building a council majority.[6] Ward politics did not close down during Washington's tenure, but he did bring community groups in as an important liaison to the city's neighbourhoods and worked with white ethnic groups on policies of mutual concern such as the home equity proposal (Squires et al., 1987: 90; Rivlin, 1992: 248). The new relationship with neighbourhood groups was typified in the decision to give citizens open access to public records (Squires et al., 1987: 127). Mayor Washington also facilitated Chicago's venture into school reform and decentralization (Gittell, 1995).

Harold Washington offered a different style of mayoralty from Richard J. Daley. Though in office for only a short time and plagued with an enormously high level of resistance to change, Harold Washington pushed his city well along the road to reform, enlarged the role of community groups in the governance of the city, and substantially broadened the city's governing coalition. Considering the short time that he was in office, Washington may have had a more lasting impact than Daley did. For example, the election of Richard J. Daley's son, Richard M., to the mayoralty in 1991 did not end the broader involvement of community groups and others in the governance of the city.

While Richard J. Daley was individually powerful in the sense of exercising considerable personal control, he fell short in meeting the leadership challenge. He took a path of minimal resistance in order to consolidate his personal position, but, in doing so, left significant trends unattended. By contrast, Harold Washington had little personal control, especially over the Chicago city council, but he widened participation in city governance and thereby helped set policy change in motion. However, despite his openness and his success at coalition-building, Washington created no permanent organization to institutionalize the progressive presence in Chicago.

Leadership performance

The above sketches offer some indication of leadership impact and how it differs from individual to individual. This is not to suggest that leaders operate in a vacuum or to deny that leadership is situational.[7] Because leadership is interactive, situation is important. But because leadership is also creative, the personal factor is important as well. Leadership study is about human agency and its role in social causation. How, then, do we think about leadership impact? The suggestion earlier was to make use of the notion of change or movement from a base point. While no quantitative measure is available, we can imagine various ways one might be crudely approximated. The total number of policy initiatives enacted might be one alternative, but, because such a measure reveals nothing about resistance overcome, it is unsatisfactory. Hence we might employ diving competition as an analogy. In such competitions, each dive has a rating of degree of difficulty so that the score for any one dive is determined by multiplying the performance on that dive by the degree of difficulty. In this way, the disincentive to attempt a difficult dive is taken away.

Although leadership study lacks a comparable rating system, the notion of degree of difficulty can be employed. Consider Hugh Douglas Price's reassessment of Richard Lee's leadership in New Haven. Vastly celebrated by Robert Dahl (1961), Mayor Lee's leadership reputation rested mainly on New Haven's large urban renewal programme. Price's response is to suggest that 'spending federal funds on a programme desired by the economic notables' is not a very 'compelling test of ability' (1962: 1594). Significantly, Mayor Daley's policy leadership parallels Mayor Lee's.

In this view, Lee's leadership is not redistributive and thus warrants a modest score because the degree of difficulty is too small. Lee sought no significant concession from the area's business class, from those best able to give but well-situated to resist. In short, Lee went for the easy 'victory'. By contrast, La Guardia took on a number of business interests in New York to negotiate lower interests on long-term borrowing by the city, to keep various prices down for Depression-hit city residents, and to impose higher taxes (Kessner, 1989: 270, 343, 390). The redistributive nature of La Guardia's actions provided a more demanding test than Lee attempted.

Promoting change is always difficult because it involves overcoming resistance. Redistribution serves as a gross indicator of the amount of reallocation and therefore of the resistance overcome. Denoting reallocation from haves to have-nots, redistribution is accorded a high degree of difficulty because it is likely to activate the opposition of those especially well positioned to defend the status quo. While promoters of redevelopment, like Lee and Daley, engaged in a form of reallocation in land use, it was from have-nots to haves. Hence, although they were promoting change that involved overcoming resistance, the resistance was relatively minor. Have-nots are poorly positioned to resist changes, especially the kinds that are too piecemeal to affect the whole class of have-nots.

What other criteria might be applied in addition to the nature of policy changes sought? Two seem especially appropriate. One involves the nature of the interaction with followers – the scope of who is involved, the degree to which followers are actively engaged, and the extent to which they are moved by the leader to see themselves in a different and less narrow way. Another test of leadership performance is the extent of institutional change achieved. Note that in all three cases, leadership is being measured by *departure* from an established course, and the change is purposeful whether in policy, follower impact or institution building.

In interacting with followers, leaders can either seek passive acquiescence or they can attempt to transform followers in some way by engaging them actively in governance or by having followers view themselves and their relations in a new light. The path of least resistance is obviously one of passivity, seeking followers who are compliant and leaving them settled in their long-standing view of the world. As we have seen, Daley pursued the path of minimum resistance, taking part mainly in peak-level bargaining. He insulated decisions from popular discontent rather than undertake the more difficult task of developing a programme of citizen involvement. Consequently he found himself poorly attuned to alienation at the grass roots, particularly in Chicago's growing black community. Despite having strong black support initially, Daley concentrated on cultivating the machine's traditional base of white ethnic support.

Curley was more accessible than Daley, but also lacked a programme of citizen involvement. His mastery of the mass media was used to reinforce the parochialism and resentments of his largely poor and immigrant followers, making few efforts to enlarge their conception of the purposes they were linked to (Connolly, 1993). In contrast, La Guardia and Washington undertook the more challenging task of creating a broad coalition around big causes. Bringing together a broad coalition is a more difficult feat because it requires that followers expand their understanding of who they are. La Guardia and Washington did this in part through opening up the process of governance, not just in a 'rainbow' assortment of top appointments, but also in making government more accessible – La Guardia through replacing favouritism with a merit system and Washington by giving community groups an active part in city governance.

Institution building, the third test, is another formidable challenge, and it is also an area of activity in which the mayors discussed above all had an impact, but a limited one. None of the mayoral figures considered here spent much political energy in linking their followers to a set of purposes by means of institutionalized arrangements. For example, while La Guardia left a lasting legacy in the form of New York's expanded merit system, he built no permanent Fusion party to continue the battle against favouritism and corruption. Daley centralized the direction of the Chicago machine by occupying both the office of mayor and the position of chair of the Cook County Democratic organization. Thus the centralization was personal, and came unravelled after his death. Harold Washington gave community groups greater access to the governance of Chicago, but failed to institutionalize his 'rainbow' coalition. Consequently, with his death the progressive hold on city hall slipped away.

Curley fares worst in making an institutional impact. He inherited a patronage system and left it unchanged, except for bringing additional discredit to it. The 'Mayor of the Poor' provided wide assistance to individuals, but established no plan to alter the long-term prospects for Boston's have-nots. La Guardia and Washington, on the other hand, took on established systems of patronage and replaced them with more open forms of employment and diminished the place of favouritism. Daley engineered a regime change, centralizing control of patronage, perhaps thereby prolonging the life of the Chicago machine. But Daley's efforts rested on his personal control of the offices of mayor and party chair, and his regime did not survive long after his death.

Table 6.1 summarizes the leadership performance of our four mayors. Though all of them exercised significant personal power, Curley falls shortest on the leadership test, while Daley, despite his personal

Table 6.1

Mayor	Scope of Policy Impact	Impact on Followers	Institution Building
Curley	Minimal	Little	None
La Guardia	Somewhat redistributive	Significant	Extensive within government but not among citizens
Daley	Reallocative but not redistributive	Little	Some within government but not among citizens
Washington	Somewhat redistributive	Significant	Extensive within government including wider access to community groups

power, had modest success. La Guardia and Washington rank highest, but still had incomplete success.

The personal dimension

The four mayors discussed above were all individuals of extraordinary personal ability. Each was a highly visible figure, deemed to be powerful in important ways. Yet, all of them, even the dynamic and creative Fiorello La Guardia, operated within very substantial constraints. Many events were beyond their control, their capacity to alter established processes was limited, and each had to contend with other leaders seeking to mobilize support for competing purposes. What, then, does the personal factor of leadership add to our understanding?

By talking about a base point, we have a way of imagining the difference a leader can make. If we take existing conditions (including established trends) at the base point, we can assess the impact of a given individual in bringing about change. Suppose that the office of mayor at a given time in a given city had been occupied by a hypothetical person of ordinary ability, minimal political skill and little vision. What would have been different? In Curley's Boston, not much. In La Guardia's New York, quite a lot but in some areas more than others.

Even though Curley and La Guardia represent opposing extremes in leadership impact, we need to remember that even La Guardia faced constraints. The capacity of talented leaders to alter circumstances should not be exaggerated. Jones and Bachelor (1993: 212) offer the term 'creative bounded choice' to emphasize that leaders have room to manoeuvre but within limits imposed by the larger environment. Thus it is not surprising than even La Guardia was selective in the challenges that he undertook.

While it is in order to acknowledge that leaders are constrained by social, political, and economic structures in which they and their followers are embedded, the career of James Curley cautions us not to confine our attention to external constraints. The personal is both a strength and a weakness. Curley, for example, was an individual of extraordinary ability, but his lust for personal wealth undercut his leadership.

The desire for material gain is only one of the personal weaknesses that hampers leadership. The urge to seek revenge, hunger for personal glory, a need to be in control, and ambition for higher office also enter the picture, not just for Curley but to varying degrees for most of the mayors considered here. La Guardia's biographer recounts how the New York mayor became increasingly preoccupied with his quest for higher office. La Guardia's unwillingness to tackle intractable problems rested in part on his desire to score quick successes and move onto a larger arena. As mayor, he eventually settled into a caretaker role while pursuing various extra-city aims (Kessner, 1989: 451).

Because leadership is personal, its impact is often transitory. Particularly in the context of America's candidate-centred politics, elected office holders concentrate on personal organization and cultivate personal loyalty. Consequently, the best examples of institutionalizing the connection between followers and causes can be found outside the electoral arena, in community organizations such as the Back of the Yards in Chicago (Slayton, 1986; Horwitt, 1989) and COPS in San Antonio (Sekul, 1983).

The office of mayor is a visible office with access to significant resources, but the personal aims of its occupants often are not conducive to institution building. The personal is a two-edged sword. It can imbue the authority of office with vitality and stimulate follower involvement and growth. But the personal is just that, and the weaknesses and ambitions of individuals impinge on interactions with followers and on the choices of leaders about where and how to direct their energies.

The office of mayor is itself a two-edged sword. Typically the most powerful and visible office in American local government, the mayoralty offers substantial leadership opportunities.[8] At the same time, some of the most capable occupants of the office, La Guardia being a conspicuous example, inevitably aspire to office at a higher level of government.[9] Hence, mayoral goals, leader-follower interactions, and city-level efforts at institution building are all limited by the ambitions of local executives to move into a larger political arena. The professional politician, looking to move up the career ladder, may leave much of the leadership potential of the mayoralty undeveloped.

Career administrators like Robert Moses (Caro, 1974) and Austin Tobin (Doig, 1987) may find leadership vacuums that they can fill through their longevity and accumulated political and technical skill. They, however, have even less incentive than a mayor like Richard J. Daley to pursue redistributive aims, to develop a mass following with an expansive understanding of the role of citizen, or to institutionalize community involvement in governance. Avoiding high-degree-of-difficulty leadership challenges, administrators tend to cultivate supporting constituencies composed of a select few who are institutionally well-connected. So their leadership is limited in scope.

Professional politicians, even those operating at the ward level, also lack a strong incentive to promote an expansive understanding of the citizen role among their followers. A community activist in Baltimore gives this assessment: 'Politicians . . . don't do anything to teach people how to be citizens. They teach them how to be consumers. You want something, you go to the organization . . . . But you're not a citizen. You don't know how to do it yourself' (quoted in Crenson, 1983: 258).

Operating outside the electoral arena, community organization offers a sharp contrast. In direct opposition to the practice of ward politicians, the Industrial Areas Foundation, started by community organizer Saul Alinsky, embraces the principle: 'Never do anything for someone that they can do for themselves (Greider, 1992: 225). Community organizers operate with less visibility and in smaller arenas than mayors, but many of them would score well on tests of leadership performance. It is not incidental that one of the Industrial Areas Foundation organizations is called BUILD – Baltimoreans United in Leadership Development (Orr, 1992). Interaction with followers is a central concern.

The irony of the American situation is that the position with the largest potential policy impact, the office of mayor, is greatly underutilized as a leadership post. In the furtherance of their personal and career ambitions, mayors often go after quick successes, insulate themselves from citizen involvement, or indulge in posturing.

A note on the British experience

The leadership profiles above are all of American mayors. The British system of local government provides no counterpart. Though local government in the United States is not uniform, the 'strong' mayor form is found in most large cities.[10] It is in some ways a miniature presidency. The 'strong' mayor is an elected executive in a separation-of-powers system, and the separation is accentuated by weak party discipline. Electoral politics is candidate-centred, and most aspiring big-city mayors must build a personal organization to gain election and maintain support while in office. The popular election of an American mayor thus provides an extraordinary arena for leader-follower interaction and a highly unstructured opportunity to pursue change. The weakness of the party system emphasizes personal leadership in a manner alien to British local government.

In the United Kingdom, with disciplined parties, a strong merit-system tradition with top posts held by career civil servants, and a national context of parliamentary government, there is no twin to the popularly elected executive in the United States. Moreover, the British system is centralized to a degree unimaginable in the American federal system with its tradition of 'grass roots' democracy. Local government in Britain thus enjoys neither the institutional foundation nor the problem-solving responsibility that underlies mayoral leadership in the US.

Cross-national differences mean that personal leadership in British local government is circumscribed to a degree that precludes direct comparison with the American mayor. Local leadership is not missing in British local government, but a 'muted leadership style' prevails (Stoker and Wolman, 1992: 260). Even before the Thatcher era, policies were 'very much laid down by central government' (Game, 1979: 402). Local government typically concerns itself with details, and broad policy leadership is uncommon (Gyford, 1985: 6). When forthcoming, policy leadership sometimes emanates from councillors who are closely involved with their party groups (Game, 1979: 403). Generally, prominent local officials operate quietly in and through official channels. They tend to be concerned mainly with the particulars of policy and to contribute more to stability than change. There are exceptions, of course, but leadership tends to operate more through party channels (including intra-party struggles) or come from independent agencies and professional administrative officers rather than through extensive contact with citizens (Game, 1979: 75; Gyford, 1985: 8–9; Keating, 1988: 63; Gyford et al., 1989; Boyle, 1990).

Change does occur, of course. Typically it is mandated by central government, though local officials may contribute to a national-level debate. When not mandated, change may emanate from the cross-currents of national politics, as in the case of the 'new urban left' (Gyford, 1985; Lawless, 1990). For example, the sharp shifts in policy for Sheffield – first, towards a radical left agenda, and then into partnership with business – involved in neither case a public leader engaged directly in mobilizing popular support (Lawless, 1990; Seyd, 1990). The first shift represented a response to deindustrialization, and the second shift was a pragmatic adaptation to policies of the Thatcher government.[11] There were significant shifts in key personnel, but they were not central in the changing of policy (Lawless, 1990).

The 'muted style' of local governmental leadership in the United Kingdom has led to consideration of proposals to move Britain in the direction of an American style mayor (Stoker and Wolman, 1992). The image of the big-city mayor as a dynamic policy entrepreneur, in direct contact with and actively supported by the local citizenry, has appeal as a way of achieving urban revitalization. Especially where existing institutions lack direction and energy, a quest for leadership is understandable. After all, as defined here, a leader is someone who operates beyond as well as within official channels in order to rally followers around a cause and change an otherwise expected course of events. The low level of citizen involvement in the governance of British cities indicates a strong but still latent potential for leadership.

What can the American experience teach about leadership from popularly elected executives? This experience suggests caution and modest expectations. Although the loosely structured context of urban politics in the US is, in some ways, fertile ground for personal leadership, the personal factor is, as the profiles above show, a complex ingredient. Leadership carries with it personal ambition and individual motives. The opportunity to involve citizens and pursue large policy goals is no guarantee that leadership energies will be used for those purposes. There is an intervening factor of leadership character.

Leadership character

That elected officials engage in ambition-furthering behaviour is no great revelation, nor is it the whole story. Mayors do have broad policy goals they advance and rally supporters behind, as is evident in the careers of La Guardia and Washington. Why, then, highlight the personal shortcomings of mayors as political leaders? The answer is that mayoral performance is more complicated than is usually acknowledged. Mayors, for example, are sometimes seen as the embodiment of the corporate interests of cities, personally limited only by their level of skill in pursuing the city's structurally generated needs. Over the past several years, urban political study has given enormous attention to economic imperatives, especially the need to compete for investment in a system of global capitalism. Focusing on structural constraints affects how urban leadership is seen. Peterson, for instance, differentiates urban leaders by their adeptness in pursuing economic growth (1981: 143–8).

Economic competition among cities constrains urban actors, without a doubt – but the quest for business investment is not the complete picture. The point made here, drawing heavily on biographical material, is that, despite the structural constraints imposed by a global economy, mayors pursue a variety of aims; and their relationship to the corporate interests of their cities is extremely complex. The imperative to respond to economic competition is not so all-encompassing or even so clear on many occasions as to dictate a mayor's actions. Thus mayors have room to pursue a variety of aims, *some of which may derive from personal wants and ambitions.* On the citizenry side, they too have a variety of needs and wants, and mayors can be more attentive to their constituents' well-being or less so.

Thus, despite the pressures from a global economy, the interaction between mayor and citizenry can take alternative forms. Consider the following potential mayoral goals:

- Furthering the city's corporate economic interests.
- Seeking to expand life chances for constituents through human investment, especially for the disadvantaged.

- Maximizing the development of constituents as capable, involved, and broad-minded citizens.
- Pursuing easy victories and quick successes in order to enhance appeal in a larger electoral arena.

A mayor can bring more skill and vision or less to these tasks. A mayor can also give overriding priority to any of these goals or achieve some degree of balance among them. The handling of multiple responsibilities, including career aspirations, is a matter of character (see Barnard, 1968: 258–84). The variations in performance among the four mayors considered above are not based primarily on unequal abilities, but rather in differences in willingness to incur personal costs and risks in the pursuit of socially worthy aims. As the case of Curley illustrates so clearly, it is not the absence of social aims that is crucial. Rather, it is that social aims have a high degree of difficulty, and Curley lacked the discipline to forgo personal pursuits for socially worthy ones – even though he saw himself as champion of the poor.

Curley differs in degree, but not in tendency, from the others. Because many socially worthy aims have a high degree of difficulty, they tend not to be pursued in a sustained manner because of the personal costs and risks. Interactions between a mayor and the urban citizenry thus leave the city's leadership potential only partially used and significant needs unattended to. Therefore it should not be surprising that community groups may be at cross purposes with city hall and that community-based organizations can accomplish goals that city hall is often unwilling to attempt. (Freedman, 1993: esp. 307–44). It is not that community-based actors are necessarily more ethical as individuals. It is that they operate in a different context, one in which aims of personal ambition play a lesser role and the need to energize followers is greater. That changes the claims on a position of urban leadership.

Focusing on the personal dimensions of mayoral behaviour is not to deny the importance of structural constraints, but it is to suggest that we look at mayoral leadership in a different way. Skill in dealing with structurally generated demands is not the full story. Biographical material on urban leadership shows that mayors often fail to make full use of the opportunities available. For this reason, the study of urban leadership in the United States needs to look beyond the office of mayor, to look beyond elected office in general, and consider other sources of follower activation and development.

In judging leadership performance, we should acknowledge structural constraints. No leader has a blank tablet on which to write at will. At the same time, leadership performances are limited by the personal preoccupations and weaknesses of the individuals who occupy leadership roles. It is appropriate that the negative side of the personal be considered along with the positive side. Success in meeting the leadership challenge is influenced by the balance point between the positive and negative. Mayor

Curley's career illustrates how the negative can undermine leadership effectiveness despite exceptional abilities. The other mayors have negatives also, but not so many as to bankrupt their leadership capacity. Elected offices contain great potential and wide opportunity for leader-follower interaction, but the personal ambitions that attach so strongly to elected office are a mixed blessing at most. The careers of big-city mayors remind us that elected offices serve the cause of democracy imperfectly. An open and personal style of leadership by itself is little assurance that policy impact, citizen involvement, or institution building will be substantial.

The British situation presents different issues. Though the circumstances are not static, greater central control and a tighter party system leave less room for personal leadership than in the US. The level of citizen involvement has been an issue inside the Labour party, but no basic transformation has occurred. There has been some policy innovation, but initiatives to pursue redistributive strategies, such as those in Sheffield, have not fared well in the face of both inter-local economic competition and counter strategies by the central government. It is not apparent that a shift to an elected chief executive would have substantially altered the British urban experience.

Notes

1 Much of the groundwork for such a theory has, however, been laid in *Leadership* by James MacGregor Burns (1978) – a book remarkable for both its sweep and keen insights. Other especially valuable works are those by Barnard (1968) and Selznick (1957). None of these books has a specific urban focus, and two of the three are focused on organizational leadership.

2 Other things being equal, established ways of acting are easier to maintain than to change. Limited cognition reinforces habit. In addition, an established way of acting provides benefits to an array of people who will resist any change that threatens these benefits. Moreover, as Machiavelli observed, whoever would introduce a new order 'has all those who benefit from the old order as enemies' and they are more zealous in their opposition than those who would benefit from, but have yet to experience, a new order (1985: 23–4).

3 Arendt observes that 'it is disaster, not salvation, which always happens automatically and therefore always must appear to be irresistible' (1961: 170).

4 Although there is no authoritative biography of Richard J. Daley, there are several major treatments of Chicago politics during his mayoralty: Gleason (1970), Royko (1971), O'Connor (1975, 1977), Rakove (1975), Kennedy (1978), Kleppner (1985) and Grimshaw (1992).

5 There is an excellent biography of Washington by Rivlin (1992). Other treatments of his administration are contained in Alkalimat and Gills (1984), Kleppner (1985) and Squires et al. (1987).

6 In the Shakman decree, a federal judge made patronage hiring and firing illegal, except for a small number of policy sensitive positions.

7 The search for universal leadership traits long ago gave way to the conclusion leadership is situational (Burns, 1978: 79–80). With regard to mayoral leadership, Ester Fuchs makes the essential point that given political personalities could thrive only in certain environments. In comparing politics in New York and Chicago, she observes: 'John Lindsay would never have been elected mayor of Chicago, while Richard Daley would never have resided at Gracie

Mansion in New York City. The structure of politics in these two cities explains why these men were elected mayor' (Fuchs, 1992: x).

8 This applies mainly to 'strong' mayor forms of government, and even these mayoral positions have limitations that vary from locality to locality. Some cities, for example, have a term limitation, but there are others as well (Pressman, 1972; Preston, 1976; and Svara, 1990). See also Reed (1988).

9 Note that the French system allows a mayor to hold office in the national assembly at the same time, hence the ban on dual office holding is not a universal feature of urban governance (Keating, 1991).

10 The 'strong' mayor form refers to the scope of administrative control exercised. Under this form, the mayor is a true chief executive, possessing line control of the administrative structure including budgetary power.

11 See also the examples of Glasgow (Keating, 1988; Boyle, 1990) and Liverpool (Parkinson, 1990).

References

Alkalimat, A. and Gills, D. (1984) 'Chicago', in R. Bush (ed.), *The New Black Vote*. San Francisco, CA: Synthesis Publications.

Arendt, H. (1961) *Between Past and Future*. Cleveland: Meridian.

Banfield, E.C. (1961) *Political Influence*. New York: Free Press.

Barnard, C.I. (1968) *The Functions of the Executive*. Cambridge, MA: Harvard University Press.

Bayor, R.H. (1993) *Fiorello La Guardia: Ethnicity and Reform*. Arlington Heights, IL: Harlan Davidson.

Beatty, J. (1992) *The Rascal King*. Reading, MA: Addison-Wesley.

Boyle, R. (1990) 'Regeneration in Glasgow', in D. Judd and M. Parkinson (eds), *Leadership and Urban Regeneration*. Newbury Park, CA: Sage.

Burns, J. (1978) *Leadership*. New York: Harper and Row.

Caro, R.A. (1974) *The Power Broker*. New York: Knopf.

Connolly, J.J. (1993) 'Reconstituting ethnic Boston, 1909–1925', Paper presented at the Annual Conference of the Social Science History Association, Baltimore, MD, 6 November.

Crenson, M.A. (1983) *Neighborhood Politics*. Cambridge, MA: Harvard University Press.

Dahl, R.A. (1961) *Who Governs?* New Haven, CT: Yale University Press.

Doig, J.W. (1987) 'To claim the seas and skies', in J.W. Doig and E.C. Hargrove (eds), *Leadership and Innovation*. Baltimore, MA: Johns Hopkins University Press.

Erie, S.P. (1988) *Rainbow's End*. Berkeley: University of California Press.

Freedman, S.G. (1993) *Upon This Rock*. New York: HarperCollins.

Fuchs, E.R. (1992) *Mayors and Money*. Chicago, IL: University of Chicago Press.

Game, C. (1979) 'Review essay: On political leadership', *Policy and Politics*, 7: 395–408.

Gittell, M. (1995) 'School Reform in New York and Chicago', *Urban Affairs Quarterly*, 30: 136–51.

Gleason, B. (1970) *Daley of Chicago*. New York: Simon and Schuster.

Greenstone, J.D. and Peterson, P.E. (1973) *Race and Authority in Urban Politics*. New York: Russell Sage Foundation.

Greider, W. (1992) *Who Will Tell the People*. New York: Simon and Schuster.

Grimshaw, W.J. (1992) *Bitter Fruit*. Chicago, IL: University of Chicago Press.

Gyford, J. (1985) *The Politics of Local Socialism*. London: Allen and Unwin.

Gyford, J., Leach, S. and Game, C. (1989) *The Changing Politics of Local Government*. London: Unwin Hyman.

Horwitt, S.D. (1989) *Let Them Call Me Rebel*. New York: Knopf.

Jones, B.D. and Bachelor, L.W. (1993) *The Sustaining Hand* (2nd edn). Lawrence, KA: University Press of Kansas.

Keating, M. (1988) *The City that Refused to Die*. Aberdeen University Press.

Keating, M. (1991) *Comparative Urban Politics*. Aldershot: Edward Elgar.

Kennedy, E. (1978) *Himself! The Life and Times of Mayor Richard J. Daley*. New York: Viking Press.

Kessner, T. (1989) *Fiorello H. La Guardia and the Making of Modern New York*. New York: McGraw-Hill.

Kleppner, P. (1985) *Chicago Divided*. DeKalb: Northern Illinois University Press.

Lawless, P. (1990) 'Regeneration in Sheffield', in D. Judd and M. Parkinson (eds), *Leadership and Urban Regeneration*. Newbury Park, CA: Sage.

Machiavelli, N. (1985) *The Prince*, Trans. By H.C. Mansfield. Chicago, IL: University of Chicago Press.

O'Connor, L. (1975) *Clout*. New York: Avon Books.

O'Connor, L. (1977) *Requiem: The Decline and Demise of Mayor Daley and His Era*. Chicago, IL: Contemporary Books.

Orr, M.E. (1992) 'Urban regimes and human capital policies', *Journal of Urban Affairs*, 14: 173–87.

Parkinson, M. (1990) 'Leadership and regeneration in Liverpool', in D. Judd and M. Parkinson (eds), *Leadership and Urban Regeneration*. Newbury Park, CA: Sage.

Peterson, P.E. (1981) *City Limits*. Chicago, IL: University of Chicago Press.

Pressman, J.L. (1972) 'Preconditions of mayoral leadership', *American Political Science Review*, 66: 511–24.

Preston, M. (1976) 'Limitations of black urban power', in L. Masotti and R. Lineberry (eds), *The New Urban Politics*. Cambridge, MA: Ballinger.

Price, H.D. (1962) 'Review of *Who Governs?*', *Yale Law Journal*, 71: 1589–96.

Rakove, M.L. (1975) *Don't Make No Waves – Don't Back No Losers*. Bloomington: Indiana University Press.

Reed, A. (1988) 'The black urban regime', in M.P. Smith (ed.), *Power, Community and the City*. New Brunswick, NJ: Transaction Books.

Rivlin, G. (1992) *Fire on the Prairie*. New York: Henry Holt.

Royko, M. (1971) *Boss*. New York: Signet.

Schneider, M. and Teske, P. (1995) *Public Entrepreneurs*. Princeton, NJ: Princeton University Press.

Sekul, J.D. (1983) 'Communities organized for public service', in D.R. Johnson, J.A. Booth, and R.J. Harris (eds), *The Politics of San Antonio*. Lincoln: University of Nebraska Press.

Selznick, P. (1957) *Leadership in Administration*. New York: Harper and Row.

Seyd, P. (1990) 'Radical Sheffield: from socialism to entrepreneurialism', *Political Studies*, 38: 335–44.

Slayton, R.A. (1986) *Back of the Yards*. Chicago, IL: University of Chicago Press.

Squires, G.D., Bennett, L., McCourt, K. and Nyden, P. (1987) *Chicago*. Philadelphia, PA: Temple University Press.

Stoker, G. and Wolman, H. (1992) 'Drawing lessons from US experience', *Public Administration*, 70: 241–67.

Svara, J. (1990) *Official Leadership in the City*. Oxford: Oxford University Press.

7

Size, Efficiency and Democracy: Consolidation, Fragmentation and Public Choice

Michael Keating

The argument about size

There is a perennial debate among students of local government about the appropriate size for municipalities. Although there are many variations and nuances, the central argument pits the consolidationists, who wish to merge small local governments into larger units, against the defenders of fragmentation. Each side has at times displayed a certainty, even self-righteousness, about its convictions and their universal applicability. Yet, the argument is immensely complex and the 'right' size for a municipal government is a matter of the local circumstances and the value judgements of the observer. Like so many issues in politics, this involves matters of ideology and of interest. It is for this reason that an apparently dry matter such as administrative reorganization can arouse such passion, and that change has proved so difficult to achieve. This chapter reviews the main arguments of supporters and opponents of consolidated local government and examines some of the practical difficulties in achieving it.

There are four great issues of principle which have animated the debate on consolidation. First, there is the question of efficiency, of which scale of structure can produce most service at least cost. Second is the issue of democracy, of what structures can best secure citizen control over government and proper accountability. Third is the question of distribution, of which structure can achieve the most equitable distribution of services and tax burdens. Fourth is the issue of development, of which structures are best equipped to promote economic growth. Each of these concepts, efficiency, democracy, distribution and development, is highly value-laden so that it becomes difficult to secure agreement on their definition, let alone whether they are being secured in particular circumstances.

These conceptual difficulties are compounded by the strong vested interests at stake in reorganizing governmental arrangements. The interests of local government elites may not be the same as those of senior governments or of citizens. Different social classes will usually have

conflicting interests in the question; so may ethnic groups. Neighbourhoods will have their own interests, which may conflict with those of
others. Career officials in local governments and ad hoc agencies may have
their own interests. Business leaders may favour particular types of
structure, or they may be divided among themselves, for example between
small, local businesses and larger enterprises.

It is also important to place the debate in its historic context. Certain
arguments have been framed or have gained support because they chimed
with the intellectual fashion of the era, met the needs of governments faced
with specific policy problems, or responded to current economic or
demographic trends. So local government consolidation periodically
arrives on and disappears from the political agenda in western industrial
democracies. The outcome in each case has been determined by a complex
interplay between theoretical ideas and vested interests in states and local
communities. One generalization which it is safe to make is that
reorganization always and everywhere has proved extremely difficult to
achieve.

There were consolidations of local government in the late nineteenth
century, such as the establishment of the London County Council and
New York city, but the first great movement to consolidation in the
contemporary era in Europe and North America took place in the 1960s
and 1970s. The context was the expanding role of government, especially
in economic and physical planning, and the establishment of the modern
welfare state. It was widely asserted that traditional forms of small-scale
local government were ill-fitted to the needs of a modern, complex society
in which they would have to engage in large scale planning and deliver a
large range of new services to citizens. Discussion was conducted in a
highly technical mode, focused on questions of efficiency and planning.
The balance of the academic debate strongly favoured consolidation. By
the 1980s, this consolidation movement was largely exhausted. There was
widespread disillusion with planning and large-scale organization. Arguments for fragmented local government, which had often rested on
sentiment and tradition, began to be framed in more rigorous terms. The
1990s may be seeing yet another turn in the debate, as consolidation comes
back onto the political agenda.

The case for consolidation

At one time it was widely asserted that larger units would be more
efficient, since they could exploit economies of scale in operation.
Sometimes, this has been justified by no more than a vague analogy with
manufacturing production where long runs of standard products can bring
down unit costs. In other cases, it was argued that there would be savings
on capital equipment and in the specialist staff which were needed for the
new sophisticated services which local governments were providing but

which small municipalities could not afford or justify. For all the importance of the issue, there was surprisingly little hard evidence about whether economies of scale actually exist. The Wheatley Commission on local government in Scotland, surveying conflicting evidence on the efficiency of small housing authorities, declared that 'arguments of this kind tend to miss the mark' since they were based on past performance, and asserted that large authorities would be needed in the future (Wheatley, 1969: 109). (One small burgh at that time had a single council house to manage.) The English Redcliffe-Maud Commission advanced a similar argument in the face of contrary evidence from its own research unit (Dearlove, 1979). In the United States, the Committee for Economic Development insisted that 'The burden of proof must rest, however, with those who argue for population levels below 50,000' (CED, 1966: 35).

Some of those involved in local government reorganization in the 1960s were more careful to avoid making claims about efficiency or cost saving. For them, the priority was to ensure that services were developed in areas, especially rural communities and small towns, which had not provided them in the past. It was argued that in the modern era, the distinction between cities and rural communities, with the latter requiring fewer services, was outdated, and that many small municipalities had neglected both service development and infrastructure investment.

It is sometimes argued that large-scale units will be more democratic since they can be given greater powers and functional competence, thus giving more local control over policy. The debate on reform is replete with references to the need for stronger local government. A more controversial issue concerned the quality or 'calibre' of elected councillors. It was widely asserted that first rate people were not attracted to local government because of the small scale and trivial matters which occupied the councillor's attention. With larger units and a greater use of strategic planning, councillors could rise from administrative detail to a concern with broad policy matters. This is turn would attract a better quality of councillor, to the improvement of local democracy.

A dominant concern in the 1960s was the need for large-scale and comprehensive planning. The pace of economic and social change, demographic trends and new technology had put existing arrangements under strain. It was believed that planning should be long-term and broad in its scale. This applied particularly to cities, which had in many cases outgrown their administrative boundaries. Planning, it was argued, needed to be conducted on the basis of economic regions or labour market areas. It should encompass the whole area in which individuals lived, worked and played, implying a metropolitan or regional level of action (CED, 1966; Wheatley, 1969). The arguments for planning, like those about economies of scale, had a strong technocratic bias, an underlying assumption being that planning was a matter for enlightened professionals who would know what the right solution to social and economic problems was. Later it was recognized that, if plans are to be more than statements on paper, they need to be tied into the wider decision-making process and especially to the allocation of resources; and that they need to be given the political weight of elected governments. So the argument for regional planning grew into an argument for regional or metropolitan government. Later still it was recognized that planning is not merely a matter for professional planners but is a highly political process, involving important decisions about who gets what.

The issue of strategic planning is closely tied to that of economic development. In the 1960s, the emphasis was on the need to accommodate growth and distribute it evenly. By the late 1980s, the emphasis had shifted to the need to promote growth in cities, in the context of global competition. There has been a marked increase in inter-city competition to attract mobile capital, at national, continental and global levels and local governments have responded with an array of economic development policies. Yet there is a mismatch between the needs of economic development and the political incentives facing local politicians, especially in fragmented metropolitan areas. Politically, local leaders have an interest in highly visible development projects, in the short term. The best way to achieve this is often to lure businesses from neighbouring municipalities. It seems that local government policies are much less effective in attracting businesses from other labour markets or in stimulating new enterprise. This leads to local governments engaging in beggar-my-neighbour policies which do not benefit the metropolitan area as a whole. Indeed, they may damage it, since there is a growing consensus that regional factors such as educational levels, infrastructure and inter-firm linkages may be important to growth and development. So there is a move to consolidate local governments in order to enhance the competitive advantages of the metropolitan area as a whole. Senior governments have encouraged this since they recognize an interest in having their own metropolitan areas performing well in international competition.

An important argument for consolidation concerns distribution. In Britain and the United States especially, the middle classes had tended to move out of central cities after the Second World War, establishing themselves in suburbs which often had their own municipal institutions. This enabled them to escape heavy city taxes, to exclude low cost or public sector housing, and to maintain class and racial segregation in their school systems. Central cities, for their part, were left with the burden of central place functions, a low income population, social stress and a depleted tax base (Ladd and Yinger, 1989). The American Advisory Commission on Intergovernmental Relations spoke of the 'near apartheid conditions now existing in many metropolitan areas' (ACIR, 1973). If central city and suburban jurisdictions were merged, a more equitable distribution of services and taxes could be achieved. This, of course, was political dynamite which risked upsetting the consensual and technocratic tone of the official debate, which is probably why the issue was treated with such discretion in official government statements.

Most of the arguments in favour of consolidation have come under critical scrutiny. The argument about economies of scale has been widely questioned. There are almost insurmountable problems in measuring whether larger or smaller local governments are more efficient. In the absence of a controlled experiment, it is possible to measure municipalities only against other municipalities or against their own past performance. Yet other municipalities may not face the same conditions or demands; after all one of the arguments for having local government is that these differ from place to place. Similarly, to measure a new municipality against the performance of its predecessors, we would have to assume that the circumstances had not changed in other relevant respects. Measurement itself poses further problems, especially in the social service area. Efficiency is not simply a matter of the cost of services. Strictly, it refers to the amount of output produced for each unit of input. So if one municipality is spending more than another, this may be because it is inefficient, or because it is producing more. To assess this, we need measures both of expenditure and of outputs. Yet measuring the output of government is notoriously difficult. It is commonly found, for example, that increasing the number of police officers results in a higher rate of reported crime, not because police officers cause crime, but because they discover more of it. How then can we measure the real effect of more policing on the crime rate? Similarly, it is very hard to measure the impact of spending on social services, particularly in the short term.

The argument that larger units will enhance local democracy has been criticized on the ground that these will be more remote from the citizen and discourage active participation. The idea of strong local government has also been subject to critical scrutiny. While all sides in the debate agree that strong local government is desirable, there are contrasting views on just what it was. For local government elites, it has meant local government which is more independent of senior governments and able to make its own policies. For senior governments, at least in western Europe and Canada, it has meant rather that local government should be functionally strong, able to implement policy and undertake development, but not necessarily to determine policy itself. Local governments should be strong in relation to their environment, not necessarily in relation to the centre; or, as one former Scottish Office official indiscreetly put it 'we wanted local governments to be powerful enough to do what we told them to do' (Ross, 1980). Senior governments have certainly wanted to unburden themselves of the irksome necessity to intervene in detailed local matters; but this is usually so that they could better control at the strategic level. This distinction, however, was glossed over in the 1960s and 1970s debate. In the United States, where state governments have had less interest in detailed policy intervention within cities, this issue was less salient.

As for concern about councillor calibre, Dearlove (1979) sees here a parallel with the American reform movement at the turn of the century and, like other left-wing commentators (Giard and Scheibling, 1981;

Clément, 1988) suspects a plot to reduce working-class representation in favour of business interests. There is certainly something to be said for this point of view. Working-class and minority representation in local government had advanced in the 1950s and 1960s in several countries (Keating, 1991) and there were frequent references in the debate to the need to encourage local business people back into local government. The arguments for planning and service development were often cast in technocratic terms and there is astonishingly little in official documents about the role of political parties. The attempt to push councillors back from administration into policy rests on a discredited idea that the two can be separated; a vital representative role for councillors is precisely to mediate between the citizen and the administration. On the other hand, there was a genuine concern in many places about patronage and corruption in local government and about the habit of councillors spending hours discussing minor matters of administrative detail, while passing gigantic spending plans on the nod.

Another objection to consolidation is that, while it might make coherent planning and redistribution possible, it did not guarantee it. That would depend on the politics of the consolidated municipalities. By merging the middle-class suburbs with the inner city areas, consolidation might push local politics to the right and prevent these policies coming into effect. In the United States, racial minorities in the 1970s and 1980s used urban government, the only level which they could hope to control, as a means of advancement and came to resist consolidation, which would dilute their voting power. In the UK, Labour opposed the creation of the Greater London Council in 1963, seeing it as a mechanism to break their urban power base by merging it with the suburbs. By the 1980s, minority and working-class interests in cities could make common cause with affluent white suburbs to protect existing boundaries and power bases. In France, the social geography of cities differs, with the middle classes remaining in the centres and the poor dispersed to the periphery, but the political argument is *mutatis mutandis*, the same.

By the late 1970s, political opposition had halted consolidation in most countries. The decline of planning in the face of disillusionment with its results and the unpredictability of economic futures revealed by the oil crises removed much of the reason for consolidation. Large-scale local government, like other large-scale organizations, came to be blamed for all manner of problems and political and intellectual fashion moved back to the 'small is beautiful' philosophy. In economics, there was a revival of faith in markets, and governments of all political stripes adopted neo-liberal policies. The context for local government restructuring was radically altered by globalization, which has reduced the capacity of national governments to manage their spatial economies, and by capital mobility, which has increasingly placed cities in competition against each other for investment. This provided the political and intellectual climate for the advance of public choice theory.

Public choice

Public choice theory, like Marxism before it, now comes in so many varieties that it presents an elusive target. Its central tenets are based upon individualist premises and utilitarian philosophy. That is, it holds that the unit of analysis is the self-interested individual and that the public good is no more than the aggregate of individuals' aspirations. Individuals define their own self-interest and pursue it. Democracy is seen less as a system for taking collective decisions than as a mechanism for allowing individuals maximum scope for choice. So public choice theorists support local government structures which approximate as closely as possible to markets, allowing individuals to make choices about services, taxes and other policies. Efficiency is seen as best promoted by competition, among individuals and among service providing units. Since bureaucrats are also seen as self-interested utility-maximizers (Niskanen, 1973), it is important to subject them to competitive discipline by allowing individuals and communities to shop around for the best services. Development is best promoted by encouraging competition among places and allowing capital to find its most profitable location undistorted by government regulation. Generally, this leads to support for small-scale, fragmented local government.

One of the earliest exponents was Tiebout (1956) who sees local governments as analogous to firms and citizens as consumers. Local governments seek to provide the services desired by their populations at minimum cost. Individuals shop around for the jurisdiction which provides the mix of services and taxes to suit their preferences. If there is a large number of local governments, this provides a set of price and quality signals analogous to those of the market, so both satisfying consumer choice and promoting efficiency through competition. Unfortunately, to make the model work, Tiebout had to make some simplifying assumptions. He had to assume that mobility was costless and, to cope with the objection that people's choice of residential location is based on work rather than the pattern of local government services, he assumed that all citizens lived on dividends.

More recent public choice approaches to local government structure build on the Tiebout assumptions about matching individual preferences with service provision through market mechanisms, but put less emphasis on personal mobility. Instead, they look at ways in which individuals and groups can shop around for services while remaining in place and the competition among governments to provide these. The local public economy school (ACIR, 1987; Ostrom et al., 1988; Parks and Oakerson, 1989) supports fragmentation and competition among local governments. This, in their view, enhances allocative efficiency by attracting capital to those places where it will be most productive. At the same time, it encourages efficiency in service provision and the maximum of citizen choice. They favour not only territorial fragmentation but also functional fragmentation in the form of special-purpose agencies. A distinction is drawn between the *provision* of public services and their *production*. Service provision may be organized according to communities of interest which will vary from service to service. They could be territorial communities, or groups of service consumers. In order to secure efficiency, however, the unit which organizes the provision of the service does not have to produce it. Services can be bought in from other communities, special agencies or the private sector. Service producing agencies will compete for custom, thus driving down costs.

Public choice can be criticized on general theoretical grounds as well as in its practical application. The status of the premise that humans are rational individual utility maximizers is not always clear. If it is intended as a descriptive statement about human motivation, then it is demonstrably false. Human motivation is immensely complex and there are countless examples of individuals engaging in altruistic behaviour or subordinating their own impulses to moral principles. Some public choice theorists cope with the altruism problem by counting altruism as merely another form of self-indulgence. In that case, the statement becomes a mere tautology and prevents us making a distinction, recognized in the political economists of the eighteenth century (Ferguson, 1966), between self-oriented and publicly-oriented behaviour. A great deal of social and political behaviour does appear to follow a collective rather than an individual logic. If the statement that people pursue their self-interest is intended as a normative one, as it really should be, then, like other normative statements, it is subject to value judgements and may be contested. Like Marxism, public choice tends to conceal its normative judgements behind ostensibly objective statements about the world, or deductive principles. Its normative element is, however, revealed in the hostility of many public choice theorists to collective institutions, such as trade unions, which are seen merely as obstacles to individual choice or good government (for example, in Ostrom et al., 1988). Scholars who see society as structured by class divisions, by contrast, see trade unions as instruments for liberation and collective self-expression.

The notion of interest, too, is a difficult one. Individuals' perceptions of their self-interest in a particular matter is governed in many ways by the structure in which they find themselves. Two gladiators in a ring may have an interest in killing each other but this is purely an artefact of the situation in which they have been placed. We cannot read into this anything about their inherent interests. Similarly, citizens placed in governmental structures which present a particular array of threats, opportunities and constraints, may define their immediate interests in relation to these, but this does not prevent the outside observer imagining a different structure in which they would perceive their interests differently. As Stone argues, 'we radically alter our understanding of politics if we think about preferences as being formed not in the context of a static social structure, but rather in a context of dynamic social interactions that sometimes reveal new possibilities and offer changing opportunities' (1993: 10).

Measuring the public choice school's claims to allocative and service efficiency has proved as difficult as measuring those of the consolidationist school. The evidence for the effect of local spending and taxation on economic growth is patchy and inconsistent. It is widely believed that local policies are more effective in relocating businesses over short distances than in bringing new ones into being, and there is no evidence on whether these relocations increase allocative efficiency in the national economy as a whole. It is more widely noted that competition for economic development does tend to drive down social expenditures in cities (Peterson, 1981; Keating, 1991, 1993). Whether this is desirable is a matter for value judgement.

Assessing the evidence about the costs of services faces the old problems about measuring service outputs and controlling for other factors which may be present at the same time. Merely because smaller jurisdictions have lower costs does not mean that they are more efficient. Schneider (1989) finds municipalities in fragmented metropolitan areas have lower costs, which he attributes to the reduced opportunities for bureaucrats to extract monopoly rents. It might equally reflect the tendency for the American middle classes to retreat into small, homogeneous communities which do not face the high costs of areas with more social stress or central place functions, and to provide more services privately. Low costs can also be viewed, from a different political perspective, as the exploitation of the workforce by local taxpayers, especially through the discouragement to unionization. Ostrom et al. (1988) report various studies to support their contention that smaller units are more efficient. One of their examples is policing. Their measure of police output is twofold, the number of police patrol cars on the street; and the number of arrests for serious crimes. The former might be criticized as being an input rather than an output measure; the latter, as noted earlier, cannot be used as a measure of efficiency unless we also know the number of crimes unreported or not investigated. In their discussion of education, they cite evidence that smaller schools may be more efficient; but this tells us nothing about the optimum size of education authorities or school districts. They note that private schools are more efficient, because parents are more motivated; but these are a self-selecting group. They can merely 'conjecture' that these findings might be extended to the public sector. What all this again demonstrates is that judgements about size and efficiency cannot be separated from broader political and value judgements.

A serious objection sometimes raised against public choice approaches is that they do not allow for redistributive policies. It is not true that public choice theorists all deny the need for or possibility of redistribution. Parks and Oakerson note that 'if citizen preferences support resource distribution to distressed communities within large, general-purpose units, they may also support redistribution to smaller, autonomous units by overlying jurisdictions' (1989: 22–3). The problem with this is that it ignores entirely the political process by which redistributive policies are formed and sustained. Redistribution does not occur because of abstract concerns with equity – or else it would operate on a global scale. Nor does it happen because some individuals derive self-gratification from indulging their altruistic instincts. It happens because the political and social systems sustain notions of solidarity and common interest in which the individual feels some responsibility for the whole. Consolidating local governments cannot bring this into existence in the absence of the political and social preconditions; but fragmented local government can certainly discourage it by forcing communities into competition and providing incentives for politicians to stress particularistic rather than common interests. The problem with local government fragmentation may not be that it produces a poor 'quality' of leadership as the consolidations argued in the past, but that it produces a parochial leadership and defines the policy agenda in narrow terms. Local politics is closed and political competition is displaced from the municipality to reappear in the form of inter-jurisidictional competition.

Public choice theory sees citizens as consumers concerned largely with qualitative issues, seeking out the mixtures of services and taxes which correspond to their preferences. So some people prefer parks, others schools and others again would like fewer services but lower taxes. In practice, however, preferences are structured by need. Families with children need education, old people need special health and social services, people without cars need public transport. Most choice therefore is not among the preferences of a homogeneous electorate, but among the needs of specific groups, which can be identified in class, ethnic, generational and gender terms. The key question in policy is not, therefore, the tastes of individuals but the distribution of resources and services among groups. These questions can be resolved in broad political forums, and outcomes legitimized through a concept of solidarity and community interest; or they can be fought out in a pluralistic setting. In both cases, outcomes will reflect differences in power and access but at least in the former case it is possible to bring some overall judgements and conceptions of social justice to bear.

It used to be argued frequently that fragmentation makes coherent urban planning impossible. This is not a valid objection for those public choice theorists who do not believe in planning. Others argue, rightly, that in a fragmented system it is possible to build highways, assemble land and provide infrastructure. What is difficult, however, is to relate land use planning to social and political priorities. Policy tends to disintegrate into functionally-defined policy communities, each determining its own priorities. There is a denial of territorial community with an ability to take decisions across functional boundaries.

Similarly, it can be argued that fragmentation does not prevent coordination in service delivery. In the local public economy model, public entrepreneurs and citizens seek out the best way of providing services just as in the private market, that is through a mixture of cooperation and competition within a set of understood rules. This approach bears comparison with analyses of French administration by the organizational sociology school (Dupuy and Thoenig, 1985). An apparently uniform and centralized regime is reduced by pluralist scholars into a complex system of agencies and individuals linked less by formal regulation than by a set of unwritten rules and understandings. Coordination comes about not by hierarchical order but through mutual accommodation and negotiation. This is a pluralist view of the world, in which democracy and efficiency are secured not by overall design but by partisan mutual adjustment.

Both European and American versions of pluralist theory in territorial government suffer from the level-of-analysis problem. At some level of analysis, any organization can be proved to be pluralist, even if this means reducing it all the way to the level of the individual member. This, however, can lead us to neglect overarching or underlying structures or assumptions which mould behaviour and shape power relations. Careful analysis often indicates that within apparently pluralist systems, there is a pattern of power relations. Stone (1989), in his study of Atlanta, shows that in a system characterized by complexity those interests with a minimum of organizational capacity, in this case the downtown business elite, can exercise disproportionate influence. In other cases this capacity may be held by service producers. Public choice theorists hold that fragmentation reduces the power of bureaucrats by forcing them to compete. It can equally plausibly be argued that it increases their power. This is because citizens do not in practice have the time or inclination to assemble all the information necessary to make policy choices. Professionals, especially when they control specialized production agencies, are able not only to determine what sorts of service can be delivered but to frame the definition of the problems at which the policies and services are addressed. Only where choice is simplified, through party systems or other means of aggregating choices, can the elector hope to come to terms with the issues.

Another difficulty with much of the writing on organizational complexity and self-regulation is its functionalist bias. That is, it is assumed that because a system is functioning, it is working well. Informal networks and the inventive devices which individuals use to get around obstacles are cited as evidence that all is well. In such a perspective the only criterion for success is an internal one, the very fact that the organization continues to function. To judge whether it is working well, however, we need an external standard of evaluation. This again takes us back to the need to make explicit normative judgements.

Public choice theory about local government tends to generalize excessively from American experience, rooted in a specific set of assumptions and historical traditions. The United States is characterized at one level by pluralism, represented by the myriad vertical, horizontal and functional divisions of government. At another level, however, it is politically homogeneous, since the ideological span of politics is extremely narrow. Pluralism thus works within strict parameters, making it manageable and reducing competition to incremental bargaining. In European states, there is a larger ideological and programmatic gap between political parties and philosophies. It might theoretically be possible to allow the full range of political ideologies in European countries to receive full expression simultaneously in policy but the result would be probably be chaotic – and the American experience of partisan mutual adjustment would provide few lessons here.

The problem of community

Many of the approaches to local government structure in the 1960s and 1970s were rather technocratic, concerned with the technical needs of service delivery and leaving democratic participation as an afterthought. Some critics complained that large-scale local governments were 'remote' from the citizen and emptied local democracy of its content. The debate came to focus on the issue of 'community.'

This is a notoriously difficult area. Lyon (1987) identifies 94 different meanings of the term 'community.' Here I will restrict myself to three. The first is traditional community, or *Gemeinschaft*, based on affective solidarity and an attachment to place which overrides other loyalties. This is characteristic of pre-industrial societies and is generally assumed to be in decline, though it continues to be celebrated both by some conservatives and by some postmodernist thinkers who see community as a means of combating the alienation and powerlessness of the masses in urban society (Cooke, 1990). They are suspicious of technocratic recipes for consolidation and prefer small and traditional units. On the other hand, small communities may be an oppressive restriction on the freedom of individuals. Supporters of consolidation also noted that, while small local governments in which the citizens all knew their representatives personally might be more participative and accountable, local democracy required that they be functionally effective, which they were not.

The second meaning of community is as an extension of private space, which can be created and recreated to suit the needs of individuals at the moment. It is this conception which is dominant in suburban America, where local government fragmentation is largely a mechanism for preserving racial and social segregation and protecting private property values. Metropolitan fragmentation is used most frequently, not to provide a range of choices and encourage mobility, but precisely to discourage residential mobility by erecting barriers to people of different class or ethnic backgrounds. Tiebout did admit that one motive which individuals might have is to associate with 'nice' people (Tiebout, 1956: 418n) but sees this entirely in terms of inclusion rather than the segregation and exclusion which is a pervasive feature of American cities.

The third meaning of community is as a space for social interaction in which political exchange can take place (Mabileau et al., 1989) but there is enough social solidarity to guarantee cohesion and legitimacy to political outcomes. In this type of political community, there is scope for individual liberty, but at the same time a capacity for collective action in defining problems and framing solutions. That is to say, decisions are not all reduced either to the logic of individual consumer choice or to that of a dominating collective interest. If local government units are not based on recognizable communities, they may not command consent and loyalty or be the basis for legitimate public decisions. A sense of community is also needed if the social solidarity which underpins redistributive policies is to develop. Some of the complaints about the loss of community may have represented nostalgia for an idealized past, or a pre-industrial world of personal contact (the first meaning), or a desire to entrench economic and social privilege by placing a jurisdictional boundary around private property (the second meaning). Yet community in the third sense is an important element in the politics of a liberal democracy. It implies that local government boundaries must recognize cultural and historic loyalties and be recognizable to the citizens. Neither the technocratic, consolidationist approach, in which boundaries are derived from the technical needs of services, nor the public choice approach, based on individual utility maximization and complexity, can secure this.

Achieving consolidation

Governments committed to consolidation have always found it extremely difficult to achieve. Change affects the interests of politicians, bureaucrats and residents. It shifts burdens and opportunities and creates fears and uncertainties. Since there are so few votes to be had in it, governments usually approach it circumspectly. In the United States, consolidation is typically a voluntary matter, needing the consent of the affected municipalities and sometimes of the electorate through referendum. This reflects the strong home rule tradition and the status of local government as an expression of the local community rather than an agency of the state. European countries and Canadian provinces are more able to act unilaterally, with few requirements for local consent. The wishes of the local inhabitants and politicians are not the paramount factor. Instead, issues of functional efficiency and planning have tended to dominate the debate. The capacity of European states to act unilaterally is influenced, however, by the weight which local elites carry in national politics. In France, the very centralization of the state gives local politicians a key role in national politics. Most members of parliament simultaneously hold local office, as have seven of the last nine prime ministers, usually as mayor. France is thus the only major European country which has not consolidated its local governments since such a reform would never get through parliament even if a party were to propose it. Britain presents the opposite case, a system in which national and local political elites are quite separate, allowing the centre to alter local government almost at will. Major structural reforms were undertaken in the mid-1970s, the mid-1980s and the 1990s. The most striking case of central government autonomy is in Scotland where the Conservatives, almost totally lacking a presence in local government, were in the early 1970s able to put through a radical programme of reform designed for them by the bureaucracy (Keating, 1975). In southern England, by contrast, they had to bend to local pressures from within their own ranks.

When it comes to capital cities, senior governments have been less keen on consolidation, fearing that a rival might be created. It was the high political profile of the Greater London Council, located directly across the river from parliament, which determined the Thatcher government on its abolition in the 1980s. Around the same time, the Mitterrand government in France tried to carve up Paris, power base of the opposition leader Jacques Chirac. Given the constraints of the French system, Chirac emerged with his powers almost entirely intact. In Catalonia, the autonomous regional government abolished the metropolitan council of Barcelona. For large and expanding cities generally, consolidated government can soon be outdated. Both Metropolitan Toronto (Frisken, 1993) and the Montreal Urban Community (Trépanier, 1993) exclude the areas where most development occurred in the 1980s.

Consolidation may take the form of a single-tier or a two-tier system. Governments have frequently resorted to two-tier arrangements in order to gain the advantages of consolidation while leaving intact local power bases and community-based local government. In this case, they must decide on how to elect the upper tier and what powers it should have. Often, they have provided for the upper tier to be indirectly elected from the lower tier. This respects local power bases and assuages the fears of local politicians that they will be dominated by the upper tier. On the other hand, it deprives the upper tier of the political status and legitimacy which comes from direct election. The upper tier may become a mere confederation of the constituent units without a sense of policy and strategic direction. Resources may simply be spread proportionally around the lower tier municipalities in a process which the French call *saupoudrage*, rather than targeted at strategic priorities.

In two-tier systems, the upper tier is usually assigned strategic planning functions, with the lower tier looking after local matters and much of the service delivery functions. The problem here is that, unless the upper tier has real powers over the implementation of plans and particularly financial authority, then its plans are liable to remain mere good intentions. Yet, the more powers that are assigned to the upper tier, the more political opposition will be created from those losing out. The result tends to be a compromise. In the Scottish case, the weakness of local interest within the governing party allowed the upper tier to be assigned extensive powers in planning, including the right to intervene in local planning matters, together with all the most expensive services, including education, police and social work. In England, local opposition led to the metropolitan counties receiving fewer powers than originally intended, and to their boundaries being more tightly drawn. In France, where it has been impossible to impose consolidation, central government has been able only to set up rather weak urban communities, drawn from the existing local governments and with strictly limited powers.

Resource sharing is another critical matter. One of the main arguments for consolidation is that larger units have access to a broader tax base. If the upper tier has extensive taxation powers and spending responsibilities, it can redistribute resources − which is not to say that it always does. Opposition, however, often forces the most redistributive resources to be assigned to the lower tier, so undermining one of the principal objectives of reform. This was the case in Britain with housing.

Relationships among the tiers are critical to the success of two-tier government. Since local government functions are intimately connected, they must be coordinated in some way. Yet, if two tiers are separately elected, they must answer to their own electorates and local politicians will not take kindly to having a tutelage imposed on them from the upper tier. Senior governments have been somewhat schizophrenic about this. In both France and Britain, ministers insisted at the time of local government reform that there should be no hierarchy between the tiers of government; yet at the same time, insisted on the need for lower tier governments to implement the strategic plans of the upper tier. In partisan systems of local government, conflict can arise when two tiers are controlled by rival parties. Yet even where both are in the hands of the same party, difficulties have been known.

These political and structural problems have made consolidation extremely difficult and ensured that even governments committed to it have had to compromise, so undermining some of the objectives of the reform.

Conclusion

The technical arguments about consolidation versus fragmentation have proved inconclusive. This is partly for lack of data, partly because of difficulties in measurement but mainly because the items which are to be measured are themselves politically contested or normative. In any case, the effects of structures on policy outputs are mediated by local politics and intergovernmental politics. It may be that the effects of consolidation on altering political assumptions and patterns are therefore more important than any direct effects on service delivery or planning. These effects themselves can vary from case to case. For example, we have seen that consolidation may provide the resource base for more redistribution and the sense of community which could sustain such a policy. On the other hand, it might bring into the city suburban and conservative votes disinclined to vote for politicians favouring redistribution. There is no universal answer to the question of whether large structures or small ones are better. The answer will depend on the circumstances of particular cases and on the value judgements of whoever is asking the question. Generally speaking, people with a beneficent view of government will support consolidation. This includes social democrats and those described in the United States as 'liberals'. People who regard government as a necessary evil, who are suspicious of its claims and who want to restrict its scope, will tend to favour small-scale, fragmented local government. This includes conservatives, European 'liberals' (that is, supporters of the free market). It also includes many on the anarchist and utopian left such as Greens and communitarian socialists.

Certain national and international trends can be discerned in all this. In the 1960s and 1970s there was a spirit of optimism about the potential of government to solve social and economic problems. Large-scale organization was in fashion and governments in Europe and even North America were committed to long-term planning. The expansion of the welfare state had raised questions about the efficiency and professionalism of local government, which played a large part in the delivery of its services. So consolidation came on the political agenda. By the late 1970s, political opposition had generally caused governments to downplay the issue. In the 1980s, with the advance of neo-liberalism and the 'new right', public choice arguments became more fashionable. The two oil crises had shown the limitations of long-term planning in an unpredictable world. Governments were seeking to downsize and limit public commitments, rather than expand the welfare state. Progress to consolidation was generally halted and even reversed in the cases of Greater London, Metropolitan Barcelona (Morata, 1991) and the Rijnmond in the Netherlands (Netherlands Scientific Council, 1990). By the early 1990s, however, the issue had come back on the agenda in a number of countries. The need for long-term planning, at least on a project basis, was illustrated dramatically in deregulated Britain by the experiences of the London Docklands development, the Channel Tunnel and the Third London airport. In France, the central government introduced new incentives for the formation of urban communities. Opposition parties in Britain were committed to looking at metropolitan and regional forms of government. In Canada, the government of Ontario launched a new programme for consolidation. In the United States, there were some attempts at county restructuring, though the issue of consolidating cities with suburbs was still generally regarded as too difficult to handle (Rothblatt and Sancton, 1993).

Note

I am grateful to Andrew Sancton for comments on an early draft of this chapter.

References

ACIR [Advisory Commission on Intergovernmental Relations] (1973) *Substate Regionalism and the Federal System*, vol. 1, *Regional Decision Making: New Strategies for Substate Districts*, Washington, D.C.: ACIR.

ACIR [Advisory Commission on Intergovernmental Relations] (1987) *The Organization of Local Public Economies*, Washington, D.C.: ACIR.

CED [Council for Economic Development] (1966) *Modernizing Local Government*. Washington, D.C.: CED.

Clément, R. (1988) 'Les élections municipales. Une démarche unitaire conforme aux intérêts des habitants', *Economie et Politique*, 140: 46–9.

Cooke, P. (1990) *Back to the Future: Modernity, Postmodernity and Locality*. London: Unwin Hyman.

Dearlove, J. (1979) *The Reorganization of British Local Government*. Cambridge: Cambridge University Press.

Depuy, F. and Thoenig, J.-C (1985) *L'administration en miettes*. Paris: Fayard.

Ferguson, A. (1966) *An Essay on the History of Civil Society, 1767*. Edinburgh: Edinburgh University Press.

Frisken, F. (1993) 'Planning and servicing the Greater Toronto Area: the interplay of provincial and municipal interests', in D.N. Rothblatt and A. Sancton (eds), *Metropolitan Governance: American/Canadian Intergovernmental Perspectives*, Berkeley: Institute of Governmental Studies Press, University of California.

Giard, J. and Schiebling, J. (1981) *L'enjeu régionale*. Paris: Messidor.

Keating, M. (1975) 'The Scottish Local Government Bill', *Local Government Studies*, 4 (1): 49–61.

Keating, M. (1991) *Comparative Urban Politics: Power and the City in the United States, Canada, Britain and France*. Aldershot: Edward Elgar.

Keating, M. (1993) 'The politics of economic development: political change and local development policies in the United States, Britain and France', *Urban Affairs Quarterly*, 28 (3): 373–96.

Ladd, H. and Yinger, J. (1989) *America's Ailing Cities: Fiscal Health and the Design of Urban Policy*. Baltimore, MA: Johns Hopkins University Press.

Lyon, L. (1987) *The Community in Urban Society*. Chicago, IL: Dorsey.

Mabileau, A., Moyser, G., Parry, G. and Quantin, P. (1989) *Political Participation in Britain and France*. Cambridge: Cambridge University Press.

Morata, F. (1991) 'La redefinició metropolitana de Barcelona: xarxes polítiques, pla estratègic i macroregió', in F. Morata (ed.), *El Govern Local, Annuari 1991*. Universitat Autónoma de Barcelona.

Netherlands Scientific Council for Government Policy (1990) *Institutions and Cities: The Dutch Experience*. The Hague: author.

Niskanen, W.A. (1973) *Bureaucracy: Servant or Master?* London: Institute of Economic Affairs.

Ostrom, V., Bish, R. and Ostrom, E. (1988) *Local Government in the United States*. San Francisco, CA: Institute for Contemporary Studies.

Parks, R. and Oakerson, R. (1989) 'Metropolitan organization and governance: a local public economy approach', *Urban Affairs Quarterly*, 25 (1): 18–29.

Peterson, P. (1981) *City Limits*. Chicago, IL: University of Chicago Press.

Ross, J. (1980) 'Local government in Scotland: some subversive reflections', mimeo, University of Strathclyde.

Rothblatt, D.N. and Sancton, A. (eds) (1993) *Metropolitan Governance: American/Canadian Intergovernmental Perspectives*. Berkeley: Institute of Governmental Studies Press, University of California.

Schneider, M. (1989) *The Competitive City: The Political Economy of Suburbia*. Pittsburgh, PA: University of Pittsburgh Press.

Stone, C. (1989) *Regime Politics: Governing Atlanta, 1946–1986*. Lawrence: University of Kansas Press.

Stone, C. (1993) 'Urban regimes and the capacity to govern: a political economy approach', *Journal of Urban Affairs*, 15 (1): 1–28.

Tiebout, C. (1956) 'A pure theory of local expenditures', *Journal of Political Economy*, 64 (4): 416–24.

Trépanier, M.-O. (1993) 'Metropolitan government in the Montreal area', in D.N. Rothblatt and A. Sancton (eds), *Metropolitan Governance: American/Canadian Intergovernmental Perspectives*, Berkeley: Institute of Governmental Studies Press, University of California.

Wheatley (1969) Royal Commission on Local Government in Scotland, 1966–69, *Report*, Cmnd. 4150, Edinburgh: HMSO.

8

Local Government Institutions and Democratic Governance

Harold Wolman

Nature of the problem

This chapter is concerned with theories of local government and their relationship to local political institutions. The debate over the best institutional structure for urban government has a long history, going back at least as far as Aristotle's consideration of the most appropriate constitution for the Greek city-state. Institutional structure achieves such an importance because it is the vehicle through which the basic purposes and values a society wishes to pursue through local government are carried out. It is, thus, presumed that institutions matter – that political and policy outcomes will differ as institutional structure differs.

Theories of democratic government, including those of local democratic government, are embedded in institutions designed to carry out these values. By institutions and institutional structure I mean not only the internal structure of local government (that is, its council, its executive arrangements, its departments and bureaux and their relationship to each other, the nature of the electoral system, etc.), but also informal norms, roles, relationships and operating practices that are so stable, structured and accepted that they can be said to be 'institutionalized'.

A consideration of theories of local government institutions has both a *normative* and an *empirical* component. Normatively, the concern is with the appropriate values to be pursued through local government institutions; empirically the question is whether governmental institutions in fact effectively promote these values, or, more broadly, what is the relationship between structure and values. Therefore, the questions on which this chapter focuses are: (1) how does institutional structure reflect the basic purposes and values society wishes to pursue through local government (that is, what set of structures are deemed most appropriate in the light of these objectives?); and (2) does local government structure, in fact, promote these basic purposes and values (that is, does structure matter in that it produces intended results?). As this suggests, any discussion of structure must be undertaken in the context of the values which inhere in local government, values that will differ from one society to another.

The chapter will proceed by first setting forth the basic values animating local government in the United States and the way in which local government institutions have been shaped to promote these values. The next section addresses the same set of questions for the United Kingdom. The following two sections then examine the nature of the debate as it exists in the literature on the relationship between local government structure and local government values in each of the two countries. The terms of the debate are set forth and, where appropriate, empirical evidence is brought to bear (that is, what values do different kinds of institutional structure in fact promote?). The chapter concludes with a critique and assessment of the debate in each country.

Values and local government structure in the United States

In the American context there are several strands of thought that relate fundamental values to local governmental institutional structure. The fundamental values, at least as traditionally expressed, include the sometimes contrasting ones of individual participation, pluralism and representative democracy, and efficiency, each of which has differing consequences for local government structure.

In the United States, as Sharpe (1973) points out in his insightful essay on American democracy, all authority resides in the people. The bedrock of American local democratic theory is that the role of the local government is to reflect the will of the people and that direct individual participation in local government is the best means of achieving this end.

Jefferson's 'sovereignty of the individual' was the animating force behind early American municipal government. His concern for direct democracy and individual participation as primary values led him to advocate a system of 'little republics' (which he termed a 'ward System'). Wards should be small enough that every citizen could attend ward meetings and 'act in person' (Syed, 1966: 39). The New England township governments were celebrated by Jefferson as the perfect manifestation of the principle of sovereignty of the individual: 'These wards, called townships in New England, are the vital principles of their governments, and have proved themselves the wisest invention ever devised by the wit of man for the perfect exercise of self-government and for its preservation' (quoted in Syed, 1966: 39). Indeed, it is Jefferson's sovereignty of the individual that is reflected in de Tocqueville's classic description of New England local government, written in 1835:

> In the township, as well as everywhere else, the people are the source of power; but nowhere do they exercise their power more immediately. In America the people form a master who must be obeyed to the utmost limits of possibility . . . in the townships, where the legislative and administrative action of the government is nearer to the governed (than at the state level), the system of representation is not adopted. There is no municipal council; but the body of voters, after having chosen its magistrates, directs them in everything that exceeds the simple and ordinary execution of the laws of the state. (1954: 64)

The individual participation celebrated by Jefferson and de Tocqueville is justified by the fundamental tenet of republican government that all authority resides in the people; the people should rule. The Jeffersonian tradition lives on, not only in deeply held and expressed populist values related to the role of the individual and local government, but also in the widespread use of some institutional mechanisms that are found in few continental systems of local government – the referendum and the initiative (a device that allows the people, by petition, to place an issue on the ballot for decision). In addition, city institutions to promote citizen participation – a by-product of the 1960s – and neighbourhood decentralization – to the extent the concern is participation rather than efficient administration – continue to reflect a Jeffersonian concern.

The values of pluralism and representative democracy both flow from the Jeffersonian concern with participation and are a reaction to it. In the pluralist version, local democracy consists of the expression of and conflict among diverse views and values held by contending groups attempting to shape local government decisions to meet their ends, with all important groups having the ability to gain access to and exercise some degree of influence over decision makers. Local government's role is thus concerned with, in Easton's terms, the authoritative allocation of values, or, in Lasswell's classic language, 'Who gets what, when and how?' Local democracy is thus a free flow of group political conflict and local government is its arena.

The critical role of participation in American local democracy remains in pluralist theory, but the emphasis shifts from individual participation to group participation. As Sharpe notes:

> The condition of American liberal life that group theory reflects is the populist doctrine of the autonomous individual. Crick has put his finger deftly on the link between the two: Bentley's groups are no more than individuals writ large, individuals organically associated according to their interests, interests that are the personality of the individuals, and thus of the groups. (1973: 137)

However, American pluralist theory also reflects Locke's concern for controlling and limiting government and, as reflected through Madison, for controlling popular majorities and 'factions'. Madison's concerns led him to emphasize separation of powers, checks and balances, and representation rather than direct democracy. As Samuel Huntington notes:

> The Jeffersonian ideal of grass roots democracy stands in direct contrast to the Madisonian concept of extensive republicanism. To Jefferson, republicanism became purer as it came closer to the people. To Madison, it became purer as it was farther removed from the people. To Jefferson, the ward republics embodied the republican ideal in its purest form. To Madison, the ward republics embodied the evils of factionalism in their worst form. To Jefferson, the principal threat to republicanism was the tyranny of arbitrary centralized autocracy. To Madison, the principal threat to republicanism was the tyranny of arbitrary local majorities. (1959: 189–90)

The Madisonian emphasis on limiting government power through separation of power and checks and balances is reflected in the separation of executive (mayor) and legislative (council) power characteristic of American municipal government as it developed beyond New England township government in the nineteenth century. In addition, Madison's focus of attention was on interest groups ('factions') rather than individuals: 'All civilized societies are divided into interests and factions' (quoted in Abbott, 1991: 84). The structure of government, under the Madisonian system, must serve both to moderate and to control factional conflict, but also to provide for adequate representation of group interests.

Thus, in the context of representative rather than direct democracy, the relevant unit of participation shifted from the individual to the group and focused concern on the representation of the interests of various groups through local government. This meshed well with the socioeconomic development of American cities in the last part of the nineteenth and first part of the twentieth centuries. The waves of European immigration brought to the cities successive ethnic groups, all of which demanded participation and representation of their interests in municipal government as a part of the process of becoming American. The mayor-council structure, within a context of rapid immigration, lent itself to the integration of the newly arrived ethnic groups into the local political process through the formation of 'machine politics'.

The advent of economy and efficiency as core values for local government represented a reaction to machine politics and the corruption that frequently accompanied it. Arising as a product of the Progressive movement in the early part of the twentieth century, the role of municipal government was defined to be primarily that of the efficient delivery of local services. As the National Municipal League, the primary advocate of municipal reform, saw it:

> Local government exists to perform functions and render services which the people of the community demand and which can be performed more cheaply by government than any other way ... the citizen's questions should be (1) Am I receiving all the services which government should, by reason of economy and convenience, rightfully perform? (2) Are these services being efficiently rendered? and (3) Is government sufficiently subject to democratic control, sufficiently responsive to public opinion, in performing those services? (1939: 1)

The reformers drew the analogy to the business corporation which pursued economy and efficiency through application of experts and scientific techniques rather than through 'political' considerations. A typical expression of this view is displayed by an early reformer, John Patterson, who wrote:

> A city is a great business enterprise whose stockholders are the people ... Our municipal affairs would be placed upon a strict business basis and directed, not by partisans either Republican or Democratic, but by men who are skilled in

business management and social science; who would treat our people's money as a trust fund, to be expended wisely and economically, without waste and for the benefit of all citizens. (quoted in Stillman, 1974: 8)

The advocates of this conception of local government proposed a series of structural changes as the best means of implementing these values: a council-manager form of government (the manager to be appointed by the elected council and to be the source of expertise on the efficient delivery of services), non-partisan elections (to reduce or eliminate the influence of parties and politics), and at-large rather than ward elections (to eliminate the politics associated with small area interests and to encourage the council to focus on the general good of the community). As Richard Childs, the 'father of the manager plan', wrote:

The position of city manager of course is the central feature of the council-manager plan and the ultimate theory of the scheme contemplates that he should be an expert in municipal administration, selected without reference to local politics. (written in 1915 and quoted in Stillman, 1974: 5)

This . . . plan corresponds to the general manager under the board of directors in a business corporation. It gives the stability of the combined judgment of many men on matters of policy, but leaves execution to a single-headed controlled executive establishment. (written in 1913 and quoted in Stillman, 1974: 8)

Concerns with group representation and checks and balances, the Madisonian tradition in American local government, are absent from the reform ethos (though the Jeffersonian value of direct democracy lives on in the Progressives' support for the referendum, initiative and recall). In the reformers' conception, the primary role of the citizen is that of voter, the source from which the elected council members obtain their legitimacy and from which they derive the values local policy should embody.

Values and local government structure in Britain

In Britain the most frequently cited values attached to local government are pluralism (local government as a counterweight to national government rather than group politics in the American sense), participation, and efficiency in the delivery of local services (see Sharpe, 1970). The Widdicombe Commission states:

The value of local government stems from its three attributes of:
(a) pluralism, through which it contributes to the national political system;
(b) participation, through which it contributes to local democracy;
(c) responsiveness, through which it contributes to the provision of local needs through the delivery of services. (1986: 47)

An earlier report, the Royal Commission on Local Government in England (known as the Redcliffe-Maud report) emphasized much the same set of values, though differently expressed:

The pattern and character of local government must be such as to enable it to do four things: to perform efficiently a wide range of profoundly important tasks concerned with the safety, health, and well-being, both material and cultural of people in different localities; to attract and hold the interests of its citizens; to develop enough inherent strength to deal with national authorities in a valid partnership; and to adapt itself without disruption to the present unprecedented process of change in the way people live, work, move, shop and enjoy themselves. (1969: vol. 1: 1)

However, it is clear that pride of place among these various rationales for local government in Britain belongs to efficient and effective local service delivery. Participation and responsiveness are, more often than not, simply handmaidens to these ends. The Widdicombe Commission, for example, concludes: 'Clearly the three attributes of local government – pluralism, participation and responsiveness – provide a strong case for its continued existence as the principal means of *local service delivery*' (1986: 53, emphasis added).

In its response to the Widdicombe report, the government noted:

Local government has a very important role to play in the democratic life of this country. Local authorities provide or promote a wide range of public services that are best administered locally, under democratic control. They are able to do so in a way that is responsive to local needs. (quoted by Leach, 1989: 103)

Sharpe (1970: 154) cites W.J.M. MacKenzie, a leading student of British local government, who states simply that local government is justified 'because it is an effective and convenient way to provide certain services'. The primacy of local service delivery over values of participation and democratic governance is expressed in the report of the Committee on the Management of Local Government: 'The local administration of public services is essential, that the local organs of administration should be democratically elected bodies is not' (Maud, 1967: 68).

Indeed, the historical development of British local government indicates that it developed to some extent as an agency to deliver public services on behalf of the central state. Sharpe refers to the 'Benthamite' tradition 'that sees local government primarily as a series of agencies for providing national services as efficiently as possible to national minimum standards' (1970: 159). Stewart observes that, over time, 'Local authorities came to be seen as first and foremost agencies for the provision of separate services required by national legislation' (1989: 238).

Despite this, much of the discussion of local government and its values does argue that local government is concerned with more than simply service delivery and that responsiveness and participation are key values as well. The Redcliffe-Maud report, for example, states:

Local government is not to be seen merely as a provider of services. If that were all, it would be right to consider whether some of the services could be more efficiently provided by other means. The importance of local government lies in the fact that it is the means by which people can provide services for themselves; can take an active and constructive part in the business of government; and can decide for themselves, within the limits of what national policies and local resources allow, what kind of services they want and what kind of environment they prefer. (1969: 10)

The Widdicombe Committee, writing nearly two decades later, concurred: 'Proponents of local government argue that it is an effective means of delivering services because it has the ability, unlike a non-elected system of local administration, to be responsive to local needs' (1986: 50).

However, it is evident from the above quotations that responsiveness is a valued aspect of local government because it leads to better service delivery. Much the same is true with the value of participation. In its recent Local Government Review consultation paper on the internal management of local authorities in England, the Department of the Environment stated: 'Good local government has an important role to play not just in securing services but also in encouraging local participation in the political system' (1991: 1).

Concern for participation as an important value of British local democracy derives originally from Mill's interest in local political participation as civic education. This differs fundamentally from the American emphasis on individual participation (discussed above) as an expression of the 'sovereignty of the individual' and the republican principle that all authority resides in the people. Indeed, in practical terms the emphasis on participation as an important value in British local government has been more rhetorical than real and subordinated to the concern for representative rather than participatory democracy. Boaden et al. begin their book on participation and local government by observing: 'Quite clearly, the idea of widespread public participation in the process of government is contrary to the idea of representative government on which so much of British central and local government is based' (1982: 1).

If local service delivery is the primary rationale for British local government, it is important to note that the value of efficiency in the delivery of local services has a broader meaning than the narrow businessman's definition. It encompasses the concept of 'responsiveness' (to the needs of local citizens) and what Sharpe terms 'functional effectiveness' as well as the delivery of a unit of service at the lowest possible cost. By 'functional effectiveness' Sharpe (1973) means the ability of local government to act so that it is able to accomplish its purposes. (Sharpe argues that this concern for 'functional effectiveness' is conspicuously absent from American discussions of local democracy.)

The structure of British local government reflects these concerns for efficient, effective and responsive delivery of local services. Responsiveness is brought about through the mechanism of representative democracy. As Leach and Stewart state:

Local government has been based on representative democracy. The electorate does not act direct, but through its elected representatives. The council of the local authority is constituted by election, but once so constituted acts on behalf of the electorate, for which actions it can be held to account at the next election. (1986: 3.13)

Dearlove calls this the 'electoral chain of command theory' of local government: 'policy demands flow from electors to councillors (through the agency of regular elections) and then on from councillors to officers' (1979: 29–30). The internal organization of local government is thus critical to its ability to efficiently and effectively deliver local services responsive to the citizenry's needs as determined through local elections. Stewart (1989: 172 ff.) argues that local governments have traditionally structured themselves in terms of their operational practices not simply as agencies of local service delivery but as agencies of *direct* service delivery.

> There has been a remarkable uniformity in the past organization and management of local authorities. Although local authorities as local government are constituted for local choice, that choice has been limited by a set of organizational principles . . . Those principles supported and expressed their role as agencies for the delivery of a series of services . . . Local authorities have been organized for the direct provision of services. That responsibility became so dominant in their working that many have come to see it as their only role . . . If the direct provision of services is seen as an organizational necessity, then it is not surprising that the management of local authority reflected that necessity. The local council organized service provision through a series of committees centring on the services provided. Inevitably much of the work of these committees focused on the running of services. (1989: 172–3)

Thus, in the British system of service delivery oriented representative local government, the electorate chooses a council in partisan elections with party candidates pursuing office on the basis of their party's manifesto or platform. The council is organized into a committee structure with the dominant party or coalition controlling each committee. Traditionally each committee was responsible for a specific service. Decisions with respect to the service were made by the committee (in most cases highly dominated by the committee chair) in conjunction with the senior official (civil servant) who served as department head for the department responsible for service delivery. Reforms in the 1970s resulted in the appointment of a chief executive (equivalent to some extent to the American city manager, but without executive authority) and a committee responsible for policy planning and strategy. These reforms were meant to improve functional coordination across service delivery areas through encouraging 'corporate planning and management'. Although each council has a council leader, the leader does not serve as an executive or have executive powers; instead, the leader is simply the spokesman for the dominant party or coalition in the council. Indeed, it is striking that there is no single locus of executive authority within British local government; executive authority is invested in the council as a whole. The council delegates authority to act to individual committees, which, with the advice and consultation of local officials representing the relevant department, set the direction for policy for individual services and these are carried out by service delivery departments.

The nature of the debate: a review of the literature

With this extensive background we can now ask what is the nature of the debate in each country as it concerns the question of local government structure and democratic values? In the American context the debate over structure centres primarily around the impact of the structural change brought about by the reform movement and particularly the impact of reform structures on the distribution of outputs (who wins and who loses) and on responsiveness (the extent to which cleavages and differences in interests that exist in the community are reflected through and dealt with by the political system).

These are concerns that are rarely reflected in the British debate over structure. Instead, in the British context the debate over structure has centred on the question of how local government organization can better contribute to efficient and effective delivery of local services and the likely impact of various changes in structure on these goals.

In both the US and the UK debate has also focused on more narrow efficiency concerns: which structural features will result in allocative efficiency and/or efficiency in a least cost sense? To some extent – and particularly in Britain – this debate has been concerned with the structure of the *system* of local government – the number of local governments, their relationships to each other, the functions to be performed, the appropriate size of local government, etc. These concerns are covered in depth in Chapter 7.

In this section I review the literature both to illustrate the nature of this debate and to present empirical evidence that addresses itself to it as well as to the broader question of whether and how differences in local political institutions matter.

The debate in the US

In the American literature debate has centred largely on the reform movement, the motivations of the reformers, and the impact of the structural features they created at the local level. Richard Hofstadter argues that the reform movement arose from the reaction of the indigenous Yankee-Protestant population to the challenge of mass immigration and reflected a clash of two different sets of political ethics:

> One, founded upon the indigenous Yankee-Protestant political traditions, and upon middle class life, assumed and demanded the constant, disinterested activity of the citizen in public affairs, argued that political life ought to be run, to a greater degree than it was, in accordance with general principles and abstract laws . . . and expressed a common feeling that government should be in good part an effort to moralize the lives of individuals . . . The other system, founded upon the European backgrounds of the immigrants, upon their unfamiliarity with independent political action, their familiarity with hierarchy and authority, and upon the urgent needs that so often grew out of their migration, took for granted that the political life of the individual would arise

out of family needs, interpreted political and civic relations chiefly in terms of personal obligations, and placed strong personal loyalties above allegiance to abstract codes of law or morals. (Hofstadter, 1955: 9)

This clash of political ethics also reflected a clash in basic values related to local democracy; the reformers' primary concern was for the values of economy and efficiency as opposed to the representation of group interest through the operations of pluralist democracy. Stone et al. (1986: 110) summarize the three fundamental principles of the local government reform movement as follows:

1 There is an overriding public interest that is superior to the particular interests of the various segments of the urban community.
2 This general interest is more easily discovered through cooperation than through conflict and competition.
3 Technical problem solving is the central task of local government; 'politics' is therefore to be minimized.

Furthermore, the reformers believed that these general principles could be realized through changes in the structure of local government. As Richard Childs, one of the leading municipal reformers, stated, 'The difficulties of democracy . . . are mechanistic, not moral, and respond to mechanistic corrections' (quoted in Stone et al., 1986: 109). The three most important structural changes they favoured were the council-manager system of government, at large (rather than ward or district) elections and non-partisan ballots. The nature and rationale for the council-manager system has been discussed above (see p. 139); at-large elections and non-partisanship were both viewed as means of eliminating conflict based on narrow interests and permitting problem solving based on the public interest. At-large elections were preferred to elections by wards which, the reformers believed, encouraged the pursuit of narrow geographic (and, given patterns of residential segregation, group based) interests rather than the general interest. In addition, ward elections led to a focus on constituency favours and a politics of political trade-off and logrolling among the representatives of the various districts rather than a politics of deliberation. Partisan politics interjected irrelevant partisan political considerations into what properly should be deliberations concerned with economy and efficiency in the provision and delivery of local services. As Andrew White, one of the earliest proponents of municipal reform, observed:

My fundamental contention is that the city is a corporation; that as a city it has nothing to do with general political interests; that political party names and duties are utterly out of place there. The questions in a city are not political questions. They have reference to the laying out of streets; to the erection of buildings; to sanitary arrangements, sewerage, water supply, gas supply, electrical supply; to the control of franchises and the like; and to provisions for the public health and comfort in parks, boulevards, libraries and museums. (1890: 271–2)

The institutional structures favoured by the reformers reflected the values of economy and efficiency rather than the values of participation and pluralism and representative democracy. Indeed, the reform movement and the institutional reforms it spawned have been heavily criticized for this emphasis and for its presumed consequences. Judd (1984), Judd and Swanstrom (1994), Stone et al. (1986) and others have attacked the class basis of the institutional reforms. Reformers were predominantly upper middle class and business oriented and their concern for economy and efficiency coincided nicely with their own self-interest, even if expressed in universalistic terms of the general good. Judd and Swanstrom argue that:

> Reform was inspired by class antagonisms. Changes in electoral rules and in the structure of city government were designed to undercut the power of lower-class groups. . . . Analysis of the social class background of reformers reveals, especially in the big cities, a uniformly upper-class bias. Studies of the origins of reform movements show that business and upper-class elements normally championed reform, while lower- and working-class groups usually opposed it . . . These groups were keenly aware of their political interests. The expectation that new forms of government would result in the election of a 'better' class of citizens, meaning businessmen or their favored candidates, was usually fulfilled . . . Opponents of the . . . manager plans were just as aware of their political interests. Machine politicians, socialists, and trade unionists opposed the plans because they rightly perceived that centralized electoral systems and decision-making processes would make it more difficult for working-class candidates to gain public office. (1994: 98–9)

Judd and Swanstrom argue, in effect, that the pursuit of the values of economy and efficiency in the name of the general interest had distributional implications that were not neutral in terms of the values of pluralism and representative democracy. To what extent does the evidence bear out these contentions?

There has been a substantial volume of empirical research on the impact of local government institutional reform (see Welch and Bledsoe (1988) and Svara (1990) for reviews of much of this literature). In briefly reviewing this literature, I will focus on the effects of reform of institutional structures on the various values that have been predominantly associated with local government in the United States – namely, (1) participation, (2) representation, (3) responsiveness (particularly to group concerns), and (4) economy and efficiency. I will also address the more general question of the effect of reform structures on policy outcomes and the distribution of these outcomes, an important concern of the critics of reform.

It seems clear that non-partisan election systems do reduce voter participation since they eliminate party 'cues' for voting choice; controlling for other variables, turnout is consistently lower in non-partisanship systems (Karnig and Welch, 1983: 498). With respect to representation, Welch and Bledsoe cite literature suggesting a 'strong negative effect of at-large elections on black representation (1988: 106). This is because black population is likely, in nearly all American cities, to be concentrated in specific geographic areas that are easily outvoted in at-large elections but would be represented in district elections. Welch and Bledsoe also cite studies indicating that black representation is likely to be adversely affected by non-partisan elections (1988: 11).

Welch and Bledsoe (1988: 37 ff.) and Svara (1990: 62) both report empirical research showing that 'reform' characteristics are associated with somewhat higher council representation by higher income and more highly educated council members. Based on their own study of a sample of over 1600 council members in cities between 50,000 and one million in population and analysis of the data to control for confounding factors, Welch and Bledsoe (1988: 106) found that council members from at large systems tended to have higher income and more education than those from district systems and that council members in non-partisan systems tended to have higher income than those from partisan systems. They attribute this to the importance of name recognition and media (requiring financial resources to purchase) in the absence of party cues and to the lower turnout associated with non-partisan elections, since low turnout usually is associated with higher rates of non-voting among low income and less well educated voters.

Early research also found that non-partisan political systems resulted in a higher proportion of Republican council members (that is, members whose personal political preferences were Republican) than did partisan systems. Welch and Bledsoe (1988: 50–1) found that a *general* bias of non-partisan systems towards Republicans did not exist; however, they did find that such a bias was present in smaller cities, in the West, and in cities that had both non-partisan systems and at-large elections.

Welch and Bledsoe conclude:

> It is clear that, with the low turnout to municipal elections . . . few councils can claim to be fully representative of the population. The lower classes, probably largely Democratic in their predispositions, are underrepresented no matter what the electoral system. But our findings support the argument that some kinds of structures block representation of these groups more than do others. When nonpartisan and at-large structures are combined, both lower income and educational level groups and Democrats are strongly disadvantaged. The Republican advantage occurs most strongly under conditions that inhibit the organization and size of groups representing neighbourhood and ethnic interests. (1988: 52–3)

Critics of reform have argued that not only are reform structures unrepresentative, as discussed above, but they are also unresponsive to the variety of groups that make up the community. Lineberry and Fowler (1967) used a variety of community characteristics reflecting interest differences in the community (for example, percentage non-white, percentage foreign born, percentage owner-occupied dwellings, percentage high income and percentage low income) as predictors of municipal outputs in both reformed and unreformed cities. They found that these variables were able to predict outcomes much better in unreformed than in reformed cities. They conclude:

> The translation of social conflicts into public policy and the responsiveness of political systems to class, racial and religious cleavages differ markedly with the kind of political structure . . . Through these [reform] political institutions, the goal of the reformers has been substantially fulfilled, for nonpartisan elections, at-large constituencies and manager governments are associated with a lessened responsiveness of cities to the enduring conflicts of political life. (Lineberry and Fowler, 1967: 715)

Dutton and Northrup (1978) examined the relationship of government structure (reformed structure, unreformed and mixed) to group influence in cities over 50,000 and found there was a positive association between council-manager cities and the influence of business and middle-class groups such as bankers, developers, real estate brokers and good government groups. They also found a negative association between council-manager cities and the influence of labour unions, ethnic groups and church leaders. No relationship was found between form of government and the influence of minority groups. Reviewing the literature following Lineberry and Fowler, Svara concludes that there is less responsiveness to population characteristics in reformed cities and that 'reform institutions . . . mute the translation of environmental factors into policy and may diminish responsiveness to ethnic groups in the city, but do not necessarily diminish response to need based on race or socio-economic status' (1990: 66).

The effect of structure on policy outcomes has proven controversial and elusive in the empirical literature. Welch and Bledsoe (1988: 104) found no consistent differences in policy *attitudes* among council members by type of government structure. In terms of policy *output* the results are mixed. Lineberry and Fowler (1967) found that cities with reform structures were associated with lower spending per capita than were unreformed cities, a result they attributed to the relative lack of responsiveness of public officials to groups in the environment discussed above. Clark's research (1968) yielded exactly the opposite results. Morgan and Pelissero (1980) examined 11 cities in which government structure had changed from unreformed to reformed or vice versa. Using interrupted time series analysis they were unable to find any relationship between change in government structure and per capita spending.

Although it is widely believed that council-manager systems with professionally trained city managers provide more efficient and low cost service delivery than do unreformed systems, Svara (1990: 61) notes that there are almost no empirical studies on the effect of government structure differences on efficiency. He does cite Stone et al.'s (1986) finding that unit prices for services were lower in council-manager cities. However, a recent study by two economists (Hayes and Chang, 1990) found no difference in the relative efficiency of mayor-council and council-manager systems of government when environmental variables were controlled for.

In sum, it does appear that characteristics associated with the reform structure have adverse consequences for several of the values underlying American conceptions of local democracy, in particular participation and representation and pluralist democracy. Its ethos certainly supports the values of economy and efficiency and it may be that reform governments do indeed provide local services more efficiently. However, while they may be more efficient, they are also less responsible. In summarizing the consequences of the reform movement, Stone et al. observe:

> reform politics weakens the representation of particular groups, especially if those groups are of lower status, have no citywide base of operation, or rank low in civic prestige. Citizen participation in making policy tends to occur through blue-ribbon committees, that is, committees composed mainly of upper-status business and professional purposes ... Reform politics appears in its purest form in affluent suburbs. The homogeneous, middle-class setting produces the least tension between reform institutions and the clientele that those institutions serve. In a large-city setting, the story is different. Because reform structures and practices are not attuned to the diversity of city life, minorities, especially those of lower status, have no easy avenues of political expression. Reform represents majority views more easily than the views of discrete segments of a large community. Moreover, by weakening overtly political institutions, reform dims the public voice of the lower-class. Middle- and upper-class groups retain a channel of expression through various civic organizations, but the lower class has need for direct political representation – for the personal link between constituent and representative. (1986: 117)

The debate in the UK

In Britain the empirical literature on the effect of government structure is sparse. The debate has been carried on primarily through reports of and responses to various government commissions and government issue papers. The most significant of these include the Maud Report on Management of Local Government (1967), the report of the Royal Commission on Local Government chaired by Redcliffe-Maud (1969), the Bains Study Group on The New Local Authorities: Management and Structure (1972), the Widdicombe Commission on the Conduct of Local Authority Business (1986), and the Department of the Environment's consultation paper on The Internal Management of Local Authorities in England (1991).

Since, as has been emphasized above, the British place primary concern on efficiency as the value local government is to pursue, the debate has focused on the structural and institutional changes that would increase that end. The terms of reference for the Bains report, for example, reflects this concern: 'To set out the considerations which, in the Group's opinion, should be borne in mind by local authorities in determining their structures of management at elected member and officer levels including particularly internal arrangements bearing on efficiency' (1972: 1).

members who would serve as political heads of individual service departments and would be responsible to the council; and (3) a separation of power system involving either an elected executive such as a mayor or an appointive executive such as a city manager. Ultimately the Commission rejected all three of these proposals as inappropriate for British local authorities, arguing (1986: 35) that the defects flowing from the lack of a formal executive structure were substantially mitigated by informal processes and devices, particularly those related to the party/partisan nature of British local government. Thus, meetings of party groups, party based informal briefing groups, and members of informal 'inner circles' or, as Stoker (1991: 92) terms them 'joint elites' (consisting of a small group of leading councillors and officers) serve to provide a greater degree of priority-setting and coordination than is conventionally thought to occur. Indeed, the Commission found such 'inner circles' to exist in about two thirds of all local authorities. They concluded:

> we believe that the onus of proof should always be on those who propose institutional change, especially where this is of a major structural character. Great Britain has a strong tradition of evolutionary change and improvisation in its institutional arrangements and a healthy suspicion of solutions that are theoretically logical or transplanted from elsewhere. Unless there is a clear case to the contrary it is preferable to build on what is already there. (1986: 76)

In 1991 the Department of the Environment issued a consultation paper on the internal management of local authorities in which it invited comment and discussion on a number of proposed options including retention of the present system, adaptation of the existing committee system (for example, allowing councils to delegate decision-making authority to committee chairmen), or institution of a new system such as a cabinet system, appointment of a council manager, a directly elected plural executive, or a directly elected mayor. Indeed, the then Secretary of State for the Environment, Michael Heseltine, indicated substantial interest in the directly elected mayor option. The consultation paper, perhaps for the first time, elicited a public debate about possible changes in the basic internal structure of local government, with editorials in papers such as *The Times* supporting the concept. However, the subsequent government report was much more timid, calling for only incremental adjustments in the present system. It did, however, support legislation that would permit a local authority, if it wished, to experiment with more radical departures, including the replacement of the existing political structure by executive models. A more recent (Department of the Environment (1993) Departmental Working Party argued that the need for a political executive had implicitly been recognized by local authorities and was in the process of evolutionary development from within the existing system in the form of a collective political executive based on majority party control. It urged local authorities to experiment with a variety of models of collective political executives.

In addition to concern about placement of the executive function in British local government and the need for policy coordination, there has also been a rather low level though persistent debate over the appropriate size for local councils and the methods for electing them. This debate, too, has been pursued primarily with a concern for its efficiency considerations. Various commissions have suggested that the relatively large size of local councils (ranging, according to the Widdicombe Commission, from 20 to 117 members for English local authorities and averaging above 50) is unwieldy and impedes management efficiency. It has also been argued that the large size of councils results in lowering the calibre of council members. However, opponents argue that reduction of council size would reduce democracy by increasing the number of constituents that each councillor represents and thus increasing the distance between elector and representative. The Widdicombe Commission lamely concludes: 'There is no simple solution to the question of council size. We consider that it should be reviewed in greater depth to see whether some reduction, to increase efficiency, would be compatible with maintaining the quality of democracy' (1986: 173).

As the above discussion undoubtedly suggests, the nature of the British debate, consumed as it is with its concern for efficiency, seems relatively tame when placed beside the American debate over the impact of structure on local government values. Dearlove (1979) has attacked both the nature of the debate and the academic research related to it, particularly with respect to the unarticulated assumptions underlying it. His critique, which is in much the same tradition as Judd's and Swanstrom's and Stone's critiques of the American reform movement cited above, is worth quoting at length.

> It is of political significance that *the* problem of local government has continually been defined as one of inefficiency and that the goal of reorganizations has been to increase it. (p. 78)

> I reject that apolitical presumption entrenched in the reformist literature which sees government reform as bringing the benefit of efficiency, effectiveness, and democracy to all at the same time as it harms absolutely no one. The reformist orientation has been dominant for so long that it does not admit the possibility of overtly political questions about reorganization that centre on its inevitable implications for the control of governmental power and public policy to the advantage of some groups over others. (p. 12)

> A political perspective on reorganization has to recognize that new boundaries, new structures, and new processes all have implications for the access of different interests to local government, and, therefore, for the likely direction of public policy. (p. 14)

> The goal of efficiency is the natural political objective of those classes which, in seeking to minimize both conflict and politics, also seeks to minimize government. (p. 78)

> Advocates of reorganization have been intent on relocating local political power away from the working class. (p. 8)

The concern about declining council calibre embodies a bitter lament that a variety of changes have conspired to result in a situation in which there is now a less close and direct relationship between economic power, social status, and the political control of local government than was once the case in the Victorian age when local government enjoyed the leadership of businessmen and local notables . . . In effect, the concern to increase calibre embodies a concern to recapture the social relations, style of politics, and class of leadership, that existed before the franchise was extended and before the working class rose to some sort of position of local political power through the Labour Party. (p. 8)

There is no study which discusses the various facets of reorganization as they relate to each other, which sees reorganization as about who will control and benefit from local government, and which seeks to understand it all by looking at it in the context of the developing political economy. (p. 6)

Critique and assessment

The traditional debate over structure appears to have reached somewhat of a dead end in both countries, although for different reasons. In the United States, the debate has been interesting and productive; it has been concerned both with normative theory – what values should local government promote – and empirical theory – to what extent do various local government institutional forms and structures promote these values? With respect to the latter, there is widespread agreement that local government institutional structure does make a difference in terms of some important values and that, in particular, reform structures are more likely to promote efficiency values and unreformed structures are more likely to promote values of participation and pluralist democracy. There remains substantial contention about the extent to which structure actually affects policy outputs (expenditure per capita is the measure of output most frequently utilized), but the literature appears to have degenerated into methodological disputation, a sure sign that sterility has set in.

In Britain, the debate has traditionally been overwhelmingly about means rather than ends. The concern has been with structural characteristics that will best promote the goal of efficiency; the question of whether efficiency should be the predominant value local government should promote has not been seriously contested. The terms of the debate have been highly technocratic, although the recent concern with more fundamental structural change has been invigorating.

In both countries there has been a very useful change in the focus of debate from more formal institutional structure to institutional norms underpinning local government activity. In Britain the traditional organization of local government has come under questioning recently, particularly with respect to the role of local government as *direct* service provider. From all sides of the political spectrum there have been calls for local government to think of itself as an 'enabler' rather than a direct provider of services (see Cochrane (1991) for a review of this discussion). On the right, Nicholas Ridley has argued that government must restructure itself as an 'enabling authority', commenting that, 'Authorities will need to operate in a more pluralist way than in the past, alongside a wide variety of public, private and voluntary services. It will be their task to stimulate and assist these other agencies to play their part instead of, or as well as, making provision themselves' (quoted in Cochrane, 1991: 283). Local government's role thus would be to arrange for the provision of services in response to local needs, but not necessarily to produce and deliver every service itself. In short, local government might *purchase* services, but would not necessarily *provide* all of them. Indeed, the Thatcher government moved this from a mere exhortation to a mandate with legislation requiring local authorities to subject a wide range of traditionally directly provided local government services and activities to compulsory tendering (that is, to a process in which private firms – along with local authority units – were permitted to bid on the provision). The emphasis on local services and efficiency as the rationale for local government remains, but the changed emphasis has led to debate over different structural forms – such as greater decentralization – as well.

On the left there has also been discussion about the need for local government to assume a responsibility much wider and broader than simply that of service provider or enabler. John Stewart, who has been perhaps the leading voice in this debate, advocates the concept of 'community government':

> If one abandons the assumption that the primary role of local authorities is to act as agencies for the administration of a series of separate services, then a new basis for the future of local government can be explored . . . As community government, local authorities' primary role is concern for the problems and issues faced by local communities. They are the means by which communities confront and resolve those problems and issues that are beyond the scope of individuals or other modes of social action. The concept of community government is not based on the idealistic picture of local communities. It recognizes within communities many differing interests and values. Conflicts exist as well as shared purposes. Community government is achieved through political processes that express different interests and values and seek their resolution in political action. A local authority is a political institution for the authoritative determination of community values. (Stewart, 1989: 240–1)

Stewart's conception of 'community government' (which begins to resemble the American version of pluralism discussed above) also implies changes in local government structure and organization. Stewart questions not only the existing committee structure as the basis for internal decision making, but also the extent and degree of citizen involvement, since without more citizen involvement differences in community values will be stifled. He supports such structural changes as proportional representation, referenda, user involvement in the provision of services, and elected neighbourhood councils.

The similarities and tensions between the two different concepts of enabling authorities are captured by Stewart and Stoker:

The Government has argued that local authorities should increasingly become enabling authorities, securing provision rather than providing services directly themselves ... The Government's proposals limit the concept of the enabling authority, because far from being based on extending the powers and resources available to a local authority they are directed at weakening its present leverage through direct provision ... The enabling role offered by the Government is a negative one, defined by what a local authority may *not* do. It is not a positive one extending the capacity of a local authority to meet the needs of those who live and work within its area, either directly or through another agency. This is not to argue for the rejection of the enabling role. Local authorities have too often assumed that their only role is direct provision and have let themselves become more concerned with the administration of services rather than with the needs of their areas. (1988: 5)

In the United States a similar shift in the debate about appropriate local government institutions, away from a concern with formal structure and towards more informal operational norms, has occurred. Although the terms of the debate in the United States have been more explicitly dominated by public choice theorists, the similarity to British concerns described above is striking. Ostrom et al. (1988), Savas (1987) and others distinguish between the *provision* of services by local government and their *production*. They note that traditionally local governments have provided services by establishing and managing their own producing bureaucracies. They argue, however, that there are a variety of other logically possible ways of producing services and that, in many circumstances, one or more of these may be more appropriate (efficient) than direct service delivery. Ostrom et al. cite: 'contracting with a private producer, contracting with another government, establishing a producer organization in cooperation with other governments, licensing private firms to operate on a franchise basis, and providing citizens with vouchers to make their own arrangements with producers' (1988: 99). They note that many local governments already engage in these activities and call upon ever greater consideration and use.

Osborne and Gaebler (1992b) go even further in their popular and influential book, *Reinventing Government*, a book which has been widely read and cited in Britain as well as the United States. In their catch phrase, local government should be concerned with *steering* rather than *rowing*. Rather than a new set of formal institutional structures, they call for a new ethos and set of operating norms that they characterize as entrepreneurial local government, a concept that bears much in common with Stewart's conception of community government discussed above. Entrepreneurial local governments:

promote *competition* between service providers. They *empower* citizens by pushing control out of the bureaucracy, into the community. They measure the performance of their agencies, focusing not on inputs but on *outcomes*. They are driven by their goals – their *missions* – not by their rules and regulations. They redefine their clients as *customers* and offer them choices – between schools, between training programs, between housing options. They *prevent* problems before they emerge, rather than simply offering services afterward. They put their energies into *earning* money, not simply spending it. They *decentralize* authority, embracing participatory management. They prefer *market* mechanisms to bureaucratic mechanisms. And they focus not simply on providing public services, but on *catalyzing* all sectors – public, private and voluntary – into action to solve their community's problems. (Osborne and Gaebler, 1992a: 47, original emphasis)

It is fair to say that the values underpinning the reinventing government approach, like those of Ostrom et al. and Savas, are primarily those of efficiency, but unlike the latter they are broader than more narrow economistic efficiency concerns. Instead the focus is on creating a government with the capacity to act effectively to achieve its objectives.

Another recent approach to institutions challenges both traditional normative conceptions of the role of local government and the nature of appropriate institutions. Its concern is with political structures to bring about greater democratic participation, but in communitarian rather than in classical liberal terms. Both Barber (1984) and Elkin (1987) have argued that local government ought to promote 'thick' or 'strong' rather than 'thin' democracy, involving the active participation of citizens, interacting with each other to address community concerns. As Barber argues, 'To be a citizen *is* to participate in a certain conscious fashion that presumes awareness of and engagement in activity with others' (1984: 155). Berry et al. summarize the communitarian participation argument:

There is widespread agreement that democracy in America needs renewal. Too few people participate in the governmental process . . . Rebuilding citizenship in America means that reform must move beyond getting more people into private voting booths to getting more people to public forums where they can work with their neighbors to solve the problems of their community . . . In face-to-face meetings, men and women can learn from each other, reason with one another, and search for common interests. Face-to-face democracy moves politics away from its adversarial norm, where interest groups square off in conflict and lobbyists speak for their constituents. Instead, the bonds of friendship and community are forged as neighbors look for common solutions to their problems. Political participation becomes an educative device rather than an occasionally exercised civic obligation. (1993: 1–3)

Elkin, in a similar vein, argues that the purpose of local government is the creation of a citizenry able and willing to engage in reasoned public debate about public issues. He argues that this has direct implications for urban political institutions. Such institutions should be structured 'to help form a citizenry that has a concern for the public interest' (1987: 150) so that the citizenry will engage in – and encourage local public officials to engage in – reasoned debate about the public interest and public policy. Elkin criticizes existing city political institutions, which he characterizes as executive-centred, as not conducive to reasoned public debate. Instead, he advocates institutions 'legislative in form and public in debate'. Such institutions include neighbourhood assemblies with real powers, city-wide referenda, and city legislatures, also with significant powers.

As Elkin's discussion suggests, the institutional implications of communitarian participation involve decentralized, neighbourhood political institutions. (This connects with reinventing government and community government discussed above, although the emphasis of the communitarians is certainly not efficiency related.) Stewart (1989) and Stewart and Stoker (1988) have advocated similar devices as part of democratic participation in a British community government. And, in both countries the new academic literature coincides with recent increases in the formation and activity of neighbourhood and community groups involved in the political process.

However, the impact of decentralized neighbourhood institutions may not necessarily lead to the informed and reasoned debate among citizens envisioned by the communitarians. There are a series of concerns: will decentralized institutions indeed increase the rate and level of citizen participation or will they merely provide a venue for a small number of self-selected community activists? Will such institutions promote reasoned public debate about community issues or will they result in defensive actions to preserve the character of their community, at the extremes excluding 'others' from entering or participating? How can decentralized political control be reconciled with wider community interests, particularly over questions such as the location of unwanted facilities or services (the NIMBY – 'not in my backyard' – syndrome)? Will decentralized institutions contribute to or detract from efficiency values? Will decentralized political institutions lead to effective government – that is, government capable of pursuing successfully its objectives – or will it lead to increased fragmentation, political conflict and gridlock?

Berry et al. (1993) have examined some of these questions empirically. They identified five US cities with strong well-functioning neighbourhood political institutions structured formally as part of the city political system. In addition, each of these cities was matched with two others similar in both size and socioeconomic characteristics. Interviews were then conducted with a random sample of citizens in each of the cities. While Berry et al. strongly support neighbourhood political institutions, they nonetheless report such institutions do not result in increased political participation: 'The data are unequivocal: overall participation in the five cities is similar to that in the comparison groups. The structures of strong democracy do not bring people out of the woodwork' (1993: 294). However, they also report that city politicians and administrators accept the neighbourhood associations as legitimate participants in city politics and do not engage in excessive conflict with them. They observe that these neighbourhood associations are effective participants in city politics and that decentralized political institutions promote the participation of groups in city politics to a greater extent than is the case in other cities where political scientists have found politics to be largely devoid of organized group activity. They also find that decentralized political institutions did not lead to governmental paralysis, gridlock and ineffective government.

Lowndes and Stoker (1992) come to similarly modest conclusions about neighbourhood decentralization in England based on their study of Tower Hamlets, a London borough that engaged in substantial neighbourhood decentralization after the 1986 electoral victory of the 'community politics' oriented Liberal Party. They note that participation did indeed increase through the decentralized advisory structures, but that participation on such advisory bodies did not imply control or even influence. Nor, according to Lowndes and Stoker, did decentralization necessarily result in improved service delivery, at least as measured by citizen satisfaction.

Thus, in both countries the debate about the appropriate nature of local government institutions (in relation to the values they are expected to promote) has begun to shift towards new and provocative directions. Nonetheless, the debate over institutional structure in the United States continues to be also much more explicitly a debate over values, while the debate in Britain continues to take place mostly within the presumed accepted value structure of local government's role as an efficient and effective provider of services.

References

Abbott, P. (1991) *Political Thought in America*. Itasca, IL: F.E. Peacock.
Bains, M. (Chairman) (1972) *The New Local Authorities: Management and Structure*. London: HMSO.
Barber, B. (1984) *Strong Democracy*. Berkeley: University of California Press.
Berry, J.M., Portnoy, K.E. and Thomson, K. (1993) *The Rebirth of Urban Democracy*. Washington, D.C.: Brookings Institution.
Boaden, N., Goldsmith, M., Hampton, W. and Stringer, P. (1982) *Public Participation in Local Services*. Harlow: Longman.
Clark, T. (1968) 'Community structure, decision making, budget expenditures, and urban renewal in 51 American cities', *American Sociological Review*, 33: 576–93.
Cochrane, A. (1991) 'The changing state of local government: restructuring in the 90s', *Public Administration*, 69: 281–303.
Dearlove, J. (1979) *The Reorganization of British Local Government*. Cambridge: Cambridge University Press.
Department of the Environment (1991) *The Internal Management of Local Authorities in England*. London: Department of the Environment.
Department of the Environment (1993) 'Working party on the internal management of local authorities', *Community Leadership and Representation: Unlocking the Potential*. London: HMSO.
de Tocqueville, A. (1954) *Democracy in America. Vol. 1*. New York: Vintage Books.
Dutton, W. and Northrup, A. (1978) 'Municipal reform and the changing pattern of urban party politics', *American Politics Quarterly*, 6: 429–52.
Elkin, S. (1987) *City and Regime in the American Republic*. Chicago, IL: University of Chicago Press.
Hayes, K. and Chang, S. (1990) 'The relative efficiency of city manager and mayor council forms of government', *Southern Economic Journal*, 57: 167–77.
Hampton, W. (1987) *Local Government and Urban Politics*. London: Longman.
Hofstadter, R. (1955) *The Age of Reform*. New York: Vintage Books.
Huntington, S. (1959) 'The Founding Fathers and the division of powers', in A. Maas (ed.), *Area and Power*, Glencoe, IL: The Free Press.

Judd, D. (1984) *The Politics of American Cities*. Boston, MA: Little Brown.

Judd, D. and Swanstrom, T. (1994) *City Politics: Private Power and Public Policy*. New York: HarperCollins.

Karnig, A. and Welch, S. (1983) 'Decline in municipal voting turnout', *American Politics Quarterly*, 11: 491–506.

Leach, S. (1989) 'Strengthening local democracy? The government's response to Widdicombe', in J. Stewart and G. Stoker (eds), *The Future of Local Government*. London: Macmillan.

Leach, S. and Stewart, J. (1986) 'The workings of local government', in H. Davis (ed.), *The Future Role and Organization of Local Government*. Birmingham: Institute of Local Government Studies, University of Birmingham.

Lineberry, R.L. and Fowler, E.P. (1967) 'Reformism and public policies in American cities', *American Political Science Review*, 61 (Sept.): 701–16.

Lowndes, V. and Stoker, G. (1992) 'An evaluation of neighborhood decentralisation', *Policy and Politics*, 20: 47–61.

Maud, Sir John (Chairman) (1967) *Committee on the Management of Local Government*. Vol. 1, London: HMSO.

Morgan, D. and Pelissero, J. (1980) 'Urban policy: does political structure matter?', *American Political Science Review*, 74: 999–1006.

National Municipal League (1939) 'Forms of government: how have they worked?', New York: National Municipal League.

Osborne, D. and Gaebler, T. (1992a) 'Bringing government back to life', *Governing*, 5 (5): 46–50.

Osborne, D. and Gaebler, T. (1992b) *Reinventing Government*. Reading, MA: Addison Wesley.

Ostrom, V., Bish, R. and Ostrom, E. (1988) *Local Government in the United States*. San Francisco, CA: ICS Press.

Redcliffe-Maud (Chairman) (1969) *Royal Commission on Local Government*. Vol. 1 Report, Cmnd. 4040, London: HMSO.

Savas, E. (1987) *Privatization: The Key to Better Government*. Chatham, NJ: Chatham House.

Sharpe, J. (1970) 'Theories and values of local government', *Political Studies*, 18 (2): 153–74.

Sharpe, J. (1973) 'American democracy reconsidered', Parts I and II, *British Journal of Political Science*, 3 (1–2): 129–67.

Stewart, J. (1989) 'The changing organization and management of local authorities', in J. Stewart and G. Stoker (eds), *The Future of Local Government*. London: Macmillan.

Stewart, J. and Stoker, G. (1988) 'From local administration to community government', Fabian Research Series, No. 351, London: College Hill Press Ltd.

Stillman, R.J. (1974) *Rise of the City Manager*. Alburquerque: University of New Mexico Press.

Stoker, G. (1991) *The Politics of Local Government*. London: Macmillan.

Stone, L., Whelan, R. and Murin, W. (1986) *Urban Policy and Politics in a Bureaucratic Age*. Englewood Cliffs, NJ: Prentice-Hall.

Svara, J. (1990) *Official Leadership in the City*. Oxford: Oxford University Press.

Syed, A. (1966) *The Political Theory of American Local Government*. New York: Random House.

Welch, S. and Bledsoe, T. (1988) *Urban Reform and Its Consequences*. Chicago, IL: University of Chicago Press.

White, A. (1890) 'The government of American Cities', *Forum*, reprinted in E. Banfield (ed.) (1969), *Urban Government*. New York: Free Press.

Widdicombe, D. (1986) *The Conduct of Local Authority Business. Report of the Committee of Inquiry into the Conduct of Local Authority Business*, Cmnd. 9797, London: HMSO.

Part III

URBAN POLITICS AND ITS CITIZENS

9

Citizenship and Urban Politics

Vivien Lowndes

Until quite recently citizenship was considered a rather 'old fashioned' term in social science. As part of the formal language of constitutions, it conjured up an image of 'model citizens' who bore little resemblance to the diverse, and often unruly, populations of our towns and cities. In the 1990s we are witnessing a revival of interest in citizenship. This interest arises out of a renewed concern with the 'triangle' of relationships between individuals, communities and government. Specifically, it reflects a concern that such relationships are breaking down: that individuals are alienated from their communities and that government institutions are inaccessible and unresponsive. An old fashioned term is being resurrected to address an old fashioned problem: what is the nature of the bond which links individuals, communities and government, and how can it be sustained? Drawing on ideas from philosophy and political theory that date back to the ancient Greeks, social scientists are reinterpreting the concept of citizenship to help us understand the dynamics of urban politics today.

The first part of this chapter looks at the classic arguments linking citizenship and urban politics, focusing on the themes of community identification, political participation and political education. The second part of the chapter considers the current revival of interest – in theoretical and policy terms – in citizenship, distinguishing between an 'individual rights' and a 'community membership' perspective.

Citizenship and urban politics: key arguments

What do theories of citizenship have to offer an understanding of urban politics? To be a citizen is to be a member of a political community with rights and responsibilities in respect of that community. While it is the nation state that ascribes the status of citizenship to the individual, many of the rights and duties of citizenship are exercised at the local level. It is at the level of the town or city that people usually come into contact with politicians or public officials, receive services and benefits from the state, and organize together in communities.

The link between the concepts of citizenship and city life goes back to the Athenian city state, where democracy had a 'face to face' quality, based upon public meetings and open debate. In medieval times, the term 'citizen' referred simply to a city-dweller, who had certain rights not available to those who lived beyond the city wall. As Rousseau put it in *The Social Contract*: 'houses make a town, but citizens a city'. Today the dictionary still defines citizen as 'inhabitant of city'.

The link between citizenship and urban politics has a long theoretical history and rests upon three propositions:

1   Citizenship derives from community identification and membership.
2   Civic action and political participation is concentrated at the local level.
3   Local governance and urban politics provide an 'education for citizenship'.

I look at these three, overlapping, arguments below, seeking to trace their origins and assess their contemporary relevance.

Citizenship and community identification

Marshall (1964) argues that citizenship involves 'the sentiment of belonging directly to a community, based on loyalty *vis-à-vis* a civilisation which is truly common to all'. Held (1993: 45) notes that the history and practice of citizenship has traditionally been centred on the idea of geographically defined communities. In modern democracies, citizenship operates at different 'levels'. While the nation is the principal collectivity which ascribes citizenship status to its members, certain rights and obligations are derived at other levels too – the municipality, the region, the state (within federal systems), and even at the supranational level (for instance the European Union). As Prior et al. put it: 'Which level of collectivity is most appropriate to citizenship will vary over time and according to the particular aspect of citizenship under consideration' (1993: 2). While the right to travel freely between countries may be based upon international conventions, the right to receive welfare benefits is likely to be based upon national laws which are then interpreted and implemented at the municipal level.

The significance of local governance and urban politics for citizenship can be expressed in both 'practical' and 'moral' terms. For practical and technical reasons, political and administrative functions are decentralized to the local level. The right to free education, for instance, may be guaranteed at the national level, while the allocation of school places and the management of schools are local matters. The obligation to pay taxes may be established nationally, while tax collection is decentralized to the local level. This practical argument sees our towns and cities as key arenas for the acting out of the rights and duties of citizenship. Municipalities are seen as useful subdivisions of the larger, primary political community.

Alternatively, the significance of the local arena for citizenship can be understood in 'moral' terms. According to this view, identification with local communities is seen as fundamental to citizenship. Rather than seeing the national political community as divided into local communities, such communities can be seen as the building blocks for national democracy. Local political institutions may be seen as a reflection, and continuation of, 'a prior and more natural form of democracy than national democracy' (Smith, 1985: 24). Citizenship at the national level can be seen to flow from community identification and membership at the local level, not vice versa. According to this view, local governance and urban politics have a moral and symbolic significance as well as a practical relevance. In short, the local community is seen as the well-spring of citizenship.

The link between citizenship and community identification dates back to the idea of the Athenian city state or 'polis'. Citizenship was expressed through practical and direct participation in the democratic process – attending public meetings, debating issues, carrying out decisions – all without the mediation of a government bureaucracy. Plato advises that the number of citizens should not exceed 5,000 as this would hinder face-to-face contact. The link between community and citizenship dominates de Tocqueville's commentary on democracy in nineteenth-century America. In his study of the New England township, de Tocqueville highlights the role of the 'town father' who, moved initially by self-interest, involves himself in local civic associations and self-government. Through this process he learns the practice of citizenship and democracy. As de Tocqueville explains:

> In the restricted sphere within his scope, he learns to rule society; he gets to know those formalities without which freedom can advance only through revolutions, and becoming imbued with their spirit, develops a taste for order, understands the harmony of powers, and in the end accumulates clear, practical ideas about the nature of his duties and the extent of his rights. (1946: 66)

The link between community identification and citizenship is the subject of much debate. Sceptics ask how relevant community identification is in the cities of the 1990s. Does a sense of community exist in the face of today's aggressive individualism? If community *is* important, is it any longer based on locality? Or are 'communities of interest' more important – based on identities like age and ethnicity, or particular interests and causes (like sport, music or environmental campaigning)? And, most importantly, does community membership and feeling give rise to any sense of civic culture and citizenship?

The classic argument about citizenship and community identification is itself contradictory. Weber saw citizenship as the *antithesis* to traditional community loyalty. He linked the spread of urban living and the development of the formal status of 'citizen' to the broader 'rationalization' of life. As Turner explains: 'to become urban was to "citizenize" the person' (1992: 49). Citizenship was seen in terms of the liberation of individuals from ancient ties of locality and tradition. De Tocqueville (1946: 66) himself saw the basis of the New England township as the recognition of interdependence among *self-reliant* individuals and families. This reflects the Jeffersonian tradition within American politics which sees self-government as the expression of the sovereignty of the individual (Wolman and Goldsmith, 1992: 10). According to this tradition, a commitment to local self-government and participation does not preclude a belief in individualism and minimal government. This uneasy balance between the rights of individuals and the needs of communities is mirrored in city life itself, which is characterized both by individualism and anonymity and by interdependence and proximity to others.

The relationship between community and citizenship is still more controversial in the face of changes in urban life. One line of argument, which resonates with many popular and 'common sense' conceptions, casts doubt over the continued relevance of community membership and identification in the 1990s. It is argued that local community is less significant in the context of broad social and economic trends. Patterns of industrial restructuring often mean people work far from home, and the fate of local economies is determined by international capital flows and investment decisions. At the same time the globalization of culture and the explosion of communications suggests that people are less tied to their immediate localities. In urban areas particularly, increasing social heterogeneity can mean that the immediate locality is less important as a focus for identification and involvement than non-geographical 'communities of interest'. Localities are increasingly made up of many different communities, each with their own identity, civic associations and political agendas. As community is progressively delinked from locality, its relevance as an organizing principle in urban politics decreases. It is argued that the new realities of urban life are associated with a new cluster of ideas – around choice, diversity, pluralism and competition – which constitute new organizing principles for urban politics and citizenship.

In contrast, a second line of argument claims that social and economic changes are leading people to become *more* rather than less attached to their locality and immediate community. At the corporate level, the marketing of 'place' becomes more important as businesses (in conjunction with government institutions and development agencies) seek to attract investment within a world market (Cochrane, 1991). The differentiation of one place from another becomes ever more important, whether expressed in terms of 'objective' factors like labour costs, land prices, communication links and tax breaks, or 'subjective' factors relating to its culture, appearance and general ambience. For individual citizens, place also gains in importance. Among the better-off, those with more leisure time and those who have invested heavily in the infrastructure of consumption (home ownership, private schooling and so on) feel practically and emotionally attached to their locality (Gyford, 1991). At the same time, those who are poor and dependent on the benefits and services delivered by local government find their mobility severely restricted: they are, in effect, 'trapped in space' (Harvey, 1989). In addition, those subject to discrimination – minority ethnic groups or gay people, for example – may feel safe only within their immediate neighbourhood or community and seek vigorously to defend that territory. According to this line of argument, community continues to have a local focus and constitute a potential basis for urban politics and citizenship.

Elements of both arguments ring true, and their respective relevance will vary in different countries and different localities. It is certainly the case that localities and communities are changing and that there is no clear one-to-one relationship between community and citizenship. As Hill puts it: 'In modern society, the assumed identity between locality and community is at best too facile and at worst positively misleading' (1994: 28). Any conception of urban citizenship needs to recognize the diversity as well as the common experience of city life. It also needs to take into account that for many – the poor, homeless, or unemployed – the city is experienced in terms of exclusion and marginality, rather than membership and identification.

Perhaps it is most useful to see community as a *potential* basis for bonds of citizenship and civic culture. There is a two-way relationship between municipal institutions and the communities and localities they serve. As well as reflecting the character of the communities it serves, urban government has 'the capacity to shape an area, to preserve it, to develop it, to change it and in so doing, to give it a new identity' (Clarke and Stewart, 1991: 29). As Prior and Walsh explain: 'Civic pride and community life will take a good deal of creation and maintenance in a world of potential fragmentation and mobility' (1993: 10). An attachment to 'community' cannot be taken for granted among today's diverse and mobile city populations. Yet there remains among many people 'a profound yearning for the idealized small town' – for 'meaning and coherence' despite the fragmenting and individualizing tendencies of modern city life (Bellah et al., 1985: 283). While the New England township cannot in itself be recreated, Bellah et al. argue that 'communities of memory' persist and that the traditions of local citizenship can be 'reappropriated in ways that respond to our present need'.

Citizenship and participation

Another, linked, element in the relationship between citizenship and urban politics concerns participation. Put simply, the argument is that participation is most likely to take place at the local level where people live and work and socialize, raise their families, and draw upon the services and benefits of the state. The significance of this argument is dependent, however, on the importance ascribed to active participation in our understanding of democracy and citizenship. If participation is seen as an essential feature of democracy, it is likely that urban politics will be regarded as central to the realization and expression of citizenship.

Two broad approaches to democracy can be distinguished, both within the liberal tradition but with different implications for popular participation. On the one hand, associated with the Athenian city state and the ideas of Rousseau and de Tocqueville, there is the approach which stresses 'direct democracy'. Voting is but one, highly episodic, element of democratic life. Democracy involves wider participation in 'the processes of formulation, passage and implementation of public policies' (Parry et al., 1992: 16). Participation involves contacting politicians or government officials, joining pressure groups, attending meetings, signing petitions or demonstrating. It refers to the right of citizens to be involved in the processes of government – to express views, to have them listened to, to be informed of decisions and the reasons behind them, to criticize and complain (Prior et al., 1993: 7). This is in many ways the classic pluralist vision of a polyarchy – a 'porous' political system which maximizes points of access for people and groups to express their views to leaders and to be involved in the process of governing. Such access is intended to guard against the concentration of political power. Local democracy and political activity are all-important in such a vision – a vision taken up enthusiastically by contemporary political theorists like Pateman (1970) and Barber (1984).

A contrasting view of democracy, associated particularly with Schumpeter (1943), argues that widespread popular participation is impractical in modern society and, moreover, destabilizes democratic political systems. Participation is impractical because traditional ways of life are breaking down; people no longer have the time nor the inclination to involve themselves in the day-to-day life of their locality. Participation is undesirable because it is likely to be defensive or promotional of sectional interests; any notion of the common good may be lost in the context of a participatory free-for-all. This approach emphasizes 'representative democracy' rather than direct democracy. Democracy is distinguished by political competition between groups of leaders (particularly political parties) for the support of electors, which is expressed at periodic elections. Democratic politics works on the basis of a 'division of labour'. Citizens elect representatives to govern for them and, between elections, their involvement in politics is limited to checks upon their leaders. Elected representatives are in a unique position to plan for society as a whole and, in the context of social democracy, to redistribute resources between more and less well-off groups and/or regions. Such a role prioritizes the representative role and takes a national rather than a local perspective.

Classical theorists who point to the centrality of popular participation in theoretical terms also express doubts about the *practice* of direct democracy. Mill (1951) emphasizes the 'educative' potential of popular participation, but doubts that direct democracy can form the basis for governing a modern political system. In accordance with much of the liberal tradition, Mill sees the Greek idea of the 'polis' as unsustainable in modern society. The argument is that self-government by means of direct participation is hampered by the sheer numbers who would need to be involved, and by the geographic and physical limits this imposes. Mill sees a representative system as the only practical and desirable option for democratic government. While participation through voting and jury service educates citizens about the working of democracy and government, such opportunities constitute the limits of active involvement.

De Tocqueville points to the centralizing tendencies of government and the likelihood of locally-based participation being squeezed out of modern political systems. He warns in the nineteenth century of the dangers of 'administrative despotism' (1946: 564). Government increases in scale and centralization and, while largely benevolent and 'protective', it is deeply paternalistic and non-conducive to participation. Administrative despotism sapped the independence and initiative of citizens. As de Tocqueville explains, in language remarkably relevant today, big government 'does not break men's will, but softens, bends and guides it . . . it does not destroy anything, but prevents much from being born; it is not at all tyrannical but it hinders, restrains, enervates, stifles and stultifies' (1946: 580). De Tocqueville sees the ballot box as an inadequate check on such developments, noting that 'under this system the citizens quit their state of dependence just long enough to choose their masters and then fall back into it' (1946: 581).

Are the doubts of the classical theorists realized in the cities of the 1990s? The evidence conveys mixed messages. Within political systems in general, voting is indeed the dominant form of political action. However, there is less interest in voting at the local than the national level. In Britain, 40 per cent turnouts are the norm for local elections, as against 70 per cent for national elections. In the United States, local turnouts are as low as 25 per cent of the electorate. These figures do not mean, however, that modern cities are a participatory desert. In fact, it is at the local level that forms of political participation *other than voting* are concentrated. Research conducted by the British Political Participation Study confirms that the public are more likely to be in contact with politicians and officials at the local level (38 per cent of respondents) than the national level (17 per cent) (Parry et al., 1992).

Participation at the local level may be motivated by practical concerns. As municipal government tends to have responsibility for 'everyday' services like education, roads and housing, it is the appropriate target of much citizen activity. Local participation may also relate to community identification and self-organization, as discussed earlier. 'Civil society' is expressed through local pressure groups, neighbourhood watch schemes, pubs and community centres, church activities, sports clubs, tenants' associations, youth groups, Chambers of Commerce, Rotary Clubs, charitable activities, community centres, playgroups, pensioners' groups, and so on. The frequency of interaction among urban dwellers may be a stimulus to political participation, even in the absence of community sentiment. Berry et al.'s (1993) research in five US cities highlights the importance of 'face-to-face' contact in nurturing participation. Parry et al.'s (1992) UK research found participation to be higher in inner city areas with high levels of interaction but low levels of community identification than in localities with high levels of community identification but less frequent interaction.

While the local arena may be the focus of much of the day-to-day contact that occurs between citizens and government, this does not necessarily amount to evidence of meaningful direct democracy. It is one thing to have the opportunity to claim benefits and services, complain when things go wrong, and lobby and petition; it is quite another to be involved in establishing priorities for local policy making, or take part in planning, running and monitoring local services. In short, there is a 'ladder of participation' (Arnstein, 1969) which takes the citizen from simple 'contacting' activities, to consultation and information exercises, to community involvement in policy making and service management.

Participation varies in volume and depth according to the culture and design of political systems. One aspect of this is the autonomy accorded to municipal government in respect of the wider political system. As Hill explains: 'The local arena provides a framework for the exercise of individual and group participation but it can do so only if significant decisions are taken at local level' (1994: 238). This makes local participation problematic in the UK where local government has seen its autonomy and authority reduced in the context of increasing central controls over revenue raising and modes of service management. There is a contrast here with the more decentralized US system of local government, based upon more firmly held traditions of localism and participation. Hambleton observes that: 'Americans when they learn of the UK arrangements for central control shake their heads in disbelief. Such a regime would never be tolerated within a US state, still less within the country as a whole' (1994: 15).

Another factor relates to the provision for direct democracy within local electoral systems. In the US, local elections may include ballots on an 'initiative' (arising out of a public petition in favour of a legislative measure of constitutional amendment), a 'referendum' (the referral to voters of a law or statute for approval or rejection), or a 'recall' (arising out of a public petition requesting a 'vote of confidence' in an elected official). While some argue that the significance of such ballots lies primarily in their symbolic reaffirmation of US localist traditions (Wolman and Goldsmith, 1992: 131), their use is increasing and spreading to states where they were not previously allowed. As Cronin (1989: 4) notes, public opinion data show widespread support for the opportunity to vote directly on key policy issues and a belief among citizens that they are capable of casting informed votes. In 1988, voting took place on 50 citizen initiatives in 18 states (Cronin, 1989: 3). The influence of the Californian 'Proposition 13' on tax policy in that state, and on wider policy debates, demonstrates the potential political importance of citizens' initiatives and direct democracy at the local level.

In the UK, local elections are concerned solely with the selection of representatives. However, there remain opportunities for municipal institutions to develop structures and ways of working which facilitate local participation – an 'infrastructure for citizenship' as Gyford (1991) puts it. Traditionally, the design and culture of municipal institutions have been dominated by the 'three pillars' of representative democracy, bureaucracy and professionalism. As Prior et al. explain: 'Bureaucracy becomes the force which defines and shapes citizenship; expert officials dominate; power is centralised and exercised over, rather than with, people' (1993: 6). Under criticism from both left and right, new structures and processes are being introduced to make local government more accessible to individuals and to organized groups – longer opening hours and better designed offices, clearer information, new neighbourhood assemblies and consultative fora, support and resources for community groups, and so on (Gyford, 1991; Lowndes and Stoker, 1992). As Berry et al. explain, local opinion on local issues will be 'heard loud and clear at city hall, not by osmosis, but by institutional arrangements that facilitate input' (1993: 288). They point to the need for 'rich, dense communication networks' between municipal government, political leaders and citizens. The fine-grain of organizational design will, however, be influenced by the particular political and civic culture of different cities (Leach and Lowndes, 1993).

Concerns are expressed, however, about the desirability as well as the practicality of direct democracy, mirroring Schumpeter's earlier reservations. Cronin's research on direct democracy shows the public to be 'in two minds about populist democracy. They want more of it in the abstract, yet they are often cautious and concerned about its excesses in practice' (1989: x). Paradoxically, direct democracy may threaten citizens' rights as well as increase citizens' voice. Direct democracy presents difficult questions in terms of the practice and principle of urban politics. How can the interests of minorities be protected in the face of vociferous majorities? How can long-term strategies be developed in the face of short-term demands? How can the needs of the city as a whole be balanced against the interests of particular neighbourhoods, and the demands of one neighbourhood evaluated against another? How can elite manipulation of direct democracy devices be avoided, given the costs involved in organizing petitions and campaigns?

While participation may form an important basis for citizenship, it is perhaps most valuable in the context of a strong and vibrant representative democracy – where accountable representatives have the authority to evaluate needs, balance demands, establish priorities, and monitor the outcomes of the political system. As Cronin explains: 'More than any other form of government, democracy requires a healthy blend of faith and skepticism: faith that if people are informed and caring, they can be trusted with self-government; and a persistent questioning of leaders and majorities' (1989: x).

Urban politics and citizen-education

The local arena has long been seen as a 'school' for citizenship. The argument has a 'practical' dimension based on the idea that training in citizenship at the local level prepares people, especially potential leaders, for political involvement at the national level. The emphasis here is on learning the skills of participation and debate. As Mill (1974) remarks: 'we do not learn to read or write, to ride or swim, by being told how to do it, but by doing it, so it is only by practising popular government on a limited scale, that the people will ever learn how to exercise it on a larger scale'. Mill sees participation in 'free and popular local and municipal institutions' as part of 'the peculiar training of a citizen, the practical part of the political education of a free people'. De Tocqueville argues that: 'town meetings are to liberty what primary schools are to science: they bring it within people's reach, they teach men how to use and enjoy it' (1946: 57). Mill notes that urban politics provides experience in citizenship for the 'lower grades' of society, who might otherwise not gain access to the political process.

There is also a 'moral' element to the argument that citizenship is learnt at the local level. This is based on the notion that democratic values are inculcated through participation in the affairs of the immediate community. De Tocqueville believes that the 'spirit of liberty' is 'imbibed' through the practice of citizenship at the local level. He argues that 'municipal institutions constitute the strength of free nations . . . A nation may establish a free government, but without municipal institutions it cannot have the spirit of liberty' (1946: 57). There is a clear link here to the arguments about citizenship and community identification reviewed earlier. Local citizenship and participation are seen less as 'practice' for politics at higher levels, than as the very well-spring of democratic values. More recently, Oakeshott (1975) has argued that civility 'denotes an order of moral (not instrumental) considerations', while Wildavsky (1980) defines citizenship as 'moral development'.

So, de Tocqueville and Mill see urban politics as 'formative of the citizenry' (Elkin, 1987: 10). Municipal institutions are more than tools with which to achieve material outcomes and solve social problems; they help to create the type of citizenry necessary for a liberal democracy to flourish. Modern day political theorists continue this theme, seeing participation in urban politics and community life as a potentially transformative experience. As Barber puts it: 'Citizens are certainly not born, but made as a consequence of civic education and political engagement in a free polity' (1984: xvii).

Research by Bledsoe and Stoker (1991) in Detroit offers useful pointers as to the determinants of citizen knowledge of local government. They found that 100 per cent of city residents could identify the mayor of Detroit – considerably more than the 66 per cent who knew the identity of the vice president of the United States! Other council members were far less readily identified, but the research revealed interesting differences in the 'cognitive structures' of citizens. Bledsloe and Stoker found that citizens' ability to name office holders was greatest for office holders with whom they shared societal characteristics, notably race and gender. The ability to name office holders was also related to the personal attributes of the citizen, increasing with age, length of residence, income and education. These findings suggest ways in which the 'making' of citizens might be influenced – how local 'citizen education' programmes might be designed to enhance civic competence in general, and among particular groups. Targeting information programmes on younger people, or those who have recently moved into a neighbourhood, could be important. Ensuring that all communities are represented in nominations for political office could also help to foster citizen awareness and involvement.

Citizen education clearly involves more than just passing on information about how government systems work. Berry et al. (1993: 256) identify three elements of citizen education: a practical dimension, referring to knowledge of how to participate; a psychological dimension, referring to a belief that one can influence the political system; and an experiential dimension, referring to the drawing of lessons from political activity leading to the repetition of certain acts. Berry et al. argue that: 'The logic is simple and compelling: one learns to be a citizen through experience' (1993: 256).

Experience in local politics affords important opportunities for developing 'citizen capacity' in a practical, psychological and experiential sense. Such opportunities are important in themselves, given the relationship between local politics and the immediate concerns of basic services and neighbourhood life. They are also important in providing a route into national politics. In the United States and many European countries (notably France) political involvement at the local level can form a springboard to national political office. Such a springboard may be of particular importance for activists and leaders from minority communities who find it hard to break on to the national stage. Mill's argument that local politics affords access to decision making and leadership training for disadvantaged groups remains relevant today. As Wolman and Goldsmith argue:

> the decentralized small scale of much American local government ensures that minorities are likely to be in a majority in some place at some time. The obvious example is the way in which blacks have used local government as a route to political control, at least partially securing their status from threat from other, possibly larger and more hostile groups. (1992: 11)

However, high levels of knowledge about local political processes, or interest in urban politics, cannot be assumed. The recent British review of local government structure was justified partly on the grounds that the public is confused about 'who does what' in the existing two-tier system. Ironically, while central government is supportive of a move to 'unitary' (single-tier) local government in Britain, it is at the same time overseeing a proliferation of special purpose local agencies as functions are taken away from elected local authorities (Stewart, 1994). It is by no means clear that single-tier local government will increase citizen understanding and capacity within this broader context of fragmentation. Local government is *potentially* an important arena for the development of 'citizen competence', but citizen knowledge and participation cannot be taken for granted. Rather, they will be related to the design and culture of municipal institutions and the autonomy and authority of local government vis-à-vis the wider political system.

A revival of interest in citizenship?

Clearly many of the the classic arguments linking citizenship and urban politics can no longer be taken for granted, if indeed they ever could. In today's cities, the triangular set of relationships between individuals, communities and municipal institutions appears fragile. This fragility is stimulating a renewed interest in the concept and practice of citizenship. New approaches to citizenship vary, however, in the way they conceptualize the links in the triangle. Some approaches draw upon the classic arguments reviewed above, others take a rather different line. In this section I consider new agendas for citizenship, exploring theoretical dilemmas and debates within urban policy and politics.

The theoretical debate

In the current debate on citizenship, approaches tend to cluster around a 'liberal' and a 'communitarian' pole. The theoretical debates are complex and each cluster includes a variety of nuanced positions. My aim here is only to introduce the main lines of debate. Put most simply, the key debate concerns the respective emphasis placed upon *individual rights* and *community membership* as a basis for citizenship.

Communitarians (like Sandel and MacIntyre) see citizenship in terms of community membership and communal provision. Liberals (like Rawls) see citizenship in terms of the rights and freedoms of the individual. Liberals define citizenship in terms of the 'natural' rights of each individual, while communitarians define citizenship in terms of rights arising from membership of a particular community. While liberals see rights as absolute, inhering in each individual, communitarians see rights as dependent upon community membership. For communitarians, citizenship involves duties as well as rights – citizenship carries with it obligations to take part in the development and working of their community. Such duties are not freely chosen but inhere in particular social positions and roles.

The two approaches have different implications for the role of government. For liberals, the main role of government is to protect the rights of individuals to pursue their own interests without interference from others (for instance, by ensuring freedom of speech and association). Government is a neutral arbiter and exercises only those powers which individuals wish to cede to it. In the liberal vision, the freedom of the individual is the paramount goal. For communitarians, government has a more active role; it intervenes to ensure all individuals are able to exercise their rights (for instance, through the provision of welfare benefits). The state constitutes an expression of shared values and needs. It is a 'necessary embodiment of solidarity' in a modern, complex society where individuals are strangers to one another and community is fragile and partial (Prior and Walsh, 1993). Rather than being neutral, the government carries out social purposes. Equality between citizens, rather than the freedom of each individual, is the key goal.

Both sets of ideas have long theoretical histories, although communitarian arguments have a closer link with classic arguments about citizenship at the local level. Communitarians' stress on community membership and collective action locates the practice and identity of citizenship firmly within the local arena. The liberal position, on the other hand, has little to say about the link between citizenship and urban politics – the urban arena is simply one stage upon which individuals' rights are expressed, and protected by government. For liberals there is no fundamental link between locality and citizenship, although they may see decentralized government as enhancing individual liberty to the extent that it prevents a concentration of government power.

While philosophically distinct, the 'individual rights' and 'community membership' approaches are not mutually exclusive in practice. They can usefully be seen as reflecting two dimensions of citizenship – dimensions which achieve a different balance in different historical periods and in different countries, depending upon political and cultural traditions. The relationship between the two 'faces' of citizenship can be understood in different ways. Marshall (1964) takes a historical approach to the question. He traces the evolution of citizenship over time, pointing to a shift from a focus on individual rights and liberty to a concern with 'social citizenship' and equality. He sees the evolution of citizenship as involving three stages. In the eighteenth century *civil rights* emerged, which concerned the liberty of the individual (eg. freedom of speech and access to the law). In the nineteenth century *political rights* were won, concerned with political equality through elections and wider access to political institutions. In the twentieth century, *social rights* developed, concerned with claims to welfare (entitlements to social security and other services) in the name of social equality. Marshall sees the three types of citizenship rights as coexisting, but implies that social rights represent a kind of 'highest stage' of citizenship.

Recognizing the specificity of Marshall's analysis to the British case, other writers have studied the emergence of different conceptions of citizenship (or mixes of conceptions) in different nation states. Esping-Anderson (1990: 22–3) distinguishes between liberal, corporatist and social democratic welfare states, each of which rests upon a different interpretation of citizenship. In the *liberal* case (characterized by the United States, Canada and Australia), the welfare state plays a residual role, catering for the needs of those unable to secure their welfare through the market. 'Social rights' and government intervention are limited; individual liberty is prioritized. In the *corporatist* case (characterized by Austria, France, Germany and Italy), social rights and state provision are accorded a greater role but are not universally available, in the context of a complex system of insurance-related entitlements. In the *social democratic* case (characterized by the Nordic countries), social rights are of the highest priority; the welfare state provides universal benefits in the pursuit of equality.

Esping-Anderson (1990: 26–7) takes care to note that there is no 'pure' case of the liberal, corporatist or social democratic welfare state; rather he identifies 'clusters' of regime type. The actual development of welfare states and social citizenship depends upon each country's history of political struggle and institutional development. The balance between rights based on liberty and equality, or the individual and the community, shifts over time. In the case of Britain, for example, the 1980s saw a shift from a relatively social democratic approach to a more liberal model of citizenship and the welfare state (Roche, 1992).

Debates in urban policy and politics

The way that citizenship is understood influences the development of municipal institutions and the practice of urban politics. In turn, such institutions and practices shape the expression and experience of citizenship. The current intellectual contest between 'individual rights' and 'community membership' approaches to citizenship is reflected in competing policies and initiatives to revive urban citizenship. As Prior et al. put it: 'Fundamental differences of political and social philosophy underlie this tension in the concept of citizenship; and the struggle between these philosophies, translated into political programmes, determines the meaning that citizenship has at any particular time and in any particular society' (1993: 4).

Two images are dominating current debates about citizenship and urban policy: the image of the citizen as *consumer*, and as *community participant*. I seek to show below that, despite the polarization of the debate, both 'faces' of citizenship may need to be reflected in any revitalization of relationship between citizens and government institutions.

The citizen as consumer   There is a clear resonance between the image of citizen as consumer and the 'liberal' position reviewed above. If the principle of individual freedom is paramount, choice is the defining activity of the citizen, and the institutions of citizenship exist to facilitate freedom of choice and guarantee formal entitlements and procedures. Those who promote this view of citizenship look to the market mechanism as the pre-eminent mechanism for the expression of choice. Civic involvement is seen in terms of consumer processes (Prior et al., 1993: 8). This view of citizenship argues that citizens' rights will be strengthened by opening up public services to market forces. On the 'supply side' competition among service providers is intended to act as a spur to improved service quality and efficiency, and – in some cases – to allow consumers some degree of choice between alternative providers. On the 'demand' side, consumers are to be provided with better information about their entitlements, the standard of service to be expected, and opportunities for complaint and redress. The aim is to change the relationship between the citizen and the state from passive recipient to active consumer. The 'empowerment' of the citizen-consumer and the end of state monopolies are intended to discipline service providers and put an end to 'bureaucrat knows best' attitudes.

The image of the citizen as consumer is influencing urban policy in both the UK and the US. Policies set out to re-style relationships between citizens and government, drawing inspiration from market models. The UK's 'Citizen's Charter' (Prime Minister 1991: 2), for example, explains that the charter 'is not a recipe for more state action; it is a testament of our belief in people's right to be informed and to choose for themselves'. In the US, *Reinventing Government* (the inspiration behind the 'Gore Report', *Creating a Government that Works Better and Costs Less*) explains that the key question 'is not how much government but what kind of government', and that the key answer lies in 'tapping the tremendous power of the entrepreneurial process and the force of the free market' (Osborne and Gaebler, 1993).

The 'Citizen's Charter' – with its subsidiary charters for health care patients, social housing tenants, public transport passengers, users of community care services – concentrates upon themes of choice, accessibility, service standards and redress. Municipal authorities, along with transport agencies, hospitals and other public bodies, are required to incorporate these themes into their own charters and 'service promises'. The main mechanisms promoted by the government for meeting charter requirements include: public information systems and complaints procedures; performance monitoring and the comparison of agencies' performance through 'league tables'; and the extension of competition and privatization in public services.

Reinventing Government proposes that government should be 'competitive', 'enterprising' and 'market-oriented', and above all 'customer-driven'. The book argues that 'clients' should be 'redefined as customers'. Public bodies should 'listen to customers' by means of surveys, focus groups and so on, while also putting public funds into individuals' hands to allow them to make choices between service providers. Competition between providers is intended to stimulate innovation and efficiency within government while 'empowering' citizen-consumers. As Osborne and Gaebler put it: 'Our public sector can learn to compete, or it can stagnate and shrink, until the only customers who use public services are those who cannot afford an alternative' (1993: 19).

A number of problems arise for the citizen-as-consumer approach. The consumer image is not appropriate to the full range of relationships that exist between citizens and municipal institutions. It may be a useful analogy for services where there is a clear relationship between an individual consumer and a local authority (for example, borrowing library books, renting social housing, attending a leisure centre). In these cases, the identity of the 'consumer' is clear, a clearly defined transaction takes place, and competition between providers exists or could be developed. However, there is a range of municipal services in which it is difficult to define who the consumer is and the precise nature of the transaction, and where there exists no market in service provision. It is difficult to apply the consumer model of citizenship for services which are consumed collectively (such as a clean and healthy local environment), for services where there is little possibility of individuals exercising choice or judgement about their own interests (as with the mentally ill or young children), or for services which are regulatory or even coercive. As the Chief Executive of Birmingham City Council asks: 'Who is the customer when we intervene to remove a child from its parents or to close down a restaurant?' (*Local Government Chronicle*, 19 Feb. 1993).

In addition, not all relationships between citizens and municipal institutions are about service delivery. The citizen is, at least potentially, an active participant in the process of government as well as a user of public services. The consumer analogy takes the politics out of citizenship and local government. This creates practical as well as 'moral' difficulties. If citizenship is reduced to consumerism and governance to shopkeeping, how are issues of collective choice to be resolved? How are decisions to be made about the condition of our towns and cities and the future of communities? How are rationing decisions to be made and conflicts between citizens' interests resolved? In an environment of rationing and financial constraint, collective choice may involve the *denial* of services to particular citizens, or group of citizens. As Hill points out: 'The concern for quality in services still leaves unanswered the issue of power; that is, who has power to take decisions, to assess standards of service and to evaluate outcomes' (1994: 6).

The consumer image captures only one aspect of citizenship. When authorities in Michigan announce that 'customer service is our reason for being' (Osborne and Gaebler, 1993: 17), they are downgrading other important aspects of citizenship and governance. The 'Citizen's Charter', when confronted by the dilemmas of collective choice, proposes 'panels of lay assessors' to arbitrate in disputes. This sounds like reinventing the wheel rather than reinventing government. Do we need lay assessors when we already have elected local politicians? In short, the citizen as consumer is a partial vision; it seems unlikely that choice and charters will render the ballot box and the protest meeting unnecessary. As Barber (1984) notes, citizenship involves a 'practical dialectic' – individual freedom and collective choice are two sides of the same coin.

The citizen as community member An image of citizen as community member is also present in current debates in urban policy and practice. Resonating with the 'communitarian' arguments discussed earlier, this approach sees citizens as having a meaningful existence only as members of communities, bound together by ties of loyalty and mutual obligation (rather than by market exchange). Individual purposes can only be formed and realized within this context; citizen activity is defined by participation in collective purposes rather than by individual choice. The institutions of citizenship exist to guarantee citizens a right to participate in the processes of government and to receive as entitlements their share of public goods. Citizens participate in the formation of community norms and are obliged to conform to them.

Advocates of the 'community membership' approach to citizenship do not necessarily reject charters and markets, but express doubts that 'a focus on individual consumers can ever be sufficient to create genuinely responsive and accountable public services' (Prior et al., 1993: 9). Rather, 'Their argument draws attention to the role of local government *as government*; that over and above the provision of specific services, local authorities embody a process of decision-making about local affairs which gives voice to the needs, wants and aspirations of the collective citizenry' (Prior et al., 1993: 9, original emphasis).

In fact, many who promote consumerist images also see the significance of these being rooted in a concept of community. *Reinventing Government* argues that government should be 'community owned' – issues of public safety, for example, are not just technical or professional matters but need to be related to community responsibilities. In the UK, the 'Citizen's Charter' concept has been developed by individual local authorities to include commitments to community involvement in setting standards and monitoring outcomes. One city's charter states that: 'Leicester City Council exists to ensure that local services reach the highest possible standards within the resources available for citizens, visitors and those who work in the city; to provide a focus for civic pride and community life; and to listen, identify and respond to agreed local needs' (cited in Prior and Walsh, 1993: 9).

The difficulty with a concept of citizenship based on community membership is the assumption that community does indeed exist. There is always the danger that 'the emperor has no clothes'. As I discussed earlier in the chapter, there is great controversy concerning the character and relevance of community in the towns and cities of the 1990s. At best, community constitutes a *potential* basis for urban citizenship. Unleashing this potential requires strategies for change, and not just wishful thinking!

While today's community-based approaches to citizenship resonate with traditional *arguments* stressing community membership, participation and citizen education, they are based upon a critique of traditional *practices*. Like 'consumerist' reformers, they argue that municipal government has become bureaucratized, inaccessible, unresponsive, and dominated by professional and producer interests. The remedies they propose, however, are based not on markets and charters but on a reaffirmation of community identity as a basis for citizen rights and civic action. Strategies focus upon action by municipal government to stimulate community identity, membership and participation: for example, the setting up of consultative fora bringing communities together to comment on and participate in local decision-making, or the support (through funding and training) of community development and self-organization involving, perhaps, the 'co-production' or community management of local services. Such an approach is not focused on individual services and individual service users; it embraces broader aspects of citizenship and governance. As Prior and Walsh explain:

> The pursuit of citizenship can be seen as an objective of the local authority itself, rather than a characteristic of the way that specific services are delivered. It will involve not only entitlements, but also participation in decision making, promotion of the ability to live autonomously and independently, and direct involvement in the delivery of services within the community – the role of local government must be to attain an appropriate balance between the rights of the individual and the commitment to the collectivity. (1993: 26–7)

In addition to government-led strategies to revive community as a basis for urban citizenship, there are approaches which seek 'bottom-up' change. The self-styled 'communitarian movement' in the US argues that it will take more than well-meaning governments to unearth or rediscover community. A 'moral reconstruction' – a fundamental 'change of heart' – is required to redress the balance between individual rights and community obligations (Etzioni, 1993). Etzioni argues that: 'the cause of the individual has gotten out of hand, jeopardizing community needs and public safety'

(1993: 16). As a result, he claims that: 'People feel alienation, that we are atomised, all living separately without enough common bonds. This creates a void. They say, "We are supposed to have a community, but we don't, and we want to do something about it"' (quoted in the *Guardian*, 23 June 1994).

Etzioni restates Kennedy's famous maxim as the rallying call for a new type of citizenship based on community obligation: 'Ask not what your country can do for you. Ask what you can do for your country' (1993: 4). However, the call for a new sense of community responsibility within education, neighbourhood life and governance relies on moral exhortation, leaving unanswered fundamental questions about the nature of urban communities. Communitarians assume a potential homogeneity of interest within communities in their urge to rediscover 'the values we all share', 'the public interest' and 'the community at large'. How *relevant* are such assumptions in real-life urban communities characterized by inequality and conflict? How *desirable* is the communitarian vision in urban communities whose energy and strength may rest precisely in their diversity?

Conclusion

The current revival of interest in citizenship relates to concern for the triangular set of relationships between individuals, their communities and the institutions of local governance. In the first part of the chapter I reviewed the classic theoretical arguments linking citizenship, community and self-government. I argued that in today's urban environment the links between corners of the 'triangle' cannot be assumed. The integrity of the triangle is threatened by the limited interest and involvement of individuals in local politics and civic life, the loss of relevance and coherence in local communities, and the inaccessibility and unresponsiveness of local political institutions.

These threats have led to, or been accompanied by, a revival of interest in the concept of citizenship. Theoretically, this has involved renewed enquiry into the fundamental nature of citizenship and the citizen bond, played out in chief through the liberal/communitarian debate. In policy terms, concern has focused on strategies for re-engaging individuals in urban politics and the civic life, re-invigorating local communities, and re-inventing municipal government.

Both the theoretical and policy debates have been highly polarized. There are sharp disagreements between liberals and communitarians in intellectual circles, and between 'marketeers' and 'community developers' in the world of policy and practice. Despite this polarization, and the politicization of 'opposing' positions, the debates reveal surprising areas of overlap and consensus. Theoretically, the liberal/communitarian debate has been described as 'misconceived', understating the subtlety and adaptability of both frameworks (Caney, 1992). It seems more profitable to see individual rights and community membership as two 'faces' of citizenship, with the relationship between the two faces embodied in different ways in different historical periods and political systems.

In policy terms, it is hard to maintain a clear separation between 'consumer' and 'community' approaches. A stress on individuals' right to information, redress and service choice and quality is unsustainable in the absence of some collective framework for the arbitration of disputes between individuals and government, the establishment of priorities and rationing criteria, and the brokering of competing demands from different groups and interests. At the same time, a stress on community membership and participation requires an understanding of the diversity of communities and of what motivates individuals to get involved, and stay involved, in local politics and civic life. Ultimately, theoretical and policy debates are underpinned by a common interest in what links the three points of the citizenship 'triangle'. Debates about citizenship stimulate students of urban politics to consider the character and determinants of relationships between individuals, communities and local political institutions.

References

Arnstein, S. (1969) 'A ladder of citizen participation', *Journal of the American Institute of Planners*, XXXV: 216–24.

Barber, B. (1984) *Strong Democracy: Participatory Politics for a New Age*. Berkeley: University of California Press.

Bellah, R., Madsen, R., Sullivan, W., Swindler, A. and Tipton, S. (1985) *Habits of the Heart: Middle America Observed*. London: Hutchinson.

Berry, J., Portney, K. and Thompson, K. (1993) *The Rebirth of Urban Democracy*. Washington, D.C.: Brookings Institution.

Bledsoe, T. and Stoker, G. (1991) *Citizens' Knowledge of Local Government in the Detroit Metropolitan Area*. Detroit Metropolitan Area Public Policy Surveys, Detroit, MI: Center for Urban Studies, Wayne State University.

Caney, S. (1992) 'Liberalism and communitarianism: a misconceived debate', *Political Studies*, XL: 273–89.

Clarke, M. and Stewart, J. (1991) *Choices for Local Government for the 1990s and Beyond*. Harlow: Longman.

Cochrane, A. (1991) 'The changing state of local government', *Public Administration*, 69 (3): 281–302.

Cronin, T. (1989) *Direct Democracy*. Cambridge, MA: Harvard University Press.

de Tocqueville, A. (1946) *Democracy in America*. London: Oxford University Press (first published 1835).

Elkin, S. (1987) *City and Regime in the American Republic*. Chicago: University of Chicago Press.

Esping-Anderson, G. (1990) *The Three Worlds of Welfare Capitalism*. Cambridge: Polity.

Etzioni, A. (1993) *The Spirit of Community: Rights, Responsibilities and the Communitarian Agenda*. New York: Crown.

Gyford, J. (1991) *Citizens, Consumers and Councils*. London: Macmillan.

Harvey, D. (1989) *The Urban Experience*. Oxford: Blackwell.

Hambleton, R. (1993) 'Not reinvented here', *Local Government Management*. 1 (7): 13–15.

Held, D. (1993) 'Democracy: from city-states to a cosmopolitan order?' in D. Held (ed.), *Prospects for Democracy*. Cambridge: Polity.

Hill, D. (1994) *Citizens and Cities: Urban Policy in the 1990s*. Hemel Hempstead: Harvester Wheatsheaf.

Leach, S. and Lowndes, V. (1993) *Fitness for Purpose: Shaping New Patterns of Organisation and Management*. Report of the LGMB Working Party on Internal Organisation and Management. Luton: Local Government Management Board.

Lowndes, V. and Stoker, G. (1992) 'An evaluation of neighbourhood decentralisation: consumer and citizen perspective', *Policy and Politics*, 20 (2): 47–61.

Marshall, T. (1964) *Class, Citizenship and Social Development*. Chicago, IL: University of Chicago Press.

Mill, J.S. (1951) *Considerations on Representative Government* in H. Acton (ed.) *Utilitarianism, Liberty and Representative Government*. London: Dent.

Mill, J.S. (1974) *On Liberty*. Harmondsworth: Penguin (originally published 1859).

Oakeshott, M. (1975) *On Human Conduct*. Oxford: Oxford University Press.

Osborne, D. and Gaebler, T. (1993) *Reinventing Government*. New York: Plume.

Parry, G., Moyser, G. and Day, N. (1992) *Political Participation and Democracy in Britain*. Cambridge: Cambridge University Press.

Pateman, C. (1970) *Participation and Democratic Theory*. Cambridge: Cambridge University Press.

Prime Minister (1991) *The Citizen's Charter: Raising the Standard*. Cm 1599. London: HMSO.

Prior, D. and Walsh, K. (1993) *Citizenship and the Quality of Local Government*. Partnership Paper, Birmingham: Institute of Local Government Studies.

Prior, D., Stewart, J. and Walsh, K. (1993) *Is the Citizen's Charter a Charter for Citizens?* Belgrave Paper No. 7. Luton: Local Government Management Board.

Roche, M. (1992) *Rethinking Citizenship: Welfare, Ideology and Change in Modern Society*. Cambridge: Polity.

Rousseau, J.J. (1973) *The Social Contract and Other Discourses*. London: Dent.

Schumpeter, J. (1943) *Capitalism, Socialism and Democracy*. London: Allen and Unwin.

Smith, B. (1985) *Decentralisation: The Territorial Dimension of the State*. London: Allen and Unwin.

Stewart, J. (1994) 'The flawed process', in S. Leach (ed.), *The Local Government Review: Key Issues and Choices*. Birmingham: Institute of Local Government Studies.

Turner, B. (1992) 'Outline of a theory of citizenship', in C. Mouffe (ed.), *Dimensions of Radical Democracy: Pluralism, Citizenship, Community*. London: Verso.

Wildavsky, A. (1980) *The Art and Craft of Policy Analysis*. London: Macmillan.

Wolman, H. and Goldsmith, M. (1992) *Urban Politics and Policy: A Comparative Approach*. Oxford: Blackwell.

10

Urban Social Movements

Susan S. Fainstein and Clifford Hirst

Before the protests and civil disturbances that swept through American and European cities from the mid-1960s into the 1970s, scholars had a largely non-conflictual view of urban political life.[1] American political scientists, who dominated the subfield of urban politics in the 1960s, focused their attention on who made political decisions and who influenced government. The problematic in which they worked referred to social movements only historically, tracing the contemporary urban institutional system to the struggle between the political machine and the progressive movement at the beginning of the century. Their principal preoccupation was the debate over who controlled decision making; their work implicitly assumed that their findings applied universally and that the patterns of authority that they discovered would persist. Scholars on the left and right split according to whether they thought a power elite of influential business people dominated governance or whether they believed that all important decisions were made by publicly accountable, elected officials. But neither side discerned overt conflict beyond the normal bounds of pluralist bargaining within the urban arena.

Among urban sociologists the ecological paradigm prevailed, with its assumptions of an evolutionary process of change determined by demographic variables and 'natural' market processes. The study of social movements was left to specialists in 'collective behaviour,' who attributed no particular importance to the urban setting beyond its conduciveness to riotous behaviour, which could spread through contagion.[2] Scholars within this tradition regarded social movements as collective manifestations of irrational or deviant behaviour. Traumatized by the European experience with fascism and communism, they equated all mass movements with the mobilizations that led up to totalitarian regimes.[3]

Changes in the political terrain of American and European cities, however, caused the old approaches to lose their relevance. As formal political institutions appeared increasingly unable to handle the demands generated by urban societies that were splintered and united along a variety of dimensions, urban social movements (USMs) became agents for social change through their effects on popular consciousness and their actions challenging both the process and outcomes of social and political decision making. Their very existence undermined the assumptions of consensus and stability that had characterized the earlier period. Moreover, the moral foundation of movements demanding racial justice, respect for the environment, and community participation made it hard to dismiss them as deviant elements to be equated with Nazis and the Ku-Klux-Klan. Widespread participation by 'respectable' people in movement activities further subverted their dismissal as aberrant acts.[4] Marxist structuralists, who *did* expect to find deeply rooted antagonisms but had not previously concerned themselves with cities, responded to urban crisis by examining the ways in which resistance to class exploitation extended into urban conflict (see especially Castells, 1978). They developed theories showing how the capitalist economy shaped urban governance and spatial form; they then demonstrated how conflict developed along the 'trenches' created within urban space (Castells, 1977; Katznelson, 1981). Among this group of thinkers initial debate revolved around the issue of whether increased public services, welfare provision, and community participation simply amounted to legitimation of the ruling class or constituted genuine progress. They took for granted that the class cleavages of the industrial city would continue to dominate urban social life. The massive decline of manufacturing in cities occurring at that time, however, made discussions based on the divide between the industrial working class and capital increasingly tangential to the issues splitting urban areas. Moreover, the orientation of USMs towards cultural, racial-ethnic and quality-of-life issues made the economistic underpinnings of the Marxist analysis unsatisfactory for examining the genesis and effects of these new movements.

Analyses of the formation and objectives of groups actively seeking urban transformation based on commonalities of race, belief or life style thus did not fit easily into either the intellectual scaffolding provided by earlier theories of urban politics, community life and collective behaviour, or by more recent, Marxist treatments of social movements. Even after the overt militance of the 1960s–70s protests subsided, 'new social movements' continued to affect urban social and political life. Their existence challenged the earlier preoccupation with decision making at the top, forced recognition of social divisions resulting from other bases of solidarity besides class, and broadened the definition of urban politics to include interactions within the realm of civil society that were not necessarily tied to the state (Boggs, 1986; Fisher and Kling, 1993: 320).

In this essay we first define USMs, discuss some of the major issues in analysing them, and present some instances of their operation. We then look at the state of the field today and conclude with our own analysis of their significance.

Urban social movements defined

Social movements are collective social actors defined by both their (dis)organization and their aims. Although movements may encompass organizations with dues-payers and membership lists, their overall structure is not fixed and is forever in process of becoming – movements are emergent phenomena. Their aims are always oppositional to established power, but the specific content of their objectives and whether their stance is resistant or transformative, reactionary or progressive, may shift according to their context and internal development.[5] While the 'old' social movements emanated from the class structure of industrial capitalism and aimed at uprooting the material inequalities produced by the mode of production, the *'new'* social movements cut across classes and are guided by non-material considerations (Offe, 1987; Scott, 1990; Touraine, 1992).

Urban social movements are a category of new social movement in their non-class basis, operation outside the realm of production and participatory ethos. They typically challenge government's role in producing or reinforcing an uneven distribution of power and resources; they are thus more explicitly political than formations around feminism or cultural radicalism, which Touraine (1981) identifies as most exemplary of the movement phenomenon in postindustrial societies. Nevertheless, their objectives transcend specific policy concessions. Thus, Manuel Castells (1983: 319–20), in his influential study of USMs, characterizes their aim as changing the 'urban meaning'. By this locution he means that they break down the material and social hierarchies structuring urban life and produce in their stead a city organized around use values, autonomous local cultures and decentralized participatory democracy:

> The city is a social product resulting from conflicting social interests and values. Because of the institutionalization of socially dominant interests, major innovations in the city's role, meaning, and structure tend to be the outcome of grassroots mobilization and demands. When these mobilizations result in the transformation of the urban structure, we call them urban social movements. (Castells, 1983: 291)

Castells distinguishes between urban movements and urban social movements; only the latter are system transforming.[6] We, however, like most other writers use the term urban social movement to refer to any urban movement, regardless of whether it has produced a transformation in the urban structure or culture. Although USMs *in toto* have a transformative effect, individual mobilizations are usually narrowly focused, demanding particular services or specific powers. Castells (1983: 319) terms mobilizations limited to demands for service provision 'collective consumption trade unionism'.[7] The fragmented, parochial nature of most urban movements limits their capabilities, causing them to be issue dependent and resistant to becoming effective elements within broad coalitions.

Issues

The recent emphasis on USMs and the concomitant downplaying of the role of the class-based party in fostering urban change has raised a number of issues among scholars generally sympathetic with movement aims of social transformation. Three of them will be addressed here: (1) Have USMs in fact displaced class-based movements? (2) Are USMs necessarily progressive? (3) To what extent can movements be analysed independently of their context?

Social movements and class

In *The Urban Question* Castells (1977: 376–7) argues that USMs are a displacement of class struggle from the workplace into the city; as a consequence urban issues are 'secondary structural issues' and are limited by their inability to transform class relations. The importance he gives to information as a social resource and to consumption as an autonomous realm, however, makes class less central to his analysis than that of other Marxists (see Saunders, 1986: 226). In his later work, Castells (1983) departs even further from orthodox Marxism, repudiating his previous reduction of all urban strife to class conflict and introducing culture as a motivating force.

Other scholars place even less weight on the political economy as the determinant of USMs, so that culture, identity, the shaping of space, and the remaking of everyday life become the principal foci of their analyses (see, for example, Gottdiener, 1985). For those concerned not just with USMs but with the new social movements more generally, the role of state and economy are submerged by questions of culture, consciousness and identity (see, for example, Touraine, 1981; Melucci, 1989).

Nevertheless, the relationship between mode of production, class and USMs remains an open issue. The grounding of the study of USMs in concepts like civil society and identity provokes criticism of scholars using these terms for their vagueness (Bartholomew and Mayer, 1992; Pakulski, 1993). More seriously, participants in USMs are accused of misunderstanding how the logic of capital forms urban processes and how class position affects popular consciousness (Katznelson, 1981: Ch. 8; Harvey, 1989: Ch. 5). Following this line of reasoning, Kling and Posner (1990) criticize 'neo-populist' urban movements, which aim at participatory democracy but which eschew a substantive, class-based agenda. They contend that the neo-populists fail to trace the causes of their grievances to the political economy and consequently are unable to bring about meaningful change.

The progressive character of urban social movements

Much of the literature on USMs takes it for granted that they embody a progressive tendency: for example, Castells (1983: Ch. 33) maintains that USMs develop an alternative to structures of domination. Harry Boyte, in his history of the 'citizen movement' in the US during the 1970s, claims that it produced 'a renewed vision of direct democracy coupled with a mistrust of large institutions, both public and private' (1980: 7). He implies that realization of this vision would create cities run by and for the benefit of urban communities and does not question that neighbourhood power represents social progress. Yet, neighbourhood groups seeking to maintain their cultural identity may stifle diversity in the name of community. And, at their worst extreme of defensive oppositionism, urban movements can be dominated by property owners who exclude lower-income people and socially desirable land uses from their communities (Plotkin, 1990). While the original 'mass society' critics of social movements falsely assumed that all movements nurtured deviant personalities and authoritarian tendencies, a number of recent social movement theorists have fallen into the parallel trap of taking for granted well-meaning participants and socially inclusive goals.

Movement autonomy

Although no one asserts that the success or failure of USMs depends only on their internal resources, a debate has arisen over whether it is possible to develop a general theory of such movements that would encompass all cases regardless of their historical context. Castells (1983, 1985) proposes a trans-historical, cross-cultural theory of social change achieved by USMs mobilized around the three goals of collective consumption, cultural identity, and political self-management. In a critique of Castells, Pickvance (1985, 1986) argues, in essence, that the incidence, militance and character of urban movements is as much a function of their circumstances as of their internal dynamics; therefore, no useful theory of USMs can derive from simply an examination of the movements separate from their context. Moreover, he contends, an understanding of the determinants of movement success and failure is crucial to any theory of USMs: 'His [Castells's] ... systematic concentration on characteristics of the movement itself, to the exclusion of contextual features ... [implies] that movement success is due solely to the movement, and not at all to the economic and political environment in which it occurs' (Pickvance, 1986: 226). To some extent the debate boils down to a question of semantics – by Castells's strict definition of an urban social movement, it exists only if it is successful. Otherwise it is simply an urban movement rather than an urban *social* movement. Nevertheless, the two approaches lead to different methodologies in the comparative study of USMs: the first approach produces a focus like that of *The City and the Grassroots*, wherein Castells (1983) dwells almost exclusively on the movements themselves, while the second leads to a much more extensive examination of political institutions and cultural understandings as significant contextual variables shaping USMs.

Illustrations and applications

In this section we amplify our theoretical discussion with examples of recent USMs in the United States and Western Europe, considering in turn their aims, composition, tactics, and effects. Our analysis divides the history of these movements into two stages: first, the period of peak mobilization – 1965–73; and second, the period of episodic movement activities and tendencies towards routinization – 1974 to the present. Since the history of the German Greens does not conform to this scheme, we deal with it separately. The section concludes with a discussion of patterns of convergence among USMs.

Movements of the 1960s and early 1970s

United States In the late 1960s protest movements erupted in many cities throughout the United States, coalescing around the three bases of race–ethnicity, client status and territory (Fainstein and Fainstein, 1974). They took as their targets local state agencies in their roles as providers of collective-consumption services such as housing, health and education, and as sponsors of physical redevelopment.

These movements emerged in the context of massive economic dislocations for African Americans, caused by the capitalization of Southern agriculture. Black migrants, who had moved to the inner areas of older American cities seeking work, found that despite overall national economic growth, they were excluded from participation in primary labour markets. Further, although they were particularly dependent on public services, they suffered neglect and discrimination from the mainly white providers of these services. Lacking any effective way of attacking their employment problems, they directed their attention to the public bureaucracies that intruded into their residential neighbourhoods (Lipsky, 1970). Because their increasing electoral strength had not yet translated into political influence, they resorted to disruptive tactics such as mass demonstrations, sit-ins, and the take-over of schools and other public buildings.

African Americans had always suffered extreme deprivation within US cities. Mass mobilization in northern cities, however, only took place when national and local political forces provided it with an opening (Piven and Cloward, 1971). The civil rights movement had heightened racial consciousness among northern blacks and increased black national political power. The War on Poverty and provisions of the revised federal urban renewal programme led to the introduction of participatory mechanisms and community organizer positions within urban neighbourhoods, producing an infrastructure of leaders, organizations and facilities that could be employed for movement purposes. Thus material conditions of deprivation, solidarity based on race and territory, resulting cultural awareness, and political opportunity combined to stimulate movement formation during this period (Fainstein and Fainstein, 1985).

The militancy of the 1960s–70s was short-lived. Movement leaders moved into elected office or remunerative agency positions, and movement organizations shifted from direct action to service delivery (see, for example, Gittell, 1980). The reliance on race as a base for mobilization, while extremely important for enhancing solidarity among movement participants, seriously restricted the potential for coalition formation. Moreover, the USMs, combined with the civil disorders of the 1960s, also produced a significant backlash directed against African Americans that undermined the New Deal Democratic coalition and led directly to the Republican presidential victories after 1972 (Mollenkopf, 1983; Edsall and Edsall, 1992). The capture of national office by a regime wholly out of sympathy with the aims of USMs produced pessimism over the likely efficacy of movement actions and a consequent ratcheting down of mobilization.

Nevertheless, the movements and the governmental response to them left an enduring legacy of community activism that would develop into a national neighbourhood movement. Federal citizen participation pro- grammes developed during the War on Poverty spawned community-based organizations, many of which survived subsequent cutbacks in federal funding and still provide a source of leadership in minority communities. Finally, while the 1960s–70s movements failed in their efforts to produce a spatially equitable city, they did substantially limit the ability of the national and local Democratic party apparatus to pursue growth-oriented redevelopment strategies without paying heed to the displacement of low- income minorities.

Europe In Europe, urban mobilizations erupted in the 1965–73 period in response to the socialization of consumption in the housing sector. In the Paris region, for example, the government developed huge low-rent housing complexes, the *grands ensembles*, on the periphery of the city. The buildings were designed and constructed with cost-minimization a paramount goal and lacked basic services (Castells, 1983). Issues of amenity and safety subsequently provided a significant basis for resident mobilizations directed against the state as provider and manager of housing.

In contrast to the US, these public housing projects were occupied by both working- and middle-class residents, thus lending themselves to cross- class alliances. Although tensions did exist between middle-class residents' demands for enhanced amenities and the working-class imperative for low rents, tenants' movements organized and sought to maintain both low rents and improved services, as well as demanding collective resident participation in management. In many cases, tenants also mobilized in the electoral arena, with many middle-class residents aligning with left parties. In addition to stimulating a number of left electoral victories at the local level, the impact of the Parisian mobilization was first to alter, and eventually to put an end to *grands ensembles* development policy. However, the failure of such 'collective consumption trade unionism' to move beyond the narrow issues of rents, repair and maintenance, rather than attacking urban problems more generally, narrowed the scope of their success and limited the appeal of their programme. Left parties also blunted the forcefulness of these mobilizations by absorbing them into their own electoral agenda (Castells, 1983: 96).

Indeed, the presence of left-leaning social democratic parties in Western Europe, itself a reflection of a rich tradition of working-class politics, provides a key distinction between the experience of USMs in Europe and the US. In the United States the resistance of 'reformed', 'non-partisan' urban political systems to the demands of working-class and minority populations stimulated an emergent mobilization around urban issues directed against urban bureaucracies outside party channels. In Europe USMs either were more easily absorbed within party frameworks or frequently directed their energies against the left parties themselves, when the party hierarchies were dominated by other interests.[8]

The US neighbourhood movement

During the 1970s the militance and prominence of USMs in both the United States and Europe declined dramatically (Ceccarelli, 1982).[9] Taking their place was an array of mobilizations which, in the US, collectively were termed the neighbourhood movement (Boyte, 1980). Many of the community organizations that participated in this American movement were dominated by homeowners. In contrast, in Europe, where movements aimed at affecting collective consumption continued to crop up, activists were typically drawn from renters of social housing. The 'backyard revolution' (Boyte, 1980) in the US evolved in the context of growing economic insecurity, fear of the expansion of corporate power, and disillusionment with government. It has drawn heavily from an American populist tradition that rejects all ideologies, emphasizing instead grass-roots democracy and a concomitant distrust of all large institutions, both public and private.

The US neighbourhood movement is an eclectic phenomenon. It embraces city-wide progressive coalitions, ethnically-based community organizations, life-style groups such as gays seeking autonomous cultural territories in urban space, and conservative homeowners' movements. Movement aims reflect this diversity of membership. They include making both publicly- and privately-led redevelopment responsive to community concerns; blocking both decay and gentrification of neighbourhoods; and achieving 'community control'. While early movement hopes for 'neighbourhood power' and even 'neighbourhood government' (Kotler, 1969) were never fully realized, the movement has strongly influenced a variety of national and local policies, including the regulation of bank lending practices in poorer areas, the continuation of neighbourhood planning and citizen participation programmes in many local jurisdictions throughout the US, as well as governmental and philanthropic support for community development corporations.

City-wide progressive coalitions   During the 1970s and 1980s some USMs succeeded in circumventing regular political party organizations and bringing about the election of a series of progressive governments in medium-sized and large cities across the US. Under progressive leadership, these municipalities pursued downwardly-redistributive taxation and expenditure policies, promoted public control of development, opposed the domination of local growth coalitions and developed innovative programmes in housing and urban services. They also pursued economic development strategies designed primarily to benefit existing residents rather than owners of extra-local capital (Clavel, 1986).

Two examples suggest both the accomplishments and the limits of such progressive cities: Santa Monica, California, and Burlington, Vermont. In Santa Monica, a southern California city of 90,000 people, a progressive slate backed by a middle-class movement of renters and fixed-income seniors captured the municipal government in 1981 (Heskin, 1983). Upon its victory, the newly progressive city council imposed a moratorium on development approvals, implemented rent control and expanded formal channels for citizen participation in municipal decision making (Clavel, 1986).

Also in 1981, in the much smaller city of Burlington, Vermont, a socialist candidate was elected as mayor. His coalition comprised middleclass and business elements who had broken with the existing regime along with opponents of the previous governing coalition's neighbourhoodthreatening strategy of highway construction and higher-income housing development (Conroy, 1990). Over the next several years the mayor enhanced the administrative capacities of the local government, wrested control of redevelopment policy from an obstructionist planning commission, developed an economic development strategy less harmful to the city's residential districts, instituted mechanisms for citizen participation in land-use planning, and went on to win several subsequent two-year mayoral terms and ultimately a seat in the US Congress.

In both cities, however, progressive coalitions lost control, and, as Conroy comments about Burlington, 'most [major] initiatives were either defeated outright or adopted in a watered-down form' (1990: 211). In general, progressive local regimes have succumbed to considerable external political opposition, economic constraints and internal weaknesses.[10] Progressive local leaders have had difficulty establishing effective governing coalitions, and often stumble in their attempts to forge a realistic strategy for growth that is acceptable to their more radical supporters. While they may occasionally take over city hall and produce substantial city-wide benefits for subaltern groups, their triumphs remain unusual and fleeting.

Community organizing in ethnic neighborhoods   Most progressive coalitions are limited to specific territories within cities and do not have city-wide impacts. Many such neighbourhood mobilizations are led by community organizers committed to the confrontational approach of Saul Alinsky (1946) and the organization he spawned, the Industrial Areas Foundation (IAF). Such community-organizing activities are frequently evident in areas with high proportions of lower-income racial and ethnic minorities. For example, in San Antonio and El Paso, Texas, IAF organizations have mobilized large but poor Latino neighbourhoods to demand such basic urban services as street paving and utilities. Key to their accomplishments have been both the substantial size of the minority populations they have mobilized and their strategy of working closely with local churches (Berry et al., 1993; Marston and Towers, 1993).

The San Antonio group, Communities Organized for Public Service (COPS), is perhaps the largest and most influential such community organization in the country (Boyte, 1980; Berry et al., 1993). Formed in 1974 and operating continuously thereafter, COPS has employed protest tactics as well as more conventional voter registration drives, lobbying of local elected officials, and candidate endorsements. Among its accomplishments have been higher funding of programmes and improved services to previously under-served areas of the city, registration of thousands of voters, and the election of sympathetic city council members. Although it has mobilized in the electoral arena, COPS has maintained autonomy from city government by refusing to accept city funds to support its organization, and it maintains a distance from political incumbents. However, COPS's success in mobilizing the Hispanic community of the city has produced resentment among the city's Anglo population, and it has not extended its efforts beyond the confines of its own cultural territory (Berry et al., 1993: 296).

The COPS model was exported to El Paso, where the IAF assisted in organizing the El Paso Interreligious Sponsoring Organization (ELPISO), which has mobilized the Hispanic community around demands for service provision, employing both confrontational tactics and electoral mobilization. ELPISO has limited itself to largely parochial neighbourhood concerns, shunning the larger issues of economic development and immigration. Thus, while ELPISO and other similar groups can point to specific, substantial victories, they refrain from challenging the broader forces that lead to neighbourhood deprivation in the first place (Marston and Towers, 1993: 95).

Homeowners' movements   While the neighbourhood movement in the US has frequently been associated with progressive aims, it also contains conservative elements. The homeowner and slow-growth movement that emerged in California in the 1970s provides a significant example of a contemporary, non-progressive USM. Indeed, the territorial mobilization of homeowners in defence of home values and neighbourhood exclusivity represents one of the most powerful social movements in contemporary Southern California (M. Davis, 1990: 153). Like their more progressive counterparts, these movements have demanded 'community control' and citizen participation in land use planning, and they have mobilized in the electoral arena, voting many traditional pro-growth politicians out of office beginning in the mid-70s. Their impacts have been considerable. Homeowners' associations and slow-growth organizations in Southern California have successfully challenged a number of regional growth-oriented regimes, have substantially shaped the socio-spatial development of a major American metropolis, and have reinforced major shifts in American national politics.

The composition of the homeowners' movement has been broadly middle-class, but it provided the grass-roots resources for a property tax revolt led by much wealthier commercial and residential rental property owners. This effort culminated in California with the passage of Proposition 13 in 1978, a tax-cutting measure that has been widely emulated in other states. The national conservative regime led by Ronald Reagan has its roots in the California taxpayers' movement. After its taxcutting success, the homeowners' movement shifted its focus to 'slow-growth' objectives and eventually collided with its former allies' interests. Typically conflicts erupted over the construction of multi-family rental, condominium and commercial projects that threatened previously exclusive single-family-home districts. As these conflicts and the movements they spawned gained momentum in the late 1970s, many local governments responded to homeowner demands by imposing limits on apartment construction, large developments and the trend towards smaller lots.

In reaction, real estate developers, traditionally opposed to government regulation, and not usually allied with minority and low-income groups, began to call for regional planning to overcome the obstructionism of local slow-growth forces. Developers, although not previously known as advocates of the poor, successfully portrayed slow-growth and homeowner activists as selfish, elitist and racist. Such delegitimizing tactics, combined with heavy developer spending in the electoral arena, have represented a powerful but not invincible counter-movement to homeowners' grass-roots initiatives. In addition, the slow-growth movement was weakened by its own failure to reach out to lower income and minority groups in coalition against real-estate investors, and by its tendency to restrict mobilization to individual locales and controversies.

The homeowners' movement exhibits a number of characteristics that are common to other USMs: its aims and tactics have been largely parochial and defensive, and its leadership tends to come from higher socioeconomic strata. Like other urban movements, it has called for democratic controls over local policy making. Further, local political and economic elites have employed strategies of division and delegitimation against this middle- and upper-middle class movement strikingly similar to those used against other lower-class and minority USMs. Pro-development forces have accused the slow-growth movement of undermining the public interest, while local governments have pursued policies that serve to fragment protest and discourage city- or region-wide mobilization. Presently, the conjunction of ongoing regional environmental and infrastructural crises with a serious recession, including substantial real estate deflation, suggest an indeterminate future for mobilizations around taxes and opposition to growth. At the moment the preoccupation of the homeowners' movements appears to be crime, and their support has underlain recent stringent anti-crime legislation at both state and national levels and the election of candidates running law-and-order campaigns.

Europe

In Europe, as the militant atmosphere of the 1960s receded, urban movements cropped up only sporadically as neighbourhood-based demands either subsided or became part of broader party programmes.[11] Pressures for community participation in planning did arise, however, in connection with various redevelopment schemes. In some exceptional cases, community groups moved beyond simple opposition to public- or private-sector plans and developed sophisticated schemes of their own, in what amounted to 'popular planning'. However, as in the US, some European USMs emerged in the 1970s that had aims quite inconsistent with progressive principles.

'Popular planning' in London and Paris   In both London and Paris in the 1970s, community groups emerged to oppose large-scale office redevelopment schemes that threatened existing residents and the character of their neighbourhoods. While these cross-class mobilizations are more exceptional than illustrative of USMs in Europe during this period, they do suggest that USMs continued to hold the potential for achieving broadly progressive aims – under suitable conditions.

In the London district of Waterloo, government plans and developers' proposals for office development on and near Coin Street provoked community opposition (Brindley et al., 1989: Ch. 5). Residents sought to block the offices, employing both mass demonstrations and more traditional approaches. Over a period of years and with extensive resident participation, the community groups developed sophisticated plans of their own for the district. These plans called for low-rent housing, parks and open space, and commercial and light-manufacturing development that would benefit the many poor and working-class residents of the area. By the late 1980s, the coalition of Waterloo community groups could point to substantial progress in having implemented their plans.

Despite a somewhat different political context, a similar pattern of aims, tactics, and effects can be seen in the mobilization of the Parisian neighbourhood of Maison Blanche (Body-Gendrot, 1987). Residents opposed the environmental effects of large office towers being constructed in their midst under an urban renewal plan. They organized mass demonstrations and a sit-in that temporarily brought construction to a halt. While the group continued to employ confrontational tactics, it also deployed the resources of its middle-class leadership in taking the developer to court. By 1985 it had won its legal battles, secured the financial support of several state agencies, and was on the way to seeing its scheme for public housing, stores, a daycare centre, and recreational facilities come to fruition.

Thus in both London and Paris, community groups were able to overcome the substantial power of public and private actors who sought to transform their neighbourhoods. In both cases, stable cross-class alliances emerged that exhibited few internal conflicts. These groups were able to deploy the divergent resources of their members: the *savoir faire* of the middle class and the social networks of workers and old-time residents. Both mobilizations employed similar tactics, switching back and forth between protest and more conventional means; in both cases, organizational flexibility and coalitions with other neighbourhood groups were essential for success. Yet contextual factors were determinative: sympathetic local (and as of 1981 in France, national) governments, along with changing economic conditions that reduced the appeal of office development proposals, contributed substantially to both victories. The very infrequency of such incidents of popular planning, however, suggest that the convergence of internal and contextual factors favourable to movement success is quite rare.

Ratepayers' movements in Britain   Although incidents of popular planning suggest that the progressive potential of USMs continued in Europe through the 1970s and 1980s, other USMs from this period have promoted rather different aims. One significant example of a European, non-progressive USM is the ratepayers' movement in Britain. The latter, along with more recent anti-foreigner and rightist movements, reinforces the point that '*tout ce qui bouge, n'est pas rouge*' (Pickvance, 1985: 39).

Organizations opposed to the rates (the local property tax) existed in Britain well before the 1970s, but after 1974 a wave of more militant ratepayers' organizations emerged across the country; they were spurred by rates increases associated with both rapid inflation and local Labour spending on public housing and services (Lowe, 1986: Ch. 5). The ratepayers demanded reductions in, or even the abolition of, the rates, along with the public spending these local taxes supported. Their political platform was populist and 'non-partisan', reflecting their frustration with seemingly-entrenched Labour domination of the authorities within which they mobilized. Among their goals were the sale of council housing, private provision of public services, and increased spending for law and order.

Professionals and the self-employed held leadership positions within ratepayer associations, but the bulk of their membership has typically been middle- and lower-middle-class, homeowning persons from the skilled manual trades. Analysis of electoral behaviour during this period suggests that voters often abandoned their national party allegiance, most closely associated with occupational status, to vote for ratepayer candidates in local elections. These findings reinforce the general conclusion that housing status cleavages have emerged to displace class conflict as the principal division in local politics in at least some British communities (Lowe, 1986: 137–8).

Ratepayers' movements have had a conservative impact on local politics, pointing to how consumption-sector interests can undermine progressive aims. These movements, however, have tended to be rather ephemeral, as internal factionalism has undercut their capacity to press their issues.

Xenophobic and right-wing movements   Non-progressive mobilizations in Western Europe have not been limited to a middle-class or homeowning base, as recent anti-foreigner and right-wing political movements, particularly in the reunited Germany, suggest. Participants in these locally-based movements, largely unemployed and working-class youth traditionally excluded from the 'alternative movement scene' (of which more below), have resented the social service and housing claims of refugees and have regarded foreigners as competitors for jobs (Mayer, 1993). They have employed 'ritualistic' rioting as well as squatting as tactics. Although officially repudiated by national governments, these emerging movements have succeeded in placing immigration controls squarely on national agendas and in bringing right-wing politicians into prominence. Urban social movements with non-progressive aims are thus common to both Europe and the US, although their composition, aims and effects have differed considerably.

The Green movement in Germany

The Green movement in Germany differs from the others we have discussed in combining local initiatives with an important national presence. The rise of the Greens began at the local level, spread to the states and culminated, in 1983, with the election of Green candidates to the Bundestag. It has inspired both emulation and controversy among radical intellectuals and activists in Europe. Recently the incorporation of the Greens into the parliamentary and administrative arenas has called into question the organic connections of Green elected officials to their grass-roots base. At the same time, it has succeeded in giving the movement significant influence over policy and social norms. In some respects, the triumphs of the Greens suggest the potential for a non-class-based radical politics that rejects consumerist and productivist values, even as Green activists grapple with establishing working relationships between the movement, political parties and the state.[12]

The history of the Green movement, and the citizens' movement with which it is closely associated, can be divided into three major periods from the 1960s to about 1990; these periods are largely defined by the state response to movement initiatives and the consequent influences these responses had on the movement itself (Roth, 1991; Mayer, 1993). During the first period, from the late 1960s to about 1974, middle-class urban residents fought defensive battles against state-sponsored redevelopment programmes. After first pressing their demands through conventional channels, activists later adopted more confrontational tactics when established political institutions failed to respond to their demands. They were joined by the youth movement in a series of squatting incidents in a variety of German cities in the early 1970s. Although the government responded with some concessions, their substantive value was limited (Roth, 1991).

In the second phase of the citizens' movement, which began in 1974 and lasted into the 1980s, the government retreated from its moderately accommodationist stance and sought to delegitimize movement activities. In the face of global economic restructuring, the German government adopted urban redevelopment and welfare policies intended to stimulate capital investment and reduce social welfare expenses; these policy shifts reinforced uneven urban development and exacerbated the conditions which first spawned the movement. The West German government singled out the citizens' movement as an obstacle to state policies aimed at making the nation more competitive in the global economy.

The disparate governmental traditions of Germany and the United States led to divergent policy positions with respect to citizen participation under similar global economic pressures (Franz and Warren, 1987). During the 1970s the US government sought to co-opt dissent through provisions for citizen participation in urban redevelopment and environmental programmes. In contrast, German political institutions completely rejected the movement's demands – in even their most middle-class and accommodating permutations. The result was yet another wave of protests and squatting incidents throughout German cities, and disparate, particularist protest movements coalesced around 'the environment' and its symbol, the colour green (Roth, 1991). In the early 1980s, these movements were joined by peace and anti-nuclear movements, but the Greens failed to incorporate labour into their coalition, and, despite recent efforts, they maintain a reputation for being anti-working class (Boggs, 1986: 209).

Despite some successes, particularly in opposing nuclear facilities, movement participants increasingly found protest tactics inadequate in the face of a united government/growth coalition opposition. Thus, in the third phase, the Green movement entered the electoral arena, forming Green and 'alternative lists' in many jurisdictions. Local victories led to the formation of a national party in 1980; in 1983, the Green Party gained seats in the Bundestag. The movement had moved into the realm of institutional politics at the local and national levels, and its tactics began to switch from protest to lobbying (Roth, 1991). The Green Party has consciously struggled to keep its links to its grass-roots base (Boggs, 1986), but recent developments suggest that its pursuing a dual strategy of grass-roots mobilization and electoral/institutional politics is exacerbating rifts in the party (which was renamed the Alliance 90/Green Party after reunification). Another source of tension has been the selective adoption of Green issues by other political parties and by the state administration. Thus the third period of the Green movement in Germany encompasses the incorporation of much of the movement leadership into institutional politics as well as the diffusion and perhaps dilution of the movement's agenda into public policies, including labour, social services and environmental management.[13]

The tensions and contradictions of incorporation in the third phase described above foreshadow yet a fourth in the 1990s: a period in which the incorporated components of the movement will face increasing pressures from socially marginal groups, particularly unemployed and working-class youth (Roth, 1991; Mayer, 1993). A strategy of incorporation necessarily produces winners and losers within a movement, creating cleavages between the new insiders and those left out. This split currently manifests itself in protest actions by lower-class youths, who have attacked many Green and grass-roots state-sponsored programmes, particularly those aiding the massive waves of immigrants into the West after reunification, as well as the participatory housing provision programmes that the more radical, 'autonomous-sector' movement perceives as gentrification (Mayer, 1993: 164).

Patterns of convergence

This review of USMs in both Europe and the US since the 1960s suggests a number of commonalities across an otherwise disparate set of phenomena. First, despite the undeniable and substantial impacts of the USMs reviewed here, they are severely limited by their inability to sustain both mobilization and programmatic gains without being routinized. Although this tension developed earlier in the United States, with its remarkably permeable political system, on both sides of the Atlantic USMs have become absorbed into regular politics and the administration of state-funded programmes.[14] Second, movements, typically characterized by a distrust of government, are frequently at odds with local authorities. While cooperation with the local state does tend towards co-optation, failure to do so undermines the ability of movements to harness the unique resources of the public sector. Third, 'collective consumption trade union' movements show a systematic inability to establish lasting coalitions with other groups. The relation of movements to political parties is consistently problematic. Saunders's (1979) early review and Goss's (1988) more recent work both highlight this, as did Castells's (1983) account of the Parisian mobilization against the *grands ensembles*. Such stresses continue to plague the Green movement.

There is an overall trend towards middle-class movements in the West (Mayer, 1993). The exception here are movements that are held together by ethnic or other identities, but such movements tend also to be circumscribed in their aims and restricted to narrow social groups. Although USMs do not pursue only progressive aims, their most striking commonality across both space and time, and even the left/right divide, has been their demand for participation in municipal decision making and management. Notwithstanding their limitations, USMs in both Europe and the US have made significant changes in local polities in a variety of cities and halted some of the more destructive kinds of state redevelopment activities. They have expanded the boundaries of local politics and have occasionally altered the balance of power among national political forces.

Recent theoretical developments

The various theorists of urban social movements, and of social movements more broadly, approach their subject matter with varying objectives and therefore do not necessarily address the same questions. We examine in this section one principal question: the reasons for the success or failure of USMs.

Resource mobilization theory

The most influential theoretical formulations of the issue of success and failure rest in 'resource mobilization theory' (RMT). RMT derives from Mancur Olson's (1968) analysis, which has as its premise that individuals will only participate in forms of collective action, including social movements, when the benefits that accrue to them as individuals outweigh the costs.[15] Olson develops his argument within the paradigm of neo-classical economics: like all neo-classical economic models, his places the individual prior to the community and defines rationality as the maximization of individual self-interest. Consequently his formulation is susceptible to criticism for an overly narrow conception of self-interest (see Mansbridge, 1990). Other scholars using RMT to analyse social movements, however, do not necessarily operate within a strict neo-classical framework. Rather, they include personal satisfaction achieved through the act of participation itself and the attainment of collective goals as a benefit to individuals. They therefore see looser constraints on behaviour than does Olson, who regards any participatory act as a cost and providing gains to free riders as an irrational act.

According to RMT, movement leaders must act as entrepreneurs, enticing others to 'invest' in the movement; participants are more or less likely to join depending on their calculations of the movement's potential effectiveness. Movements are successful when they are able to mobilize sufficient resources to either overcome or co-opt their opposition. According to Jenkins:

> Resource mobilization theories have adopted an 'open system' approach, arguing that the outcomes of movements are critically shaped by the larger political environment [from which many resources are drawn]. The outcomes of challenges depend not only on strategic choices but also on the stance of political elites and the support/opposition of established interest organizations and other movements. The balance of supports and social controls is, in turn, shaped by changes in governing coalitions, the structure of regimes, and societal changes that give rise to regime crises. (1983: 543)

Pickvance (1995) applies the less constrained version of RMT to his analysis of the rise and decline of urban movements. In his discussion he restricts his definition of USM success to the ability of movement organizations to mobilize participants.[16] He identifies two main factors in the urban context which go far to explain the decline of those urban movements demanding an expansion of collective consumption: first, a new policy environment in which budgetary constraints, buttressed by market-based ideologies calling for reductions in government social welfare efforts, lowered participation in movements calling for more state spending; second, a new emphasis on the privatization of public services and a consequent absorption of movement organizations and leaders into the service delivery sector. The former change reduced the potential returns of activism, the latter increased the likely costs.

Pickvance (1995) differentiates himself from Castells, who, while recognizing the variability in the strength of USMs from place to place, argues that worldwide there is an upward trend. Pickvance maintains, in contrast, that movements within different contexts have different roots and therefore 'it is not sensible to debate whether there is a "clear comparative upward trend" as Castells suggests or whether "large-scale urban social movements have faded out as rapidly as they originated" [as Ceccarelli argues]'. What matters is to understand the relationship between the movement and its context. Consequently the contingent factors that differentiate USMs from one locale to another are theoretically as important as the commonalities that Castells (1983) seeks to identify.

Our recapitulation of the experience of some European and American social movements corroborates Pickvance's insistence on the interaction between movement activities and context. The subsidence of American USMs based on the convergence of race, client status and territory; the subsequent rise in both the US and the UK of taxpayers' revolts; and the mutations of the citizens' movement in Germany as it responded to alternative government policies of concessions and hostility all indicate how much a movement's strength and tactics depend on the sociopolitical framework in which it operates. Nevertheless, to the extent that movement activities shape this framework, the consciousness and tactics of participants have an independent role in affecting outcomes.

Economic versus other bases for mobilization

We noted earlier in this chapter that analysts have largely agreed that the wellsprings of contemporary USMs do not spring from specifically economic grievances. Disagreement, however, persists over how to evaluate the effect of cross-class urban mobilizations.

Kling and Posner assert that the neo-populists, who do not seek to change the economic framework, are engaged in a highly problematic, possibly retrogressive endeavour:

> In the absence of a commitment to some larger concept of social justice, mobilization for collective action based on these most readily accessible 'dispositions' (i.e., familiar identities and beliefs like property rights and community self-determination) does not necessarily move people in the direction of greater equality or democracy. . . . It is precisely these readily accessible mobilizing sentiments that . . . assimilate protest into the structures of politics as usual. (1990: 36)

The American neighbourhood movement thus has only limited egalitarian potential. Offe, when speaking of the radical middle-class movements in Europe, comments that they embody 'typically a politics *of* a class, but not *on behalf of* a class' (1987: 77, original emphasis). In contradistinction, the US neighbourhood movement is frequently dominated by homeowners, which, while not a class in the Marxian sense, are a group with very specific property interests (see J.E. Davis, 1991). Thus, the neighbourhood movement, even though strongly democratic in its aims, often acts on behalf of an economic group in ways that oppose egalitarian outcomes. When urban movements do have more redistributive goals, as in Burlington and Santa Monica, they are seriously limited by higher levels of government and forces in the broader society and economy.

Castells, although less critical of movement aims than Kling and Posner, also views urban movements as limited by their localism. He argues that 'urban movements are unable to put forward any historically feasible project of economic production, communication, or government' (Castells, 1983: 329). Social transformation therefore depends on the success of 'central' movements like feminism and self-management (Castells, 1983: 327). For Castells, as well as for Kling and Posner, the base of USMs in residential communities separate from the world of work precludes their acting on a world economic system that determines the flow of material resources. Our synopsis of the experience of USMs strongly supports Castells's argument.

The Green movement comprises the most developed synthesis of locally based activism with a nationally defined social and cultural tendency. Although the Greens' programme for democratizing society rests on a middle-class base and does not constitute a direct attack on capitalism, its ecological and cultural precepts undercut capitalist hegemony. But, as we indicated earlier in this chapter, it has failed to forge meaningful links with working-class organizations, and it is doubtful whether any movement with an anti-growth stance could do so. The fundamental problem of environmentalist movements is that they confront not only the capitalist drive for profits but also the interests of a working class dependent on economic expansion for employment. Thus, the possibility of environmentalism becoming the mobilizing aim for an egalitarian social movement founders if the prerequisite is a serious blockage of economic expansion.

Assessment

An assessment of the theory of USMs looks at only a fragment of the theory of social movements more generally. Whereas Touraine or Melucci are analysing seismic changes in whole societies, analysts of USMs are discussing a very specific type of social actor – one based in a small piece of territory that usually does not encompass a centre of power. Hence, Castells must be correct in his argument that at best such movements by themselves have only the capability of resistance and attainment of specific benefits. There are a number of strategic questions that arise beyond this broad one of movement potential: Can USMs continue to be effective if they become connected to party organizations or professionalized staffs? Will participation in elections necessarily destroy their transforming potential? Can a cross-class base allow them to confront capitalist hegemony? In other words, does a social movement remain a social movement if its constitutive organizations participate in normal politics or administration (Fainstein and Fainstein, 1991)? And can it be truly transformative if it encompasses a broad coalition of groups with varying economic interests? None of these questions can be answered yes or no in general, since all entail irresolvable tensions. The price that USMs pay if they do not become fully involved in the political system is 'a marked incapacity for confronting the imperatives of political power' (Boggs, 1986: 75). But the cost of involvement is co-optation and compromise.

The constraints on USMs imply that locally based movements only affect the structural forces impinging on cities when they are fused into national forces. The civil rights and black power movements in the US were once such forces; the homeowner-based anti-tax movement in the US has had major effects on the revenue-raising capabilities and social welfare role of US state and federal governments; the more inclusive movement against the poll tax in Britain did force the Conservative government to adopt a more equitable tax policy; and the Greens today have the potential to affect the culture and polity of Germany as a whole.

At present the greatest impact of urban movements is to make urban decision making more democratic. Nonetheless, increased citizen participation in local government and service delivery has not dramatically changed the outcomes of urban processes beyond decisions on immediately mobilizing issues. This does not mean that local politics and urban movements are of no importance or that the urban community is a meaningless base for mobilization, but it does imply that USMs, to be transfotmative, must develop a set of aims that goes beyond a content-free demand for local democracy. If they do so they are no longer simply *urban* social movements but are elements of social movements more generally.

Notes

1 We restrict our discussion to North America and Western Europe. Urban social movements have been significant actors in cities in Eastern Europe and in the less developed countries as well, but, given important differences in their origins and theoretical treatments, we cannot include them within the space limitations of a single chapter.

2 This viewpoint traces back to Gustave LeBon (1960), who in 1895 argued that in a crowd men forsake reason and responsibility.

3 The field of collective behaviour identified a serious threat to liberal democracy in any incidence of 'mob' behaviour. Smelser's (1962) is the best known of the irrationalist interpretations of social movements. He collapses movements, riots and panics into a single category and asserts that all such forms of collective behaviour have connected with them a 'generalized', or 'exaggerated' belief containing irrational elements: 'A norm-oriented movement involves elements of panic . . ., craze . . ., and hostility' (Smelser, 1962: 271). Among political scientists Seymour Martin Lipset (1960), in a widely read volume, dismissed social movements because they injected the mass of people directly into decision making and tended to avoid bargaining and compromise.

4 In particular, studies of the student movement contradicted assertions concerning the irrationality and marginality of movement participants. See Bay (1967).

5 For definitions of social movements see Fainstein and Fainstein (1974: Appendix); Eyerman and Jamison (1991: Introduction); Scott (1990: Introduction); Diani (1992).

6 Pickvance (1986), however, criticizes Castells for failing to maintain this distinction consistently.

7 By 'collective consumption' Castells (1977: 460) refers to goods and services that reach consumers by way of the state sector, for example, public housing, parks, community health services, etc.

8 For example, in the London Borough of Croydon, which had a long tradition of Conservative party dominance, the local Labour councillors of the 1970s were largely middle class. They opposed the demands of their working class constituency when they conflicted with abstract socialist principles. When the Conservative local council proposed a limited programme of selling council housing units to long-term residents in the early 1970s, the Labour councillors obstructed the programme on ideological grounds, leading their working-class constituents to mount a protest against them (Saunders, 1979: 285). Goss (1988) tells a contrasting story of the take-over of the local Labour organization in the London Borough of Southwark by middle-class professionals and cultural radicals, who wrested control from the old male-dominated working-class leadership.

9 Exceptions to this general observation include a number of militant outbursts in Britain (Benyon and Salomos, 1987), while in Germany the squatting movement experienced a revival in the early 1980s (Roth, 1991).

10 Stone (1989) has documented the rise and fall of the neighbourhood movement in Atlanta, Georgia, while Reed (1988) reviews the constraints on minority-controlled local governments in the US more generally. Notwithstanding the limits of electoral mobilization, in its absence, sustained local policy shifts that favour subordinate groups are not likely (Browning et al., 1984).

11 Recent social movements have primarily directed their attention to broader issues, such as the peace, anti-nuclear, and feminist causes.

12 For an early position on the general relation of social movements to political parties and the state, see Gorz (1982).

13 Local governments throughout Germany are increasingly employing the services of local 'grass-roots' groups in housing and social services provision as an 'innovative reserve' (Mayer, 1993: 160). Gyford (1991) describes similar local government adoption of grass-roots initiatives in the UK.

14 The assimilation of social movement innovations by the local state in response to economic restructuring has been observed in Britain, on the Continent and in the US (Franz and Warren, 1987; Gyford, 1991; Roth, 1991).

15 Olson's discussion breaks sharply with the earlier analyses of social movements that regarded them as essentially expressive and irrational. Like collective behaviour theory, however, it attempts to treat all forms of non-institutionalized collective action as alike, regardless of social background of participants, aims of the collectivity, or method of action.

16 Hannigan (1985: 446) criticizes Touraine and Castells for failing to recognize the role of social movement organizations in determining the movements' fate.

References

Alinsky, S. (1946) *Reveille for Radicals*. Chicago, IL: University of Chicago Press.

Bartholomew, A. and Mayer, M. (1992) '*Nomads of the Present*: Melucci's contribution to "New Social Movement" Theory', *Theory, Culture and Society*, 9: 141–59.

Bay, C. (1967) 'Political and apolitical students: facts in search of a theory', *Journal of Social Issues*, 23 (July): 77–85.

Benyon, J. and Salomos, J. (eds) (1987) *The Roots of Urban Unrest*. Oxford: Pergamon Press.

Berry, J.M., Portney, K.E. and Thompson, K. (1993) *The Rebirth of Urban Democracy*. Washington, D.C.: Brookings Institution.

Body-Gendrot, S. (1987) 'Grass-roots mobilization in the Thirteenth Arrondissement of Paris: a cross-national view', in C.N. Stone and H.T. Sanders (eds), *The Politics of Urban Development*. Lawrence: University Press of Kansas.

Boggs, C. (1986) *Social Movements and Political Power*. Philadelphia, PA: Temple University Press.

Boyte, H. (1980) *The Backyard Revolution*. Philadelphia, PA: Temple University Press.

Brindley, T., Ryder, Y. and Stoker, G. (1989) *Remaking Planning: The Politics of Urban Change in the Thatcher Years*. London: Unwin Hyman.

Browning, R.P., Marshall, D.R. and Tabb, D.H. (1984) *Protest Is Not Enough: The Struggle of Blacks and Hispanics for Equality in Urban Politics*. Berkeley: University of California Press.

Castells, M. (1977) *The Urban Question*. Cambridge, MA: MIT Press.

Castells, M. (1978) *City, Class and Power*. London: Macmillan.

Castells, M. (1983) *The City and the Grassroots*. Berkeley: University of California Press.

Castells, M. (1985) 'Commentary on C.G. Pickvance's "The rise and fall of urban movements . . ."', *Environment and Planning D: Society and Space*, 4: 221–31.

Ceccarelli, P. (1982) 'Politics, parties, and urban movements: Western Europe', in N.I. Fainstein and S.S. Fainstein (eds), *Urban Policy under Capitalism*. Beverly Hills, CA: Sage.

Clavel, P. (1986) *The Progressive City*. New Brunswick, NJ: Rutgers University Press.

Conroy, W.J. (1990) *Challenging the Boundaries of Reform*. Philadelphia, PA: Temple University Press.

Davis, J.E. (1991) *Contested Ground: Collective Action in the Urban Neighborhood*. Ithaca, NY: Cornell University Press.

Davis, M. (1990) *City of Quartz: Excavating the Future in Los Angeles*. London: Verso.

Diani, M. (1992) 'The concept of social movement', *Sociological Review*, 40 (February): 1–25.

Edsall, T.B. with Edsall, M.D. (1992) *Chain Reaction: The Impact of Race, Rights, and Taxes on American Politics*. New York: Norton.

Eyerman, R. and Jamison, A. (1991) *Social Movements: A Cognitive Approach*. University Park: Pennsylvania State University Press.

Fainstein, N.I. and Fainstein, S.S. (1974) *Urban Political Movements*. Englewood Cliffs, NJ: Prentice-Hall.

Fainstein, S.S. and Fainstein, N.I. (1985) 'Economic restructuring and the rise of urban social movements', *Urban Affairs Quarterly*, 21 (2): 187–206.

Fainstein, S.S. and Fainstein, N.I. (1991) 'The changing character of community politics in New York City: 1968–1988', in J.H. Mollenkopf and M. Castells (eds), *Dual City*. New York: Russell Sage.

Fisher, R. and Kling, J. (1993) 'Conclusion: Prospects and strategies for mobilization in the era of global cities', in R. Fisher and J. Kling (eds), *Mobilizing the Community*. Newbury Park, CA: Sage.

Franz, P. and Warren, D.I. (1987) 'Neighborhood action as a social movement', *Comparative Political Studies*, 20 (2): 229–46.

Gittell, M. (1980) *Limits to Citizen Participation: The Decline of Community Organizations*. Beverly Hills, CA: Sage.

Gorz, A. (1982) *Farewell to the Working Class: An Essay in Post-industrial Socialism*. London: Pluto Press.

Goss, S. (1988) *Local Labour and Local Government: A Study of Changing Interests, Politics and Policy in Southwark from 1919 to 1982*. Edinburgh: Edinburgh University Press.

Gottdiener, M. (1985) *The Social Production of Urban Space*. Austin: University of Texas Press.

Gyford, J. (1991) *Citizens, Consumers, and Councils: Local Government and the Public*. London: Macmillan.

Hannigan, J.A. (1985) 'Alain Touraine, Manuel Castells and social movement theory: a critical appraisal', *Sociological Quarterly*, 26 (4): 435–54.

Harvey, D. (1989) *The Urban Experience*. Baltimore, PA: Johns Hopkins University Press.

Heskin, A.D. (1983) *Tenants and the American Dream: Ideology and the Tenant Movement*. New York: Praeger.

Jenkins, J.C. (1983) 'Resource mobilization theory and the study of social movements', *Annual Review of Sociology*, 9: 527–53.

Katznelson, I. (1981) *City Trenches*. New York: Pantheon.

Kling, J.M. and Posner, P.S. (1990) 'Class and community in an era of urban transformation', in J.M. Kling and P.S. Posner (eds), *Dilemmas of Activism: Class, Community and the Politics of Local Mobilization*. Philadelphia, PA: Temple University Press.

Kotler, M. (1969) *Neighborhood Government*. Indianapolis, IN: Bobbs-Merrill.

LeBon, G. (1960) *The Crowd*, New York: Viking.

Lipset, S.M. (1960) *Political Man: The Social Bases of Politics*. Garden City, NJ: Doubleday.

Lipsky, M. (1970) *Protest and City Politics: Rent Strikes, Housing, and the Power of the Poor*. Chicago, IL: Rand McNally.

Lowe, S. (1986) *Urban Social Movements: The City after Castells*. New York: St. Martin's Press.

Mansbridge, J.J. (1990) 'On the relation of altruism and self-interest', *Beyond Self-Interest*. Chicago, IL: University of Chicago Press.

Marston, S. and Towers, G. (1993) 'Private spaces and the politics of places: spatioeconomic restructuring and community organizing in Tuscon and El Paso', in R. Fisher and J. Kling (eds), *Mobilizing the Community*. Newbury Park, CA: Sage.

Mayer, M. (1987) 'Popular opposition in West Germany', in M.P. Smith and J.R. Feagin (eds), *The Capitalist City*. Oxford: Blackwell.

Mayer, M. (1993) 'The career of urban social movements in West Germany', in R. Fisher and J. Kling, (eds), *Mobilizing the Community*. Newbury Park, CA: Sage.

Melucci, A. (1989) *Nomads of the Present*, J. Keane and P. Mier (eds). Philadelphia, PA: Temple University Press.

Mollenkopf, J.H. (1983) *The Contested City*. Princeton, NJ: Princeton University Press.

Offe, C. (1987) 'Challenging the boundaries of institutional politics: social movements since the 1960s', in C.S. Maier (ed.), *Changing Boundaries of the Political*. Cambridge: Cambridge University Press.

Olson, M. (1968) *The Logic of Collective Action*. New York: Schocken.

Pakulski, J. (1993) 'Mass social movements and social class', *International Sociology*, 8 (June): 131–58.

Pickvance, C. (1985) 'The rise and fall of urban movements and the role of comparative analysis', *Environment and Planning D: Society and Space*, 3: 31–53.

Pickvance, C. (1986) 'Concepts, contexts and comparison in the study of urban movements: a reply to M. Castells', *Environment and Planning D: Society and Space*, 4: 221–31.

Pickvance, C. (1995) 'Where have urban movements gone?', in C. Hadjimichalis and D. Sadler (eds), *In and around the Margins of a New Europe*. London: Belhaven Press.

Piven, F.F. and Cloward, R.A. (1971) *Regulating the Poor: the Functions of Public Welfare*. New York: Pantheon.

Plotkin, S. (1990) 'Enclave consciousness and neighborhood activism', in J.M. Kling and P.S. Posner (eds), *Dilemmas of Activism: Class, Community and the Politics of Local Mobilization*. Philadelphia, PA: Temple University Press.

Reed, A. Jr. (1988) 'The black urban regime: structural origins and constraints', in M.P. Smith (ed.), *Power, Community and the City*. Vol. 1. *Comparative Urban and Community Research*. New Brunswick, NJ: Transaction Books.

Roth, R. (1991) 'Local Green politics in West German cities', *International Journal of Urban and Regional Research*, 15 (1): 75–89.

Saunders, P. (1979) *Urban Politics: A Sociological Interpretation*. London: Hutchinson.

Saunders, P. (1986) *Social Theory and the Urban Question* (2nd edn). New York: Holmes and Meier.

Scott, A. (1990) *Ideology and the New Social Movements*. London: Unwin Hyman.

Smelser, N. (1962) *Theory of Collective Behavior*. New York: Free Press.

Stone, C. (1989) *Regime Politics: Governing Atlanta 1946–1986*. Lawrence: University of Kansas Press.

Touraine, A. (1981) *The Voice and the Eye*. Cambridge: Cambridge University Press.

Touraine, A. (1992) 'Beyond social movements?', *Theory, Culture and Society*, 9: 125–45.

11

Women Redefining Local Politics

Susan E. Clarke, Lynn A. Staeheli and Laura Brunell

The feminization of the city through a confluence of economic, demographic and political trends argues for a more gendered perspective on urban politics. In this essay we discuss some of the gendered consequences of the restructuring of local political economies and the implications these trends hold for women's involvement in local politics during the 1990s. We argue that gender relations mediate citizens' experiences with state and economic restructuring. In doing so, we note the inadequacies of established urban theories in dealing with gender as an analytic category. Yet we must also concede the need for more empirically grounded feminist theories of the changing position of women in localities, particularly differences among women in diverse class, race, sexuality and cultural positions. A more gendered research perspective is essential to appreciating the trends that are reshaping cities and to understanding how gender relations segment local economic and political changes.

Urban research and feminist theory

We contend that citizens' experiences with state and economic restructuring are mediated increasingly by gender relations, although the particular configurations and responses to these trends will be shaped by variations in local political, economic and social settings. Understanding the involvement of women in local politics, therefore, requires a larger sense of how economic and political restructuring processes have reshaped the local political terrain. Although established urban theories, as detailed in other contributions to this volume, provide a rich and vigorous account of restructuring effects on local politics, inattention to gender relations restricts their theoretical and empirical value. In this section, we briefly note some of the limitations of established theories of urban politics and indicate the features of a more gendered framework. The following section sketches the gains from a greater theoretical and empirical sensitivity to gender issues in urban analyses, drawing on empirical studies that demonstrate how women are redefining local politics. The concluding section notes the issues raised by feminist urban analyses and assesses the potential contributions of a more gendered approach to urban analysis.

Why a gendered approach to local politics?

Neither urban political economy nor pluralist theories are particularly well equipped to analyse and understand the gendered implications of restructuring changes. Certain limitations are a matter of inadequate theoretical frameworks (Jones, 1988; Abrahams, 1992; Silverburg, 1992; Staeheli and Lawson, 1994). Two features of political economy approaches (such as regime analysis and growth machine approaches) are especially troublesome: the overly economistic perspectives (see Swanstrom, 1993) and the state-centred, elite orientations (Staeheli and Clarke, 1994) that encourage almost an exclusive emphasis on land and capital (Logan and Molotch, 1987; Cox and Mair, 1988) and slight other systems of stratification (but see Smith et al., 1991; Fainstein et al., 1992). As a result, most political economy approaches remain partial theories: while they continue to be of use, they are unable to address fully the political implications of increasing social complexity (Dahlerup, 1986; Harloe and Fainstein, 1992). For example, as Harloe and Fainstein (1992: 248) point out, the fragmentation of the new working class by gender, race and ethnicity dampens working class representation in institutionalized local political structures. As a consequence, the voices of capital and the 'productive', less vulnerable occupational groups are magnified in local political affairs. But the failure to incorporate gender as an analytic category stymies the use of political economy frameworks for investigating these socially marginalized groups and political shifts (Bondi and Peake, 1988; Brownhill and Halford, 1990; McDowell, 1991).

Pluralist approaches are more limited still. The pluralist portrayal of local politics centres on groups organized around exchange values and material interests in competition for public benefits. It presumes that narrow and instrumentalist groups, generally reflecting economic bases, form to influence policy on distributional issues (Young, 1992). But it can tell us little about the emergence of new social groups, the changes in local institutions (Horan, 1991), or the conflicts over non-economic issues such as cultural signifiers and social relations now characteristic of contemporary community politics. In particular, pluralist assumptions about group origins and self-interest maximization motives are less relevant in analysing local identity politics or groups with social movements bases. Indeed, the question of women's 'interests' is contentious; even a feminist reading of women's interests as eliminating patriarchal domination is complicated by the overlay of class, race and ethnicity with gender relations. These differences among women can obscure the political meaning and significance of their organizational strategies (Acklesburg, 1984, 1988; Dickson, 1987). In addition, women's organizations with both cultural change and service goals do not fit easily in conventional typologies of local interest groups as single purpose or public good organizations. Nor are the processes through which movement-based groups engage the state (Costain, 1992a) captured by pluralist bargaining models of political activity. Women's groups in the United States often eschew political parties as vehicles for mobilization and political incorporation: instead, women's groups and non-profit organizations are important non-electoral political features in many American cities, with 'interests' in social and cultural change that extend beyond influencing local policies (Sapiro, 1986: 122; Young, 1992: 531).

Feminist critiques of urban analyses

But how useful is feminist theory in urban analyses? Feminist social theories are, after all, rooted in fundamental critiques of patriarchal society and capitalist economies, not concerns with local politics. From a feminist perspective, however, local politics are shaped by these gendered social and economic relations: while all cities are patriarchal, patriarchy is not invariant but differs across time and place, contingent on struggles over gender inequalities (Appleton, 1994). This feminist perspective contributes three important features to urban analysis: an *epistemological critique* of the dualisms embedded in conventional frameworks that result in a gendered knowledge of localities, an evolving *theoretical debate* on gendered local restructuring processes, and a *normative perspective* on gender and citizenship. Feminist theorists argue that it is not just accidental that women are overlooked and undertheorized in social research but a consequence of key dichotomies in social and political theory that implicitly relegate women to 'inferior' realms that do not require social or political explanation (McDowell, 1992: 410; Staeheli and Lawson, 1994). By continuing to work in ignorance of the gendered associations of these dualisms, urban scholars construct a view of localities that is partial and misleading. Furthermore, gender relations are integral to the restructuring processes that *are* of interest to urban scholars; by failing to take into account how restructuring processes alter the conditions under which both patriarchal and capitalist systems function, urban scholars' understanding of local restructuring processes and consequences is severely diminished. Finally, feminist perspectives provide a normative perspective on urban governance and citizenship that promises to reinvigorate both urban analyses and democratic theory.

The dualisms critique   Dualist distinctions between the workplace and the community, the community and the local state, the individual and the community, the individual and the organization are rampant in urban research but rarely recognized as gendered. These familiar dichotomies are gendered both because they universalize the particular experiences of some males and because they link implicit gender associations with each dichotomy. In most empirical urban research, individual motives are ascribed as if people are independent of other relations and responsibilities; studies of political attitudes and activities were based, until recently, primarily on male respondents and assumed women thought, believed and acted the same as men. This assumption now seems remarkably ill-founded, but the feminist critique requires more than 'adding women' to urban research. A feminist perspective demands rethinking the dualistic, gendered assumptions underlying the dichotomies central to established frameworks: in particular, these include the notions of public/private, formal/informal, and insider/outsider characteristic of most approaches to local politics.

The public/private dualism tends to replicate the distinction of public and private spheres common to liberal democracies (Jaggar, 1983) by accepting differentiations between the so-called 'public' sphere of male-dominated production activities, wage labour and political life, and the private sphere of domestic activity, unpaid domestic labor and everyday life (Viaou, 1992). This limits the scope of analyses of restructuring processes by uncritical acceptance of a restrictive definition of politics that literally renders women and marginal groups invisible (Bondi and Peake, 1988; Brownhill and Halford, 1990; Staeheli and Clarke, 1994). The gendered impacts of economic restructuring underscore the intertwining of these spheres: in particular public laws and institutions such as divorce laws, family policies and welfare programmes shape the private sphere and women's 'public' actions are moulded by their household settings (Okin, 1992).

Formal/informal dichotomies are also employed to distinguish male and female political spheres (Brownhill and Halford, 1990). While women's historical participation in place-based local voluntary associations is recognized, it is discounted as informal rather than formal political involvement. This informal involvement in community politics can be seen as a safe haven for women: it is legitimated by the role continuity with family responsibilities and may be preferred by some women because of the greater accessibility and flexibility of local politics (Bondi and Peake, 1988). Yet women's lower rates of participation in more formal politics may well speak to the lack of other opportunities, the barriers of systemic bias towards male powerholders, and the marginalization of women's issues and demands in formal politics (Bledsoe and Herring, 1990; Brownhill and Halford, 1990: 412). Contemporary increases in women's political participation in both formal (Chaney and Nagler, 1993) and informal arenas indicate that changing perceptions of efficacy (Beckwith, 1986) and shifts in political opportunity structures (Brownhill and Halford, 1990; Costain, 1992b) may be more robust explanations of local political participation than assumed individual preferences for informal politics.

Similarly, the insider/outsider distinction fails to describe adequately women's organizations. As described below, intermediary organizations operating between the market and the state are especially important features of local states (Horan, 1991) and characteristic of the niches occupied by many women's groups; many women's groups are neither insiders nor outsiders and resemble neither classic interest groups nor state units. Similarly, it is unhelpful to categorize women's activities as insider or outsider strategies: the interactions of political insiders and women's groups outside the political process are key elements in women's political involvement (Franzway et al., 1989). Costain (1988) describes this interaction as a process by which insider groups and politicians guide the strategies of outsider groups and effectively subsidize their learning costs. Women's broader political effectiveness is contingent on the continued presence and pressure of groups remaining outside the system, the cooperation of existing groups willing to supply tactical advice and support, and the presence of insider political allies able to guide groups in their new contacts with the state.

The restructuring debate As McDowell points out, restructuring trends challenge earlier feminist assumptions of the interdependence of capitalism and patriarchy (1991: 101). Whereas male industrial workers were seen as supported by the unwaged domestic labour of the wife and the welfare state institutions complementing the worker's 'family wage', neither the industrial worker nor the family wage nor the welfare state institutions appear essential to the capitalist relations attendant to restructuring economies. Furthermore, the increased participation of women as waged and unwaged workers reflects a gender division of labour that is, as McDowell puts it, 'a constitutive element' (1991: 101) rather than just a consequence of these economic trends. These changes in the position of women in the home and the workplace alter, although they do not eliminate, patriarchal relations.

As a gendered local economy emerges from economic restructuring processes, these feminist perspectives become especially salient. In North America, Britain and Europe, women's increased labour force participation is a fundamental aspect of these economic restructuring processes; it is concentrated in employment structures characterized by working arrangements that allow firms to adjust flexibly to labour needs rather than be bound by labour contracts. This includes the more vulnerable middle and lower service occupations and the unskilled working class employed in service and manufacturing jobs (Pratt and Hanson, 1988; Christopherson, 1989; Harloe and Fainstein, 1992; Jezierski, 1994; Johnston-Anumonwo et al., 1994). The employment structure now characteristic of many cities – a new service class segmented by different skill levels and marketability, a fragmented working class of skilled and unskilled workers, a shift to non-standardized work regimes with 'flexible' wages and hours – has differential effects on women, ethnic and racial communities (Christopherson, 1989; Staeheli and Clarke, 1994).

This feminization of the city is articulated through employment structures, familial patterns and spatial relations. It is especially pronounced in older American cities where ecologically defined communities of the poor, the vulnerable, racial minorities and female heads of households are concentrated (Farkas et al., 1988; Harloe and Fainstein, 1992; Appleton, 1994; Johnston-Anumonwo et al., 1994). Indeed, the majority of all female headed households in the Unites States live in central cities (Appleton, 1994: 11); it is a distinctly urban and local grouping, one often also characterized by low income status and racial and ethnic identities. In the United States, the urban concentrations of dual income families, childless couples, and female-headed households in themselves present a demographic counterpoint to most models of urban politics and service delivery. Although waged employment is generally associated with greater political participation (Andersen, 1975), it is not clear it will result from these new configurations if women continue to bear major household responsibilities as well, nor if political participation channels remain structured for a different economic era (Rowbotham and Mitter, 1994; Staeheli and Clarke, 1994). Furthermore, the complex communal and gender fragmentation of these vulnerable groups hampers mobilization on the basis of their common circumstances rather than a narrower identity politics. Thus it is not the increased waged employment of women that is economically and politically significant, it is their segmented flexible employment status and their consequent peripheralization in work and politics (Staeheli and Clarke, 1994). Women's economic, social and political needs are rooted in these macrostructural changes; as in the past, they are not needs associated with any essentialist definition of women's special concerns for family and children but with how the nexus of work and community and family is challenged by the gendered impacts of economic change.

The normative perspective

In addition to these critiques, a feminist perspective offers normative views of local citizenship and urban governance. Generally, these views reject liberal democratic pluralist assumptions of a neutral state arbitrating among competing class-based interests. They are also likely to argue against a politics of emancipation and redistribution (Phillips, 1992; Giddens, 1993) through centralized state actions that leave patriarchal relations intact. Rather, they tend to advocate a purposeful public philosophy in which the state promotes gender justice (for example, Young, 1990, 1992). One version begins by 'rewriting Rawls', as Nussbaum (1992) describes it: theorists adopt Rawls's device of the Original Position but argue that gender justice is not a matter of the distribution of particular goods to women on the basis of their objective (and universal?) interests but the distribution of capabilities to take action found in a gender-friendly society. Not only does this view leave the content of interests, and thus of a 'women's agenda', variable according to the self-definition of different subcommunities, it redirects attention to the political form in which interests are represented. This echoes arguments for 'rational' or 'reflective' liberalism made by Smith (1989), Sen (1982), Nussbaum (1992), Galston (1982) and others; it assumes an active state promoting citizens' potential for reflective choice (Smith, 1989: 291). Thus gender justice arguments (Sen, 1982; Jonasdottir, 1988; Okin, 1992) would return urban analysis to a normative consideration of democratic values rather than narrower concerns with producer or consumer efficiency.

Using the feminist lens in urban research

By looking at localities with this feminist lens, we bring into focus a number of features neglected by other perspectives. Women's growing involvement in local politics must be interpreted in the context of gendered changes in employment structures and work regimes but also in the context of the new institutional arrangements emerging in post-welfare state communities, the overlay of local groups with class-based interests and those with roots in new social movements, and the volatile resource bases of these new groups. These changes suggest greater local complexity and shifting political opportunities but do not necessarily imply more pluralistic local power relations (Lovenduski and Randall, 1993: 173) since a systemic bias towards patriarchy persists.

Few, therefore, would anticipate that the increasing participation of women in local economies and polities will fundamentally change local power relations or redress gender inequalities. But by sketching out analyses of three political dimensions (Dahlerup, 1986: 16), we illustrate the importance of understanding the interaction of gender relations and local political systems: local political leadership and the concomitant values and ideas expressed in local politics; tensions between feminist principles and interest group politics; and local state institutional change. The empirical studies noted here indicate that women's activism is transforming how women view themselves and how the political system views women's interests. As a consequence, women are rethinking traditional categories of political action and characterizing their political activities in new categories that do not necessarily correspond to state definitions. In this process of self-definition and invention of their relation to the state (Foucault, 1982), women are redefining local politics as a sphere of action.

Gender and political leadership

Women's greater political participation presumably brings more direct introduction of gendered values into local politics (Bers and Mezey, 1981). Women are an increasingly active electorate (Chaney and Nagler, 1993) although the participation of women with feminist values is mediated by race (Fulenwider, 1981; Jennings 1991; but see Kay, 1985), class (Ackelsburg, 1988) and ethnicity (Hero, 1992; MacManus and Bullock, 1994; Rabrenovic, 1994). Differences among women hamper coalition formation and the effective use of gender gaps as an electoral strategy to induce greater support for women's concerns from elected officials (Mueller, 1988; Evans, 1993). They also complicate expectations of the effects of having more women in elected and appointed political positions.

Nevertheless, it does appear that there are significant differences between male and female public officials' role perceptions, problem-solving styles and policy priorities in American subnational politics. The findings of gender differences in state politics – women have different policy priorities, including women's rights and family issues; women are more active on women's rights legislation; women are more 'feminist' and 'liberal' in their policy orientations; women are more likely to bring citizens into the governing process; women are more responsive to outsider groups; women use more contextually-oriented problem-solving styles; women define power in cooperative rather than coercive terms (Carroll et al., 1991; Kathlene, 1994; MacManus and Bullock, 1994) – are also evident in more limited studies of local public officials in the United States (Acklesburg, 1984; Antolini, 1984; Flammang, 1984, 1985; Darcy and Hadley, 1988; Beck, 1991; Boles, 1991; Jennings, 1991; MacManus and Bullock, 1994, but see Rinehart, 1991), as well as in England (Barry, 1991) and Ireland (Wilford et al., 1993).

Thus bringing more women inside the local political system promises to make a difference, especially if they have had close ties to women's organizations (Flammang, 1985; Franzway et al., 1989; Carroll et al., 1991) and are sustained by outsider women's groups (Katzenstein, 1984; Dahlerup, 1986). Yet there is some evidence that women's numerical gains promote a negative 'intrusiveness' response in masculinized institutions that can temper the influence women politicians may have (Kathlene, 1994). While earlier fears that women will be restricted to a token status in government (Flammang, 1984) are receding, the effects of gendered local institutions and socially prescribed gender roles on women's actual influence must be taken into account in assessing their effects on policies. Indeed, two-tier gendered local leadership structures remain a possibility. Jezierski (1994) suggests that the absence of women in the local industrial and corporate leadership structures leads to a default dualism: private sector and selected local officials dominate long-term economic policy-making processes while neighbourhood and women's groups, as well as the school boards and local legislative councils where women have made the greatest gains in representation, cope with operational, primarily consumption, issues.

Although empirical evidence of gender differences among political leaders is compelling, it is not yet clear whether there are more differences than commonalities among women activists. There is very little research on the interactive effects of gender, race and class in local politics (see Darcy and Hadley, 1988; Jeanette Jennings, 1991; James Jennings, 1992; MacManus and Bullock, 1993). African American women and Latinas are showing steady gains in local elected office: in 1992, there were 75 black female mayors and more than half the black female office holders were on city councils while in 1993 Latinas held 319 local offices and three times that number of school board seats (MacManus and Bullock, 1994; see also, Hero, 1992). At a minimum, this suggests the inadequacy of feminist theories that assume the primacy of patriarchal relations and do not take into account the differences among women stemming from their multiple locations (McDowell, 1992: 412).

Feminism and group politics

Women's local economic and political activities are occurring within a new cultural and institutional context created by political restructuring processes. This raises a number of analytic issues. Since avenues for women's political participation differ historically from those available to men (UN, 1992), analysing women's formal political participation and incorporation with models derived from white male experience at a different historical period is problematic. Women will have different 'interests' and varying mobilization paths due to the historical context of their increased labour force participation, the segmented employment structures in which they work, and their increased contacts with a local state undergoing political restructuring and retrenchment from earlier welfare state arrangements. Thus the modern white male experience of political mobilization and incorporation through labour union activity and electoral organizations may be less relevant to understanding women's contemporary mobilization and incorporation into local politics. This argues not only against generalizing on the basis of historical male experiences but also cautions against assuming a universal female politics, since experiences will vary across settings, depending on the economic and cultural aspects of gender relations in different locales, and by class, race and ethnicity as well (see, for example, Dickson, 1987; Kofman and Peake, 1990).

Local political activity now occurs in the context of political restructuring processes involving decentralization, devolution, privatization and retrenchment of the welfare state. Local governments are faced with vulnerable workers, changing new family structures, and emergent identity politics of non-class based groups with diverse agendas; yet they are saddled with new fiscal responsibilities and dwindling resources. The new political terrain in many cities is shaped by the social complexity resulting from restructuring processes and the institutional complexity generated by devolving and decentralizing state structures. This new political context has important consequences for groups seeking to influence local political decisions, especially those with 'new social movement' origins (Fainstein and Hirst, Chapter 10, this volume; Fincher and McQuillen, 1989; Scott, 1989). In their concerns with transforming values and enhancing personal autonomy, these groups often preferred, as Offe puts it, 'politicizing the institutions of civil society' (1985: 820) instead of directly engaging the state. Indeed, the values of non-hierarchical organization and consensus decision styles nurtured by the feminist movement promised little success in dealing with state structures.

While some groups in North America and especially in Britain and Europe maintained an anti-statist stance, many others moved from the initial social movement phase of the 1960s and 1970s to other forms of local political involvement. But the funding support necessary for new activities often depended on developing tactical priorities and accountable business management structures that threatened movement-oriented operating styles (Costain, 1988; Brunell, 1993). The influence of such funding dependencies became a contentious issue: the patron relationship may threaten the displacement of group goals by patron goals (Piven and Cloward, 1979; McAdam, 1982), undermine local initiatives (Gittell, 1980), and prompt a narrowing of participatory decision making within the group (Jones et al., 1982). Those groups overcoming the potential factionalism generated by these organizational transformations were often accused of abandoning the radical edge and the purposive and solidary incentives that sustained their membership in favour of 'liberal' strategies that failed to challenge the fundamental causes of gender inequalities (Jones et al., 1982; Gelb, 1989). To some, these organizational changes were so grave that they signalled the death of the feminist movement itself. To others, these changes signified organizational maturation, generational changes, or fragmentation processes that are part of any movement's trajectory over time (Dahlerup, 1986). This is a continuing issue for British groups (Lovenduski and Randall, 1993); in both American and British feminist groups, divisive debates on funding not infrequently contributed to the factionalization and instability of many organizations.

Anne Costain (1988) characterizes American women's groups as shifting from equity to 'special needs' agendas in the 1980s. These new agendas signalled a new role for many women's groups; their demands for distributional benefits were more easily accommodated by politicians, especially at the local level where the dominant discourse includes responsiveness to local needs. Throughout the 1970s and early 1980s, in North America and Britain, local women's groups and alternative institutions proliferated (Sapiro, 1986; Lovenduski and Randall, 1993), often supported by national and local funding. Local projects important to women – rape crisis centres, health clinics, etc. – received Federal start-up funding in the United States and local women's committees formed within local authorities in Canada and Great Britain. There clearly are costs associated with this greater group access. Most basically, there is continuing concern that greater political integration leads to deradicalization (Lovenduski and Randall, 1993). Groups formed by women as survival strategies now exist as organizations continually threatened with collapse from loss of funding or membership support. Groups concerned with tactical priorities, material incentives, political and financial accountability, special needs and coalition building may lose sight of goals for transforming gender relations. They may also lose members attracted by these original goals and sustained by the purposive incentives associated with more radical empowerment efforts. Indeed, Lovenduski and Randall (1993) attribute the decline of the women's movement in Great Britain to these deradicalization trends although they recognize that more liberal strategies may also encourage broader participation as well as state accommodation. Through accommodation and political integration, women's groups, like any other groups, lose a measure of control over the definition of their issues.

Gender and the potential for local state change

Although many women's organizations moved from movement politics to seemingly more conventional political modes, their organizational strategies and niches differ from those of conventional interest groups. In comparison with other contemporary interest groups in American cities Clarke and Brunell (1994) find women's organizations are differentiated from other groups, and somewhat from each other, by their resource bases and strategies. While national women's organizations enjoy outside patron support and funding autonomy (Walker, 1991: 189), local women's groups are characterized by high dependence on either internal funding or hybrid funding, including revenue generation activities. Women's groups with outside funding tend to emphasize service agendas while those relying on internal dues pursue empowerment strategies. The latter groups reflect organizational networks that may provide the experience and skills for women to move more rapidly into local elected and appointed office (Lovenduski and Randall, 1993; Wilford et al., 1993; MacManus and Bullock, 1994). But rather than viewing service-providing women's groups as beholden to and potentially compromised by external patrons, it is important to recognize their dense agendas. These groups generally do not distinguish between service provision and empowerment categories in a facile way; their political style and framing of policy issues recognizes the empowering capacities of service provisions, particularly those involving alternative institutions (Clarke and Brunell, 1994). These women's organizations see providing alternative services as part of empowerment: their organizational strategies synthesize mobilization, representation, and empowerment agendas (Katzenstein, 1984). In contrast to the deductive arguments of many group theorists, these local women activists do not see these as mutually exclusive goals or strategies.

Links with the state also differ. In contrast to earlier periods where groups were politically incorporated into a primarily bureaucratized state (Browning et al., 1984; Gelb and Gittell, 1986; Naples, 1991), women's links with the local state through non-profit organizations may provide greater potential for challenging the organization of the state. Although incorporation into a bureaucratic welfare state created an infrastructure facilitating political mobilization (Piven, 1985), the gender subtext of the welfare state limited organizational change efforts (Siim, 1988; Naples, 1991). With recent decentralizing and privatizing trends, shifts away from state bureaucratic forms reduce the emphasis on credentialled knowledge as the basis of local decision making and on narrow, state-defined interpretations of needs that hampered these earlier change efforts (Naples,

1991). These non-bureaucratic organizational niches allow women's groups to clarify their self-definition relative to the state as well as to increase their infrastructural power, both essential to bringing about social and cultural change (Barrows, 1993). While debate on the effects of the 'contract culture' on voluntary organizations remains contentious (Brindle, 1994), women in non-bureaucratic organizational niches have greater flexibility in creating political identities and discourse that may change the local political systems in which they operate.

Issues in research on gender and local politics

Taking gender seriously in urban research means relaxing the usual analytic boundaries of public/private, formal/informal and insider/outsider activities; it also requires sensitivity to the gendered dimensions of economic, social and political inequalities within and across communities. Although there is significant progress in doing so, a number of issues are raised in the course of these efforts. Three concerns are addressed here: universalizing women's experiences and slighting differences among women; clarifying the concept of women's interests; and incorporating contingent contextual features into feminist analyses.

Gender and differences

All mainstream political theory abstracts agents from their history, gender, class, race and geographical contexts. This 'view from nowhere', as Harding (1991) puts it, has been privileged as objective, impartial and universal. In so doing, difference is reduced to unity – anything that does not fit is ignored and reduced to subjectivity. Not only does this devalue the subject positions from which women – and other non-dominant groups (see Hero, 1992; Jennings, 1992) – act, it reinforces oppression. Refusal to recognize the partial perspectives from which individuals inevitably act universalizes the position of the dominant group and silences the voices of the oppressed (Young, 1990).

The challenges facing feminist urban theorists, therefore, are no different from those facing any social theorists in the coming decade: they include theorizing unstable and multiple subjectivities, accepting multiple and flexible feminisms situated in different circumstances, and constructing partial and situated knowledges (Massey, 1991; McDowell, 1992; Staeheli and Lawson, 1994). At a minimum, this precludes the possibility of meeting feminist critiques by 'adding women' to established frameworks (McDowell, 1991; Silverberg, 1992). Understanding difference and partiality is important in analysing relations between women and men, but also in analysing relations between women. Our social location is a function not only of gender but of class, ethnicity, sexuality, colonial history, and so on. The task ahead for feminist and mainstream political theorists alike is to formulate democratic institutions and processes that allow the articulation of interests of different individuals and social groups according to what Mouffe (1988) terms 'democratic equivalence'. This requires first that more voices from different subject positions be heard in political discourse, and second that the perspectives of one group not be privileged. A first step towards this is to rework the notion of interests.

Gender and interests

Just as restructuring trends compel a reworking of feminist theories of capitalism and patriarchy, they also demand more historically and empirically grounded feminist theories of interests (Diamond and Hartsock, 1981; Sapiro, 1981). In contrast to the political economy focus on economic interests and the pluralist assumption of overt subjective interests, feminists question whether 'women's interests are interesting'. That is, do women have objective interests that merit recognition and legitimation of women's interests as a group in conventional political terms (Sapiro, 1981) or is 'needs' a more appropriate analytical category than 'interests' (Diamond and Hartsock, 1981)? Even those agreeing that women as a group have an interest in overcoming the injustices of a patriarchal system of sexuality may still disagree on whether those objective interests include particular allocations of goods and privileges that can be gained from state authority. Molyneux, for example, asks whether interests are strategic gender interests derived in a deductive analysis of women's subordination and focused on changing gender relations or practical gender interests constructed inductively from women's experiences and using gender differences to make claims for public activism if not necessarily for redressing gender inequalities (Molyneux, 1986). The former does not necessarily lead to political action while the latter places women in contestation with the state (Jonasdottir, 1988: 36). Accepting that women as a group have interests that merit political attention can lead to design of political representation institutions, such as Young's (1990) corporatist mechanisms, that directly voice those concerns in agenda-setting and policy formulation processes.

But Sapiro (1981) points out that these debates and deductive interests typologies have limited value in the face of the multiplicity of women's interests. Chowdhury and Nelson (1993) also note that such typologies, including Molyneux's original formulation, tell us little about the development of these strategies or how tactics might change over time. And, we would add, across different communities. These critiques are especially germane at the local level, where multiple interests are rooted in the complex, fragmented employment and family structures experienced by women with different class, race and ethnic identities. In American cities, this includes gender differences in labour market segmentation, poverty status and residential segregation complicated by race and ethnicity (Johnston-Anumonwo et al., 1994) that contribute to divergent issue agendas among women (Jennings, 1991; Naples, 1991; Johnston-

Anumonwo et al., 1994; for British cities, see Harloe and Fainstein, 1992; Lovenduski and Randall, 1993). Together with the growing scepticism among feminist theorists about universalizing women's experiences, this suggests rethinking women's interests in terms of the distribution of capabilities for action and reflexive choice and the political forms in which these needs might best be represented.

Gender and context

These multiple identities and interests must be analysed in the context of specific historical and geographical circumstances (McDowell, 1992: 412). Two particular contemporary circumstances must be incorporated into feminist urban analyses of why, how, when and where women's political role is strengthened: frictions in existing political institutions and power networks and increased institutional complexity creating new decision spaces. These contextual features suggest that destabilizing changes in local political processes that allow and invite women's inclusion may, at times, be as important in explaining women's political effects as the resources or entrepreneurial leaders posited by interest group theorists (Costain, 1992b).

Changes in political opportunity structures (McAdam, 1982; Costain, 1992a, 1992b), open up new grounds for women. Competitive bidding for women's votes and allegiances emerged in American and British (after the 1992 general election) politics with the perceived 'gender gap' in voting patterns (Mueller, 1988). While this gap is not stable over time (Kofman and Peake, 1990; Chaney and Nagler, 1993) parties are becoming more aware of women's electoral concerns as well as the growing pool of educated women with professional and political experience. Competing for women as voters and electoral coalition partners induces contests over the rules of the game that allow women to emerge as effective participants in male power networks (Lovenduski and Randall, 1993: 174). It includes struggles over establishing women's quota systems for internal party offices and nominations. But it also encompasses ideological differences within parties. In France, the ascendance of the Second Left in the socialist party in the mid-1970s and 1980s amplified interest in less centralized state power, enhancing women's position, and partnerships with citizen associations (Ullman, 1993: 23) just as the new urban left in local Labour parties in England stressed more participatory, more inclusive policy forums and funding of community-based voluntary service groups (Gyford, 1975).

The reform movements of the 1960s and 1970s stepped up the politicization of American local government (Stone et al., 1986). While civil rights pressures resulted in court-ordered reapportionment and redistricting at the national level, as well as affirmative action requirements for federal contracts, court rulings in many cities forced shifts to district or mixed election formats rather than at-large elections, to larger city councils, and to more elected rather than appointed positions. These changes in electoral laws and the enlargement of the available pool of positions expanded political opportunities for minorities and women. Although women candidates generally are not necessarily more successful in single member district elections (MacManus and Bullock, 1994: 29), minority women are (Darcy and Hadley, 1988); the number of African American women and Latina local office holders has increased dramatically since the mid-1970s (MacManus and Bullock, 1993).

'Elite disarray' in existing organizations also expands political opportunities for women. Lovenduski and Randall argue that the decline in trade union strength (particularly the dominant role of traditional, patriarchal trade unions) in the Labour party in Great Britain created opportunities for women to gain power. In their bid to gain new members, trade unions reached out to women workers, shifting power towards more 'women-friendly' unions within the movement. The decline of the traditional industrial trade unions allowed soft left reformists within the Labour party to push for rule changes in 1993 giving party constituencies rather than trade unions a greater internal voice (Lovenduski and Randall, 1993: 138).

Although trade unions are not as important in structuring American political life, similar organizational incentives were created indirectly by the advent of neo-conservative governments in the United States, Canada and Great Britain in the early 1980s. As public discourse shifted to decentralization and privatization, public funding and political support for local groups declined; the fate of local projects and innovations became problematic (Bashevkin, 1993; Andrew, 1994). The equation of decentralization with greater democracy supported a shift towards an ideology of consumer (rather than producer) efficiency; this encourages decentralized, specialized service delivery (Sharpe, 1993). Similarly, the privatization rhetoric encouraged a receptivity to non-bureaucratic, non-profit organizations and more legitimacy to new arrangements and values. In federal systems, the discourse of limited local responsibility (due to inelastic tax base or legal frameworks) and the discourse of local government responsiveness and responsibilities to local electorates could be used to encourage local officials to be more receptive to, and to give priority to, women's demands (see Andrew, 1994).

As state responses to fiscal and political crises (Smith and Lipsky, 1993; Ullman, 1993), these organizational adaptations to new restructuring environments (Sharpe, 1993) result in greater institutional complexity. In the United States (Smith and Lipsky, 1993), and Europe (Sharpe, 1993) this includes greater reliance on partnerships among national, local, quasi-governmental and private institutions (Sharpe, 1993: 11) particularly in social policy arenas. These para-statal structures are 'between' or 'beyond' the market and state; in decentralized systems such as the United States, this institutional strategy allows even weak states (such as the fragmented American state) to increase their effectiveness. This occurs not by extension of central governmental power (limited by the fragmented institutional design of the American system) but by legitimating and coordinating para-statal, or intermediate, organizations (Barrows, 1993). In centralized systems like Great Britain, they emerge as centrally designed and controlled 'quangos' or, as in France, as local associations whose formation is supported by the state. Whether these organizations operate in a democratic, representative and accountable manner is a matter of political choice rather than a structural issue. As Lovenduski and Randall (1993: 142) point out, establishing these new expanded structures is less troublesome than disrupting the patronage and incumbency dynamics in established organizations by forcing integration of new groups and demands. But they may operate in ways that maintain, rather than challenge, existing biases.

While this increasing institutional complexity may stem from state crises and functional restructuring pressures (Sharpe, 1993: 14), it creates new local 'decision spaces' that may encourage women's inclusion in a reconfigured political sphere. Even though national governments pursue the vertical partnership strategy to devolve fiscal responsibilities, avoid political demands, and gain 'central advantage', at the local level these strategies destabilize political processes and alignments in important ways. In particular, they introduce national political norms on women's equality as well as organizational preferences for non-profit and quasi-governmental groups (Goetz, 1993) that may override more patriarchal local configurations. As Hernes (1988: 211) sees it, the absence of clear institutional boundaries facilitates women's entry into public space so the inherent fuzziness of these public/private boundaries may be advantageous. And, as noted above, women's unpaid activism in health, employment, education and other local arenas make them likely participants in paid employment and leadership in the third sector as local government transforms. Not that women will automatically gain these positions. But the gendered division of labour and the historical pattern of women's voluntarism in social and educational programmes ironically increases the likelihood that women will be able to move into this new decision space. Thus, given the gendered impacts of local economic and political restructuring processes, local political change cannot be understood without recognizing how gender relations interact with local political and economic structures.

Does gender make a difference in urban research?

But could one ask these questions or come to these conclusions about cities in the absence of feminist sympathies? Not if one continues to work uncritically with the dualisms of established models or merely 'updates' a research approach by 'adding' in women. As we've sketched out here, seemingly gender-neutral urban theories incorporate a number of dualist assumptions that limit both their theoretical value and their adequacy in fully understanding urban change. Understanding cities as gendered spaces requires that we recognize and accommodate the partial position from which all agents act.

On both epistemological and empirical grounds, we contend that tinkering with established models is not sufficient: women redefine politics in ways that challenge accepted notions about the nature and locus of political activity. At a minimum, theories slighting gender relations are partial and often inaccurate. Pluralist theories, for instance, assume that women's groups are seeking a diffuse range of subjective interests through state-allocated policy benefits. But feminist theorists emphasize the primacy of social and cultural change; engaging in distributional politics may be part of the agenda but it does not drive the agenda as in classic interest group models. Political economy approaches are also troublesome since they tend to relegate women's interests and concerns to the so-called 'private' sphere of non-political concerns. As McDowell puts it, 'only a male definition of politics' could have ignored the issues and new organizational forms advocated by women in a misplaced focus on the apparent decline of working class action (1991: 101). An enlightened political economy perspective that incorporated family issues may well continue to slight the political implications of women's changed employment status. Even refining the approach to include a broader definition of public activities, the elite governing coalition formation focus neglects some of the distinctive non-electoral aspects of women's political involvement. Many women seek public leadership roles, but most women's organizations are involved in alternative institutions and their organizational strategies do not conform to conventional interest-group politics. Relying on established pluralist or political economy frameworks means asking questions that underestimate and distort women's involvement in local politics.

Yet applying a feminist perspective to urban analyses merely by 'reading off' urban politics from patriarchal relations would be equally unproductive. While there is reason to assume a systemic patriarchal bias in urban politics, there is nothing gained by only doing so. For feminist theories to be more useful to urban analysts, several issues must be addressed. Feminists must reconsider the relations of capitalism and patriarchy in the face of restructuring if they are to describe fully and 'make visible' how women's reproductive and productive roles are socially constructed in contemporary cities (McDowell, 1992). For example, conceptualizing patriarchal relations as a loosely-coupled system producing gender inequalities, rather than a monolithic, invariant structure, opens up the analytic space to account theoretically and empirically for variations in gender regimes over time and space (Appleton, 1994). And in order for a gender justice perspective to be articulated as an urban public philosophy promoting more than resource allocation principles, feminists' philosophical and theoretical arguments must undergo empirical scrutiny. Given the patriarchal bias in political institutions (Kathlene, 1994), there is the possibility that women activists will not pursue gender justice but will act in conformance with conventional models of political participation to achieve power. In order to consider the likelihood of women-friendly polities, feminist theorists must rework the notion of interests and develop a more careful understanding of how and why such communities might differ from those described by established models of local politics.

But feminist urban research entails more than theorizing about differences between men and women in cities. Analysts must redress the reductionist and universalizing elements in feminist theorizing that overlook differences between women stemming from race, class, sexuality and cultural differences. The concern with differences among women that is characteristic of contemporary feminist theory does indeed call into question the continued utility of gender as an analytic category (McDowell, 1992: 412). Yet treating gender as a question of 'women' in cities implies a unity and homogeneity that is unlikely to be true and defies theorization (Elson, 1991a: 1). Better urban theory will require rethinking existing theories in terms of their sensitivity to gender relations and then attempting to disaggregate analytic categories by gender (1991b: 198). This deconstructing and disaggregating is necessary for thinking further about socially determined differences that intersect with gender relations. Bringing a gender relations perspective to urban politics makes it more likely that differences *among* women will be addressed because it centres on the gender dimension of various social relations structuring people's lives. By beginning with an assumption that gender relations are asymmetrical and disadvantage women relative to men in similar economic and social positions, one can address differences in these gendered experiences by race, sexuality, class, and so on (Elson, 1991a: 2). It is not possible to do so if one limits the analysis to 'women' or fails to recognize gender relations as a constitutive stratification system of contemporary cities. The gendered restructuring trends described here bring into question the value of urban analyses that remain insensitive to gender and other socially constructed differences.

Note

This research has been supported in part by the Center for Public Policy Research at the University of Colorado, Boulder, and the National Science Foundation, Grant No. SES-9112359.

References

Abrahams, N. (1992) 'Towards reconceptualizing political action', *Sociological Inquiry*, 62: 327–47.
Ackelsburg, M.A. (1984) 'Women's collaborative activities and city life: politics and public policy', in J. Flammang (ed.), *Political Women: Current Roles in State and Local Government*. Beverly Hills, CA: Sage.

Ackelsburg, M.A. (1988) 'Communities, resistance and women's activism: some implications for a democratic polity', in A. Bookman and S. Morgan (eds), *Women and the Politics of Empowerment*. Philadelphia, PA: Temple University Press.

Andersen, K. (1975) 'Working women and political participation, 1952–1972', *American Journal of Political Science*, XIX, 3: 439–53.

Andrew, C. (1994) 'Getting women's issues on the municipal agenda: violence against women', in J. Garber and R. Turner (eds), *Gender in Urban Research*. Newbury Park, CA: Sage.

Antolini, D. (1984) 'Women in local government: an overview', in J. Flammang (ed.), *Political Women: Current Roles in State and Local Government*. Beverly Hills, CA: Sage.

Appleton, L.M. (1994) 'The gender regimes of American cities', in J. Garber and R. Turner (eds), *Gender in Urban Research*. Newbury Park, CA: Sage.

Barrows, C.W. (1993) 'State autonomy, state strength, and state capacities: a problem of theory in the new institutionalism', paper presented at the Annual Meeting of the Western Political Science Association, Pasadena CA, March.

Barry, J. (1991) *The Women's Movement and Local Politics*. Aldershot: Avebury.

Bashevkin, S. (1993) 'Confronting neo-conservatism: Anglo-American women's movements under Thatcher, Reagan and Mulroney', paper presented at the Annual Meeting of the American Political Science Association, Washington D.C.

Beck, S.A. (1991) 'Rethinking municipal governance: gender distinctions on local councils', in D.L. Dodson (ed.), *Gender and Policymaking: Studies of Women in Office*. New Brunswick, NJ: Center for the American Woman and Politics, Eagleton Institute of Politics, Rutgers University.

Beckwith, C. (1986) *American Women and Political Participation*. Westport, CT: Greenwood Press.

Bers, T.H. and Mezey, S. (1981) 'Support for feminist goals among leaders of women's community groups', *Signs*, 6: 737–48.

Bledsoe, T. and Herring, M. (1990) 'Victims of circumstances: women in pursuit of political office', *American Political Science Review*, 84: 213–23.

Boles, J. (1991) 'Advancing the women's agenda within local legislatures: the role of female elected officials', in D.L. Dodson (ed.), *Gender and Policymaking: Studies of Women in Office*. New Brunswick, NJ: Center for the American Woman and Politics, Eagleton Institute of Politics, Rutgers University.

Bondi, L. and Peake, L. (1988) 'Gender and the city: urban politics revisited', in J. Little, L. Peake and P. Richardson (eds), *Women in Cities: Gender and the Urban Environment*. New York: New York University Press.

Brindle, D. (1994) 'Rich cup or poison chalice?' *The Guardian*, 18 May: 11–12.

Brownhill, S. and Halford, S. (1990) 'Understanding women's involvement in local politics: how useful is a formal/informal dichotomy?' *Political Geography Quarterly*, 9: 396–414.

Browning, R., Marshall, D.R. and Tabb, W. (1984) *Protest is Not Enough*. Berkeley: University of California Press.

Brunell, L. (1993) *Feminism, Funding, and Agenda-Setting: The Relationship of Goals, Funding, and Action in Feminist, Community-based Groups*. Master's Thesis. University of Colorado at Boulder.

Carroll, S., Dodson, D.L. and Mandel, R.B. (1991) *The Impact of Women in Public Office: An Overview*. New Brunswick, NJ: Center for the American Woman and Politics, Eagleton Institute of Politics, Rutgers University.

Chaney, C. and Nagler, J. (1993) 'Women, issues, and participation', paper presented at the Western Political Science Association Annual Meeting, Pasadena, March.

Chowdhury, N. and Nelson, B.J. (1993) 'Redefining politics: patterns of women's political engagement from a global perspective', in B.J. Nelson and N. Chowdhury (eds), *Women and Politics Worldwide*. New Haven, CT: Yale University Press.

Christopherson, S. (1989) 'Flexibility in the US service economy and the emerging spatial division of labour', *Transactions of the Institute of British Geography*, 14: 131–43.

Clarke, S.E. and Brunell, L. (1994) 'New decision spaces in local politics: women's organizations and the new terrain of local politics', *Working Paper*. Boulder, CO: Center for Public Policy Research, University of Colorado at Boulder.

Costain, A.N. (1988) 'Representing women: the transition from social movement to interest group', in E. Boneparth and E. Stoper (eds), *Women, Power, and Policy: Toward Year 2000* (2nd edn). New York: Pergamon.

Costain, A.N. (1992a) 'Social movements as interest groups: the case of the women's movement', in M. Petracca (ed.), *The Politics of Interests*. Boulder, CO: Westview Press.

Costain, A.N. (1992b) *Inviting Women's Rebellion: A Political Process Interpretation of the Women's Movement*. Baltimore, MD: Johns Hopkins University Press.

Cox, K.R. and Mair, A. (1988) 'Locality and community in the politics of local economic development', *Annals of the Association of American Geographers*, 78 (2): 307–25.

Dahlerup, D. (ed.) (1986) *The New Women's Movement*. London: Sage.

Darcy, R. and Hadley, C.D. (1988) 'Black women in politics: the puzzle of success', *Social Science Quarterly*, 69: 629–45.

Diamond, I. and Hartsock, N. (1981) 'Beyond interests in politics: a comment on Virginia Sapiro's "When are interests interesting? The problem of political representation of women"', *American Political Science Review*, 75: 716–21.

Dickson, L.F. (1987) 'Toward a broader angle of vision in uncovering women's history: black women's clubs revisited', *Frontiers*, 9: 62–8.

Elson, D. (1991a) 'Male bias in the development process: an overview', in D. Elson (ed.), *Male Bias in the Development Process*. Manchester: Manchester University Press.

Elson, D. (1991b) 'Overcoming male bias', in D. Elson (ed.), *Male Bias in the Development Process*. Manchester: Manchester University Press.

Evans, G. (1993) 'Is gender on the new agenda? A comparative analysis of the politicalization of inequality between men and women', *European Journal of Political Research*, 24: 135–58.

Fainstein, S.S., Gordon, I. and Harloe, M. (eds) (1992) *Divided Cities*. Oxford: Basil Blackwell.

Farkas, G., Barton, M. and Kushner, K. (1988) 'White, black, and Hispanic female youths in central city labor markets', *The Sociological Quarterly*, 29: 605–21.

Fincher, R. and McQuillen, J. (1989) 'Progress report: women in urban social movements', *Urban Geography*, 10: 604–13.

Flammang, J. (ed.) (1984) *Political Women: Current Roles in State and Local Government*. Beverly Hills, CA: Sage.

Flammang, J. (1985) 'Female officials in the feminist capital', *Western Political Quarterly*, 38: 98–117.

Foucault, M. (1982) 'The subject and power', *Critical Inquiry*, 8: 777–95.

Franzway, S., Court, D. and Connell, R.W. (1989) *Staking a Claim: Feminism, Bureaucracy, and the State*. Cambridge: Polity.

Fulenwider, C.K. (1981) 'Feminist ideology and the political attitudes and participation of white and minority women', *Western Political Quarterly*, 34: 17–30.

Galston, W. (1982) 'Defending liberalism', *American Political Science Review*, 76: 621–9.

Gelb, J. (1989) *Feminism and Politics: A Comparative Perspective*. Berkeley: University of California Press.

Gelb, J. and Gittell, M. (1986) 'Seeking equality: the role of activist women in cities', in J.K. Boles (ed.), *The Egalitarian City*, New York: Praeger.

Giddens, A. (1993) Presentation. University of Essex.

Gittell, M. (1980) *Limits to Citizen Participation*. Beverly Hills, CA: Sage.

Goetz, E. (1993) *Shelter Burden*. Philadelphia, PA: Temple University Press.

Gyford, J. (1975) *The Politics of Local Socialism*. London: Allen and Unwin.

Harding, S. (1991) *Whose Science? Whose Knowledge: Thinking from Women's Lives*. Ithaca, NY: Cornell University Press.

Harloe, M. and Fainstein, S.S. (1992) 'Conclusion: The divided cities', in S. Fainstein, I. Gordon and M. Harloe (eds), *Divided Cities*. Oxford: Basil Blackwell.

Hernes, H.M. (1988) 'The welfare state citizenship of Scandinavian women', in K.B. Jones and A.G. Jonasdottir (eds), *The Political Interests of Gender*. London: Sage.

Hero, R. (1992) *Latinos and the U.S. Political System*. Philadelphia, PA: Temple University Press.

Horan, C. (1991) 'Beyond governing coalitions: analyzing urban regimes in the 1990s', *Journal of Urban Affairs*, 13: 119–35.

Jaggar, A.M. (1983) *Feminist Politics and Human Nature*. Sussex: Rowman and Littlefield.

Jennings, James (1992) *The Politics of Black Empowerment*. Detroit, IL: Wayne State University Press.

Jennings, Jeanette (1991) 'Black women mayors: reflections on race and gender', in D.L. Dodson (ed.), *Gender and Policymaking: Studies of Women in Office*. New Brunswick, NJ: Center for the American Woman and Politics, Eagleton Institute of Politics, Rutgers University.

Jezierski, L. (1994) 'Women organizing their place in restructuring economies', in J. Garber and R. Turner (eds), *Gender in Urban Research*. Newbury Park, CA: Sage.

Johnston-Anumonwo, I., McLafferty, S. and Preston, V. (1994) 'Gender, race, and the spatial context of women's employment', in J. Garber and R. Turner (eds), *Gender and Urban Research*. Newbury Park, CA: Sage.

Jonasdottir, A.G. (1988) 'On the concept of interest, women's interests, and the limitation of interest theory', in K.B. Jones and A.G. Jonasdottir (eds), *The Political Interests of Gender*. London: Sage.

Jones, D., Montbach, J. and Turner, J. (1982) 'Are local organizations local?' *Social Policy*, 13: 42–5.

Jones, K.B. (1988) 'Towards the revision of politics', in K.B. Jones and A.G. Jonasdottir (eds), *The Political Interests of Gender*. London: Sage.

Kathlene, L. (1994) 'Power and influence in state legislative policy making: the interaction of gender and position in committee hearing debates', *American Political Science Review*, September: 560–76.

Katzenstein, M.F. (1984) 'Feminism and the meaning of the vote', *Signs*, 10: 4–26.

Kay, S.A. (1985) 'Feminist ideology, race and political participation: a second look', *Western Political Quarterly*, 38: 476–84.

Kofman, E. and Peake, L. (1990) 'Into the 1990s: a gendered agenda for political geography', *Political Geography Quarterly*, 9: 313–36.

Logan, J. and Molotch, H. (1987) *Urban Fortunes*. Berkeley: University of California Press.

Lovenduski, J. and Randall, V. (1993) *Contemporary Feminist Politics: Women and Power in Britain*. Oxford: Oxford University Press.

MacManus, S.A. and Bullock, C.S. (1993) 'Women and racial/ethnic minorities in mayoral and council positions', *The Municipal Year Book 1993*. Washington, D.C: The International City Managers Association.

MacManus, S.A. and Bullock, C.S. (1994) 'Electing women to local office', in J. Garber and R. Turner (eds), *Gender in Urban Research*. Newbury Park, CA: Sage.

McAdam, D. (1982) *Political Process and the Development of Black Insurgency, 1930–1970*. Chicago, IL: University of Chicago Press.

McDowell, L. (1991) 'Restructuring production and reproduction: some theoretical and empirical issues relating to gender, or women in Britain', in M. Gottdiener and C. Pickvance (eds), *Urban Life in Transition*. Newbury Park, CA: Sage.

McDowell, L. (1992) 'Doing gender: feminism, feminists and research methods in human geography', *Transactions of the Institute of British Geography*, 17: 399–416.

Massey, D. (1991) 'Flexible sexism', *Environment and Planning D: Society and Space*, 9: 31–57.

Molyneux, M. (1986) 'Mobilization without emancipation? Women's interests, state, and revolution', in R.R. Fagen (ed.), *Transition and Development: Problems of Third World Socialism*. Boston, MA: Monthly Review Press.

Mouffe, C. (1988) 'Radical democracy: modern or postmodern?' in A. Ross (ed.), *Universal Abandon? The Politics of Postmodernism*. Minneapolis: University of Minnesota Press.

Mueller, C. (1988) *The Politics of the Gender Gap: The Social Construction of Political Influence*. Newbury Park, CA: Sage.

Naples, N. (1991) 'Contradictions in the gender subtext of the war on poverty: the community work and resistance of women from low income communities', *Social Problems*, 18: 316–32.

Nussbaum, M. (1992) 'Justice for women!' *New York Review of Books*, 8 October, 39: 43–8.

Offe, C. (1985) 'New social movements: challenging the boundaries of institutional politics', *Social Research*, 52: 817–68.

Okin, S.M. (1992) *Justice, Gender, and the Family*. New York: Basic Books.

Phillips, A. (1992) 'Must feminists give up on liberal democracy?' *Political Studies*, XL: 68–82.

Piven, F.F. (1985) 'Women and the state: ideology, power, and the welfare state', in A.S. Rossi (ed.), *Gender and the Lifecourse*. New York: Aldine Press.

Piven, F.F. and Cloward, R. (1979) *Poor People's Movements: Why They Succeed, How They Fail*. New York: Pantheon.

Pratt, G. and Hanson, S. (1988) 'Gender, class and space', *Environment and Planning D*, 6: 15–35.

Rabrenovic, G. (1994) 'Political participation of women in urban communities', in J. Garber and R. Turner (eds), *Gender and Urban Research*. Newbury Park, CA: Sage.

Rinehart, S.T. (1991) 'Do women leaders make a difference? Substance, style, and perceptions', in D.L. Dodson (ed.), *Gender and Policymaking: Studies of women in Office* New Brunswick, NJ: Center for the American Woman and Politics, Eagleton Institute of Politics, Rutgers University.

Rowbotham, S. and Mitter, S. (eds) (1994) *Dignity and Daily Bread*. London: Routledge.

Sapiro, V. (1981) 'When are interests interesting? The problem of political representation of women', *American Political Science Review*, 75: 701–16.

Sapiro, V. (1986) 'The women's movement, politics and policy in the Reagan era', in D. Dahlerup (ed.), *The New Women's Movement*. London: Sage.

Scott, A. (1989) *Ideology and the New Social Movements*. London: Unwin Hyman.

Sen, A. (1982) *Choice, Welfare, and Measurement*. Oxford: Blackwell.

Sharpe, L.J. (1993) 'The European meso: an appraisal', in L.J. Sharpe (ed.), *The Rise of Meso Government in Europe*. London: Sage.

Siim, B. (1988) 'Towards a feminist rethinking of the welfare state', in K.B. Jones and A.G. Jonasdottir (eds), *The Political Interests of Gender*. London: Sage.

Silverberg, H. (1992) 'Gender studies and political science: the history of the behavioralist compromise', in J. Farr and R. Seidelman (eds), *Discipline and History: Political Science in the United States*. Ann Arbor: The University of Michigan Press.

Smith, M.P., Tarallo, B. and Kagiwada, G. (1991) 'Colouring California: new Asian immigrant households, social networks and the local state', *International Journal of Urban and Regional Research*, 15: 250–68.

Smith, R.M. (1989) '"One United People": second-class female citizenship and the American quest for community', *Yale Journal of Law and the Humanities*, 1: 229–93.

Smith, S.R. and Lipsky, M. (1993) *Nonprofits for Hire: the Welfare State in the Age of Contracting*. Cambridge, MA: Harvard University Press.

Staeheli, L. and Clarke, S.E. (1994) 'Gender, place and citizenship', in J. Garber and R. Turner (eds), *Gender in Urban Research*. Newbury Park, CA: Sage.

Staeheli, L. and Lawson, V. (1995) 'Feminism, praxis, and human geography', *Geographical Analysis*, 27 (4).

Stone, C., Whelan, R.K. and Murin, W.J. (1986) *Urban Policy and Politics in a Bureaucratic Age*. Englewood Cliffs, NJ: Prentice-Hall.

Swanstrom, T. (1993) 'Beyond economism: urban political economy and the postmodern challenge', *Journal of Urban Affairs*, 15: 55–78.

Ullman, C.F. (1993) 'New social partners: nonprofit organizations and the welfare state in France', paper presented at the Annual Meeting of the American Political Science Association, Washington D.C., September.

United Nations. Centre for Social Development and Humanitarian Affairs (1992) *Women in Politics and Decisionmaking in the Late Twentieth Century*. Dordrecht: Martinus Nijhoff.

Viaou, D. (1992) 'Gender divisions in urban space: beyond the rigidity of dualist classifications', *Antipode*, 24: 247–62.

Walker, J.L. (1991) *Mobilizing Interest Groups in America: Patrons, Professionals, and Social Movements*. Ann Arbor: University of Michigan Press.

Wilford, R., Miller, R., Bell, Y. and Donoghue, F. (1993) 'In their own voices: women councillors in Northern Ireland', *Public Administration*, 71: 341–55.

Young, I. (1990) *Justice and the Politics of Difference*. Princeton, NJ: Princeton University Press.

Young, I. (1992) 'Social groups in associative democracy', *Politics and Society*, 20: 529–34.

Part IV

URBAN POLITICS, THE STATE AND CAPITALIST SOCIETY

12

Autonomy and City Limits

Mike Goldsmith

It is a truism to suggest that urban politics matters. So many people live in cities and large urban areas, not only in the developed countries of North America and Western Europe, but in the developing world, the Far East and in Eastern Europe as well. The way in which the daily lives of urban dwellers is defined and ordered is a reflection of the processes of politics globally, nationally and locally. What is of interest is an understanding, however limited in practice, of how these different levels of politics interact, and in particular how far the local level of politics is able to operate with some degree of autonomy or discretion from other levels. This chapter will examine this question in some detail, beginning with a review of normative and empirical theories about the autonomy of subnational or city governments. Then an examination is made of the evidence of local autonomy in comparative practice. The chapter concludes with an assessment of the extent to which localities and their governments can exercise some degree of influence over the daily lives of their residents.

Local autonomy: a review of theory

The *Oxford English Dictionary* attaches two meanings to its definition of 'autonomy' – self-governing and independence. Both of these are relevant to our discussion here and at the same time contain within them the major problem with which writers about local autonomy have had to grapple. First, the notion of self-government is a long-standing idea in normative writing about local government. It is particularly strong in American writing on the subject, though is sometimes hardly less marked in what some British writers have written. For some Europeans, however, local autonomy as local self-government is not a necessary feature of local government whereas others, such as the Germans and the Spanish and the European Commission, use the concept of subsidiarity to overcome the problem of defining accurately the idea of local autonomy. One reason why this is so is because of the second element in the *OED*'s definition – the idea of independence. For, try as we may, or much as we might wish, it is abundantly clear from the experience of the last century that local governments everywhere lack independence from other agencies. Indeed the very notion of increasing economic, social and political interdependence represents a key element in most modern thinking about present day societies and their conditions. And from such a perspective the idea of any local government having sufficient independence in order to be able to be self-governing seems almost absurd. Why is this so and how is it that we can have two starkly contrasting views about how urban government should operate in theory and practice?

And why is a concern with local autonomy important? In the first place, it is important because autonomy is at the heart of the very justification of most systems of elected local government. If local governments lack the ability *to determine for themselves* the mix of local goods and services, as well as local tax rates, then, it is argued, local governments are no more than an administrative arm of the central state, and the election of local representatives serves little purpose.

But in the modern state the idea of local governments exerting complete autonomy in their activities is largely impractical, public choice arguments notwithstanding (Wolman, 1990). In this modern context, most local governments operate within an environment which is more or less constrained – more or less decentralized – and the less constrained and more decentralized the system, the more autonomy might local governments have in practice. Thus, as Wolman points out, if political decision making is decentralized, each local unit 'can tailor its tax and service package to the preference of its citizenry' (1990: 31). Equally high levels of local autonomy might enhance local responsiveness and accountability. Decentralized, local autonomous units will be closer to their citizens, more responsive to their demands, producing as a result a greater congruence between those demands and the public policies designed to meet them. Similarly local accountability should be heightened under these circumstances: failure to meet citizen demands is likely to result in voters rejecting those responsible. But where autonomy is low, then local politicians can shuffle off responsibility for their actions or non-actions onto higher levels of government at state and central levels.

High levels of local autonomy may also increase policy diversity, reflecting the wider variety of choice made at the local level. In turn this diversity may well lead to policy innovation and diffusion of new initiatives across a range of localities. But policy diversity by definition implies inequality of tax burdens and services, which may themselves be judged more or less acceptable according to local voters' preferences.

The level of local autonomy is important both because of its possible impact on the level of political interest and citizen education at the local level and because it may help protect and foster democracy by assuring a system of countervailing power – of checks and balances – in a pluralist society. Promoting liberty – as Sharpe (1970) notes – is not a value we should necessarily expect of local government – but large numbers of highly autonomous local units not only limit the extent of central power but limit the spread of local tyranny. Reserving for local government certain rights and responsibilities also places a check on the power and influence of higher levels of government, which in turn may exert a check on local excesses – if and when they occur.

For all these and other reasons the notion of local autonomy, and attempts to observe it empirically in a comparative context, are important. At the very least, ideas about local autonomy, decentralization, and local self-government are essential features of what has generally come to be regarded as a democratic society, notwithstanding the fact that local elected institutions with the discretion to decide for themselves the appropriate level of local taxes and services are only one element in such a pluralist society.

Analytic perspectives on local autonomy

In this section we turn to a consideration of different analytical writings on the issue of local autonomy, in an effort to clarify the extent to which localities can be considered to possess the ability to influence their own destinies. In so doing, it is helpful if the various approaches examined are classified into different types – definitional and classificatory; causal and empirical.

An early contribution to this literature is represented by the resource-dependency model as developed by Rhodes (1981, 1986a, 1986b, 1988). The contribution was important as a heuristic device, and remains so, for a variety of reasons. First, it highlighted the multidimensional nature of intergovernmental relations, and the consequence that this would have for local autonomy. Second, it drew attention to the wide range of resources which the different levels of government could bring to bear to the intergovernmental network. Thus, for example, Rhodes distinguishes between constitutional-legal resources; regulatory resources; political, professional and financial resources.

Rhodes suggested initially that the relationship between centre and locality was an interdependent one, in which both sides deployed their range of resources in order to ensure their position and to increase the resources available to them. He saw the relationship essentially as a bargaining one in which neither side had the ability to dominate the other, yet something of a zero sum game in which what one side gained the other lost.

Despite an initial tendency to see the relationship between centre and periphery as a symmetrical one, in which he underestimated the hegemonic power of central government to determine the rules of the relationship, Rhodes's later formulations accept the inherently asymmetrical nature of the relationship and the unequal distribution of resources between both sides, leading him to develop ideas about the nature of intergovernmental policy communities and networks of a highly specialized and sectoral nature. The world of intergovernmental relations which Rhodes portrays is thus complex, diverse and fragmented, and it is these characteristics which give rise to differing patterns of local autonomy. The result is a pluralist diversity of relationships, yet one in which the centre is dominant, reflecting the legal and constitutional resources it is able to deploy in shaping how local government operates in practice, yet leaving local government with considerable autonomy in other respects.

Writing in the early 1980s, Gordon Clark (1984) developed an interesting alternative schema enabling him to distinguish between four different types of local autonomy. In a definitional and classificatory article utilizing what is essentially a legalistic perspective, Clark identifies two primary principles of local autonomy: the power of *initiation* and the power of *immunity*. Initiation refers to the actions of local governments in carrying out their rightful duties. Such powers can, of course, be both broadly prescribed – as in the case of those countries such as Sweden and Denmark whose legislation prescribes a general competence power to local governments – or more narrowly prescribed – as in the case of Britain, where the doctrine of ultra vires ensures that local authorities can only do those things which Parliament has said they can do under legislation.

By contrast Clark defines the power of immunity as the 'power of localities to act without fear of the oversight authority of higher tiers of the state. In this sense immunity allows local governments to act however they wish within the limits imposed by their initiative powers' (1984: 198). For Clark, these two sets of powers define local autonomy: local discretion in turn is defined by the degree of local autonomy 'in terms of local government functions, actions and legitimate behaviour' (1984: 198).

Clark's perspective allows him to develop a fourfold typology of local autonomy (see Figure 12.1). Under Type 1 autonomy, local governments have both the capacity to initiate and are free (immune) from the oversight of higher levels of government. Under the opposite case (Type 4) local governments have neither the power to initiate nor do they have any immunity from oversight. Under Type 2, local governments have the power to initiate for themselves, but are constrained in that everything they do is subject to oversight by higher levels of government. Under Type 3, local governments have little or no power to initiate, but are then immune from higher level oversight. In each of these cases both the degree of autonomy and discretion which local governments have varies, being

	Initiation	Non-initiation
Immunity	Type 1 High	Type 3 Medium
No Immunity	Type 2 Medium	Type 4 Low

Figure 12.1   *Typology of local autonomy*

very high under Type 1 and virtually non-existent under Type 4, Clark suggests that the Platonic Greek city state is closest to Type 1, while Type 4 perhaps finds its expression in a 'Weberian image of a rationalized, bureaucratic, rule-oriented instrument' (1984: 200). Type 3 local governments come closest to the kind of representative and responsible local government suggested by J.S. Mill, while Type 2 'can be described as decentralized liberalism' (Clark, 1984: 201). For Clark, it is the power to initiate, rather than the power of immunity, which is of greater importance, which thus places Type 2 local governments above those in Type 3.

Clark applies his analysis to three different models of local government – Tiebout's (1956) public choice model; Dillon's 1911 judgement or rule, and the home rule provisions made in some American states (notably Illinois). His conclusion is that most United States and Canadian cities in reality fall into the Type 4 category, with most local governments effectively being 'bureaucratic extensions of state governments'. However, he sees the Tiebout perspective as one which would lead to local governments which were closer to the Type 2 category.

Given the generally critical perspective from which Clark, in association with many other geographers writing at the same time, was writing, such a conclusion is perhaps not unexpected.

Attempting to deal with the relative autonomy of the local state was a major problem for many Marxist writers in the late 1970s and early 1980s, just as it remains one today. In attempting to develop an alternative perspective, Gurr and King (1987) suggested that the autonomy of local governments was constrained by two sets of factors. The first, Type 1, referred to constraints imposed by the mix of local economic and social factors, while Type 2 constraints reflected Clark's analysis in suggesting the limits imposed upon municipalities by the higher levels of government.

Gurr and King are concerned to explore both the autonomy of the state generally and of the local state in particular. Their contribution is an important development in the literature because of the way in which it both offered alternative explanations to the Marxist contention that the state – both local and national, but often not clearly distinguished – had no or little autonomy from the interests of capital and developed a classification of different types of constraint on autonomy, especially at the local level.

The Marxist position is best characterized by the work of Cockburn (1977) Reflecting especially on the experience of Lambeth in England, Cockburn explored the way in which British local governments, far from being autonomous units able to reflect their residents' needs and desires and thus act as a force in the class struggle, were in fact prisoners of central government and capital interests concerned with reinforcing the class divide. Additionally, through the adoption of a new managerialism based on the 'corporate model' of the private firm, British local governments were seen as the unwilling slaves of a professionalism which reinforced class differences rather than reduced them.

Gurr and King's response to this line of argument was to acknowledge much of the value of the Marxist contribution to the debate about local autonomy, but to extend the argument and to highlight the ways in which local autonomy might be constrained, yet suggesting rather more autonomy for state institutions, both national and local, than the Marxists allowed. Their more refined classification of constraints between the Type 1 economic and social kind and the Type 2 legal and political kind opened up the possibility for a different kind of interpretation of the state and in particular of local autonomy. They argued that local governments had far more autonomy than Marxists and indeed traditional writers would believe, both from economic and social forces and from other sectors of the state more generally. As far as the first group are concerned (Type 1), Gurr and King identify three important constraining factors – limitations on revenue raising at the local level; the existence of powerful economic actors able effectively to control the local political agenda, and the presence of powerful local social movements able to resist the local state's policies or to influence their implementation.

Since Gurr and King were writing, the nature of Type 1 constraints, particularly of an economic nature, has become much clearer and must be seen as largely dominant. Clearly, in these times of multi national capital and corporations, the internationalization of the world economy and increasing interdependence, the extent to which local governments can exert any considerable control over their futures is very limited. The nature of some of these constraints is explored in the work of Pickvance and Preteceille (1991), who show how changes in central-local government relations have come about largely as a response to the global economic crisis of the 1970s and 1980s, with the changes being linked particularly to the policies adopted to ensure economic restructuring. They demonstrate how such policies have led to a reduction in financial and political support at the national level for the continued growth of the welfare state, often with important consequences for local government, especially in countries such as Britain and Denmark. This policy shift has also been accompanied by a increased central government 'support for policies leading to the accumulation of capital by private firms' (Pickvance and Preteceille, 1991: 197). Furthermore, they suggest that these shifts in policy preferences and resources is a consequence of changes in the nature of the world economy, with globalization, the growth of multinational companies, and the introduction of new technology all combining to produce a major shift in national government policy. This change is in turn followed by changes in the pattern of intergovernmental relations and local autonomy, especially in Western Europe. On the one hand we see declining support for welfare state services, while on the other we see both central government and local governments taking initiatives designed to position themselves so that they can compete in the new global economic conditions. As Pickvance and Preteceille put it:

> The territorial restructuring of states would then contribute to the establishment of a possible new regime of flexible accumulation by destructuring the organisation of public collective consumption in favour of a mode of functioning which is less equalising and redistributive, more fragmented, more dominated by market relations and competition, and more open to high technology capitalist processes. (1991: 198)

As the authors note, such an explanation has its limitations. For example, it neglects significant differences between countries, and would lead us to expect a uniform process of state decentralization in parallel with the increasingly flexible modes of accumulation. And it leaves open the question of how much local autonomy local governments have in practice. But the expectation would be that they would have less discretion to be redistributive through their implementation of welfare state policies, a view they share with more liberally oriented writers such as Peterson (1981).

Peterson starts from the view that local politics are limited politics – that local governments in practice have little opportunity to influence well-being, and as a result, in a modern federal system like the United States, only the federal government can affect redistributive policies relating to welfare. Writing in the period of the fiscal crises of such American cities as New York, Cleveland, Chicago and elsewhere of the mid-1970s, Peterson suggests that not only are local governments limited in their ability to be redistributive in their policies because of economic and fiscal limits on their capacity and particularly because of the mobility of businesses and residents across local boundaries, but he also stresses local political limitations, such as poor working class or ethnic organizations at the local level and the absence of strong local parties – a kind of political under-development as far as redistributive issues at the local level are concerned. For Peterson only the federal level possesses both the financial capacity and the political strength to achieve redistributive policies associated with a strong welfare state.

While such a view may accurately reflect some of the difficulties the United States faces in terms of welfare state development, it ignores the capacity of other federal systems to develop welfare, such as Germany, through a strongly decentralized system where subnational levels have considerable autonomy, and the way in which in Scandinavia a partner-ship between central and local government – albeit one in which local government is very much a junior partner – achieved high levels of welfare provision up until at least the mid-1980s. Since that time pressure has been on Scandinavian governments generally to maintain provision if not reduce it, as these countries also reflect the extent to which fiscal crisis is, as Peterson and others have put it, not only a crisis for local government but more particularly for nation states as well.

In this context, the limited role of local governments to influence the well-being of their residents more generally is further explored in Wolman and Goldsmith (1992). The latter in particular highlight the extent to which our well-being depends far more on the activities of private markets and on national governments, notwithstanding the fact that they also identify a number of ways in which local governments affect people's well-being in general. In so doing they take a different view of what is meant by local autonomy from that conventionally found in the literature, namely the discretion local governments possess to act free from control by higher levels of government. For Wolman and Goldsmith, 'local autonomy is the ability of local governments to have an independent impact on the well-being of their citizens' (1992: 45). To follow this line, they first have to define well-being, which they do as:

> the satisfaction an individual derives from the life circumstances he/she experiences. Community well-being relates to both the aggregate well-being of individual community residents (efficiency) and the distribution of that well-being among community residents (equity) ... Well-being consists of the income which permits individuals to purchase goods and services, to satisfy their desires, but it also consists of non-monetary attributes from which individuals derive satisfaction such as their personal relationships, health, self-esteem etc. (1992: 45)

As we have noted, Wolman and Goldsmith see well-being as being largely determined by a range of factors other than local government: they are concerned to ask what scope remains for local governments to have an impact at all. Local government is thus treated as a residual, but as they note it is a residual which could conceivably account for either a very small or a very large portion of what determines each of the aspects of well-being. Thus the potential for local autonomy is likely to vary from country to country, for 'reasons relating to differences in either national economic, political or social, systems and processes or to local governmental institutional characteristics' (Wolman and Goldsmith, 1992: 45). On the basis of their analysis of British and American experience, they conclude that local governments in both countries possess autonomy in limited, but not unimportant, spheres. Depending on the extent of local autonomy, local governments may exercise an influence on citizen well-being in a variety of ways. For example, local government frequently serves as a vehicle for reflecting citizen preferences for those services which cannot, organizationally, be purchased privately – the classic argument for public goods where it is impossible to determine individual benefits from the provision of such goods, despite the fact that their provision is of considerable collective benefit. Similarly, local governments will have to set priorities between different sets of expenditures: the way in which they do so may well have a considerable impact on individual well-being. For example, as writers such as Elkin (1987) have noted, the way in which local governments determine land use can have a considerable consequence for individual well-being. Equally through such activities, as well as the kind of tax and expenditure mix which they produce, local governments might make their community more or less attractive to inward investment by the private sector – and as such have some impact on community well-being.

Gurr and King's Type 2 constraints refer to the limits imposed on local governments by higher levels of government. Here the comparative work of Page and Goldsmith (1987) helps to clarify how Type 2 limits work and how they can be identified analytically. In an introductory classification, they suggest that the autonomy of local government can be considered under a number of headings. First, there is the constitutional position of municipalities, especially whether or not their competencies are considered as general or specific. Second, there are the kind and range of functions which higher levels of government expect municipalities to perform. Variations across countries may well produce differences in the degree of local autonomy possessed by local governments. Third, local governments may vary in their autonomy according to the amount of discretion they possess in determining how they perform their functions. This discretion may vary because some functions are mandatory while others are permissive, or because the kind of administrative oversight exercised by higher levels of government gives that level of greater or lesser degree of control over what municipalities actually do.

The last formal kind of constraint which may limit local autonomy is the financial regime under which the local government system operates. Are governmental grants conditional or unconditional? What limits are placed on the ability of each locality to raise its own income? The 1980s saw a general increase in the limits placed on the ability of local governments both to spend and to raise income in a number of countries, including Britain, America and some of the Scandinavian countries, but by contrast some of the Southern European countries saw a marked increase in the amount of grant income coming to local governments.[1]

Page and Goldsmith also stress the importance of a political factor in affecting local autonomy, namely the degree of access or influence which local political elites are able to exercise over higher levels of government. Page (1991, esp. Ch. 3) explores this idea in further detail. Building on ideas developed by Mackenzie (1951, 1954), Page suggests that 'the greater the influence of local elites the greater the degree of political localism' (1991: 42) and makes a distinction between direct and indirect forms of influence. In the case of the former, this form reflects direct individual contacts between local officials and national politicians and civil servants, whereas in the latter case, such influence is often exercised on a collective basis on behalf of local government as a whole. France and Italy would provide good examples revealing where individual municipalities are able to exercise direct influence, with the United States as a third example. By contrast, Britain and Scandinavia are countries where such influence is more likely to be exercised in a collective fashion through local government associations (Page and Goldsmith, 1987; Page, 1991: 42–68).

Local autonomy: theory applied and assessed

How do these models work in practice? Page, both in his collaboration with Goldsmith (1987) and his later work (1991), uses his ideas to draw an important empirical distinction between the experience of local government in North and South Europe. For Page, local autonomy depends very much on the interplay between the different legal and political factors, and it is important to realize that such factors can not only reinforce each other but also cut across one another. It is this variation which makes it so difficult to predict in theoretical terms how autonomous one system of local government is likely to be or indeed to explain why one system appears to be more or less autonomous than another. But where the extent of legal autonomy is high, either because it is guaranteed by the constitution or because there is little administrative oversight, or because the financial regime is relatively loose,[2] and where local political influence is extensive,[3] then we would expect local autonomy to be high – and vice versa. The results of such a distinction are set out in Figure 12.2.

In terms of different countries, such a differentiation would put the Spanish autonomous communities in the high autonomy category; French (and perhaps Italian) municipalities and regions in the medium autonomy category because of their high political status, the Scandinavian countries in the medium autonomy category because of their high legal status (and Britain before 1979), while Britain would now be in the last category of low autonomy – low legal status and low political status.

Examining each of these countries in turn, is there evidence to suggest that such a classification has some virtue? Clegg (1987: 151) writing about the Spanish autonomous communities stresses the importance of regionalism and of regional culture and identity. Comparing the strength of the autonomous communities with the municipalities he suggests that the process of change at the local level has been slow after the democratic transition, but clearly identifies the way in which access has opened up. However, much of it remains clientelistic in style, but despite this, Clegg suggests that the autonomy of local government in Spain has increased in comparison with the years of the Franco regime. Parejo Alfonso (1991: 490) suggests that it is at the local government level where 'the consequences of the change to democracy have been most immediately felt', but that it is still difficult to see any real increase in local autonomy, apart from (and perhaps because of) the influence of the autonomous communities, such as the Basque and Catalonian areas. He suggests that

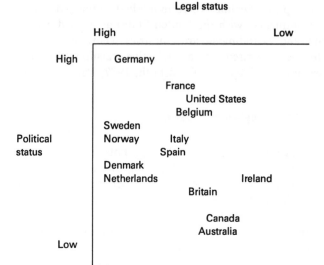

Figure 12.2   *Local autonomy: a cross national comparison*

rather more needs to be done to fulfil 'the constitutional provisions for the territorial design of the state' so that local government has greater legal powers to run services and greater recognition by central government of the role of municipalities. Mateo (1991: 154) suggests a similar conclusion in his brief review of the Spanish experience, while Morata suggests 'the urgent need for reform is becoming increasingly evident' (1992: 193), particularly to ensure better territorial representation of the regions. In terms of the legal and political dimensions of autonomy, therefore, we might wish to conclude that while the regional level of autonomous communities enjoys considerable autonomy, in effect the municipal level is much more limited.

Italy shows similar features, but its subnational government system has frequently confused observers, both Italian and foreign. Page and Goldsmith (1987) and Page (1991: 87–9) clearly placed Italy in the Southern European category, suggesting that its history of clientelism and strong party linkages led to a different pattern of intergovernmental relations as compared with its Northern European counterparts. In the same book, Sanantonio (1987: 119) suggested that the 'overall picture is particularly complex' as far as the legal status of Italian local government was concerned, concluding that the overlapping structure of some 7,000 communes, district councils, provinces and regional institutions are 'supervised in a very detailed way, and that their powers of discretion are small' (Sanantonio, 1987: 118). On the other hand, discussing the access or political status which subnational government enjoys means that the 'political channel between party headquarters and the various and multiple "localisms" is open, and allows access through a variety of routes'

(Sanantonio, 1987: 126). Dente (1991a: 517–20) highlights the degree of fragmentation and heterogeneity to be found in Italian local government, which also gives rise to a weakness of local bureaucracy. Together this can give rise to localities being captured by outside interests of various kinds. Recent scandals, such as those affecting Milan, together with the emergence of the regional political organizations such as the Lega Nord highlight this kind of danger. Dente suggests however, contrary to writers like Sanantonio and Tarrow, that 'the use of party channels for solving centre periphery conflict is fairly limited' (1991a: 547). For Dente, the problem is 'to govern the fragmentation and not to pretend it does not exist' (1991a: 548). Writing elsewhere in the same year, Dente (1991b: 121) suggests that there has been little change in the way in which local government in Italy operates, notwithstanding pressures towards privatization.

Among other commentators, Meny (1987) has seen the decentralization reforms of the early 1980s in France leading to a strengthening of the intermediate tier and of the main urban centres, mainly at the expense of the smaller communes, who have been forced to collaborate and come together in order to retain some influence and status. The relative financial health of French local government for much of the 1980s underpinned the decentralization reforms, which pushed functional responsibility for many activities from the central state downwards and at the same time weakened the central oversight of local activities which the old prefectorial system had involved. And while the limitation on the cumul de mandats might have limited the number of offices an individual might hold, it has not seriously weakened the opportunities which local politicians have to influence public policy (Preteceille, 1991: 141). While agreeing with this broad assessment, Bernier also suggests that decentralization's most striking consequence is 'the competitive environment which pits cities, departments and regions against each other as they attempt to attract profitable businesses and affluent taxpayers to their areas' (1992: 20). Such a view is also implicitly supported by Balme and LeGales (1993) who illustrate this competitiveness in the context of the European Union. However, the election of a more right-wing central government in 1993 has meant a change in the financial and political climate in which such local politicians have to operate, perhaps making it more difficult for them to compete against each other. Thus, while the 1980s saw French subnational government enjoy an increase in legal autonomy over that it had previously enjoyed, its political autonomy had always been relatively high – but in the 1990s the economic and political environment nationally might result in some limitation on local autonomy generally. The overall picture, however, leaves French localities in the middle of our figure – relatively low (but increasing) in legal status, but relatively high (but possibly decreasing) in political status.[4]

The Scandinavian countries need examining individually. Because, as Wolman and Goldsmith (1987: 199) suggest, to a large extent local autonomy is not only determined by constitutional and political factors, but by financial ones as well, and the general economic situation of a nation in terms of its GDP is a good indicator of how strong local government is likely to be. When the economic cake is growing, central government finds it much easier to finance increasing state services: when it is static or even worse decreasing, cuts in expenditure and reductions in service levels are more likely. In the late 1970s and early 1980s, Danish local government experienced both financial retrenchment and loss of political status, as the national government sought to rein in the cost and range of the Danish welfare state. While Sweden briefly echoed the Danish experience in the early 1980s, its economy recovered quickly and it was not until the late 1980s that further economic downturn threatened a reduction in local services. Norway, able to finance new services from its oil incomes, was able to protect both local government and its level of welfare state provision until the mid- to late 1980s, when its economic situation forced retrenchment and its political centre of gravity shifted towards the right.

But in all three cases, the fact that local government had a constitutional provision which gave it general powers to act at least gave the impression that the degree of legal autonomy it possessed in Scandinavia was higher than in countries like Britain. In practice, however, as writers like Bogason (1987, 1991); Lane and Magnusson (1987) and Fevolden and Sorenson (1987) show, all three countries had a system of extensive and detailed administrative control in place, which effectively ensured tight central control over what localities might do in practice. Thus, for example, the 'free commune' experiment, at least in its early years, was more a process of administrative deregulation than a liberalizing of local autonomy. The fact that most localities depended on intermediate interest organizations in the form of local authority associations further meant that the political status of individual municipalities was limited, notwithstanding their relatively small size and numbers. Certainly in Denmark, the local authority associations were not unwilling partners in securing the restrictions on local expenditure that central government wished to achieve in the early 1980s (Bogason: 1987: 67). Throughout much of the 1980s, the Danish central government imposed considerable restraint on local expenditure (Skovsgaard and Sondergaard, 1986; Schou, 1988, cited in Bogason, 1991; Nissen: 1991; Tonboe: 1991), notwithstanding the resistance to cuts in the local welfare state led by women to which Tonboe draws attention.

Norwegians came face to face with expenditure restraints and a popular move to the right later than their Danish colleagues, it being the late 1980s before the Norwegian economy felt the impact of recession. The result was that by this time Norwegian local government had 'achieved the character of a welfare service supermarket' (Hansen, 1991: 237). In terms of intergovernmental relations, this image is reflected in Fevolden and Sorenson's (1987: 30–1) description of central-local relations as being one over the period which moved from 'willing central government–reluctant local government' (1945–63) to one where it was a case of 'willing local government–reluctant central government' (post 1978). Hansen also suggests that decentralist reforms in Norway have had 'less to do with localist values than with more "centralist" ideas about welfare state development and social equality in the consumption of centrally determined public services' (1988: 21). The influence of local governments with the centre is described as formal, and despite the introduction of the free commune experiment in 1986, local discretion remains limited (Lodden, 1991; Rose, 1990). Indeed the latter sees the free commune experiments in Scandinavia generally as representing a continuation of the process of administrative regulation common in all Scandinavian countries and concludes that the experiment is best seen 'as part of a shift from direct to indirect forms of central government control' (Rose, 1990: 233).

Writing about Sweden in 1991, Agne Gustaffson similarly notes the growth of the Swedish welfare state and its domination by municipalities, as well as identifying the problems the central government has in attempting to control expenditures and services (1991: 180). Lane and Magnusson observed that the 'sharp rise in costs has become more and more burdensome in recent years' and that it was clear to the central government that 'efforts must be made to hold back local government expenditure' (1987: 28). Such a change, the authors suggest, would lead to increased local autonomy, as the central government would be forced to reduce both its administrative oversight and its financial contribution. Gunnel Gustafsson highlights the tensions which exist in Swedish local government between the idea of 'equal service delivery' and 'local self-government' (1991: 256), suggesting that the political controversies have intensified during the 1980s, even if policy making is still dominated by consensus in the local government arena. By the time Sweden's economic position had worsened, Gustafsson (1992: 3–6) suggests that the Swedish public sector was 'in the middle of a sweeping process of change' with further decentralization in a climate of local cutbacks and the introduction of alternative modes of service delivery, especially privatization, expected. Elander (1991: 49) neatly summarizes this process of change as leaving Swedish local governments as being 'freer than before to do what you want but in a narrower financial framework'.[5]

The overall result is that in all three Scandinavian countries, the degree of autonomy is limited, despite the apparently high legal autonomy which local governments possess – as demonstrated by their powers of general competence and the free commune experiment. The financial environment in which they operate has generally declined since the 1980s, while their political status has remained limited, notwithstanding the tendency noted by Hansen to push functions and responsibilities down to the intermediate county tier.

The British case is worthy of comment, albeit that it is one of the better documented cases (Rhodes, 1985, 1986a; Stoker, 1991; Cochrane, 1991,

1993). Notwithstanding that Britain involves four different systems of central-local relations, in each case the past 20 years have largely been characterized by increasing centralization and diminution in the status of elected local government. The period has seen restrictions on finance in both tax and expenditure terms, the transfer of powers away from local government, together with the requirement to contract out and offer for competitive tender many local services. There has been the disastrous reform of local taxation, with the introduction and subsequent abandonment of the community charge or poll tax, which played its part in bringing down the then Prime Minister, Mrs Thatcher. Last, but not by any means least, there is a review of structure, supposedly undertaken by an independent Local Government Commission charged with undertaking widespread local consultation, but given direction by the relevant minister to introduce unitary authorities.[6] Throughout the period, there has been a considerable increase in the number of ad hoc special purpose bodies assuming responsibility for functions previously overseen by elected local governments, including urban development, training and enterprise, among others. These bodies are largely appointed, business dominated organizations, the membership of which is often difficult to identify, while the accountability of such bodies is very limited. The political influence of local government – as exerted through the local authority associations – has moved from its high point in the 1970s as described by Rhodes (1986a) to its current low position as suggested by Cochrane (1993) among others. Given that the legal position of British local government has been diminished by the changes described above, the autonomy of British elected local government (never considered particularly high by many commentators) has reached an all-time low.

The most recent study of British local government (Cochrane, 1993) bears out this interpretation and classification. There is widespread agreement that the position of British local government has changed considerably over recent years – but that there is also room for differences in interpretation. Cochrane starts from the point that local government – and more importantly local politics – has been and remains important in Britain. But he goes on to argue that British local government in its institutional form is now but one element in a whole battery of agencies concerned with local well-being, and that the key problem is increasing the accountability of these local agencies. He sees these developments not so much as the replacement of the institutionalized welfare state by the market, as the reorganization of the local state as part of a post-Fordist and corporatist style restructuring of the British state more generally. In other words, a welfare production oriented local government has been replaced by a more flexible range of agencies concerned with (particularly) economic development and the provision of services to people now seen as consumers of services rather than clients of professional bureaucracies. The main actors – politicians, agency heads, bureaucratic professionals, major economic interests, voluntary sector organizations – come together in a kind of local corporatist network, dominating the local decision-making landscape.

But the emphasis on consumerism and the fragmentation and privatization of much of British local government reflects the concern of both the Thatcher and Major governments with the promotion of consumerism as part of their strategy designed to enable the market to replace the state as service provider. This change has been achieved by a mixed process of rolling back the welfare state; centralizing and then fragmenting the local state through the creation of a multitude of different local agencies, the autonomy of which is difficult to assess but whose accountability appears limited.

While the main emphasis of their work has been on Western Europe, both writers (Goldsmith, 1989; Page, 1991) suggest that their analytic approach can usefully be applied to federal systems such as those found in Germany, North America and possibly Australasia. Certainly Canada is a country where the degree of local autonomy available to municipalities is severely limited, given the strong constitutional and political position exerted by provincial governments in the Canadian political system and their legal, financial and political dominance of their local governments. Notwithstanding the existence of partisan politics at provincial level, their formal virtual absence at the local level gives little access and influence to local elites at provincial and federal levels. There are exceptions, mainly based on the large metropolitan cities where a dominant mayor, such as Drapeau in Montreal or a strong chairman such as Gardiner in Toronto, has been able to develop a political power base in the city which offers a significant challenge to the provincial and federal levels. But since the late 1970s onwards, the story of Canadian national and local politics has been one of dominance by the provincial level. Thus Higgins, writing in 1991, suggests that Canadians attach 'relatively low stature to local government', giving it a 'lesser role than other levels of government' and that it is little more than an 'administrative adjunct to senior government' (1991: 48). Such a picture is borne out by its non-partisan status; by its low share of public expenditure (1984: 7 per cent) and of public employment (1986: 25 per cent). Financially weak, heavily dominated and supervised by provincial government and with no real contact with the federal level, Canadian local government is essentially in the low legal and political status category resulting in its having very limited autonomy. Much of Australian local government would appear to be in a similar position: (Jones, 1991: 13) suggests it has 'survived rather than prospered', despite the fact that, as in Canada in the 1970s (Feldman and Graham, 1979), the federal government under Whitlam attempted to rescue local government from its decline and apparent irrelevance (Chapman and Wood, 1984).

To some extent a similar story could be suggested for the United States during the Reagan years. 'Getting the feds out of the cities' and 'reviving state government' were part of the Reagan strategy. While the former may have succeeded, it has left many problems – especially of housing, health and transportation – behind it, and the latter has met with varying success. Most states have chosen not to take up the challenge posed by the federal vacuum in relation to city politics and problems. But the story is more complex in reality. Reagan argued a decentralist policy, basing his arguments on a return to the constitutional principles of federalism which, he believed, required a reduction in the powers of the federal government relative to state and local government. He also supported the desirability of increasing the discretion of states and localities. Towards these ends he reduced the number of categorical grants and increased block grants, especially during his first term – later there was to be a significant increase in the number of categorical grant programmes (Wolman, 1986; ACIR, 1981). Many of these changes were explicitly designed to enhance the power of state government, not only with respect to the federal government, but also to local governments as well. But the overall reduction in grants meant that the resources available to local governments actually decreased, making it more difficult for them to support existing spending levels, thus in effect reducing their local autonomy. More recently, with the election of a Democratic president, there seems to be some return – at least on a selective basis – to greater federal involvement with selected cities, with the introduction of enterprise zones and empowerment areas by the Clinton administration likely to see considerable federal funds directed towards those American cities with major urban problems. Such a development would reinforce Peterson's view that only the federal government can produce redistributive policies which are likely to be effective.

But this story needs placing in a more general context which highlights the way in which local autonomy in the United States is constrained, formally and informally. Constitutionally, local governments are all creatures of state governments: Dillon's rule makes this quite clear in a celebrated phrase – 'They are . . . the mere tenants at will of the legislature' (ACIR, 1981: 17). But many states have gone further than Dillon's rule implied, granting their municipalities some form of home rule, which in its broadest form implies something similar to the general competence powers given to Scandinavian local governments.

This position is further complicated by other factors. First, there is the fragmentation of the municipal system in the United States, perhaps the best known feature of its metropolitan areas. Such fragmentation can isolate communities, particularly the major central city, from other areas, while at the same time leading to exclusionary zoning (by which rich areas keep out undesirables, such as the poor and the black) and to the imposition of external costs by some municipalities on their neighbours. Second, there may be internal constraints imposed upon the autonomy of localities, such as the celebrated tax and expenditure limitations enacted by some states and localities from the late 1970s onwards, such as California's famous Proposition 13 to Massachusetts's Proposition 2.5. For example, by 1985, 31 states had placed a maximum on the tax rate which their localities could apply to the assessed value of property in their areas (Wolman and Goldsmith, 1992: 79).

Having said that, the political representation of cities and municipalities remains as strong as ever, even if the degree of influence may not be as great as that exerted by state governors. Big city mayors in particular can still expect their voice to be heard in Washington, both in Congress and the White House, while different interest organizations, such as the League of Cities, possess considerable lobbying power. In terms of the distinction between legal and political status, American local government would appear to have relatively high political status, like some of their European counterparts in France and Spain for example. As a result, local government in the United States would thus fall into the medium autonomy category because of its high political status, even if its legal status is limited and relatively low.

The German case is both different and interesting. Here it is the doctrine of subsidiarity which gives the regions and localities of Germany their legal and political status. Local governments are 'guaranteed the right to "regulate on their own responsibility all the affairs of the local community within the limits set by law"' (Hesse, 1991: 364). This legal position has been reinforced over the years since 1945 by a growing political importance for local government; an increasing dissatisfaction with the policy performance of federal government, which has led to demands for a 'revival of politics for below' (Hesse, 1991: 380). While Hesse suggests that such demands underestimate the extent to which political and administrative decision making in Germany is essentially interdependent between the different levels, clearly regional (*Länder*) and municipal governments exercise considerable influence and autonomy over affairs. In his review of local government in the German federal system, Gunlicks suggests that while both constitutional and *Land* local government law have not made local governments equal partners, local governments 'enjoy constitutional protection as institutions of self-government with a guaranteed core area for self-determination' (1986: 72). As a result they might be placed in the high autonomy category.

Other writers have looked at countries such as Belgium and Holland. Until recently Belgium was very similar to France in terms of the structure and culture of its local government system and thus could reasonably be expected to show similar characteristics to the other Southern European countries, such as Spain, Italy and France. Belgian local government accounts for relatively little of total current and capital public expenditure (Page, 1991: 141), reflecting the limited responsibilities it has. Mughan also points out the extent to which 'communes have long enjoyed high popular esteem in Belgium' (1985: 280) despite their reduction in numbers over the years and that the holding of dual mandates – as with French local elected officials – 'has always provided an informal but intimate link between local and national politics in Belgium'. Recent moves to decentralize the Belgian state in the late 1980s led some writers (for example, Delmartino,

1991) to suggest that Belgium is now more like a federal than a unitary state, with a resulting increase in the status of subnational governments. One would thus be tempted to place Belgian local government in the medium autonomy category arising from its relatively high political status.

By contrast the Netherlands comes much closer to the Northern European model, with local government accounting for about 25 per cent of public spending in the mid-1980s, on a par with local government spending in Britain. Dutch local governments also have a range of responsibilities more in line with Scandinavian experience, have extremely limited financial autonomy, with over 90 per cent of their finance coming from central government, and there is a strong tradition of administrative oversight (Hoogerwerf, 1984; Toonen, 1987, 1991; Bekke, 1991). Toonen's description of Dutch intergovernmental relations as one reflecting the 'interdependency and interwovenness of intergovernmental affairs' (1991: 315), resulting in a situation in which the idea of a 'free "autonomous" municipality is obsolete' and a national government which 'has become too dependent on local government for carrying out its affairs' (1991: 319) stresses that interdependency. The result would be to suggest that the Netherlands local governments fall between the Scandinavian and British cases – relatively high legal status but low political status.

Conclusion

What this review of comparative local government suggests is that there is pressure on local autonomy in many political systems today. How that pressure is explained and how it is assessed has been a major concern for this chapter, which has ranged widely both in terms of the theories it has examined and the countries it has briefly reviewed. That it covers so much is a sign of the interest which the idea of and desire for local autonomy engenders.

This chapter has suggested that local autonomy is important in the context of normative theories about local government and central to many arguments about the democratic nature of societies. The ability of local communities, through institutional and representative forms, to act for themselves unfettered by constraints from higher levels of government remains important as a normative objective.

The different analytical theoretical perspectives we have reviewed endorse these normative objectives, notwithstanding their attempt to define, classify and explain the different patterns of local government which we find. What they do is to suggest that the pattern of inter-governmental relations in most societies is complex, differentiated and variable, giving rise to different patterns of local autonomy – and changing rapidly in the face of widespread economic and social change.

In understanding these changing patterns, the work of Gurr and King, together with that of Wolman and Goldsmith, and of Page, allows us to identify the key factors affecting local autonomy in theory and practice. The distinction between Type 1 and Type 2 constraints gives rise to a view of local autonomy and intergovernmental relations as largely conditioned and determined by two sets of variables. On the one hand, the Type 1 factors are broadly economic and social, reflecting the economic restructuring taking place across the world. New technology, shifting manufacturing centres, new formulations of capital, all impose on national states and localities in different ways, perhaps caught, however inadequately, as the results of the transition from Fordist to post-Fordist societies as explored by Pickvance and Preteceille as well as by Cochrane and Stoker. By contrast, the Type 2 constraints, as the work of Clark, Page, Rhodes, Wolman and Goldsmith, are essentially legal and political in nature: as Page would put it, local autonomy is a reflection of the differing and changing legal and political status of local government across countries, either in its formal constitutional position or in terms of its ability to exercise political influence across the political system.

The result is a complex intermingling of all four types of factors, which places interpretations of local autonomy in a highly contingent position. The balance between centre and locality is constantly changing as the different dimensions – economic, social, legal and political – themselves change, with the result that local autonomy is itself constantly changing. Relationships are unstable, and local autonomy uncertain.

Even if our comparative review helps to reinforce the uncertain and confusing picture, some order can still be seen within it. In their concluding chapter to the major survey of local government worldwide, Hesse and Sharpe (1991: 606 ff.) identify three broad groupings or types of local government systems. The first is what they call the *Franco* group in which the local government system basically follows the Napoleonic model, and in which the raison d'être of local government is essentially political rather than functional. As we have seen, and as Hesse and Sharpe conclude, 'this type of local government system is found – in addition to France – in Italy, Belgium, Spain and Portugal, and to some extent in Greece' (1991: 607). And as we have suggested, following Page (1991), these countries form a core in which local autonomy is moderate – a high political autonomy contrasted by relatively weak legal autonomy.

The second group identified by Hesse and Sharpe is what they refer to as the *Anglo* group – the UK, Ireland, Canada, Australia, possibly the US and New Zealand. Local government systems in this group enjoy little legal status and little political autonomy. Broadly one would agree with the description, though one might argue that while Canada and Australia might fit alongside Britain as a low autonomy system today, British local government formerly had wide service providing powers, and even today would enjoy greater functional autonomy than its Canadian or Australian counterparts. By contrast, American local government might enjoy greater political status than its other federal counterparts in this group – and certainly more than is the case in Britain. Without wishing to make a complete case for British exceptionalism, this author's view is that Hesse and Sharpe's Anglo group is less clear cut than they would suggest, with the result that the countries making up this group would be more widely spread in Figure 12.2 than Hesse and Sharpe's categorization would lead us to expect.

The third type of local government system identified by Hesse and Sharpe is the *North* or *Middle European* type. Here they argue that 'central-local relations broadly resemble those typical of the Anglo model, especially with regard to the emphasis placed on local functional capacity; but, in contrast to the Anglo form, equal emphasis tends to be placed on *local democracy per se*' (1991: 607, original emphasis). Among the countries we have surveyed here, Scandinavia, the Netherlands and Germany would be included – and Hesse and Sharpe add Austria, Switzerland and Japan to the group.

Again one would quibble, suggesting that the degree of political autonomy is over exaggerated by Hesse and Sharpe in some of these cases, again resulting in a wider distribution of the individual countries. But where they are correct is to stress the dependence which central government has on the local level in this group of countries, especially for local service delivery – and why it is also correct to separate Britain from this grouping. In the British case, central government has deliberately sought to move away from this dependent situation over the last 15 years – and, as we have argued, signs exist that some of this group are beginning to show the same tendency.

What one cannot deny is Hesse and Sharpe's (1991: 617) general conclusion, namely that intergovernmental relations and local autonomy have changed significantly over recent years and that they have become more problematic. What Hesse and Sharpe refer to as a 'golden age' in the case of the Middle/North European group may well be over – not only in the Anglo group but for the Middle Europeans as well. What may well replace it is another golden age – in West Europe at least, in which local autonomy at regional or city level is increasingly brought about through the process of European integration – a process which reflects more strongly the traditions of the Franco group. But this is another story, only just beginning.

Notes

1 For a much more detailed discussion of these points see, inter alia, Page and Goldsmith (1987) and Wolman and Goldsmith (1992, esp. Ch. 6).

2 By which is meant some combination of a general grant system with little attempt at capping the local tax regime, which itself would be based on a buoyant tax.

3 By which is meant that localities are able to exert direct influence on upper tiers of government, through, for example, an extensive dual mandate system.

4 A similar picture to these three main Southern European countries can be found in the limited literature on countries like Ireland, Portugal, Greece and Turkey (Kousalas, 1986;

Ayarta, 1987; Collins, 1987; Barrington, 1991; Christofilopoulou-Kaler, 1991; Heper, 1991; Pedroso de Almeida, 1991; Pereira, 1991; Coyle and Sinnott, 1992).

5 See also Elander and Montin (1990).

6 This direction is subject to legal challenge at the time of writing. Some municipalities have challenged the direction on the grounds that the Minister has changed the Local Government Commission's terms of reference as approved by Parliament, thus exceeding his powers.

References

Advisory Commission on Intergovernmental Relations (1981) *A Catalogue of Federal Grant-in Aid Program to State and Local Governments: Grant Funder FY 1989.* Washington D.C.: US Government Printing Office.

Ayarta, A. (1987) 'Clientelism and local political leadership in Turkey'. Paper presented to the ECPR Workshop on Local Political Leadership, Amsterdam, April.

Balme, R. and LeGales, P. (1993) 'French cities and regions in the wake of European integration', in J.E. Loughlin (ed.), *Europe of the Cities v Europe of the Regions.* Rotterdam: Erasmus PA Network.

Barrington, T.J. (1991) 'Local government in Ireland', in R. Batley and G. Stoker (eds), *Local Government in Europe.* London: Macmillan.

Bekke, H.A.G.M. (1991) 'Experiences and experiments in Dutch local government', in R. Batley and G. Stoker (eds), *Local Government in Europe.* London: Macmillan.

Bernier, L. (1992) 'Reading Decentralisation: Signs of Change in the French Intergovernmental System', mimeo.

Bogason, P. (1987) 'Denmark', in E. Page and M. Goldsmith (eds), *Central and Local Government Relations.* London: Sage.

Bogason, P. (1991) 'Danish local government: towards an efficient welfare state', in J.J. Hesse (ed.), *Local Government and Urban Affairs in International Perspective.* Baden-Baden: Nomos Verlagsgesellschaft.

Chapman, R. and Wood, M. (1984) *Australian Local Government: the Federal Dimension.* Sydney: Allen and Unwin.

Christofilopoulou-Kaler, P. (1991) 'Local government reform in Greece', in J.J. Hesse (ed.), *Local Government and Urban Affairs in International Perspective.* Baden-Baden: Nomos Verlagsgesellschaft.

Clark, G. (1984) 'A theory of local autonomy', *Annals of the Association of American Geographers,* 74: 195–200.

Clegg, T. (1987) 'Spain', in E. Page and M. Goldsmith (eds), *Central and Local Government Relations.* London: Sage.

Cochrane, A. (1991) 'The changing state of local government: restructuring for the 1990s', *Public Administration,* 69 (3): 281–303.

Cochrane, A. (1993) *Whatever Happened to Local Government?* Buckingham: Open University Press.

Cockburn, C. (1977) *The Local State.* London: Pluto Press.

Collins, C.A. (1987) *Local Government Managers at Work.* Dublin: Institute of Public Administration.

Coyle, C. and Sinnott, R. (1992) 'Regional elites, regional "powerlessness", and European regional policy in Ireland', *Regional Politics and Policy,* 2 (1–2): 71–108.

Delmartino, F. (1991) 'Local government in Belgium: decentralising the state', in J.J. Hesse (ed.), *Local Government and Urban Affairs in International Perspective.* Baden-Baden: Nomos Verlagsgesellschaft.

Dente, B. (1991a) 'The fragmented reality of Italian local government', in J.J. Hesse (eds), *Local Government and Urban Affairs in International Perspective.* Baden-Baden: Nomos Verlagsgesellschaft.

Dente, B. (1991b) 'Italian local services: the difficult road towards privatisation', in R. Batley and G. Stoker (eds), *Local Government in Europe*. London: Macmillan.

Elander, I. (1991) 'Analysing central-local government relations in different systems: a conceptual framework and some empirical illustrations', *Scandinavian Political Studies*, 14 (1): 31–58.

Elander, I and Montin, S. (1990) 'Decentralisation and control: central and local government relations in Sweden', *Politics and Policy*, 18: 165–80.

Elkin, S. (1987) *City and Regime in the American Republic*. Chicago, IL: Chicago University Press.

Feldman, L. and Graham, H. (1979) *Bargaining for Cities*. Montreal: Institute for Research on Public Policy.

Fevolden, T. and Sorenson, R. (1987) 'Norway', in E. Page and M. Goldsmith (eds), *Central and Local Government Relations*. London: Sage.

Goldsmith, M. (1989) 'The status of local government: a consideration of the political position of local government in Britain, Canada and the United States', in H. Pratt, C. Elder and H. Wolman (eds), *Constitutional Regimes and the City*. Detroit, IL: Wayne State University.

Gunlicks, A. (1986) *Local Government in the German Welfare System*. Durham, NC: Duke University Press.

Gurr, T. and King, T. (1987) *The State and the City*. Chicago: Chicago University Press.

Gustafsson, A. (1991) 'The changing local government and politics of Sweden', in R. Batley and G. Stoker (eds), *Local Government in Europe*. London: Macmillan.

Gustafsson, G. (1991) 'Swedish local government: reconsidering rationality and consensus', in J.J. Hesse (ed.), *Local Government and Urban Affairs in International Perspective*. Baden-Baden: Nomos Verlagsgesellschaft.

Gustafsson, G. (1992) 'Democracy in Transition – Swedish Municipalities and County Councils in the Local Territory', Umea: University of Umea, mimeo.

Hansen, T. (1988) 'Intermediate level reforms and the development of the Norwegian welfare state', paper presented to IPSA World Congress, Washington, D.C., 1988.

Hansen, T. (1991) 'Norwegian local government: stability through change', in J.J. Hesse (ed.), *Local Government and Urban Affairs in International Perspective*. Baden-Baden: Nomos Verlagsgesellschaft.

Heper, M. (1991) 'Local government in Turkey', in J.J. Hesse (ed.), *Local Government and Urban Affairs in International Perspective*. Baden-Baden: Nomos Verlagsgesellschaft.

Hesse, J.J. (1991) 'Local government in a federal state: the case of West Germany', in J.J. Hesse (ed.), *Local Government and Urban Affairs in International Perspective*. Baden-Baden: Nomos Verlagsgesellschaft.

Hesse, J.J. and Sharpe, L.J. (1991) 'Conclusions', in J.J. Hesse (ed.), *Local Government and Urban Affairs in International Perspective*. Baden-Baden: Nomos Verlagsgesellschaft.

Higgins, D. (1991) 'Canada', in J.J. Hesse, (ed.), *Local Government and Urban Affairs in International Perspective*. Baden-Baden: Nomos Verlagsgesellschaft.

Hoogerwerf, A. (1984) 'Les Pays-Bas', in Y. Meny (ed.), *La Réforme des collectivités locales en Europe: stratégies et résultats*. Paris: La Documentation Française.

Jones, M. (1991) 'Australian local government: waiting for a challenge', in J.J. Hesse (ed.), *Local Government and Urban Affairs in International Perspective*. Baden-Baden: Nomos Verlagsgesellschaft.

Kousalas, D. (1986) 'Communist mayors in Greece', in B. Szajkowski (ed.), *Marxist Local Governments*. London: Pinter.

Lane, J.E. and Magnusson, T. (1987) 'Sweden', in E. Page and M. Goldsmith (eds), *Central and Local Government Relations*. London: Sage.

Lodden, P. (1991) 'The free local government experiment in Norway', in R. Batley and G. Stoker (eds), *Local Government in Europe*. London: Macmillan.

Mackenzie, W.J.M. (1951) 'The conventions of local government', *Public Administration*, 29: 345–56.

Mackenzie, W.J.M. (1954) 'Local government in parliament', *Public Administration*, 32: 409–23.

Mateo, J.F. (1991) 'Improving access to administration in Spain', in R. Batley and G. Stoker (eds), *Local Government in Europe*. London: Macmillan.

Meny, Y. (1987) 'France', in E. Page and M. Goldsmith (eds), *Central and Local Government Relations*. London: Sage.

Morata, F. (1992) 'Regions and the European Community: a comparative analysis of four Spanish regions', *Regional Politics and Policy*. 2 (1–2): 187–216.

Mughan, A. (1985) 'Belgium: all periphery and no centre?', in Y. Meny and V. Wright (eds), *Centre Periphery Relations in Western Europe*. London: Allen and Unwin.

Nissen, O. (1991) 'Key issues in the local government debate in Denmark', in R. Batley and G. Stoker (eds), *Local Government in Europe*. London: Macmillan.

Page, E. (1991) *Localism and Centralism in Europe*. Oxford: Oxford University Press.

Page, E. and Goldsmith, M. (eds) (1987) *Central and Local Government Relations*. London: Sage.

Parejo Alfonso, L. (1991) 'Local government in Spain: implementing the basic law', in J.J. Hesse (ed.), *Local Government and Urban Affairs in International Perspective*. Baden-Baden: Nomos Verlagsgesellschaft.

Pedroso de Almeida, J.M. (1991) 'Portugal: overcoming the central government', in J.J. Hesse (ed.), *Local Government and Urban Affairs in International Perspective*. Baden-Baden: Nomos Verlagsgesellschaft.

Pereira, A. (1991) 'The system of local government in Portugal', in R. Batley and G. Stoker (eds) *Local Government in Europe*. London: Macmillan.

Peterson, P. (1981) *City Limits*. Chicago, IL: University of Chicago Press.

Pickvance, C. and Preteceille, E. (1991) *State Restructuring and Local Power*. London: Pinter.

Preteceille, E. (1991) 'From centralisation to decentralisation: social restructuring and French local government', in C. Pickvance and E. Preteceille (eds), *State Restructuring and Local Power*. London: Pinter.

Rhodes, R. (1981) *Control and Power in Central-Local Government Relations*. Aldershot: Gower.

Rhodes, R. (1985) 'A squalid and politically corrupt process?' Intergovernmental relations in the postwar period', *Local Government Studies*, 11 (6): 35–57.

Rhodes, R. (1986a) *The National World of Local Government*. London: Allen and Unwin.

Rhodes, R. (1986b) '"Power Dependence". Theories of central-local relations: a critical reassessment', in M. Goldsmith (ed.), *New Research in Central-Local Relations*. Aldershot: Gower.

Rhodes, R. (1988) *Beyond Westminster and Whitehall*. London: Allen and Unwin.

Rose, L.E. (1990) 'Nordic free commune experiments: increased local autonomy or continued central control', in D. King and J. Pierre (eds), *Challenges to Local Government*. London: Sage.

Sanantonio, E. (1987) 'Italy', in E. Paige and M. Goldsmith (eds), *Central and Local Government Relations*. London: Sage.

Schou, B. (1988) 'Udgiftsstyring eller fornlyse? Firkloverregeriingens politik over for kommunerne', in K.-H. Bentzon (ed.), *Fra vaekst til omstiing-moderningsen af den offentlige sektot*. Copenhagen: Nyt fra samfundsivendskaberne.

Sharpe, L.J. (1970) 'Theories of local government', *Political Studies*, 18 (2): 153–74.

Skovsgaard, C.J. and Sondergaard, J. (1986) 'Danish local government: recent trends in economy and administration', in M. Goldsmith and S. Villadsen (eds), *Urban Political Theory and the Management of Fiscal Stress*. Aldershot: Gower.

Stoker, G. (1991) *The Politics of Local Government* (2nd edn). London: Macmillan.

Tiebout, C.M. (1956) 'A pure theory of local expenditures', *Journal of Political Economy*, 64: 416–24.

Tonboe, J. (1991) 'Centralized economic control in a decentralized welfare state: Danish central-local government relations, 1970–1986', in C. Pickvance and E. Preteceille (eds), *State Restructuring and Local Power*. London: Pinter.

Toonen, T.A.J. (1987) 'The Netherlands: a decentralised unitary state in a welfare society', in R.A.W. Rhodes and V. Wright (eds), *Tensions in the Territorial Politics of Western Europe*. London: Frank Cass.

Toonen, T.A.J. (1991) 'Change and continuity; local government and urban affairs in the Netherlands', in J.J. Hesse (ed.), *Local Government and Urban Affairs in International Perspective*. Baden-Baden: Nomos Verlagsgesellschaft.

Wolman, H. (1986) 'The Reagan urban policy and its impacts', *Urban Affairs Quarterly*, 21 (3): 311–36.

Wolman, H. (1990) 'Decentralisation: what it is and why we should care', in R. Bennett (ed.), *Decentralisation, Local Government and Markets*. Oxford: Clarendon Press.

Wolman, H. and Goldsmith, M. (1987) 'Local government fiscal stress in a period of slow national growth: a comparative analysis', *Environment and Planning C: Government and Policy*, 5 (2): 171–82.

Wolman, H. and Goldsmith, M (1992) *Urban Politics and Policy*. Oxford: Basil Blackwell.

13

Marxist Theories of Urban Politics

Christopher Pickvance

In this chapter, it will be shown that Marxist theories of urban politics both offer alternative explanations of topics addressed by more conventional theories, and identify new objects for study. We consider in turn the main Marxist theories of urban politics and some empirical applications of these theories, and then evaluate these theories and their applications.

An exposition of Marxist theories of urban politics

Marxist theories of urban politics show a strong family resemblance but display considerable diversity. This diversity reflects the absence of a worked out theory of politics in the writings of Marx and early Marxists, the varied perspectives of those claiming a Marxist underpinning for their work, and the wide range of political contexts in which Marxist theories have been developed.

The starting point for all Marxist theories of urban politics is the view that urban political institutions are part of the state apparatus, and hence are inescapably marked by the role which the state plays in capitalist society.

Marxist writing on the state is voluminous. Its point of departure is that capitalism cannot secure its own reproduction because it has prerequisites which the market cannot be guaranteed to provide, and because it produces conflicts which cannot be regulated by economic institutions. These conflicts are class conflicts because the capitalist mode of production is an exploitative one allowing the accumulation of capital by a capitalist class at the expense of the 'working class'. The state is thus seen as playing two indispensable roles. The first is to provide the general prerequisites of production which range from a legal system, a monetary system and communications and transport systems to a healthy labour force with the skills and motivation needed by employers. The second is to maintain social order by the creation of institutions to contain social conflict, the diffusion of supportive images and attitudes, the introduction of policies containing 'concessions' to subordinate classes, and the creation of repressive institutions. The terms 'accumulation function' and 'legitimation function' were introduced by O'Connor (1973) to refer to these categories of action. (It should be noted that the boundaries of state action are flexible – reflecting the extent to which functions such as communications and transport can be provided through the market, and the extent to which there are threats to social order.)

Beyond these claims about the state, Marxist writers are divided and hence there are sharply differing conceptions of urban politics. The main division concerns the degree of autonomy in relation to the dominant classes which state institutions need in order to perform the accumulation and legitimation functions described.

'Instrumentalist' writers see the state as an 'instrument' used in the general interests of the dominant class and as having minimal autonomy from that class. This view also stresses the unity of state institutions and minimizes conflicts among them. It follows that urban political institutions are understood as being an integral part of the state and hence as having little or no autonomy from higher levels of state institution. The policies carried out at local level are seen as reflecting the interests of nationally dominant classes and local politics is seen as offering a semblance of 'participation' but no real power. As a result, the study of urban politics is of little interest since policies are a resultant of forces external to the urban arena.

An alternative view of how the accumulation and legitimation functions are performed by the state is offered by the 'structuralist' view. On this view the execution of these functions requires considerable autonomy to be placed between state institutions and the dominant class, and considerable 'looseness' to exist in the relations among state institutions. The reason is that this view places greater emphasis on the divisions among the 'fractions' of the capitalist class, and the need to 'buy off' working class strength by concessions. As a consequence, state institutions become an important object of study due to their role in reconciling conflicting pressures. Urban political institutions thus have some autonomy in relation to local class interests to create a social order which reconciles national and local class interests. The difficulty of predicting how such an order is achieved gives the field of urban politics a much greater interest than on the instrumentalist view.

Instrumentalist and structuralist views therefore differ regarding the autonomy of the state from the dominant classes (low, high), the unity of state institutions (high, low) and the determination of urban politics (and policy) by external forces (high, low).

We now turn to four specific theories of urban politics. O'Connor's theory is close to the instrumentalist view of the state; Friedland, Piven and Alford's theory is somewhat further away and Castells's theory is close to the structuralist view. Finally, we consider Saunders's theory which is partly instrumentalist but partly rejects Marxism.

The American writer O'Connor published his book *The Fiscal Crisis of the State* in 1973. It was not explicitly a contribution to urban politics but had an influence in this field since it was published at a time when 'urban fiscal crises' were breaking out in New York and elsewhere and was used to help understand these events.

O'Connor's argument started by breaking the economy into three segments – the state sector, the 'monopoly' sector and the 'competitive' sector. He then argued that the growth of the state sector and the growth of the monopoly sector were mutually interdependent. The state's accumulation function required it to spend to maintain capital accumulation. He termed such spending 'social capital' expenditure and argued that it had the effect of increasing profitability since it obviated the need for capitalists to make provision themselves. 'Social capital' expenditure was divided into 'social consumption' (for example, spending on state housing, education or health – which lifted a burden from employers) and 'social investment' (for example, spending on roads and utilities). In addition to its social capital expenditure, O'Connor argued that the state had a legitimation function which required it to spend on items which do not contribute directly to profits. Such 'social expenses' range from the maintenance of social order by means of a police force and system of social security to the provision of levels of education and health beyond what is 'necessary' for capital accumulation.

However, O'Connor's analysis of state spending was not tension-free. His central thesis was that state accumulation and legitimation functions lead to 'a contradictory process which creates tendencies towards economic, social and political crises' (1973: 9). In particular, a fiscal crisis would ensue due to the tendency for state expenditure to outrun state income. However if this was resisted by state employees and state clients, it would be translated into a social crisis.

O'Connor does not outline a theory of urban fiscal crisis, but he does provide the elements for one. He argues that both state and local governments provide crucial spending in support of capital (for example, education and highway investment), but whereas local governments are dominated by competitive capital, state governments and big cities are more likely to be beyond the control of any fraction of capital and will be objects of contention between the working class, competitive capital and monopoly capital with 'arbiter governments' emerging. O'Connor also points out that the division between suburban and central city governments means that the resources needed to pay for this spending are unequally distributed, making it more likely that central city governments will experience fiscal crisis.

O'Connor's theory has close links with the theory of state monopoly capitalism elaborated by the French Communist Party in the 1960s which regarded the state and monopoly capital as functioning as a 'single mechanism', but his comments on the functions of federal state and local governments in the US allow for some degree of unpredictability about their precise roles.

A second theory of urban politics is the theory of the distribution of state functions put forward by the American writers Friedland, Piven and Alford (1977). On the one hand, it builds on O'Connor's work; on the other hand it gives state structures much greater analytical autonomy than do instrumentalist theories.

Friedland et al. start from O'Connor's notion of a contradiction between the state's accumulation and legitimation functions and ask why this contradiction so rarely gives rise to conflict. They suggest that the answer lies in the way state functions are distributed among different levels of government, and between elected and non-elected bodies.

O'Connor himself noted that in big cities there is a tendency to set up supramunicipal non-elected bodies in order to avoid working-class majorities (1973: 87). Friedland et al. build on this insight and argue that political structures have developed which allow the potential conflicts between the municipal roles of supporting economic growth by means of capital investment, and so on, and providing channels of political participation to be avoided. The structural arrangements they identify are the decentralization of state functions and the segregation of accumulation and legitimation functions.

Friedland et al. argue, drawing on US experience, that the more decentralized a local government is – that is, the less subject to grants or controls from higher levels of government – the more dependent it is on the fortunes of the local economy. As a consequence, such local governments are more likely to take part in competitive bidding to attract or support business, thereby making fiscal stress more likely. Interestingly this is probably an unintended consequence of decentralized government which is generally advocated as a way of allowing local citizens to govern themselves.

A second mechanism by which state structure reduces potential conflict is through the segregation of accumulation and legitimation functions. Friedland et al. argue that this can happen in three ways: first, by giving responsibility for accumulation and legitimation function to different bodies, for example, as when economic development or urban renewal functions are hived off from local government and given to separate agencies; second, by insulating agencies with accumulation-related functions from citizen input and giving privileged access to business inputs; and third, by locating accumulation and legitimation functions at different levels of government, for example, by creating supramunicipal or regional structures for infrastructure investment decisions affecting economic development. In contrast, local government is highly visible and open to citizen pressure though this may to some extent be moderated as when there are conflicts between the interests of citizens as service beneficiaries and citizens as taxpayers.

Finally, Friedland et al. argue that none of these structural 'solutions' for reducing conflict over state functions is lasting. Typically each 'solution' shifts the locus and character of the conflict rather than eliminating it. In particular, they convert political conflict into fiscal strain, which in turn may lead to new temporary 'solutions'.

We now consider a theory of urban politics which is explicitly inspired by the structuralist view of the state: the 1970s work of the Spanish writer Castells (1977, 1978). Castells's writing drew from Poulantzas's (1973) structuralist theory of the state but combined this with an emphasis on social movements deriving from the influence of the French writer Touraine. Rejecting state monopoly capitalism theory, Castells's theory of advanced capitalism was centred on the role of the state. Far from seeing the state as passively responding to fractions of capital, he saw it as having a key organizing role. In particular, he argued that due to the functional pressures from capital and from the working class, the state had come to play a key role in organizing the reproduction of labour power as well as its functions in direct relation to capital. Castells coined the term 'collective consumption' to refer to this intervention, which could take the form of regulation, subsidization or direct provision. He defined 'urban' politics to refer to the struggles over such intervention. (His definition of urban was not geographical, so for example political conflicts over council housing in rural areas would form part of urban politics as he defined it.)

Castells's theory was that growing state intervention in collective consumption was an inevitable feature of advanced capitalism and that it made the state an increasingly frequent object of political demands. As regulator, financier or provider of consumption facilities, it became a political target of what previously would have been demands made against economic actors, for example, landlords.

Castells gives no space to the role of political parties in articulating such demand making. Rather, he privileges the role of social movements, introducing the terms 'participation', 'protest' and 'urban social movement' to describe the three levels of change (from 'control' to 'reform' to revolutionary) which they can bring about alone or in conjunction with other groupings. Subsequently, Castells used the term urban social movement to refer both to all such mobilizations whatever their effects, as well as to the rare cases where revolutionary changes occurred. Since the generic category of urban movements is covered in a separate chapter, they are not discussed further here.

Castells's concept of urban politics also acknowledges the role of state intervention beyond collective consumption. He used the term 'urban planning' in an idiosyncratic way to refer to all interventions which sought to ensure the extended reproduction of capitalism and the regulation of conflicts. Examples of urban planning include new town building and urban renewal.

Finally, we consider the dual state or dual politics theory of Saunders. This theory is partly inspired by Marxist theorizing but can be seen as an attempt to go beyond it. Saunders rejects the need for a choice between theoretical approaches and argues that 'we need . . . to understand their complementarity in the sense of tracing the contexts in which each of them [namely, theories such as instrumentalism, pluralism and managerialism] is most likely to apply' (1986a: 218). Saunders's 'dual theory of politics' does this by arguing for a complementarity between instrumentalism and 'imperfect pluralism'. He sets out an ideal type model of the contexts in which these two theories apply (see Table 13.1). In brief, he argues that production issues generate a politics which is class-based, which involves corporatist representation of actors, which is focused on the central state level and where allocation is based on private property rights. Consumption issues on the other hand are not class-based but based on sectoral interests (for example, council tenants', landlords', owner-occupiers'). These interests engage in competitive politics focused on the local state and allocation is based on citizenship or social need. The instrumentalist theory of the state applies in the former case and the 'imperfect pluralist' theory in the latter. ('Imperfect pluralism' refers to the facts that while elected authorities are relatively open to external pressure, this openness varies according to the interest group concerned, and that officials' values are also a means by which pressures are transmitted.)

It is important to be precise about Saunders's claims about this theory. First, it is not intended as a (Marxist) 'functionalist state theory in which the level at which a service is provided is explained in terms of the need to insulate it from, or tailor it to, this or that interest or pressure' (1986a: 302). Rather, he suggests, an explanation of the distribution of state functions must be historical. Second, Saunders does not assert that his model is realized empirically, but only that it identifies typical patterns.

Saunders's theory claims that:

> the state will operate in the interests of the dominant classes the more its interventions are directed at the process of production, the more corporatist its organizational forms, the more centralized its operations [and] will be more responsive to the weight of popular opinion . . . the more its interventions are directed towards provision for consumption, the more competitive or democratic its organizational forms, the more localized its operations (1986a: 307)

He argues that the two patterns are explained by instrumentalist theory and imperfect pluralism theory respectively.

In considering Saunders's theory of urban politics, one can either stress or ignore its linkage with Marxist theories by saying either that it is half-based on the (Marxist) instrumentalist approach, or that it is half-based on the (non-Marxist) 'imperfect pluralist' approach.

In this section, we have shown that Marxist theories of urban politics share certain common features. They start from an analysis of the necessary role of the state in the reproduction of capitalism, treat the interests of fractions of capital as the main determinants of policy outcomes, and argue that political parties have relatively little autonomy in relation to economic interests. On the other hand, we have noted significant differences among Marxist theories concerning their views of the unity of the state, the differentiation of levels of the state, the presence

Table 13.1 *Saunders's dual politics thesis*

	Politics of production	Politics of consumption
Social base	Class interests	Consumption sector interests
Mode of interest mediation	Corporatist	Competitive
Level	Central state	Local state
Dominant ideology	Capitalistic (private property rights)	Public service (citizenship rights)
State theory	Instrumentalism (class theory)	Imperfect pluralism (interest group theory)

Source: Saunders (1986a: 306)

and/or degree of autonomy of political institutions in relation to economic interests, and the scope for working-class power.

Applications of Marxist theories of urban politics

In this section, we shall describe some applications of the theories outlined above. The order of presentation will be roughly similar to that in the previous section: from instrumentalist to structuralist. As examples of work close to the instrumentalist approach we will refer to studies by Hayes, Lojkine and Cockburn.

A work which is close to the instrumentalist approach is the American study by Hayes (1972) of 'who rules in Oakland'. The book does not contain an elaborate theoretical framework, but tackles the question of 'who rules' by examining who has influence over urban politics and who benefits from urban policies. Hayes distinguishes between the 'systematic' influence of business and specific interventions by business. The former includes the establishment of structures which favour business interests, for example, the Bay Area Rapid Transit district, an autonomous board to control the city's port land, the council-manager form of government, and at-large elections. The specific interventions include the under-assessment of businesses for property tax, the virtual non-existence of public housing, the absence of rent control and business involvement in running poverty programmes. Hayes goes on to argue that businesses are the main beneficiaries of policy (including non-intervention). For example, urban renewal has led to massive destruction of low-cost housing and the displacement of its occupants, the need for low-cost housing and jobs has not been met, the welfare system in the city is minimal, and the poor pay high taxes.

Hayes does not conclude that business is the only source of influence in the city (labour and blacks have had some influence) or that it always obtains what it wants. He says that 'no ruling group in history . . . always wins exactly what it wants'. Rather 'the test of the existence of a ruling or predominant group in urban politics . . . is whether on a majority or disproportionately large number of cases in which it takes an interest, [its] wishes become official policy, while the wishes of other groups are not articulated, are ignored, or are successfully combatted' (1972: 197). On this basis, Hayes concludes that business is the dominant political force in Oakland.

The French writer Lojkine is another writer close to the instrumentalist perspective but he denies that the local state simply meets capital's needs or succeeds in regulating conflicts. Lojkine applies the theory of state monopoly capitalism to urban politics and like O'Connor, emphasizes the interdependence and unity of state and monopoly capital. Other fractions of capital such as small capital do not have the leading role taken by monopoly capital. Lojkine then argues that urban policies can be derived from class interests. Central government is the bearer of the interests of monopoly capital and can usually impose these interests at local level due to the high degree of centralization of government in France.

Local elected bodies are seen as havens of small capital and the working class and hence as political obstacles to the interests of monopoly capital. If central government cannot impose its intentions directly on local government, it will have to reach some sort of compromise with locally-dominant interests. Lojkine also insists that state intervention necessarily exacerbates the class struggle. In this respect he is seeking to convey a picture of capitalism as riven with contradictions which the state is incapable of smoothing, rather than adopt a functionalist view in which the state is sufficiently independent of these contradictions and free in its choice of means to regulate them.

Lojkine's work in Paris and Lyon uses a traditional idea of class interests and seeks to demonstrate that urban policies reflect the demands of specific classes or class fractions. In the Paris[1] study, Lojkine (1972) is concerned with urban policy on the location of jobs, the segregation of industrial and office work, and public transport up to 1970. He argues that office activity was boosted at the expense of manufacturing, that office location in central areas was encouraged while manufacturing was pushed into the suburbs, that social housing was concentrated in the suburbs and that public transport investment facilitated the above 'segregative' trends. Lojkine then argues that these policies are a direct or indirect reflection of class interests. In practice, Lojkine's analysis is far from satisfactory since direct connections are simply asserted and when this is not plausible, an appeal is made to the 'complexity' of relations between class fractions.

A third study of urban politics which is fairly close to the instrumentalist approach is the study of local government in Lambeth in inner London by the British writer Cockburn (1977). Her central thesis is that, despite the apparent diversity of state institutions, 'the state preserves a basic unity. All its parts work *fundamentally* as one' (1977: 47, original emphasis). Furthermore, she denies that local government is constitutionally independent of central government and argues that 'local authorities . . . are aspects of the national state and share its work' (1977: 46). Cockburn's introduction of the term 'local state' follows from this.

She uses the term local state to emphasize the basic unity of the state and to encompass local health, water and transport authorities, and so on, which are not part of local government but which also perform state functions at the local level.

Cockburn does not attribute any specific state functions to the local state since, on her definition, it has a multifunctional role. However, she does note that the local state is particularly involved in the reproduction of labour power (that is, people's capacity to work) through its housing, education and health activities. Finally, Cockburn sees elected bodies such as local councils as part of the 'play within the structure of the state, needed to enable the co-ordination of the interests of a divided dominant class'. She notes that this 'affords opportunity for working class militancy to win concessions' (1977: 50) but argues that the chance of this is limited since power at national level has shifted from Parliament to the Civil Service and Cabinet, and in local government from councils to policy committees made up of senior politicians and officials.

In Lambeth, Cockburn argues that the role of the local state is not to advance the interests of a locally dominant class. She argues that the dominant class in Lambeth is not locally resident but consists of the property developers, building firms and related professionals operating in Lambeth, whose interests work through the central state and who 'scarcely notice a local council' (1977: 45). In contrast, Cockburn sees the main function of Lambeth council as being to reproduce the local labour force through housing, social services, leisure facilities, and so on.

This leads Cockburn to focus on community development since she sees this as the means by which the local state manages the local population, and reproduces it as a labour force. The study focuses on the creation of neighbourhood councils as a means of improving communications, providing information, supporting local councillors and maintaining the council's authority. She analyses the way these councils helped to defuse conflicts between council and residents. A parallel focus is on how Lambeth council dealt with squatters. Cockburn shows that by introducing a 'licensing' system which gave squatters limited rights, the council reduced the conflict and created a new category of tenancy, which could be used to penalize ordinary council tenants who failed to maintain their rent payments.

Finally, in parallel with this emphasis on management, Cockburn like Lojkine emphasizes the way the local state can create new conflicts. In this respect both writers depart from a pure instrumentalist position. Cockburn argues that local state policies create opposition among employees who are asked to achieve higher productivity, and among households who consume council services and who are faced with cutbacks. She places a special emphasis on the role of women both as council employees and as the main intermediary between household and council in the receipt of services.

We now turn to Marxist studies of urban fiscal crisis for which O'Connor's (1973) *The Fiscal Crisis of the State* can be regarded as a major stimulus. An initial and central issue for these studies has been the definition of urban fiscal crisis. It appears to refer to a financially defined phenomenon such as municipal bankruptcy. However, students of the subject such as Swanstrom (1986) have pointed out that whether bankruptcy occurs is a political matter too. His analysis suggests that urban fiscal crises are the result of underlying 'fiscal stress' combined with a balance of political forces in which local government has exhausted its political capital and lenders are no longer willing to lend. This raises in turn the question of how fiscal stress is to be measured, for example, by the extent to which the yield of local taxes fails to match the growth in local expenditure (Sharpe, 1981) or by the need to raise local tax rates or cut real spending (Mouritzen, 1992).

Marxist arguments about urban fiscal crisis relate it to the conflict between local spending in favour of business and a declining ability to pay for this spending. The Marxist studies of the subject, however, all agree that the occurrence of urban fiscal crises is highly restricted. Taking a historical view, Hill (1977) denies a connection between general fiscal crisis and urban fiscal crisis, noting that the highest rate of municipal defaults since the war was in an expansionary decade, the 1960s.

The summary of Marxist studies of fiscal crisis in American cities by Rubin and Rubin (1986) shows among other things that business influence was not as strong as O'Connor suggests and in some cases business pressed for low spending and low taxation rather than high pro-business spending, that poor central cities relied on federal grants to defray the cost of urban renewal, and that high interest rates were more important than infrastructure spending as a source of rising expenditure in the 1970s (a point which Newton and Karran (1985) also make for the UK). However, Rubin and Rubin note that O'Connor was right to anticipate a decline in federal and state grants to cities. They conclude that a combination of public choice and Marxist theories is needed to make sense of the evidence on urban fiscal crisis. For example, they argue that bureaucratic interests in increased spending, and demands by groups of citizens for increased services which are paid for by other groups, are forces for urban fiscal crisis ignored by Marxists.

Turning to studies which are closer to the structuralist approach to urban politics we start with Castells's (1978) study of urban renewal policy in Paris in 1970. Castells uses statistical data to show that urban renewal barely affected central Paris where housing conditions were worst, that it was concentrated in areas characterized by their immigrant and low occupational status rather than by their poor physical state, and that there was a negative correlation between the size of urban renewal projects and the level of housing deterioration. Castells goes on to argue that the effect of urban renewal is to reinforce residential segregation by pushing lower strata out of Paris and to increase the volume of office space. However, he is not satisfied with this view and asks why state intervention should be necessary in order to strengthen what are existing trends. He hypothesizes that the answer is political: to provide electoral stability for the party of the ruling classes, and to reduce the likelihood of protest. Castells denies that this is a conscious ruling class intention and argues that the logic of the ruling class's interests 'unconsciously tends to sweep aside everything that is not useful to it' (1978: 107). Finally, Castells also documents the protests triggered by urban renewal.

A second study which gives more explicit attention to the local political system is the study of local policy in three industrial towns in North-West England between the wars by Mark-Lawson et al. (1985). This study is an application of the 'local social relations' approach to urban politics developed by the British writers Duncan and Goodwin (1988). These authors base their argument on Miliband's statement that the local state is both agent of and obstacle to the central state. Their main concern is with the degree of freedom of the local state to pursue local interests against the central state.

Duncan and Goodwin's starting point is that society develops unevenly: there is a spatial division of labour leading to economic differentiation between localities and there are equally important local differences in 'civil society' and in people's beliefs about their locality ('imagined communities'). As a result, each local area has a specific pattern of 'local social relations'. An important component of these is gender relations which may reflect the differing occupational participation of women in different areas. On the other hand, Duncan and Goodwin point out that the central state needs to manage local areas in all their diversity. The 'local state' must therefore have some capacity to reflect different local needs and interests. Combining the two perspectives, Duncan and Goodwin argue that the 'local state' responds both to central state management interests and to 'local social relations'. Unlike other Marxist-inspired writers considered here, Duncan and Goodwin do not focus on local state functions and even deny that the local state has specific functions (1988: 43).

Although the study by Mark-Lawson et al. pre-dates Duncan and Goodwin's book, it is a good example of their approach. Mark-Lawson et al. show that per capita spending between the wars on public services such as education, maternity and child welfare, and recreation was highest in Nelson, lower in Preston and lowest in Lancaster. They explain this by a causal chain in which public services depend on labour movement strength, which in turn depends on women's political involvement, which depends on women's role in the labour force. Thus, for example, in Lancaster women's employment was low, women were politically inactive and the Labour Party favoured paternalist employer provision rather than council provision. In Nelson, in contrast, there was a long history of campaigning organizations, a high level of women's employment (with women and men often working side by side) and a strong labour movement leading to Labour control of the local council during 1927–39. The differences between the two towns in their 'local social relations' thus parallel the difference in council policies. This study shows the importance of 'local social relations' in understanding local policy. The emphasis on gender relations shows how Duncan and Goodwin's theory of the local state can be applied.

These examples of Marxist studies of urban politics illustrate the differing theoretical weight given to economic forces such as fractions of capital, to the role of the state and to class struggle. They also start to indicate some of the problems in grounding Marxist arguments, which we consider in the next section.

Critical discussion

We now start a critical assessment of Marxist theories of urban politics and their applications. First it is useful to set out some ground rules. In assessing a theory and its applications, attention must be given to its four characteristic features:

1 A set of concepts, linked together by a rationale, which it takes to be the key to understanding society.
2 A set of favoured research questions or 'home domain' (Alford and Friedland, 1985) which the theory is best adapted to tackling.
3 A set of substantive explanations (sometimes themselves called theories) in which the concepts are deployed, and
4 A set of methodological assumptions, for example, about the data required to support an explanation, or about how to handle the absence of data (Pickvance, 1984).

As was shown in the first section of this chapter, concepts such as class, capital and mode of production are central to Marxist theory, and the importance of capital accumulation and the containment of class conflict are the rationale for the approach. Some of the characteristic Marxist research questions and explanations have also been seen; in particular the way the local state enhances the continuity of capitalism through its structure and policies has been emphasized. In the present section, we shall also refer to the fourth feature of Marxist theory.

The above picture of a theory is also useful in categorizing the types of criticism that can be made. The most radical type of criticism, *external theoretical criticism*, challenges the value of the basic concepts and rationale of a theory. For example, for Weber, the process of rationalization was the key to understanding society and he rejected the Marxist emphasis on capital accumulation. A second type of criticism, *internal theoretical criticism*, is made from a position sympathetic with the theory but seeks to refine it. For example, we have seen the Marxist theories of urban politics vary in the weight they give to fractions of capital, to the state and to class struggle. Debates *among* Marxist writers are frequently about whether one or other of these categories has been given sufficient weight. A third type of criticism is *technical* in nature, and does not challenge the theory. For example, criticism of the choice of city, choice of political issues, the sources of information, the size of survey samples, and so on, are of this kind.

It follows from this classification that all criticisms are not of equal weight. A study against which many technical criticisms are directed may remain theoretically intact, and the impact of 20 technical criticisms may be less than that of one external theoretical criticism. Here we shall mainly be concerned with external and internal theoretical criticisms.

Finally, before starting a critical discussion of Marxist work on urban politics, the scope of the discussion must be defined. First, we shall steer a middle path between those who regard Marxism as pseudo-science, and their opponents for whom Marxism is a self-evident 'science' to be defended against (bourgeois) 'ideology'. Second, we shall not give space to the claim that Marxist thinking requires special treatment since it is 'dialectical' or is proved by 'practice'. Rather, we shall treat Marxist theories as essentially commensurate with other theories of urban politics and hence subject to the same criteria of evaluation. This implies that we do not take a relativist position in which every discourse has its own validity and where comparison serves simply to identify similarity or difference, rather than to evaluate it by external criteria. Nor do we follow realist epistemology which preserves Marxist theory from test (Saunders, 1986a). Realist epistemology distinguishes between a 'real' level of deep structures with causal powers and a 'surface' level of observed events. The events are explained by the action and interaction of one or more deep structures. This approach has the advantage of forcing the analyst to look for deep rather than immediate or 'precipitating' causes, but it provides no method for deciding which deep structures exist or what their causal powers are. Hence it is open to the danger of establishing Marxist concepts as real structures and preserving them from challenge.

We consider in turn the basic concepts used in Marxist studies, arguments about the functionality of the local state within capitalism, and claims about the distribution of state functions.

Basic concepts

A major area of criticism concerns the basic concepts used in Marxist studies which typically argue that the local state allows specific classes or class fractions to secure their interests. External theoretical criticisms deny the usefulness of concepts such as class, class interest and class conflict and prefer terms such as lobby, pressure group and social conflict.

The concept of class is an abstract one and is translated in different ways. It may refer to phenomena ranging from silent social categories to organized groups with explicitly stated interests. When Marxists argue that local employers have an interest in building houses to increase the local supply of labour, even if employers have not said so, they are making a theoretical imputation unsupported by empirical evidence. This involves a methodological assumption about how to deal with missing data: for Marxists the absence of an explicit statement by employers is irrelevant but for those external critics for whom only stated interests count as real interests it is crucial.

The strength of the Marxist position is that it allows for the possibility that groups will deliberately conceal their interests. If this is so, statements of interest will not be a guide to real interests. Conversely external critics of Marxism accuse Marxists of ignoring stated interests and of advancing 'ready-made' analyses applied without regard to the observed 'facts'. Each makes a different assumption about the need for data on interests. In particular cases, the two views may be reconcilable (as when one group is considered a class fraction by Marxists and a lobby for anti-Marxists) but in general they are not.

This leads to a second, closely-related, external theoretical criticism of Marxist concepts, that of class reductionism. This is the claim that the only significant analytical entities are classes or class fractions and that all other groups are of secondary importance. Categories such as owner-occupiers, public transport users, local residents or women are seen by Marxists as defined in the sphere of distribution rather than production and hence as of secondary importance. Marxists acknowledge that divisions between owner-occupiers, council and private tenants are real, and may give rise to a distinctive consciousness, but argue that these divisions are 'really' between fractions of the working class (defined in Marxist terms) and show how the reproduction of labour power occurs in a segmented way. Each fraction of the working class on this analysis has its own 'reproduction space' (Harvey, 1989: Ch. 4) and housing situations can be 'read off' from workplace positions.

Class reductionism also has implications for an understanding of conflict. Class struggle is the traditional Marxian concept for conceptualizing conflict. However, as has been shown, Marxist writers have made an internal theoretical criticism of the concept of class conflict. Cockburn's focus on conflicts between consumers of council services and the local state and between female council employees and the local state, and Castells's concept of urban movements are both acknowledgements that the image of class conflict based on male workers against private employers is out of date. However, there remains a reluctance among Marxist writers to acknowledge that non-class categories such as women or ethnic minorities have specific interests beyond those of their class position.

Such criticisms have merged with those of external critics of Marxist work on urban politics who have developed the idea of 'consumption sectors' (Dunleavy, 1979) to capture non-class differentiation. The idea here is that housing, education, health, transport and other facilities can be provided by the market or by the state and people's 'consumption locations' can be in one or other (or both) for each of these facilities. Dunleavy (1979) argued that the consumption sector, as measured by public/private housing and transport locations, has a predictive effect on voting behaviour over and above occupation. The implication is that class is not the only significant basis of stratification. His claim was challenged by Franklin and Page (1984).

In brief, Marxian analyses have been justly criticized for their class reductionism from both external and internal positions but it remains an open question how far analyses must be in terms of stated interests in preference to imputed interests.

The functionality of urban politics within capitalism

A strong claim of Marxist theories of urban politics is that urban politics should not be viewed as an autonomous sphere but in terms of its functionality for capital accumulation. This functionality is expressed in various ways: in providing direct benefits to capital (grants, urban planning), in helping provide a healthy and educated labour force, in providing an arena for political participation, etc. The key issue here is how successfully such functional effects can be demonstrated. If they cannot, then the specifically Marxist claim that the local state is capitalist cannot be sustained.

To start with, it is necessary to clarify what relation is being asserted between (A) features of the local state (for example, its structure, provision of opportunities for the articulation of political interests, and policies) and (B) the continuity of the capitalist mode of production. Three cases can be identified.

The strongest relation between A and B would be that of *indispensability*. This would imply that particular features of the local state were necessary to capitalism, and that any change in A would threaten B. A second and weaker case would be where A was one among a number of *functionally alternative* ways of ensuring the survival of capitalism. This would imply that particular features or policies of the local state were not as critical to capitalism as in the case of indispensability. Both of these cases imply the functionality of the local state for capitalism.

A third type of relation between A and B is weaker still and merely asserts the *compatibility* of A and B. This means that A does not hinder B but is not very important to B either. This could be the case if urban political institutions were not after all very crucial to the survival of capitalism. Clearly this contradicts the Marxist claim of a functional relation between A and B since it does not assert any positive effects.

The question then is how Marxist theories of urban politics provide support for these claims. It should be pointed out that Marxist writers on urban politics do not make a careful distinction between these three types of relation – though generally instrumentalist-inspired studies argue for stronger relations between A and B than do structuralist-inspired studies (Pickvance, 1980a).

Three approaches can be identified, none of which, I shall argue, is satisfactory. The first is to say that as long as capitalism continues to exist without serious challenge, urban political institutions must be performing necessary functions. But this argument is equally compatible with all three of the relationships just distinguished and hence provides no evidence in itself of a functional relation between A and B. As Gouldner (1973: Ch. 7) has shown, one cannot assume that because an institution exists it is either necessary at all, or if necessary is indispensable to the functioning of capitalism: rather, systems can exist with varying degrees of interdependence between their parts.

A second approach is to try and trace out the functional effects of urban political institutions and their policies. Marxist studies frequently point to the benefits of local policies to fractions of capital and hence argue for their functionality for capitalism. Two comments can be made about this. First, a policy which benefits a local fraction of capital is not ipso facto functional for local capitalist reproduction, for example, if it involves heavy tax increases and a 'tax revolt'. Second, even if local level functionality can be demonstrated it is not necessarily synonymous with national level functionality. Attracting industry by grants may be locally functional but nationally dysfunctional in the sense that it increases the tax burden without increasing the total level of industrial activity.

A third approach is, like the first, theoretical rather than empirically grounded. Pinçon's (1976) study of social housing provision in the Paris area argues on theoretical grounds, and without any supportive evidence, that the effect of social housing is to improve the reproduction of labour power needed by the state and private employers in Paris (see the discussion in Pickvance, 1980b). This is characteristic of some Marxist studies which impute functions to a policy with minimal evidence. Such imputations will not convince external critics who demand supportive evidence, but they may satisfy Marxists who may hold strong beliefs as to why no supportive evidence is likely to exist.

An alternative to these approaches is possible but has not to my knowledge been tried. Since Marxists argue that local state intervention improves the functioning of capitalism, it should be possible to make comparisons between local state intervention and the functioning of capitalism in particular local areas. The hypothesis would be that where local states were adopting more appropriate policies, this should be reflected in better 'system performance' (Pickvance, 1980a). This could be measured by the absence of social unrest, the relative attractiveness of the locality to investment, and so on. Obviously this approach would only be relevant in so far as local level 'system performance' was a valid measure of policy effects, and as was pointed out, one cannot assume national and local functionality are synonymous.

An overall judgement on Marxist claims about the functionality of the local state and its policies must be that both for external and internal critics the claims have not been adequately demonstrated. Hence the argument that the local state is capitalist remains no more than a theoretical assertion.

So far we have examined Marxist claims about the functionality of the local state and its interventions. However, equally part of Marxist theory is the argument that the capitalist state is only able to regulate society to a partial extent. As noted earlier, for Lojkine this distinguishes Marxism from functionalism.

This is a claim supported from inside and outside Marxism. Writers such as Offe (1975), Habermas (1976) and Rhodes (1988) have drawn attention to the incapacity of the state to formulate or apply coherent policies due to a lack of economic resources, a lack of legitimacy, the exclusion of policies which significantly challenge private property rights, conflicting external pressures, the fragmentation of state departments due to their clientilistic relations with fractions of capital and insufficient coordination capacity, and so on. State policies are also seen as triggering new conflicts. These arguments have been developed about national state intervention but have relevance at local level.

The cogency of such arguments leads to an obvious problem. On the one hand, we have seen that Marxist studies of urban politics make theoretical assertions about the functionality of local state structures and policies. On the other hand, the reasons for state intervention being limited in effect are very powerful. For Marxists the two aspects are 'contra-dictory' aspects of reality. For external critics, however, they go to show the sponge-like nature of Marxist explanation since it appears that whatever happens can be explained. We return to this point in the final section of this chapter.

The division of functions between central and local state

The final part of this critical discussion concerns the theories of O'Connor, Friedland et al. and Saunders which all bear on the distribution of functions between levels of government and non-elected bodies and specifically on the scope of local government functions.

Underlying all three theories is the idea that functions concerned with capital accumulation are at risk if placed at local government level. As a consequence, they are more likely to be located at national (or federal) or regional (or state) level, or to be given to non-elected bodies, leaving local government to concentrate on 'consumption'-related issues.

A number of theoretical arguments have been developed around this subject of local state functions – some are external and some internal to Marxist theory.

O'Connor is insistent that there is a contradiction between state accumulation and legitimation functions and that the state 'must either mystify its policies by calling them something that they are not, or it must try to conceal them' (1973: 6). His reasoning is that state action in support of capital accumulation is perceived as a class policy which benefits the capitalist class at the expense of the working class. This leads O'Connor to the prediction that accumulation-related functions will be removed from local government. However, such a model applies best in political conditions where a strong communist party ensures that class analyses of state policy are prevalent. In Western Europe, since 1945, only in France and Italy have such conditions been present. In the US, they are completely absent. The more common experience is that state policies in favour of capital are presented, and understood, as being in the national interest. Hence there appears to be a mismatch between O'Connor's explanation and reality.

A similar objection can be made to Friedland et al.'s arguments. They emphasize the 'perpetual motion' in which functions are shifted about to avoid conflict, and do not believe that any final equilibrium can be reached. They argue that it is this distribution of functions which prevents the contradictions between state functions from leading to conflict. However, if we are right that O'Connor exaggerates the importance of these contradictions, then they can be no more than a contributory factor to the processes identified by Friedland et al.

Finally, Saunders's argument does not use the notion of contradiction but does posit an 'elective affinity' between production functions and national policies, and consumption functions and local policies. He envisages a more stable equilibrium in the distribution of functions than do Friedland et al. There has been a considerable number of comparative studies of local state functions (Page and Goldsmith, 1987; Pickvance and Preteceille, 1991). These conclude that there is a wide variation in the extent of functions (and spending) by the local state and that the idea that consumption-related functions are concentrated at local state level turns out to be most characteristic of non-federal Western European welfare states, but not of the US where accumulation-related functions loom much larger relatively speaking at local level. In addition, there has been a general growth in production-related functions at local government level. As well as planning powers which have a direct impact on production (though they may be shared or be subjected to some higher-level control), most local governments now have powers to attract investment. These may not involve large spending but they modify Saunders's picture of local government functions.

There is no space here to discuss fully the debate surrounding Saunders's dual state theory. Conveniently Saunders (1986b) himself has summarized his critics' views and made a response to them. His reply to those who refer to countries such as the US or Australia where consumption-related functions are not concentrated at local state level is that the 'elements' of his theory are general but the way in which they are combined is variable (Saunders, 1986b: 22–4). This in my view is a considerable concession by Saunders, since he is denying that the model set out in Table 13.1 is a general one, and claiming only that its conceptual elements are general. Does this mean that they can be found in any permutation? The logic of Saunders's approach is that the permutations are limited by the choice of theories – instrumentalism and imperfect pluralism in the Table 13.1 model. What he needs to show is whether the different permutations observed are consistent with these two original theories, or whether new theories are necessary to make sense of them.

In conclusion, it can be argued that the analyses of O'Connor, Friedland et al. and Saunders all have weaknesses. O'Connor's assumptions about opposition to state policy in favour of capital do not ring true in most capitalist countries today, Friedland et al.'s arguments address the same issue and hence are vulnerable to the same criticism, and Saunders's model needs considerable modification to cope with the diversity of ranges of local state activity.

Nevertheless, the proliferation of non-elected bodies, particularly in the local economic development field, and the continual movement of functions between levels of government are real trends. In my view, they may sometimes be explained in terms of class interests and the avoidance of class conflict, but other factors such as the pursuit of efficiency-related objectives, professional and managerial interests, and the avoidance of conflict other than class conflict, are also relevant.

Overall assessment

In this final section, I shall indicate what I see as the strengths and weaknesses of Marxist analyses of urban politics, following the four features of theoretical approaches outlined in the previous section. I will conclude by discussing the complementarity or otherwise of Marxism with other theories of urban politics.

The rationale of Marxist theory, namely, the centrality of capital accumulation and the containment of the conflicts it generates, leads immediately to a perspective which links the economic and political spheres. In an age of specialization, this is a desirable type of linkage. The question remains whether the Marxian grasp of it is adequate. Some Marxists write as though any study which rejects the boundaries of political science is by definition superior to one which accepts them. This is unfounded. The question then is whether all urban political processes can be illuminated from the Marxist standpoint.

At this point, the difference arises between instrumentalist Marxists who argue that all urban politics is 'really' about capital accumulation, and others who allow urban politics a greater autonomy. (Such differences correspond to the different levels of functional relationship discussed in the previous section.) For the latter group, capital accumulation is a key reference point for urban politics but not a total explanatory principle, and non-class interests will be acknowledged.

In terms of research questions, Marxian work in urban politics has drawn attention to impacts of policy for economic interests, and the impact on policy of economic interests and of class conflict. This was an important counterpoint to institutionalist approaches which focused on elections and did not look for external social and economic influence or at the distributional impact of policy. The Marxist approach has also been important as a contrast to approaches which focus on ideas and stated intentions. Marxists always see ideology as mediating interests rather than as describing them accurately.

However at the same time, Marxist writing has diverted attention from the study of political parties, elections and voting behaviour, and from the study of the internal functioning of the local state. Of course, one Marxist theme, the distribution of functions among levels of government, structures the topics of political debate which are likely to occur at each level but Marxists have not generally gone beyond this to study relations between officials and politicians. Marxists have also generally steered clear of the organizational level of analysis.

It can thus be said that Marxian theory has offered alternative answers to existing questions and has placed new questions on the agenda (for example, the series of questions about how class segments are reproduced, and about the role of the local state in the reproduction of labour power), but has left many questions unaddressed. In my view this reflects the distinctive 'home domain' of Marxian theory rather than any lack of diligence by Marxian writers.

Turning to the grounding of Marxist explanations, it is clear from the previous section that this is a major area of criticism because of the concepts used, the stance taken towards evidence and the apparently sponge-like character of Marxist theory. The concepts are abstract and are often 'applied' to concrete situations with little attention to mediating processes. The absence of evidence may be dismissed on the grounds that actors cannot be expected to be fully aware of the implications of their actions or that state agencies cannot be expected to keep records of the full reasons for their policies. (If a riot is followed by a new urban policy Marxists would make a causal inference that they were connected even if politicians denied it.) Internal and external critics of Marxism thus differ as to the evidence they regard as sufficient to ground an explanation. Hence 'appealing to the evidence' will leave unresolved important differences between writers of different persuasions.

Finally the common criticism that Marxist theory is compatible with any event and is therefore unfalsifiable needs to be confronted. In my view this criticism is justified mainly by the poor practice of Marxist writers and only in part by problems intrinsic to Marxist theory itself. The main reason why Marxist theory appears to be sponge-like is that it is easy to impute a class interest or class conflict to 'explain' a state intervention. But this practice does not merit the label explanation, since explanation requires an analysis of the available evidence on the presence of the postulated explanatory factors. The genuine problems for Marxist theory are: the abstraction of its concepts; the assertion that contra-dictory processes co-exist; and the critical and selective stance towards evidence.

Conclusion

In conclusion, we will comment on the compatibility between Marxist and non-Marxist theories. The position taken is not uncontroversial.

First, whereas Marxian writers often claim that Marxist theory provides the key to understanding all aspects of society, the view taken here is that Marxist theory is no different from any other theory in having a 'home domain' of questions which it is particularly well-developed to ask. (Marxists may claim that questions which they cannot answer are not important, but that will not convince others.)

Marxist theory addresses questions about the reproduction of socio-economic systems at a fairly large scale. It is less able to address questions at the middle and micro-levels. It may even be asked whether Marxist theories of urban politics are not over-ambitious since they involve middle range questions in the sense that they concern the functioning of institutions between the level of the individual and the level of the whole society. Certainly Marxist attempts to understand the mobilization of actors into urban protest have been a failure.

This leads immediately to a second question, that of theoretical pluralism. Galtung (1967: 456) introduced the terms 'principle of variety of theories' and 'principle of co-existence between theories' to acknowledge that different theories could explain a given set of data and that it was not necessary to choose between them. An obvious objection to these principles is that data are always conceptualized and that different theories use different concepts. However, like Saunders (1986a: 352–62), I consider that this does not prevent the commensurability of theories because the reconceptualization of data using different concepts is an everyday experience (for academics at least). The implication of Galtung's principles is that the fact that there is a Marxist explanation of an aspect of the local state does not exclude the possibility of rival explanations.

A more controversial question is that of 'eclecticism' or the simultaneous holding of theories of different kinds. For anyone who considers one theory can illuminate every aspect of society and social change – as do many Marxists (see Saunders, 1986b: 19–22) – eclecticism is a sin. Saunders denies that his own dualistic theory of politics is eclectic since each theory applies in a restricted domain (instrumentalism for production, imperfect pluralism for consumption) (1986b: 20). However, it is debatable whether such restriction is possible: it implies that what happens in the production sphere does not have implications for the consumption sphere. My own view is that eclecticism can avoid such inconsistency only if theories at different levels nest inside each other (Pickvance, 1982). This can happen if the different theories operate at different levels of analysis which are relatively cut off from each other. For example, to hold a Marxian theory at the societal level is not inconsistent with holding a resource mobilization theory of urban protest since Marxist theory contains no theory of social action at this level. On the other hand, with reference to Saunders (1986b: 22), given Galtung's principles, there may be several rival theories at the societal level.

In sum while Marxist theories of urban politics have not offered rival analyses in all parts of the field, they have widened the questions asked and suggested new explanations. Their concepts have proved controversial but parallels to the very real problems of grounding Marxist analyses are to be found in all theories of urban politics.

Note

1 Central and local state functions are intermingled in this study. Lojkine's work on Paris and Lyon is discussed in Pickvance (1977)

References

Alford, R.R. and Friedland, R. (1985) *Powers of Theory: Capitalism, the State and Democracy.* Cambridge: Cambridge University Press.

Castells, M. (1977) *The Urban Question: A Marxist Approach.* London: Edward Arnold.

Castells, M. (1978) *City Class and Power.* London: Macmillan.

Cockburn, C. (1977) *The Local State.* London: Pluto.

Duncan, S. and Goodwin, M. (1988) *The Local State and Uneven Development.* Oxford: Polity.

Dunleavy, P. (1979) 'The urban bases of political alignment: "social class", domestic property ownership, or state intervention in consumption processes?', *British Journal of Political Science*, 9: 409–43.

Franklin, M.N. and Page, E.C. (1984) 'A critique of the consumption cleavage approach in British voting studies', *Political Studies*, 32: 521–36.

Friedland, R., Piven, F.F. and Alford, R.R. (1977) 'Political conflict, urban structure and the fiscal crisis', *International Journal of Urban and Regional Research*, 1 (3): 447–71.

Galtung, J. (1967) *Theory and Methods of Social Research.* London: Allen and Unwin.

Gouldner, A.W. (1973) *For Sociology.* London: Allen Lane.

Habermas, J. (1976) *Legitimation Crisis.* London: Heinemann.

Harvey, D. (1989) *The Urban Experience.* Oxford: Basil Blackwell.

Hayes, E.C. (1972) *Power Structure and Urban Policy: Who Rules in Oakland.* New York: McGraw-Hill.

Hill, R.C. (1977) 'State capitalism and the urban fiscal crisis in the United States', *International Journal of Urban and Regional Research*, 1: 76–100.

Lojkine, J. (1972) *La Politique Urbaine dans la Région Parisienne 1945–1972.* Paris: Mouton.

Mark-Lawson, J., Savage, M. and Warde, A. (1985) 'Gender and local politics: struggles over welfare politics 1918–1939', in L. Murgatroyd (ed.), *Localities, Class and Gender.* London: Pion.

Mouritzen, P.E. (1992) 'What is a fiscal crisis?' in P.E. Mouritzen (ed.), *Managing Cities in Austerity.* London: Sage.

Newton, K. and Karran, T.J. (1985) *The Politics of Local Expenditure.* London: Macmillan.

O'Connor, J. (1973) *The Fiscal Crisis of the State.* New York: St. Martins Press.

Offe, C. (1975) 'The theory of the capitalist state and the problem of policy formation' in L.N. Lindberg, R. Alford, C. Crouch and C. Offe (eds), *Stress and Contradiction in Modern Capitalism.* Lexington, MA: Lexington Books.

Page, E.C. and Goldsmith, M.J. (eds) (1987) *Central and Local Government Relations.* London: Sage.

Pickvance, C.G. (1977) 'Marxist approaches to the study of urban politics: divergences among some recent French studies', *International Journal of Urban and Regional Research*, 1 (2): 219–55.

Pickvance, C.G. (1980a) 'Theories of the state and theories of urban crisis', *Current Perspectives in Social Theory*, 1: 31–54.

Pickvance, C.G. (1980b) 'The role of housing in the reproduction of labour power and the analysis of state intervention in housing', in *Political Economy of Housing Workshop, Housing, Construction and the State*. London: Conference of Socialist Economists.

Pickvance, C.G. (1982) 'Review of Saunders, *Social Theory and the Urban Question*', *Critical Social Policy*, 2: 94–8.

Pickvance, C.G. (1984) 'The structuralist critique in urban studies', in M.P. Smith (ed.), *Cities in Transformation*. Beverly Hills, CA: Sage.

Pickvance, C.G. and Preteceille, E. (eds) (1991) *State Restructuring and Local Power: A Comparative Perspective*. London: Pinter.

Pinçon, M. (1976) *Les HLM: Structure Sociale de la Population Logée* (2 vols). Paris: Centre de Sociologie Urbaine.

Poulantzas, N. (1973) *Political Power and Social Classes*. London: New Left Books.

Rhodes, R.A.W. (1988) *Beyond Westminster and Whitehall*. London: Unwin Hyman.

Rubin, I.S. and Rubin, H.J. (1986) 'Structural theories and urban fiscal stress', in M. Gottdiener (ed.), *Cities in Stress: A New Look at the Urban Crisis*. Beverly Hills, CA: Sage.

Saunders, P. (1986a) *Social Theory and the Urban Question* (2nd edn). London: Hutchinson.

Saunders, P. (1986b) 'Reflections on the dual politics thesis: the argument, its origins and its critics', in M. Goldsmith and S. Villadsen (eds), *Urban Political Theory and the Management of Fiscal Stress*. Aldershot: Gower.

Sharpe, L.J. (1981) 'Is there a fiscal crisis in Western European local government? A first appraisal', in L.J. Sharpe (ed.), *The Local Fiscal Crisis in Western Europe*. London: Sage.

Swanstrom, T. (1986) 'Urban populism, fiscal crisis and the new urban political economy', in M. Gottdiener (ed.), *Cities in Stress: A New Look at the Urban Crisis*. Beverly Hills, CA: Sage.

14

Regulation Theory, Post-Fordism and Urban Politics

Joe Painter

In seeking to interpret some of the broad shifts in urban politics during the 1980s, a number of urban theorists, urban and political geographers and political scientists began to turn to the writings of a small group of French economists working in the tradition of Marxist economics and known as the 'regulation theorists'. At first sight, this seems a strange move, because the regulation theorists' main concern was with explaining economic changes, and their ideas, at least at first, did not include much consideration of the state, government and politics.

The appeal of regulation theory for urban political theorists, however, stems from three main sources. First, it presents an account of the changing character of capitalist economies and of the role of cities within them. It thus provides a context against which to discuss urban political change. Second, it examines the connections and interrelations between social, political, economic and cultural change. This potentially avoids some of the problems encountered by those theories which focus on one aspect of the political whole (such as elections, leadership or bureaucracy). Third, it tries to avoid a rather different set of difficulties associated with some versions of orthodox Marxism, which accord only a secondary role to political processes. For regulation theory, economic change depends upon, and is partly the product of, changes in politics, culture and social life.

Not all of these advantages have yet been realized in full by urban political theorists, as this chapter will make clear. However, in comparison with many other theoretical traditions, regulation theory is still very young and there is much scope for further development. In this chapter I will discuss the progress that has been made so far in applying the ideas of regulation theory in the sphere of urban politics. After outlining the key concepts of the approach I will consider three of them in relation to urban politics: the labour process, the 'Fordist mode of regulation', and the 'post-Fordist mode of regulation'. I will then look at some of the criticisms that have been made of these ideas, before concluding with an evaluation of the current position.

Regulation theory: an exposition

The concept of regulation

Regulation theory originated in France in the 1970s and early 1980s in the work of a number of Marxist economists including Michel Aglietta, Robert Boyer and Alain Lipietz. It has subsequently been developed by economists, geographers, political theorists and others working in a variety of countries. As a result it has become a rich, but highly diverse, school of thought. There is no one unified 'regulation theory' and many writers now prefer to talk about a 'regulation approach'.[1]

Central to all regulation theory is the concept of regulation itself. There is a certain amount of confusion about the nature of regulation theory, which has arisen partly because of a misinterpretation of this central idea. In English, the term 'regulation' usually refers to 'conscious and active intervention by the *state* or other collective organizations' (Boyer, 1990: 20). However, in French, this sense is conveyed by the word '*réglementation*', and not by '*régulation*' (the word used by the regulation theorists). A further problem arises as the term 'regulation' is often used in the context of general systems theory and biology to mean *self*-regulation. (The kind of regulation provided by the regulator on a steam engine.)

By contrast with both the deliberate rule-making of *réglementation* and the auto-regulation of a negative feedback system, regulation theory looks at the kinds of regulation of economic life which are neither wholly deliberate nor automatic. According to the regulationists 'successful' regulation of the crises and contradictions of capitalism does not occur automatically and inevitably but neither does it occur purely by conscious and deliberate design. Instead, when it does occur, it is the often *unintended* consequence of the interaction of activities and processes which may have been undertaken deliberately, but perhaps for quite other reasons. This general principle is given substance by two further core concepts, the *regime of accumulation* (which specifies the nature of the economic relationship between investment, production and consumption) and *mode of regulation* (which specifies the political and sociocultural institutions and practices which secure that relationship).

These two key ideas mean that temporal and spatial variations in the character of capitalism play an important part in regulation theory. Capitalism has been marked by a series of different regimes of accumulation and modes of regulation. The *regime of accumulation* refers to a set of macroeconomic relations which allow expanded capital accumulation without the system being immediately and catastrophically undermined by its instabilities. Within a regime of accumulation, the imbalances in the cycle of reproduction, production, circulation and consumption are postponed or displaced. Acute crises and sharp irregularities are replaced for a time by chronic crisis tendencies and muted economic cycles. A regime of accumulation may be identified when rough balances between production, consumption and investment, and between the demand and supply of labour and capital allow economic growth to be maintained with reasonable stability over a relatively long period.

However, this stability cannot arise simply as the result of the operation of the defining core processes of capitalism. When stabilization does occur (and it is not inevitable that it will) it is the contingent outcome of social and political activities. A sustained compatibility between production and consumption, for example, is not an automatic feature of capitalism. Rather it is generated in and through social and political institutions of various sorts, cultural norms and even moral codes. Such norms and codes are not set up *for the purpose* of sustaining a regime of accumulation, but they can sometimes interact to produce that effect. When this happens, they constitute a *mode of regulation* also referred to as the 'mode of social regulation' or MSR. (Bob Jessop now uses a still more precise term, the 'social mode of economic regulation' in order to stress that it is economic activities which are being regulated, and that they are regulated socially.[2])

'Fordism', 'neo-Fordism' and 'post-Fordism'

The term 'Fordism' was first used in the 1930s by the Italian Marxist, Gramsci (1971). It is most often used today to refer to the 'long-boom' in Western development which lasted from 1945 to 1974. By extension, 'neo-Fordism' refers to an intensification of Fordist arrangements, whereas 'post-Fordism' implies a transition to a qualitatively new set of relationships.

Regulation theory is often mistakenly assumed to be synonymous with theories of Fordism and post-Fordism. Both Jessop and Boyer stress the broadly *methodological* character of regulation theory, seeing it as a set of organizing principles and as an approach to analysis, rather than a series of substantive accounts. Concepts such as Fordism and post-Fordism come lower down the hierarchy of abstraction – they are examples of ideas which some regulationists have developed to make more substantive claims about specific societies.

In relation to Fordism, Jessop (1992) distinguishes four different such categories: the labour process, the regime of accumulation, the mode of regulation, and the mode of societalization. The Fordist *labour process* involves the production of long runs of standardized commodities. Archetypally this involves a moving assembly line staffed by workers executing a limited range of production tasks and separated from the design of both the product and the production process. As a *regime of accumulation*, 'Fordism involves a virtuous circle of growth based on mass production and mass consumption' (Jessop, 1992: 47). Mass production provides economies of scale and productivity growth, which in turn allow wage increases, providing a market which can sustain mass consumption.

The *mode of regulation* is the set of social, cultural and political supports which promote the compatibility between production and consumption in the regime of accumulation. These supports operate through particular norms, networks and institutions which are the outcomes of social and political conflicts. In the Fordist mode of regulation they include: the form of the wage relation; the character of social organization within and between firms; a system of money supply based on national central banks and private credit; mass media and mass advertising, marketing and retailing to promote the connection between mass production and mass consumption; and the Keynesian welfare state which manages aggregate demand through fiscal policy and generalizes the norm of mass consumption through collective provision of certain services and transfer payments to the un- (or inadequately-) waged. Finally Fordism may be understood as a '*mode of societalization*' which specifies the overall social impact of the characteristics discussed above on wider aspects of society such as cultural life, spatial organization and the political system. Jessop also outlines a series of problems associated with each of these readings of Fordism (1992: 53–8), and argues that Fordism is best defined as a mode of regulation.

A mode of regulation can never *permanently* resolve the contradictions of capitalism, but only translate acute crises into crisis tendencies. Eventually, the contradictions *do* build up and prevent the established mode of regulation from operating to promote economic growth. Fordism developed to a greater and more complete extent in some countries than others, and the timing and consequences of its failure also varied considerably. In general, however, the 1970s was the decade when the limits to Fordism began to become apparent, and the 1980s was when a series of (often conflicting) political strategies began to be adopted in attempts to resolve the problems. In due course, if certain of these strategies, or a combination of them, succeed in securing a new phase of economic growth, it may be possible to identify a new 'post-Fordist' phase.

However, the concept of post-Fordism[3] is yet more problematic than the concept of Fordism. As Jessop notes, there is considerable asymmetry between the concepts of Fordism and post-Fordism. Most analysts are agreed that no fully-fledged post-Fordist social relations have yet emerged (while some doubt that they ever will). Therefore, only in the case of Fordism is it possible to discuss the substance within the four categories. Nonetheless, one can consider some of the potential characteristics of post-Fordism under the same four headings.

As Jessop points out, for it to make sense to speak of post-Fordism (rather than non-Fordism, for example) the new developments would have to have the potential to resolve the specific problems of Fordism. The area in which there is most evidence of post-Fordist developments in this sense is the labour process. The emphasis in the post-Fordist labour process is on the use of microelectronic technology to provide significantly increased flexibility and automation in the production process. Jessop argues that new communication and information technologies 'allow new or enhanced flexible specialization by small firms or producer networks even in small-batch production and, indeed, outside manufacturing, could promote flexibility in the production of many types of services in the private, public, and so-called "third" sectors' (1992: 61). These developments have the potential to resolve some of the contradictions of the Fordist labour process, and thus justify the label 'post-Fordist'.

In the other three categories of analysis it is more difficult to identify clear lines of development which might serve to resolve for a time Fordist contradictions in each case. However, since the concept of Fordism appeared to have most purchase when defined as a mode of regulation, it is important to consider what might be meant by a post-Fordist mode of regulation. One of the problems with this, as Jessop points out, is that the objects of regulation and the processes which regulate them emerge together. A mode of regulation can therefore only be identified with hindsight. However, some possible trends are apparent in relation to the advanced industrialized economies. It seems likely that the wage relation in a post-Fordist mode of regulation would involve increased flexibility within labour markets and increased polarization between a multiskilled (or at least multitasked) core workforce and an unskilled 'peripheral' workforce recruited from politically marginalized social groups. Corporate organization would probably shift from relatively hierarchical bureaucratic forms, to leaner, flatter structures, with a smaller central organization and a series of subcontracting relations with external bodies. Money may be supplied at least in part through new types of financial instruments and become increasingly internationalized. The link between production and consumption would increasingly become a matter of segmented rather than mass markets promoted by niche forms of advertising and retailing.

Finally, the state would have a particular role to play in a post-Fordist mode of regulation. With the internationalization of financial and productive capital, Jessop argues, the state would play a stronger role in promoting competitiveness of both specific firms and of the overall socio-economic system. Jessop argues that these changes will involve the decline of the postwar 'Keynesian Welfare States' and the emergence of 'Schumpeterian Workfare States' (1993). The state will become more involved in supply side interventions of various kinds, including in the labour market. At the same time, the state may become 'hollowed out'. Some of its powers will be passed upwards to supranational bodies, such as the European Union, which arguably have greater capacity to act in a globalized economic system. Other powers may be devolved downwards to local or regional tiers of the state (Jessop, 1992: 63–5; 1993).

Applications in urban politics

Having outlined some of the main arguments of the regulation approach I am now in a position to consider how they relate to the field of urban politics. As I have shown, regulation theory was developed as a theory of economic, not political, change. At first sight, therefore, it seems perverse to adopt it as a framework for analysing urban politics. However, political processes do play a crucial role in regulationist explanations of economic changes.[4] Furthermore, the breakdown of Fordism and the debates over its putative successor have generated considerable discussion among analysts about the implications for urban politics of the supposed transition, and about the implications for any transition of the changing character of urban politics. The emphasis in regulation theory on change and periodization holds out the promise of a theoretical account of urban politics which is historically embedded, and which can deal with qualitative shifts in the character of political processes and institutions. This is in contrast to some other theories which assume that the urban political system is essentially unchanging. Moreover, the contingent character of the emergence of regulation avoids the pitfalls of economic reductionism, while still allowing the crucial relationship between the state and economic processes to remain in the frame.

In the following discussion, I will interpret 'urban politics' as including:

1 Urban *policy* (state policies established to deal with perceived urban problems).
2 The institutions and processes of urban government and governance (involving not only the local tier of state administration, but *all* organizations exercising political authority at the local level – whether public, private or voluntary – and the relationships between these.
3 Political movements and processes operating at the urban scale, but outside institutions of governance (such as local community campaigns).

The elements of regulation theory on which I particularly want to focus are post-Fordist developments of the labour process, Fordism as a mode of regulation and the role of the 'Schumpeterian Workfare State' within a potential future post-Fordist mode of regulation.

Urban politics and the labour process

Aglietta argued that new production techniques and developments in the labour process had the capacity significantly to transform the provision of the means of collective consumption and thereby to reduce their cost (1979: 167). Picking up this idea, Hoggett (1987) was among the first to introduce the notions of Fordism and neo-Fordism to an analysis of urban politics. In his consideration of decentralization initiatives by socialist city councils in Britain, he drew an analogy between the organization of production along Fordist lines in manufacturing firms and the 'people-processing' character of the local welfare state. At the same time, the power of local government professionals added a complicating element which had something in common with pre-Fordist craft production in the manufacturing sector. Moreover, the hierarchical and bureaucratic organization of the local government institutions also resonated with corporate organization in the private sector. In Hoggett's view, decentralization might represent part of a shift from a Fordist to a neo-Fordist labour process. The decentralization of local services involved, according to Hoggett, a critique of the 'Fordist' character of welfare state production: its remoteness, inflexibility and unresponsiveness. Decentralization supposedly involved a series of key changes which were characteristic of the neo-Fordist changes in the manufacturing labour process. These included: an emphasis on customer care; leaner, flatter, managerial hierarchies; budgetary devolution; multiskilling and flexibility of the workforce; a key role for information and information technology; and the adoption of new managerial ideologies, notably those associated with Peters (see Peters and Waterman, 1982).

Stoker (1989) goes somewhat further than Hoggett in discussing the restructuring of British local government 'for a post-Fordist society'. However, like Hoggett, Stoker regards the labour process within local government as of central significance. Within this he includes the contracting out of service provision to private sector companies. Like Hoggett, he refers to the potential of information technology:

> the availability of information technology in all its forms – data processing, communications and control, computer-aided design, office automation – offers the possibility of recasting traditionally labour-intensive service activities. And one major use of such technology is to reduce the aggregate cost of a particular service and the employment within it. (1989: 160)

Geddes also discusses the labour process within the provision of public services in urban areas, through his consideration of the local state (Geddes, 1988). He comes to the same conclusion, that information technology offers opportunities to reorganize state production processes, to cut the costs of collective provision and to provide a more individualized 'product'. There is a wide range of urban public services to which information technology and other forms of technological change is being applied. While these developments are still rather patchy, some interesting examples are discussed in detail in the OECD publication *Cities and New Technology* (OECD, 1992).

Urban politics and the Fordist mode of regulation

A somewhat larger group of writers have concentrated their attention on the part played by urban politics within specific modes of regulation. As I noted above, the Fordist mode of regulation included a key role for the Keynesian welfare state, and in many ways it is in analysing the link between the welfare state and the urban arena that regulation theory has most to offer the study of urban politics.

Urban policy Florida and Jonas (1991) discuss the link between regulation theory and postwar urban policy in the United States. They argue that the Fordist mode of regulation in the United States was intimately related to federal urban policy (broadly defined). To begin with, the specific character of US Fordism was constituted in part by the ending of the social democratic experiment of the New Deal. This saw, among other things, the Cold War circumscribing the legitimate role for the state, a limited 'class accord', the growth of the military-industrial complex and the emergence of new areas of economic growth in the west and east of the country. In comparison with the situation in Europe, US Fordism was to a significant extent privatized, and depended on a spatial organization at the urban scale in which suburbanization was central: 'suburbanization was propelled by a growing demand for housing, automobiles, consumer durables and public services (eg: education and infrastructure)' (1991: 362).

The argument here is that Federal urban policies such as the expansion of education and the 1956 Highway Act promoted the shift to the suburbs, which in turn then helped to generate the demand for goods and services to sustain the virtuous circle of growth of Fordism. Suburbanization thus significantly reduced the 'need' for the state intervention characteristic of Western European modes of regulation. It was accompanied by decentralization of private production and the spatial fragmentation of labour markets. As a result, the Fordist mode of regulation in the United States was more socially-divided than in Europe. In inner-urban areas lived a population of poor and disproportionately black 'peripheral' workers, while a suburbanized, affluent and disproportionately white group provided the core, skilled labour force. When linked to the territorial fragmentation characteristic of US urban government the result was increasing fiscal stress, making it more and more difficult to provide public services in inner-urban areas. This meant that the crisis of the Fordist mode of regulation was developed relatively early, and Florida and Jonas argue that the black civil rights movements in the 1960s were an expression of this crisis. As a result the Federal government acted to mitigate some of the worst problems of US Fordism with a series of urban renewal programmes and the enhancement of the 'social wage' directed at poorer groups. By contrast, explicitly spatial policies had long been a defining part of the Fordist modes of regulation in Western Europe.

Urban government Surprisingly few regulationist writers have focused on the functions fulfilled by urban government and the local-level institutions of the state under the Fordist mode of regulation. This may reflect the genesis of regulation theory during the crisis of Fordism, and the urgency of interpreting current changes, rather than worrying about the past. Whatever the reason, while there are now several attempts to consider the links between local government, the crisis of Fordism and a supposedly emergent post-Fordist mode of regulation, most of the authors take the character of the Fordist system more or less for granted and no

comprehensive account of the local state in the 30 years after the Second
World War has so far used regulationist ideas in any detail.

Given that the concept of the Fordist mode of regulation represents one
of the richer products of regulation theory, it is disappointing that
regulationist writers on urban politics have generated so few developed
accounts of the character of local government within Fordism. The
following ideas are thus derived from general regulationist principles and
the brief accounts which have been provided elsewhere (Stoker, 1989: 149–
52; Painter, 1991a: 58–79; 1991b: 23–33).

In most countries in which the Fordist mode of regulation developed,
governmental and state institutions operating at the urban scale played a
key role in the operation of the Keynesian welfare state. First, they were
often instrumental in providing a part of the 'social wage': goods and
services provided collectively to all or to those unable to afford them
privately. Public housing is a pre-eminent example of this. The social wage
was central to the Fordist mode of regulation, because it placed a 'floor'
under popular consumption, ensuring that during times of economic
difficulty, recession did not turn into slump. This 'subsidy' to the costs of
reproducing labour power was one of the ways in which the Fordist mode
of regulation ironed out large fluctuations in the process of capital
accumulation by helping to match demand to supply.

Second, the Fordist mode of regulation involved an increased degree of
government planning of economic and social life. In many cases, urban
government was one of the primary agencies through which this planning
took place. In the United Kingdom, for example, the local government
system was the principal forum for land use and urban infrastructural
planning. Related to this, and third, the Fordist mode of regulation
involved state intervention to provide vital human and physical infrastructure, such as transportation, environmental improvement, education
and health care. Under Fordism, these were vital to the private sector but
were often unprofitable for individual firms to provide, at least on a
universal basis.

Finally, there is an area which links the mode of regulation with the
much more narrow concerns with the labour process discussed above. The
organization of state institutions at the local level under Fordism involved
the application of bureaucratic principles. Governmental institutions
tended to be hierarchical and centralized, with the performance criteria
based on procedure, rather than results. As Hoggett noted (see above),
they tended to be good at providing a relatively narrow range of services
in a fairly inflexible and standard way to a large population, which was
implicitly assumed to be fairly homogeneous. Some critics have argued
that this reflected the dominance of producer interests within the public
services sector over the interests of service users. However, while there are
clear links here with the mass consumption norm of the Fordist regime of
accumulation, it is not immediately clear whether these features of urban
government were an *essential* part of the Fordist mode of regulation.

Arguably they do reflect some of the organizational principles of the archetypal Fordist firm. However, as I have already suggested, within Fordism, the public sector in fact often played the role of 'filling-in' gaps left by private provision. In other words, it was distinctively different from the private sector, not a straightforward mimic of it, and thus where organizational form is concerned, the causal link remains obscure.

Urban political processes   Political processes at the urban scale took a particular form and played a particular role in the Fordist mode of regulation. In particular, the role of local elections played a key role, especially in those countries where Fordism was secured through a form of social democratic political settlement. This representative function conferred a degree of political legitimacy on Fordist arrangements.

According to regulation theory, the 'grand compromise' of Fordism (Lipietz, 1987) accorded a degree of political power to certain (organized) sections of the working class in exchange for a broad toleration of capitalist relations of production. This had two political consequences at the urban scale. First, the organizations of the working class struggled for, and began to be involved in, political decision making. This took place through, for example, certain forms of local corporatism involving trade unions or the development of mass working class-based political parties. The government of many major urban areas, particularly in Western Europe, was, as a result, frequently dominated by social democratic, socialist or communist politicians.

Second, the limits of the compromise circumscribed the boundaries of legitimate political struggle. It was acceptable (though sometimes only just) to fight for labour *within* the limits of the Fordist deal. However, where urban political unrest began to challenge the rules of the game itself, the state was often swift in its retribution. As the mode of regulation of Fordism began to develop its own crises, these challenges, and the retribution, became more intense. Examples include the civil rights movements in the United States, the events of May 1968 in Paris and the public sector strikes in the 1970s in Britain.

Urban politics and potential post-Fordist modes of regulation

Despite, or perhaps because of, the considerably more problematic character of the concept of post-Fordism, much more attention has been focused by regulation theorists on trying to interpret a supposed shift from Fordism to post-Fordism, than on clarifying the nature of Fordism. Moreover, Mark Goodwin and I have recently argued that not only are there empirical reasons for doubting whether a new mode of regulation is emerging, but there are also significant conceptual reasons why it may be unlikely to do so (Goodwin and Painter, 1993).

Nonetheless, the notion of post-Fordism has attracted considerable attention, and in this section I will first briefly outline the 'crisis of

Fordism' and then draw on both regulationist principles and existing accounts of change to discuss the relationships between urban politics and post-Fordist modes of regulation.

The crisis of Fordism is a key reference point for any development of the notion of post-Fordism. As I have suggested, the Fordist mode of regulation was itself a contradictory phenomenon and the subject of political struggles and conflicts. Ultimately these aspects compromised its ability to postpone economic difficulties. Most of the standard accounts of regulation theory contain a discussion of the overall character of the crisis, so I will limit myself to the role of urban politics.

The crisis involved a pincer movement in which the 'virtuous circle' of Fordism switched into a downward spiral. The productivity increases on which the regime of accumulation depended could not be sustained indefinitely given the existing technical and organizational approaches. This led to a fall in profits and the growth of structural unemployment in the industrialized countries as multinational corporations in particular shifted production overseas in search of cheaper labour. This simultaneously decreased the pool of finance from which the state drew its resources and increased the demand for public services as workers and their families increasingly faced economic distress. In addition, many of the social groups which had been marginalized in the Fordist mode of regulation began to organize and assert demands on the welfare state (Bakshi et al., 1994; Painter, 1995). In many countries, this placed strains on the urban political system as local government struggled to meet increased demand for welfare services, sometimes in the face of fiscal stringency. In addition, urban policy and the urban political process increasingly became dominated by the need to deal with economic restructuring (frequently involving deindustrialization and only limited growth of new sectors) and the social effects of these changes, such as increases in crime and poverty and shifts of population. In the face of such changes, new political strategies have been adopted by many central and local government organizations. The debate is over whether these have the capacity to secure a new mode of regulation which will resolve or sidestep the contradictions of Fordism and usher in a new phase of enhanced capitalist development.

According to Jessop the broadly neo-liberal strategies adopted by most western governments mean that it is likely that in any new post-Fordist mode of regulation, the state would be a Schumpeterian Workfare State (SWS). In contrast to the Keynesian Welfare State of Fordism, the SWS would: 'promote product, process, organizational, and market innovation and enhance the structural competitiveness of open economies mainly through supply-side intervention; and to subordinate social policy to the demands of labor market flexibility and structural competitiveness' (Jessop, 1993: 19). This would imply that urban policy would shift away from an explicit concern with social and spatial equity, full employment and welfare programmes and towards initiatives aimed at promoting workforce flexibility and the economic competitiveness of the private sector. In addition the social polarization implicit in the neo-liberal version of post-Fordism would be likely to require increasingly authoritarian measures of policing and social control (Edwards and Hallsworth, 1992).

Esser and Hirsch (1989) outline the impact of these changes in a study of the then Federal Republic of Germany. Urban policy in Germany, they argue, is increasingly a matter of managing the division in urban areas between the affluent middle-classes who are to take advantages of the growth industries and the marginalized poor and dispossessed. This intra-urban heterogeneity is, they suggest, a stronger feature of contemporary Germany than inter-regional differences. (However, with the incorporation of the former German Democratic Republic, this last point no longer holds as regards the relationship between East and West.)

In Britain, urban policy has changed distinctively towards a system of centrally imposed and non-elected agencies, such as the Urban Development Corporations (UDCs), with wide-ranging powers over specific, and usually fairly small, areas of inner-urban land. The UDCs were explicitly charged with undertaking the regeneration of their areas in ways which prioritized the needs of private investors. Considerable sums of public funding were channelled into transport infrastructure, land reclamation, office and housing developments, and environmental 'improvements'. In some cases the people originally living in the local area have gained relatively little from the changes, with many of the housing and leisure developments aimed deliberately at up-market consumers and incomers with aspirations to an affluent lifestyle (Goodwin, 1991, 1993).

Debates around the agencies of urban government and governance have focused on two connections with post-Fordism. First, some authors have considered the links between public sector organization and new forms of corporate organization in the private sector. Stoker and Mossberger (1995), for example, identify many of the new organizational attributes of urban government and governance in Britain as post-Fordist in part because they reflect management strategies adopted in the private sector in response to the economic impact of the crisis of Fordism. These include in particular: an emphasis on the consumer (often called 'customer care' in the British public sector); a stress on flexible forms of organization; a more diverse range of relationships with external private and public sector bodies.[5] I have elsewhere emphasized the role of increased contracting out in the structures of urban government in Britain (Painter, 1991a, 1991c, 1991d). Although there has not been wholesale privatization of services provided by local councils in the UK, many public utilities outside the control of elected local government have been transferred to the private sector. Privatization of public service provision would have a key role in a new mode of regulation, as it simultaneously reduces the costs of providing labour intensive services as workers are removed from the protection of collective agreements and provides new sources of capital accumulation for the private sector.

The main potential contribution of these kinds of changes to a new mode of regulation would be to help to resolve the fiscal crisis of the local state, and, arguably, its legitimation problems by making the services more responsive to user needs. The second connection is slightly different, however, and involves the *direct* functions of urban governmental organizations within the Schumpeterian Workfare State (SWS). In Britain, the 1990s saw the establishment by the central government of a large number of quangos at the urban level. Foremost among these are the Training and Enterprise Councils (TECs) in England and Wales and the Local Enterprise Companies in Scotland. These agencies are outside the system of elected local government and are dominated by appointed, private sector interests. They have the responsibility of delivering government training schemes and promoting local economic development and private sector enterprise. This would seem to place them at the centre of any move towards the SWS. Peck and Jones (1994) have studied the work of the TECs from precisely this point of view. They concluded that TECs do look and sound very much like the local level equivalent of the SWS, but they have one fatal flaw. According to Peck and Jones, they are quite efficient at 'disciplining' the unemployed workforce to accept the primacy of employer requirements in the labour market, but they are not able to provide the entrepreneurial, supply-side innovation which Jessop argues is a necessary feature of the SWS. In other words they are 'workfarist' but not particularly 'Schumpeterian', largely because the funding which the central government provides is mostly targeted at training schemes, with only very limited resources set aside for generating local entrepreneurial activities.

Mayer has usefully summarized a range of the changes underway in urban governance across the western capitalist world relating them to the possible emergence of post-Fordism as a new mode of regulation (Mayer, 1994; see also Mayer 1991). Her account emphasizes new forms of economic intervention organized around innovation and new institutional relations in which hierarchical local state structures are supposedly being replaced by more pluralistic ones. She argues that both of these developments could be part of the political strategies of the left as well as the right, with rather different social outcomes.

Goodwin et al. (1993) discuss the changing character of urban politics in three English urban areas: Sheffield, Bracknell and Camden in London. Their account is especially useful in highlighting geographical variations in urban political processes within Fordism, its crisis and its potential successor. In many ways, Goodwin et al. argue, the three locations were archetypes of Fordist urban politics, within which 'a highly skilled labour force reaped the benefits of high wages and increasing levels of service provision in return for increasing productivity' and where 'structures of local politics were in place which were conducive to continued economic growth, social stability, and increasing standards of collective consumption' (1993: 76). With the crisis of Fordism, the local political coalitions which allowed this to continue in each place have now been undermined.

In Sheffield, the catastrophic decline of the steel industry initially prompted the city council to develop regeneration strategies based on the public sector promotion of employment. The imposition of central government control of the regeneration process meant that the explicitly socialist inflection and class basis of this strategy gave way to one subordinated to private capital and based on leisure, consumption and place marketing. In Bracknell, a New Town in the South East of England, Fordist growth had been governed by the social democratic and corporatist New Town Development Corporation, which used public sector finance to develop the local infrastructure. Today, some of the characteristics of a post-Fordist mode of regulation are evident:

> owner occupation has replaced council housing as the dominant form of housing tenure in the area, which lies at the centre of the affluent M4 corridor. Per capita expenditure by the local state on public services is little more than a third of that in Camden, and around two thirds of that in Sheffield. The shift from the postwar version of a one-nation mass-consumption system, as exemplified by Bracknell's successful New Town, has now been completed here to a two-nation model based on private provision for the affluent worker, with only a minimal 'social security state' for those excluded from this. . . . The basis and institutions of collectivist local politics have been systematically challenged by social and economic recomposition, and in their place the local state now facilitates private accumulation and consumption. (Goodwin et al., 1993: 81)

In Camden, the decline of Fordism was accompanied by the rise of the 'new urban left' with its emphasis on supporting social groups marginalized by Fordism, such as women and black people. These kinds of political movements and particularly the socialist experiment at the Greater London Council in the early 1980s briefly held out the hope of an alternative transition from Fordism; one not based so whole-heartedly on the dominance of the private sector and central government. However, the defeat of many of the groups and movements both locally (Goodwin et al., 1993: 82) and nationally, culminating in the abolition of the GLC in 1986, effectively dashed that hope. Nonetheless, the evidence from Goodwin et al.'s research does not support the existence of a smooth transition to a private sector post-Fordist future. If that transition does occur, it will have been highly uneven, partial and, in some places, bitterly contested.

Critiques and responses

Almost all the authors I have cited so far are, to a greater or lesser extent, proponents of regulation theory or the concept of post-Fordism, or both. However, the regulationist approach and (particularly) the idea of post-Fordism, have also been heavily criticized. While there are some who are critical of regulation theory as a whole, the picture is complicated because many of those who accept the principles of regulation theory are themselves critical of the idea of post-Fordism or of its use by certain writers. Furthermore, there are also writers who accept the tenets of regulation theory (and in some cases, also, post-Fordism) but regard its ability to account for changes in urban politics rather limited.

Some of the most trenchant critics of regulation theory as a whole have been other Marxist economists and political theorists (for example, Bonefeld, 1987, 1993; Clarke, 1988, 1990; Bonefeld and Holloway, 1991; Brenner and Glick, 1991). Since this account is concerned specifically with urban politics, I will not discuss their criticisms in detail, but they hinge around four main issues.

First, it is argued that regulation theory is *teleological*. That is, it sees history as the unfolding of an inevitable logic of development, from one regime of accumulation to the next. This, it is suggested, reduces the scope for political intervention and political conflict, and means that contemporary political events are evaluated purely in terms of their success in advancing society towards a pre-supposed future (post-Fordism). Second, according to some writers, regulation theory is *functionalist*. In other words it explains the development of a new mode of regulation in terms of its effects in securing capital accumulation: post-Fordism has arisen because the process of capital accumulation needed it. This, it is argued, is problematic, since the effects of a phenomenon cannot serve as an explanation of its origins. Third, regulation theory is sometimes accused of *technological determinism*. That is, the concern with the labour process and product and process innovation leads regulation theorists to assume that social development is essentially driven by new technology. Fourth, critics of regulation theory argue that it overstates the *coherence* of the mode of regulation and assumes that the class compromise around which it is supposedly built is hegemonic and widely accepted. This then leads to an underemphasis on social struggle during modes of regulation, with conflict and new developments only being significant *between* modes of regulation. Once a mode of regulation has been established, the working class, and especially other oppressed groups, simply have to sit it out and wait for its inherent logical contradictions to build up to crisis point.

Regulation theorists have responded vigorously to all these criticisms. Lipietz, in particular, has been especially concerned to develop a version of regulation theory which avoids functionalism and teleology (see Lipietz, 1987). Technological determinism is arguably a feature of some regulationist writing, but it can only really apply in the sphere of the labour process, which as we have seen is but one aspect of regulation. Some accounts of modes of regulation have indeed tended to stress their coherence and unity, rather than their contradictions and diversity. Given that regulationism is a developing theory, what is required here are more detailed and nuanced accounts of particular modes of regulation operating at particular times in particular countries. In discussing concrete cases, it may well make sense to talk about 'regulatory processes' or 'tendencies towards regulation', rather than coherent 'modes of regulation'. Further-more, all those who would abandon regulation theory are still left with the conundrum posed at the beginning of this chapter, namely, how, given the inherently contradictory nature of capital accumulation, has capitalism not only survived, but from time to time generated relatively stable economic growth?

In addition to these criticisms of regulation theory as a whole, a number of specialists in urban politics have criticized its application there. Cochrane (1993: 81–93) has recently neatly summarized many of these sceptical reactions, and also considers the problems of the concept of post-Fordism. He begins by discussing the debates around post-Fordism as a technological paradigm, which I have referred to here as the labour process.

Focusing on the work of Hoggett and Geddes, he argues that the notion of post-Fordism in this narrow technical and organizational sense implies a determinism, which makes it difficult for local government to resist or affect the changes:

> However qualified the argument, political processes still tend to be relegated to secondary status. This makes it difficult to explain why particular technological opportunities are taken up at one time rather than another, and also makes it easy to under-estimate the extent to which the direction of change remains contested. (Cochrane, 1993: 84)

In addition Cochrane suggests that the analogy between private sector organizational forms and the local welfare state may be overstated. There may be parallels, though he suggests that these are sometimes more apparent than real, but parallels and analogies cannot explain why the public sector adopted certain methods at certain times.

Moreover, as I have argued elsewhere, Hoggett's argument that the production of public services approximated to Fordist production in the manufacturing sector is actually sharply at odds with Aglietta who 'insists that it is precisely those goods and services whose production cannot be organized on Fordist lines which then have to be produced by the state, given a politically-determined consumption norm' (Painter, 1991b: 33).

Unlike some critics of the regulation approach, Cochrane is careful and correct to distinguish debates around post-Fordism as labour process and organizational form from debates around shifts in the mode of regulation. In assessing the latter he outlines and discusses Stoker's (1989) description of local government under Fordism and post-Fordism. First, in Cochrane's view, the case presented by Stoker is an oversimplification of the complexities of the British local state and urban politics. He regards Stoker's account of Fordism as applying at best only to the formal structures of elected local government, but failing to allow for the informal processes of negotiation and political conflict in any real political system. On the other hand, Stoker also points out that 'the Fordist character of local government organization and management ... should not be overstated' (1989: 151). Second, contracting out is often regarded as a key element of post-Fordist local government, and yet as Cochrane points out, such arrangements can actually reduce the flexibility which is supposed to be one of its other defining features. However, 'flexibility' can apply in a number of different spheres. Contracting out does seem to be associated with a deregulation of the labour market, for example, and there is no reason in principle why a contract could not specify that the contractor should provide a service which responds ('flexibly') to public demand. Third, according to Cochrane, in some countries, including the United States, local government during the so-called Fordist period actually has a lot in common with Stoker's model of post-Fordist local government in Britain (Cochrane, 1993: 89). Finally, in the case of Britain, Cochrane agrees with the regulation theorists that local government did indeed play a key role in the welfare state. However, he argues that regulation theory underemphasizes the degree of contestation and conflict around that role.

Evaluation

The concepts of regulation theory and the idea of post-Fordism have only been applied in the field of urban politics for some six or seven years, and then somewhat sporadically. Stoker and Mossberger point out that in comparison with other available theories, 'the post-Fordist literature has a reasonable claim to have most effectively captured the broad complexity of the changes that are occurring in the system of local governance' (1995). In practice, however, the application of regulation theory to these issues has been very patchy.

First, more work is required to specify the complex and uneven relationship between urban politics and Fordism. At least some of the difficulties with the notion of post-Fordism stem, in my view, from a too glib assumption about the link between politics, the urban arena and the Fordist mode of regulation.

Second, the so far extremely limited geographical reach of most of the accounts I have discussed needs to be addressed. For example, how far is the so-called post-Fordist local government system a peculiarity of the British case where an unusually right-wing government has been in power for an unusually long time. How were different modes of regulation articulated differently with urban politics in different societies? (According to Kevin Cox (personal communication), the debate over Fordism and post-Fordism has 'little resonance' with research into urban politics in the United States.) More research will be required to address these questions.

Third, modes of regulation can only firmly be identified retrospectively. Regulation theory is much better at describing the character (and contradictions) of an established mode of regulation than it is at explaining the emergence of new forms. These, it insists, are the product of social struggles and political conflicts. What is therefore required, and what regulation theory currently lacks, is a complementary set of theoretical tools that can account for the development of potential new regulatory practices and processes, without falling into the traps of teleology and functionalism.

Fourth, the prevalence of post-Fordist forms of local governance and urban politics remains unclear and extensive empirical research is required to assess it. In Britain, at the time of writing, such research is underway as part of the Local Governance Research Programme established by the Economic and Social Research Council.

This preliminary assessment suggests, first, that changes in contemporary urban politics in all its senses can be viewed in terms of competing political strategies in response to the decline of Fordist arrangements, whether social, economic or political. A major strength of regulation theory lies in its attempt to disclose and explain the *links between* the economic, political and sociocultural spheres. However, second, there is as yet relatively little evidence that urban politics is playing any clear role in the emergence of a new, coherent, post-Fordist mode of regulation. Certain developments are certainly not incompatible with such a future. On the other hand, since, as Jessop points out, the objects and processes of regulation are mutually constituting, it is likely that a definite assessment will only be possible retrospectively. At its present stage of development, regulation theory is perhaps best seen as a specialized, rather than a general theory. It may be of only limited application in specifying the detail of political shifts, but is particularly helpful in making sense of the social and economic context within which those shifts are taking place.

Notes

1 I have space here only to outline the main concepts. Fuller accounts are provided in Robert Boyer's excellent survey of regulation theory (1990) and by Peck and Tickell (1992).

2 Jessop further distinguishes the pattern of market relations as constituting an additional '*economic* mode of economic regulation'.

3 Some writers (including the founder of regulation theory, Michel Aglietta) prefer the concept of neo-Fordism, implying that the new arrangements are a development of Fordist systems, rather than a wholesale transformation of them. While the concept of neo-Fordism is arguably more precise and less open to some of the criticisms discussed in this chapter, it has not been widely adopted.

4 Jessop (1990: 200) argues that it should be possible to use regulationist methods to develop an account of the state, rather than the economy. This would involve identifying the state as an *object* of regulation (a contradictory and unstable phenomenon which itself is regulated, or needs regulation) rather than (or as well as) something which participates in the regulation of the economy. While Goodwin et al. (1993) begin to take up this point in their discussion of urban politics, it remains the case that most regulationist writers are concerned with the regulation of the economy, rather than the state.

5 Stoker and Mossberger also consider the role of the local state in managing the changed economic and social circumstances of local areas.

References

Aglietta, M. (1979) *A Theory of Capitalist Regulation: the US Experience*. London: Verso.

Bakshi, P.K., Goodwin, M., Painter, J. and Southern, A. (1994) 'Monitoring the transition from Fordism in British local government', paper presented at the Institute of British Geographers' Annual Conference, Nottingham.

Bonefeld, W. (1987) 'Reformulation of state theory', *Capital and Class*, 33: 96–127.

Bonefeld, W. (1993) 'Crisis of theory: Bob Jessop's theory of capitalist reproduction', *Capital and Class*, 50: 25–47.

Bonefeld, W. and Holloway, J. (eds) (1991) *Post-Fordism and Social Form*. London: Macmillan.

Boyer, R. (1990) *The Regulation School: A Critical Introduction*. New York: Columbia University Press.

Brenner, R. and Glick, M. (1991) 'The regulation approach: theory and history', *New Left Review*, 188: 45–119.

Clarke, S. (1988) 'Overaccumulation, class struggle and the regulation approach', *Capital and Class*, 36: 59–92.

Clarke, S (1990) 'New utopias for old: Fordist dreams and post-Fordist fantasies', *Capital and Class*, 42: 131–55.

Cochrane, A. (1993) *Whatever Happened to Local Government?* Buckingham: Open University Press.

Edwards, A. and Hallsworth, S. (1992) 'Regulation theory and crime control: a future for Marxist criminology?', paper presented at the Political Studies Association Marxism Specialist Group Annual Conference, Leicester.

Esser, J. and Hirsch, J. (1989) 'The crisis of Fordism and the dimensions of a "post-Fordist" regional and urban structure', *International Journal of Urban and Regional Research*, 13 (3): 417–37.

Florida, R. and Jonas, A. (1991) 'U.S. urban policy: the postwar state and capitalist regulation', *Antipode: A Journal of Radical Geography*, 23 (4): 349–84.

Geddes, M. (1988) 'The capitalist state and the local economy: "restructuring for labour" and beyond', *Capital and Class*, 35: 85–120.

Goodwin, M. (1991) 'Replacing a surplus population: the policies of the London Docklands Development Corporation', in J. Allen and C. Hamnett (eds), *Housing and Labour Markets: Building the Connections*. London: Allen and Unwin.

Goodwin, M. (1993) 'The city as commodity: the contested spaces of urban development', in G. Kearns and C. Philo (eds), *Selling Places: The City as Cultural Capital, Past and Present*. Oxford: Pergamon.

Goodwin, M. and Painter, J. (1993) 'Local governance, the crisis of Fordism and uneven development', paper presented at the Ninth Urban Change and Conflict Conference, Sheffield.

Goodwin, M., Duncan, S. and Halford, S. (1993) 'Regulation theory, the local state, and the transition of urban politics', *Environment and Planning D: Society and Space*, 11 (1): 67–88.

Gramsci, A. (1971) 'Americanism and Fordism', in Q. Hoare and G. Nowell Smith (eds), *Selections from the Prison Notebooks of Antonio Gramsci*. London: Lawrence and Wishart.

Hoggett, P. (1987) 'A farewell to mass production? Decentralisation as an emergent private and public sector paradigm', in P. Hoggett and R. Hambleton (eds), *Decentralisation and Democracy: Localising Public Services*. Bristol: School for Advanced Urban Studies.

Jessop, B. (1990) 'Regulation theories in retrospect and prospect', *Economy and Society*, 19 (2): 153–216.

Jessop, B. (1992) 'Fordism and post-Fordism: a critical reformulation', in M. Storper and A.J. Scott (eds), *Pathways to Industrialization and Regional Development*. London: Routledge.

Jessop, B. (1993) 'Towards a Schumpeterian Workfare State? Preliminary remarks on post-Fordist political economy', *Studies in Political Economy*, 40 (Spring): 7–40.

Lipietz, A. (1987) *Mirages and Miracles: The Crises of Global Fordism*. London: Verso.

Mayer, M. (1991) 'Politics in the post-Fordist city', *Socialist Review*, 21 (1): 105–24.

Mayer, M. (1994) 'Post-Fordist city politics', in A. Amin (ed.), *Post-Fordism: a Reader*. Oxford: Blackwell.

OECD (ed.) (1992) *Cities and New Technology*. Paris: OECD.

Painter, J. (1991a) 'Responding to restructuring: the geography of trade union responses to the restructuring of local government services in Britain, 1979–89'. Ph.D. dissertation, Open University, Milton Keynes.

Painter, J. (1991b) 'Regulation theory and local government', *Local Government Studies*, 17 (6): 23–44.

Painter, J. (1991c) 'The geography of trade union response to local government privatization', *Transactions of the Institute of British Geographers*, 16: 214–26.

Painter, J. (1991d) 'Compulsory competitive tendering in local government: the first round', *Public Administration*, 69 (2): 191–210.

Painter, J. (1995) 'The regulatory state', in R.J. Johnston, P.J. Taylor and M. Watts (eds), *World Problems: Geographical Perspectives*. Oxford: Blackwell.

Peck, J. and Jones, M. (1994) 'Training and Enterprise Councils: Schumpeterian workfare state, or what?', paper presented at Institute of British Geographers' Annual Conference, Nottingham.

Peck, J. and Tickell, A. (1992) 'Accumulation, regulation and the geographies of post-Fordism', *Progress in Human Geography*, 16 (2): 190–218.

Peters, T. and Waterman, R. (1982) *In Search of Excellence*. New York: Harper and Row.

Stoker, G. (1989) 'Creating a local government for a post-Fordist society: the Thatcherite project?' in J. Stewart and G. Stoker (eds), *The Future of Local Government*. London: Macmillan.

Stoker, G. and Mossberger, K. (1995) 'The post-Fordist local state: the dynamics of its development', in J. Stewart and G. Stoker (eds) *Local Government in the 1990s*. London: Macmillan.

Index

popular planning (London/Paris), 192–3
Posner, P.S., 184, 199
post-Fordism, 11, 242, 247, 278–80
post-Fordism and urban politics, 11,
    276
  applications of regulation theory,
    280–9
  critiques and responses, 289–92
  evaluation, 292–3
  exposition of regulation theory,
    277–80
post-Fordist modes of regulation, 285–9,
    290–1
Poulantzas, N., 257
power
  business (control), 79–82, 85
  command, 58, 65, 69
  community, 5, 17, 32, 39–41, 44–6, 48,
    66, 67
  functional, 75, 76
  of immunity, 231–2
  of initiation, 231–2
  relations, 25, 127, 211
  social production model, 29
power, urban
  elite theory, 4, 5–6, 35–50
  pluralism, 4–5, 13–32
  regime theory, 4, 6, 54–70
Pratt, G., 209
pre-emptive power, 65
preference formation, 60–1
prescriptive theories, 2, 4
pressure groups, 22, 165, 167, 209, 265
Preston, 263
Preteceille, E., 233–4, 239, 247, 270
Price, Hugh Douglas, 106
price system, 82
principal-agent analysis, 7, 76–7, 86, 91
Prior, D., 161, 164–5, 168, 172–4, 176
private/public dualism, 208, 220
private property rights, 258, 269
privatization, 87–8, 92, 198, 219, 241, 243,
    287
production
  politics of, 258, 259, 270
  regime of accumulation, 277–8
productivity, 278, 286, 288
professionalism, 168
Progressive movement, 138, 139
progressive regimes, 61, 184–5, 189
property development, 44–5
property rights, 258, 269
public choice theory, 2, 7–8, 77–8,
    117–32
public services, 74, 123–4

quangos, 220, 288

Rabrenovic, G., 211
race, gender and, 211, 212, 213
race relations, 22
'rainbow coalitions', 104, 107
Randall, V., 211, 214, 215, 218, 219–20
ratepayers' movements, 193–4
rational authority, 37
Reagan, Ronald, 191
Reagan administration, 243–4
realist epistemology, 265
reality, 2
recall, 139, 168
Redcliffe-Maud Commission (1969), 119,
    139–41, 148, 150
Redford, E., 74
referendum, 137, 139, 167–8
reform movement (USA), 143–8, 152,
    218–19
regime of accumulation, 277–8, 279, 284,
    286
regime theory, 3, 6, 13, 44
  neo-pluralism and, 26–30, 31, 55–7
regime theory and urban politics, 54
  application of, 62–4
  conclusion, 69–70
  contribution of, 57–62
  criticisms and developments, 64–9
  pluralism, 55–7
réglementation, 277
regulation
  concept, 277–8
  Fordist mode, 282–5
  post-Fordist modes, 285–9
regulation theory and urban politics, 3,
    10–11, 276
  applications, 280–9
  critiques and responses, 289–92
  evaluation, 292–3
  exposition, 277–80
Reinventing Government (Osborne and
    Gaebler), 155–6, 174–5, 176
rentiers, 42, 43, 44–5, 47
representative democracy, 37–9, 137–8, 141,
    145, 165, 168–9
republican government, 137
reputational analysis, 5, 15, 38–40, 50
resource-dependence model, 230
resource mobilization theory, 197–200, 273
resource sharing, 131
responsiveness, 139–40, 141
restructuring processes (feminist critiques),
    207, 209–10
Rhodes, R., 230–1, 241, 242, 247, 269

Compiled by Jackie McDermott